AF898044

FIFTH EDITION

The Complete QDRO Handbook

Dividing ERISA, Military, and Civil Service Pensions and Collecting Child Support from Employee Benefit Plans

PATRICIA D. SHEWMAKER AND JAMES ROBERT LEWIS IV

AMERICAN BAR ASSOCIATION
Family Law Section

Cover design by Jill Tedhams, ABA Design

Printed in the United States of America.

28 27 26 25 24   5 4 3 2 1

A catalog record for this book is available from the Library of Congress.

Contents

About the Authors

Patricia D. Shewmaker

Patricia "Patty" D. Shewmaker, a native of Nebraska, attended the U.S. Military Academy at West Point, New York, where she earned a bachelor of science degree in political science and was commissioned as a Second Lieutenant in Military Intelligence. Patty served seven years on active duty in the U.S. Army and three years in the Georgia Army National Guard. She deployed as a Company Commander of a Counterintelligence Company in support of Operation Iraqi Freedom and Operation Enduring Freedom. Patty received the Bronze Star for her service in a combat theater of operations. With her extensive military background and understanding of the unique issues that confront military families, Patty represents many military service members in family law issues.

Patty earned her law degree from the Georgia State University College of Law, where she graduated with honors. She has an active practice in all areas of family law, including divorce litigation, modification of custody, alimony and child support, contempt actions and legitimations, and paternity suits.

Patty also specializes in dividing qualified retirement plans incident to divorce and legal separation for other practitioners and her own clients, including pensions under the Federal Employees Retirement System (FERS), military pensions, private pensions, 401(k)s, Thrift Savings Plans (TSPs), and other qualified retirement plans.

Patty also has extensive experience with cross-jurisdictional family law litigation. She represents clients whose cases span multiple states and foreign countries, be they divorces, custody actions, or modifications. Patty is well versed in the special jurisdictional requirements of the Uniform Child Custody Jurisdiction and Enforcement Act (UCCJEA) and the Uniform Family Support Act (UFSA).

Patty is admitted to practice with the State Bar of Georgia, the Georgia Court of Appeals, the Georgia Supreme Court, the U.S. District Court for the Northern District of Georgia, and the U.S. District Court for the Middle District of Georgia.

Patty is a founding member of Shewmaker & Lewis, LLC, in Peachtree Corners, Georgia.

James R. Lewis IV

James "Jimmy" Lewis was born and raised in Atlanta, Georgia. He attended Auburn University and graduated with a bachelor of arts degree in political science focusing on prelaw and conflict resolution. Jimmy received his law degree in 2014 from John Marshall Law School, where he began to learn litigation skills under two Cobb County district attorneys.

Jimmy practices in all areas of family law, including divorce litigation, legitimation/paternity, modification of custody, alimony and child support, contempt actions, and military-related family law issues. He has a practice focused on the preparation of retirement division orders, including Qualified Domestic Relations Orders (QDROs), as well as orders to divide federal civilian and military retirement. Jimmy is routinely hired to advise family law attorneys on the division of retirement plans and the preparation of QDROs, as well as for QDRO-related litigation.

Jimmy is admitted to practice in the State of Georgia, the Georgia Court of Appeals, the Georgia Supreme Court, and the U.S. District Court for the Northern District of Georgia and is a member of the State of Georgia Bar Association, Georgia Family Law Section, Georgia Young Lawyers Division, DeKalb County Bar Association, and the Family Law section of the DeKalb Bar.

Jimmy is a partner at Shewmaker & Lewis, LLC, in Peachtree Corners, Georgia.

Introduction

This is a practical handbook, not an academic treatise. It was written for people who work with Qualified Domestic Relations Orders (QDROs) every day in a hands-on capacity—lawyers representing divorce clients; Plan Administrators and their lawyers; state IV-D agencies using QDROs to collect child support; family court judges; and the paralegals, administrative assistants, and other support staff who work with them. It is designed to be a how-to manual and a cookbook filled with step-by-step recipes, with a practical approach to the subject. We hope you will find it so useful that you will keep it on your desk and so helpful that you will refer to it every day. QDROs are a complex and difficult subject, but they can be explained so that every interested party can understand them and put them to practical use.

Although its title is *The Complete QDRO Handbook*, this book also covers division of military retired pay; federal, state, county, and municipal civil service pensions; non-ERISA plans such as IRAs; and Qualified Medical Child Support Orders.

Who Needs This Handbook?

- *Lawyers in private practice*: This handbook will help you draft domestic relations orders—DROs—and get them accepted as "qualified" by the Plan Administrator so your clients get their fair share of pension benefits. To help you achieve that goal, this handbook will also teach you how to counsel your clients on their rights and keep them satisfied, how to conduct cost-effective discovery, how and where to obtain the information you need from the pension plan and how to understand it once you get it, how to deal with Plan Administrators, and other tips and techniques for turning QDROs from a headache into a profit center for your law practice.

- *Plan Administrators and their lawyers*: This handbook is designed to help you efficiently and properly deal with QDRO applications so that your company's employees view your work as a valuable part of their overall employee benefit package, not as a hostile and adversarial encounter with your legal department. To help you achieve that goal, this handbook will also help you draft and administer the Written QDRO Procedures required by ERISA for your plan to comply with recent changes in this field.
- *State IV-D agencies*: This handbook is your guide to drafting and implementing QDROs to collect child support from pension plans. Although ERISA specifically provides that QDROs can be used to collect child support, few state IV-D agencies have actually implemented a QDRO program to enhance child support collections. Strategic use of QDROs can increase both the percentage of cases in which child support is collected and the amount collected per case. This handbook teaches you how to restructure your case intake and administration procedures to do that.
- *Family court judges*: This handbook should give you a better understanding of the technical aspects of QDROs as well as of the goals and needs of all the different parties involved in QDROs—the husbands, wives, children, divorce lawyers, employee benefit plans, Plan Administrators, actuaries, plan lawyers, and IV-D agencies—so that you can help them achieve their goals and wisely resolve their disputes.
- *Paralegals, administrative assistants, and support staff*: You are the frontline troops who gather information from clients or employees, keep the files, draft the correspondence, field the angry phone calls and complaints, and make sure that what is supposed to happen really does. This handbook can help you with all of those important and valuable duties. In this handbook you'll find the checklists, model clauses, procedures, forms, and other information you need to do your jobs.

How to Use This Handbook

QDROs are a complex and difficult subject. This handbook will help you gain a basic knowledge of all aspects of the substantive law of QDROs and familiarize you with the needs and goals of all organizations involved in them and with employee benefit plans, divorce lawyers, IV-D agencies, and the judiciary.

Whether you are new to the area or have been dealing with QDROs for many years, we recommend that you do the following.

First, read the entire handbook from cover to cover. If you really must, you can read more rapidly or skim the sections that don't apply directly to you, but you should have at least a passing familiarity with them. This will help you understand the big picture—the substantive law of QDROs, the perspectives of all the different constituencies involved in QDROs, and the practical tips and techniques for qualifying and administering QDROs.

Second, keep this book nearby so that you can consult it as a handy reference when conducting pretrial discovery, drafting and qualifying orders, and considering QDRO litigation.

Throughout this handbook we have used "he" as shorthand for "he or she," "his" as shorthand for "his or her," and so on. We have also quite arbitrarily and generally made the "Participants" male and the "Alternate Payees" female. These shortcuts were taken purely for the sake of brevity, convenience, and readability; fortunately, real life is much more complex, varied, and interesting than that.

We dedicate this handbook to our colleagues at Shewmaker & Lewis, LLC, and most specifically our spouses with whom we practice: Steven Shewmaker and Alexa Lewis. Special thanks to the members of the ABA Section of Family Law Publications Development Board for their support in publishing this fifth edition.

Employee Benefit Plans and Domestic Relations

1

1.1 Pensions before Employee Retirement Income Security Act (ERISA)

Before 1974, private pension plans were not regulated by the federal government and were only sporadically regulated by the states. Common problems during this era included a lack of disclosure to employees regarding their pension rights, inequitable treatment by employers, impoverishment of elderly employees by the bankruptcy of their employers, and other abuses. Many employers reserved the right to terminate pension payments if their former employees did or said anything after retirement that was perceived to be against the employer's interests. Employees eligible to receive a pension after 40 years of loyal service could be fired a month, or even a single day, before their fortieth anniversary and receive nothing.

During this period, the state courts afforded no special treatment to pension plans in domestic relations cases. Payments from pension plans were treated, like any other income, as subject to attachment and garnishment for child support or alimony but not divisible as property.

1.2 1974: ERISA Changes the Rules

In the early 1970s, pressure mounted for the federal government to step in and begin regulating this area. The result was the enactment of the Employee Retirement Income Security Act of 1974, now universally known as ERISA, which is codified in both titles 26 (income taxes) and 29 (labor) of the United States Code. ERISA is a comprehensive statute that has made dramatic changes to every aspect of the design, creation, and operation of all private sector "ERISA-qualified" pension and benefit plans. ERISA was enacted in response to public concern over the abuse and mismanagement of employee pension and benefit plans.

Most private employee benefit plans in the United States today are ERISA-qualified plans. Substantial tax benefits flow to both the employers that sponsor qualified plans and the employees who participate in them. First, the employer may deduct contributions to the plan when they are made. Second, funds in a plan grow tax-free until withdrawn. Finally, employees are not taxed on their pension benefits until they actually begin to receive them. These significant tax benefits are available if, and only if, the plan obtains, and maintains by compliance with ERISA, its ERISA-qualified status. *See* Internal Revenue Code, 26 U.S.C. §§ 401, 402, and 414. In 2013, there were more than 765,000 ERISA-qualified retirement plans with approximately $12.8 trillion in assets for the benefit of 153 million workers and beneficiaries. *Fact Sheet: EBSA Restores over $1.4 Billion to Employee Benefit Plans, Participants, and Beneficiaries*, Dep't of Labor (Oct. 14, 2022), https://www.dol.gov/sites/dolgov/files/EBSA/about-ebsa/our-activities/resource-center/fact-sheets/ebsa-monetary-results.pdf. But not all employer-provided retirement plans are ERISA-qualified plans. In recent years, there has been a rise in the number of non-qualified plans. Employers do not get the tax beneficial treatment of these plans, but employers may use them to supplement qualified plans and to be competitive in hiring key personnel. These are most often used with senior employees or in executive compensation plans.

1.3 The Anti-Alienation Clause of ERISA vs. State Divorce Law Developments

From its enactment in 1974, ERISA has required that each pension plan ensure that the benefits it provides not be "assigned or alienated." 29 U.S.C. § 1056(d)(1). This provision was intended, at least in part, to "protect an employee from his own financial improvidence in dealing with third parties." *See Hawkins v. Comm'r,* 86 F.3d 982, 988 (10th Cir. 1996); *see also American Tel. & Tel. Co. v. Merry,* 592 F.2d 118, 124 (2d Cir. 1979).

At about the same time ERISA was enacted, the state courts, led by California, began holding that pension rights earned or accrued by one spouse during a marriage were marital or community property and were divisible as such between both spouses in divorce proceedings. *See, e.g., In re Marriage of Fithian,* 517 P.2d 449 (Cal. 1974); *In re Marriage of Brown,* 544 P.2d 561 (Cal. 1976). Today virtually every state has come to recognize this principle and treats pensions (usually only that portion of pension benefits earned or accrued while the parties were married) as property divisible in divorce proceedings. *Annotation, Pension or Retirement Benefits as Subject to Assignment or Division by Court in Settlement of Property Rights between Spouses,* 94 A.L.R.3d 176. It is malpractice to ignore or neglect a client's rights to receive a share of the spouse's pension in a divorce action. *Smith v. Lewis,* 530 P.2d 589 (Cal. 1975); *Hutchinson v. Divorce & Custody Law Center,* 449 S.E.2d 866 (Ga. Ct. App. 1994); *Bross v. Denny,* 791 S.W.2d 46 (Mo. Ct. App. 1990).

1.4 Federal and State Case-Law Development, 1974–84

The potential for conflict between ERISA's anti-assignment clause and the developing state domestic relations law doctrine of pension divisibility rapidly turned into a very serious problem early on. During the decade following ERISA's enactment in 1974, a number of cases wrestled with the issue of whether the two principles really were in conflict, and, if so, how to resolve it. Most cases held that there was an "implied exception" to the anti-assignment language of section 1056(d)(1) for family support obligations (*American Tel. & Tel. Co. v. Merry,* 592 F.2d 118 (2d Cir. 1979)), or that a state court divorce order splitting a pension between divorcing spouses merely recognized a preexisting inchoate property right, an implicit joint ownership rather than an "alienation or assignment" forbidden by ERISA. *Carpenters Pension Trust v. Kronschnabel,* 460 F. Supp. 978 (C.D. Cal. 1978), *aff'd,* 632 F.2d 745 (9th Cir. 1980), *cert. denied,* 453 U.S. 922 (1981). But other cases held that divorce-related property divisions or garnishments for family support obligations would violate section 1056(d). *Monsanto Co. v. Ford,* 534 F. Supp. 31 (E.D. Mo. 1981); *Francis v. United Tech. Corp.,* 458 F. Supp. 84, 85–86 (N.D. Cal. 1978).

1.5 1984: The Retirement Equity Act (REA) Changes the Rules Again

In response to this decade of uncertainty and rapidly proliferating federal and state litigation, Congress acted in 1984 to clarify how state domestic relations laws and ERISA should interact. It passed a new law amending ERISA, known as the "Retirement Equity Act" or "REA," P.L. 98-397 (1984). *See* H.R. Rep. No. 655, 98th Cong., 2d Sess. (1984); Sen. Rep. No. 575, 98th Cong., 2d Sess. (1984) (discussing conflicting cases at 20).

REA amended certain key sections of ERISA and the Internal Revenue Code. The provisions of REA are now scattered throughout ERISA and the Code and have become an integral part of those laws. The text of the two major provisions, sections 1055 and 1056(d) of ERISA, as amended by REA, is set forth in Appendix A. For an excellent analysis of the history and general goals of REA, *see Ablamis v. Roper*, 937 F.2d 1450 (9th Cir. 1991).

REA provides that certain orders entered in state domestic relations cases relating to the provision of child support, alimony, or property division must be accepted and honored by ERISA-qualified pension plans. These orders are known as "QDROs," which stands for "Qualified Domestic Relations Orders." REA specifies the required characteristics of QDROs, sets forth the procedures that plans must follow in determining whether an order is a QDRO, specifies the tax consequences of payments made pursuant to QDROs, and regulates many other matters concerning these orders. REA also requires the provision of survivors' benefits for spouses and former spouses of employees. All of these matters are explored in detail in later chapters.

1.6 Case Law and Regulatory Development, 1984–2000

REA has been widely recognized as a valid and useful statute. *See, e.g., Boggs v. Boggs*, 520 U.S. 833 (1997). The 1974–84 philosophical debate over the conflict between ERISA and state court domestic relations orders was over. That conflict was resolved by Congress when it enacted REA and created the concept of QDROs. An order considered a QDRO is expressly exempted from the anti-assignment and anti-alienation clause of section 1056(d)(1) of ERISA. Section 1056(d)(3) now provides that section 1056(d)(1) "shall not apply [to] . . . a QDRO." The battleground in the federal and state courts has now shifted to whether or not the parties have complied with all the requirements of REA and whether a state court order in a domestic relations case is or is not qualified. Recent cases on these topics are discussed in the appropriate chapters that follow.

Regulatory jurisdiction over ERISA matters is divided between the Department of Labor (DOL) and the Internal Revenue Service (IRS). Insolvent pension plans fall under the jurisdiction of the federal Pension Benefit Guaranty Corporation (PBGC), established in 1974. In the late 1990s, all three of these federal government agencies issued regulations and publications on QDROs, which are also discussed subsequently.

1.7 Non-ERISA Plans: Military, Federal, State, and Local Government Retirement Plans

During the same period (1974–2000) that the developments in the private pension world described previously were taking place, parallel—but not identical—developments occurred in the world of public sector pensions. It seemed both illogical and inequitable for a wife in one family to be able to receive a share of her husband's pension rights under REA because he was employed by a private company, while her neighbor received nothing at all because her husband was a military officer, a policeman, or a federal, state, or municipal civil servant.

The remedy for this obvious inequity was the enactment during the 1970s and 1980s of specific federal and state laws making such pensions divisible in a comparable, but not identical, fashion to the mechanism for private sector pension divisions created by REA. These laws include the Uniformed Services Former Spouses Protection Act and significant amendments to the federal statutes governing federal civil service pensions. These laws and their practical application are discussed in Chapters 11 and 12. The Office of Personnel Management (OPM) has published a helpful handbook for lawyers involved in dividing federal civil service pensions and benefits (see section 12.1).

In 1993, ERISA was amended to allow courts and child support agencies to obtain Qualified Medical Child Support Orders (QMCSOs) under procedures similar to, but simpler than, the procedures for obtaining QDROs. These orders, and miscellaneous types of plans such as individual retirement accounts (IRAs), are discussed in Chapter 13.

1.8 Case Law and Regulatory Development since 2000

Since 2000, it has become well accepted that private pension and employee benefit plans are subject to division incident to divorce and subject to garnishment for the purposes of child support and alimony. The case law since 2000 has further refined a spouse's interest in a Participant's employer sponsored retirement plan. The biggest development since 2000 has been the shift from defined benefit pension plans to defined contribution plans such as a 401(k). In fact, few private companies still offer pension plans for their employees, opting instead for defined contribution plans. Coinciding with this development is the addition of other employer-sponsored benefit plans such as Employee Stock Purchase Plans (ESPP).

On the public side, this shift from defined benefit plans to defined contribution plans has been regulatory. We first saw this shift when the federal government, in 1986, changed from the Civil Service Retirement System (CSRS) to the Federal Employee Retirement System (FERS). The change from CSRS to FERS reduced the pension benefit while adding a defined contribution plan, the Thrift Savings Plan (TSP), with matching government contributions. This change from CSRS to FERS was a cost-saving measure, just as this shift from defined benefit plans to defined contribution plans has been a cost-saving measure for private employers. More recently, the uniformed services have followed suit, introducing the new Blended Retirement Systems (BRS) in the National Defense Authorization Act of 2015. The BRS follows the lead of FERS, reducing the military pension benefit while enhancing the TSP with government contributions. These new changes with the BRS are discussed in further detail in this book.

1.9 Why Are QDROs So Important?

More than 150 million Americans are covered by ERISA, military, and civil service[1] employee benefit and pension plans. These plans contain well over $7.5 trillion in assets. Pension rights are usually a divorcing couple's largest or second-largest asset (the other being the family home) and are a major source of income for the purposes of paying alimony and child support payments.

---

1. When using the general term "civil service," the authors are referring to both CSRS and FERS employees.

With more than 50 percent of all marriages ending in divorce and uncollected child support being a major social problem, every divorce lawyer, state court judge, employee benefit Plan Administrator, corporate legal department, employee benefits and human resources department, and state "IV-D" (child support enforcement) agency must learn to deal effectively with QDROs and related methods of dividing military and civil service pensions.

1.10 Why Are QDROs So Difficult?

Despite the many advantages and great utility of QDROs, they have for various reasons remained a headache for many of the professionals who deal with them. First, ERISA uses a highly technical vocabulary and unfamiliar concepts. It is discouraging to diligently request plan documents in discovery and then try to wade through page after page of discussions of "accumulated actuarial funding deficiency," "attained age-normal credit method," "maximum average actual deferral percentage test," and similar incomprehensible jargon, not to mention such acronyms as TPA, SSTWB, HCE, EGTRRA, SERP, and VEBA. Chapter 2 will help you overcome this difficulty by cutting through some of these complexities and explaining them in understandable terms.

Second, each employee benefit plan is different, with different benefit schedules, options, specially defined terms, benefit payment options, and procedures for qualifying state-court domestic relations orders. ERISA is a permissive statute that allows employers to use an almost infinite variety of plan designs as long as certain minimum standards are met. This leads to wide variations in plan features and makes it difficult to learn from experience in this area, because to a certain extent each new plan you encounter requires you to "reinvent the wheel" in drafting a suitable QDRO.

Third, QDROs are a difficult and sometimes explosive mix of state and federal law. State law governs such matters as the inclusion and valuation dates for pension rights; the percentage awarded to each party; and terminating payment events such as remarriage or emancipation for alimony or child support QDROs. Federal law governs plan design and features; the form and timing of benefit payments; normal, early, and disability retirement ages and conditions; joint and survivor annuity design; and QDRO approval procedures. The two legal systems—federal and state—occasionally conflict with each other or with the wishes and desires of the parties. When you draft a QDRO you must undertake the difficult task of making sure that all aspects of state and federal law are covered in a single instrument that resolves all inconsistencies and conflicts between these laws and that is acceptable to both parties, opposing counsel, the trial judge, and the Plan Administrator. This is a challenging task under the best of circumstances.

Finally, while QDROs may seem dry and technical at times, they have a significant emotional dimension. Emotions run high in divorce and child support cases, often leading to protracted and bitter litigation over every clause and every penny involved in a QDRO.

1.11 The Top Ten QDRO Mistakes and How to Avoid Them

Listed next, in reverse order, are the ten most common mistakes divorce lawyers make in dealing with QDROs. Each mistake is followed by references to the chapters and sections in this book that will enable you to avoid it.

MISTAKE #10. Failure to discover and divide all employee benefit plans (including nonqualified plans and benefits from prior or part-time employment). *SOLUTION:* Use the discovery techniques outlined in Chapter 3 and the model discovery forms in Appendices B through I to make sure you discover all employee benefit plans. Then use the checklists at the end of Chapters 8, 11, and 12 to make sure you cover all the issues in dividing them.

MISTAKE #9. Failure to provide for cost-of-living adjustment (COLA) increases to be shared between the Participant and the Alternate Payee. *SOLUTION:* Use the model clauses in Chapters 8, 11, 12, and 13 to make sure you include these important rights.

MISTAKE #8. Blindly following the plan's model QDRO and just "filling in the blanks" (particularly when you represent the Alternate Payee). *SOLUTION:* Subsection 8.3D explains in detail the serious dangers involved in doing this.

MISTAKE #7. Failing to prorate contributions to defined contribution plans that are made at the end of the contribution year that spans the date of separation or divorce. *SOLUTION:* For tips and techniques on solving this problem, see subsection 5.3B and clause 5L in subsection 8.5, part C.

MISTAKE #6. Limiting the division of benefits to vested benefits only, rather than to accrued benefits. *SOLUTION:* See the discussion in subsections 5.3C and D.

MISTAKE #5. Failing to specify, when dividing a Defined Contribution Plan, whether the Alternate Payee will receive interest, dividends, gains, and losses on her share between the date of valuation and the date a separate account is established for the Alternate Payee. (Failure to specify whether this adjustment should be made leads to a result known in the QDRO trade as "If it goes up, I'm your partner; if it goes down, I'm your creditor," and may lead to years of litigation.) *SOLUTION:* See clauses 5L and 5M in subsection 8.5, part C.

MISTAKE #4. Not having the plan review and approve your QDRO in advance so you can bring it to court with you (with amounts or percentages left blank if necessary) or attach it as an exhibit to the separation agreement. *SOLUTION:* Unless the Participant is threatening to withdraw funds from his plan, take out a loan against his account, or retire in the immediate future—potentially placing the Alternate Payee's share of benefits in jeopardy—this is always a good practice. See subsection 8.3C.

MISTAKE #3. Automatically following the Shared Interest Approach in every case. *SOLUTION:* Most Alternate Payees prefer the Separate Interest Approach because it gives them control over when payments from a Defined Benefit Plan begin and ensures that payments will continue for the Alternate Payee's lifetime. In contrast, the Shared Interest Approach means the Alternate Payee receives no payments at all until the Participant chooses to retire, and payments to the Alternate Payee may cease on the Participant's death. See section 6.3 and section 8.5, clause 5, part B, for a full discussion of how to use both the Shared Interest and Separate Interest approaches.

MISTAKE #2. Failing to provide a qualified preretirement survivor annuity (QPSA) benefit for ERISA plans, survivor benefit plan (SBP) for military retired pay divisions, or Former Spouse Survivor Annuity (FSSA) for federal civil service plan divisions for your Alternate Payee clients. *SOLUTION:* This is an extraordinarily common omission.

Failure to expressly provide for survivor benefits for your Alternate Payee clients at trial or in a stipulation or separation agreement can be fatal to your ability to include them in a subsequent QDRO if the Participant or his lawyer objects. Failure to expressly include survivor benefits in the QDRO itself is always fatal. It takes only a few words to preserve these vitally important rights for your Alternate Payee clients in ERISA, military, and civil service plans.

See the definitions in subsections 6.2C–F, P, Q and R and the clauses in subsections 8.5(7), 11.15(7), and 12.5.

MISTAKE #1. Failure to follow through until your order has been accepted as a QDRO by the plan. *SOLUTION:* The most common form of malpractice in the QDRO area is the failure of counsel for the Alternate Payee to persevere and make sure that a QDRO is entered by the state divorce court as well as sent to and finally accepted by the plan. In my experience in plan administration, about 15–20 percent of the time when an initial QDRO application is rejected by the plan, the application is simply abandoned. The plan never hears back from the Alternate Payee's lawyers, and the Alternate Payee's rights are irrevocably lost. Chapter 9 is devoted to this problem and covers it in detail.

1.12 Common Interests and Goals

One perennial problem with QDROs is that the constituencies most actively involved in them—state IV-D agencies, lawyers in private practice, plan officials, and state court judges—rarely meet or communicate with each other. A major objective of this handbook is to encourage better communication and cooperation among these groups. We all have a common goal: using QDROs to equitably divide employee benefits and provide child support, and qualifying DROs and putting them into effect with a minimum of time, effort, expense, and friction.

Whatever your role in QDROs, it will help you do a better job if you read every chapter of this handbook. If you're a Plan Administrator, don't skip the sections on law office management and client relations. Reading them will help you better understand the concerns and difficulties faced by the divorce lawyers with whom you deal. If you work for a IV-D agency, read the material addressed to Plan Administrators. It will help you anticipate the responses your

DRO will receive as well as the responses to your requests for assistance. Every chapter will help you understand how to accomplish your own work as well as appreciate the concerns and goals of the other parties with whom you must deal in order to accomplish your QDRO goals.

"Just Enough ERISA": Core Definitions and Principles

2

2.1 Introduction

Dealing effectively with Qualified Domestic Relations Orders (QDROs) requires an understanding of certain key definitions and concepts of ERISA. There is no shortcut to learning these terms and basic principles. Their definitions are set forth in this chapter, not alphabetically, but in logical order. Use this part of the handbook as a dictionary, and refer to it as often as you need to while reading other chapters. Once a term is defined, it is thereafter capitalized as a reminder it has a special and precisely defined meaning in the world of QDROs. For example, a "Plan Administrator" is usually quite different from the "Plan Sponsor," and both in turn are different from "Plan Fiduciaries." They have different statutory duties and powers, and it is important to distinguish them. *See Guzy v. Ameritech Corp.*, 1999 U.S. Dist. LEXIS 8943 (E.D. Mich. 1999). A common reason for a plan's refusal to qualify a domestic relations order (DRO) is that the terms defined by ERISA are used incorrectly or imprecisely in the order. This is an easy mistake to avoid if you refer to this chapter while drafting QDROs.

The definitions in this chapter apply only to ERISA-qualified plans; other specialized defined terms unique to military, civil service, and other government retirement plans are set out in Chapters 11 and 12, concerning division of those types of plans. Be mindful of these different categories and keeping particular terms and language in the appropriate category.

The areas in this book addressing ERISA are only what is applicable to QDROs and QDRO procedures. ERISA is an extremely large and complex code, and if it was not relevant to the topic of this book, it was not included. There is no shortage of ERISA-based books and documentation in the event you need to reference ERISA further or are interested in learning more about ERISA.

2.2 Key ERISA Definitions

A. Employee Benefit Plan

An Employee Benefit Plan includes both Employee Pension Benefit Plans and Employee Welfare Benefit Plans as defined in subsections 2.2B and 2.2C. 29 U.S.C. § 1002(3).

B. Employee Pension Benefit Plan

An Employee Pension Benefit Plan is any plan sponsored by an employer to provide either (1) retirement income or (2) a deferral of income until the termination of employment or beyond. 29 U.S.C. § 1002(2).

C. Employee Welfare Benefit Plan

An Employee Welfare Benefit plan is any plan, fund, or program sponsored by an employer to provide life insurance, death benefits, medical care, day care, scholarships, legal services, and the like. 29 U.S.C. § 1002(1). It is not clear whether QDROs can be used to assign life insurance benefits. *Compare Metropolitan Life Ins. Co. v. Person*, 805 F. Supp. 1411 (E.D. Mich. 1992) (employee welfare plans not subject to QDROs), *with Metropolitan Life Ins. Co. v. Marsh*, 119 F.3d 415 (6th Cir. 1997); *Metropolitan Life Ins. Co. v. Wheaton*, 42 F.3d 1080 (7th Cir. 1994); and *Garland v. Metropolitan Life Ins. Co.*, 935 F.2d 1114 (10th Cir. 1991) (QDROs may be used in connection with employee welfare plans).

D. Participant

A Participant is defined as "any *employee or former employee of* an employer, or member or former member *of* an employee organization [usually a union] who *is or may become* eligible to receive a benefit of any type from an Employee Benefit Plan . . . or whose *beneficiaries* may be eligible to receive any such benefit." 29 U.S.C. § 1002(7) (emphasis added).

E. Beneficiary

A Beneficiary is "a person designated by a Participant or by the terms of an Employee Benefit Plan, who *is or may become* entitled to [receive] a benefit thereunder." 29 U.S.C. § 1002(8) (emphasis added).

Some plans automatically designate the Beneficiary (that is, surviving spouse, children if no surviving spouse, and so on). Most plans give the Participant the ability to choose his Beneficiaries by filling out a Beneficiary designation form and filing it with the plan, with a standard menu of presumed Beneficiaries if the Participant fails to file the form.

The Retirement Equity Act (REA) added significant restrictions to the ability of married Participants to designate persons other than their surviving spouses as Beneficiaries unless those spouses execute written waivers. 29 U.S.C. § 1055(a), (c)(2), (d), and (e). Former spouses have the same rights as spouses in this area but only to the extent a QDRO expressly states they do. 29 U.S.C. § 1056(d)(3)(F).

See the definition of "Alternate Payee" in subsection 2.2M on the issue of when an Alternate Payee may be considered a Beneficiary.

F. Plan Administrator

A Plan Administrator is either (1) the person or entity specifically so designated by the terms of the instrument under which the plan is operated, or (2) if no such person is so designated, the Plan Sponsor (employer). 29 U.S.C. § 1002(16)(A).

Plan Administrators have certain special statutory duties under ERISA. Outsiders usually deal with counsel for the Plan Administrator, which is sometimes a person in the legal or employee benefits department of the Plan Sponsor (see subsection 2.2G). Many Plan Sponsors have outsourced their QDRO processing to specialized firms that handle the initial screening of QDROs, subject to final approval by the Plan Administrator. It is sometimes necessary to send official notice to the Plan Administrator in connection with processing a QDRO or in litigation (see section 10.1).

G. Plan Sponsor

The Plan Sponsor is the employer that sponsors the plan. 29 U.S.C. § 1002(16)(B). Some plans, particularly those negotiated by unions, are sponsored by more than one employer and therefore are known as "multi-employer plans."

H. Normal Retirement Age

Normal Retirement Age is defined as the earlier of

- (A) The date a Participant attains the normal retirement age specified in the plan, or
- (B) The later of
  - (i) The date a Participant attains age 65, or
  - (ii) The fifth anniversary of the time the Participant began to participate in the plan. 29 U.S.C. § 1002(24).

This is a somewhat confusing definition that is best calculated backward. In other words, first decide under (B) which is later: the time the Participant reaches 65 or the fifth anniversary of his participation in the plan. Then compare that figure to part (A) of this definition—the Normal Retirement Age expressly provided in the plan—and choose the earlier of them.

For example, in a Defined Benefit Plan, first calculate the date of the fifth anniversary of the date the Participant began to participate in the plan. (Note that this is not always the date the Participant was first hired by the sponsoring employer; ERISA allows plans to defer entry of their employees up to a year after they are first hired, and many plans adopt that delayed entry policy.) Next, determine when the Participant will attain age 65. Choose the later of these two dates. Then compare that date with the Normal Retirement Age specified in the written text of the plan, and choose the earliest.

I. Earliest Retirement Age

The Earliest Retirement Age is defined as the earlier of

- (A) The date on which the Participant is first entitled to receive a distribution from the plan, or

(B) The later of
    (i) The date a Participant attains age 50, or
    (ii) The earliest date on which the Participant could begin receiving plan benefits if the Participant separated from service (ceased to be employed by the Plan Sponsor). 29 U.S.C. § 1056(d)(3)(E)(ii).

This is another somewhat confusing definition best calculated backward. In other words, first decide under (B) which is later: the time the Participant reaches 50 or the earliest date he could receive benefits if he quit or was fired (often this is immediately). Then compare that figure to the date provided in part (A).

Example 1: In a Defined Contribution Plan, if the Participant quits his job at age 35, part (B)(i) is 50 (it always is) and part (B)(ii) is 35, the age at quitting. The later of these two is 50. Part (A) is the Participant's age at termination, 35, and the earlier of (A) and (B) is 35, which is the Earliest Retirement Age.

Example 2: In a Defined Benefit Plan that provides (A) is 65, or 55 or more with ten years of service (employment), part (B)(i) is 50 and part (B)(ii) is 65, or 55 or more with ten years of service. The later of these is (B)(ii), 65, or 55 or more with ten years of service. This is the same as (A), so the Earliest Retirement Age is 65, or 55 or more with ten years of service.

This is a critically important date. Alternate Payees may usually begin receiving payments under a QDRO when the Participant attains (or would have attained, if he dies earlier) the Earliest Retirement Age, *whether the Participant actually retires at that time or not.*

J. Defined Contribution Plan, or Individual Account Plan

The Defined Contribution Plan (also called Individual Account Plan) is a plan that creates an individual account for each Participant and provides benefits based solely on the amount contributed to that Participant's account—together with any income, dividends, interest, and capital gains, and any forfeitures from the accounts of other Participants allocated to that account. 29 U.S.C. § 1002(34).

Defined contribution plans are becoming increasingly popular with Plan Sponsors. The number of defined contribution plans has doubled in the last 20 years, while the number of defined benefit plans decreased by about 40 percent. Even after this transformation, defined benefit plans still hold over half the assets on deposit in private pension plans, since union pension plans and large corporate plans tend to be defined benefit plans. One reason for the growing popularity of defined contribution plans with employers is that all risk is shifted to the Participant: the Plan Sponsor contributes a fixed percentage of salary, a cost easy for it to control, and what each Participant receives on retirement depends on how well he manages his retirement account between now and then. Defined contribution plans are very easy to value. They are like bank accounts or accounts with a stockbroker; all you have to do is get a copy of the most recent account statement and read it to learn what's in the account and how much it is worth (see Appendix L). State law may or may not permit a discount to that current value for the income tax consequences of withdrawing funds from the plan if that is intended by one or both of the parties or required by their need for immediate cash.

The following are all defined contribution plans:

Money purchase pension plans

Profit-sharing plans

401(k) plans

Stock bonus plans

Employee stock ownership plans (ESOPs)

K. Defined Benefit Plan

A Defined Benefit Plan is any pension plan that is not a Defined Contribution Plan. 29 U.S.C. § 1002(35).

In defined benefit plans, all risk falls on the Plan Sponsor. The employer promises a certain level of payments to each Participant on retirement, and the responsibility for coming up with the funds to pay such benefits rests completely on the employer. Defined benefit plans usually promise a level of monthly payments on retirement calculated by a formula using (1) the number of years the Participant worked for the Plan Sponsor, (2) the Participant's age at retirement, and (3) the Participant's salary in his last year of employment, or the average of a specified number of years of salary or contribution. Each plan uses a different formula for calculating benefit entitlements. One plan might offer 1.25 percent of your last year's salary for each year you work for the Plan Sponsor, so if you worked 30 years before retirement you would receive 37.5 percent (30 × 1.25) of your last year's salary as your pension. Another Defined Benefit Plan might promise you $50 per month for each year of service before retirement, as many union plans do. Many Defined Benefit Plan formulas set the initial monthly payment level a retiree will receive and then provide for later cost-of-living increases.

Although a Plan Sponsor is required by ERISA to put a certain amount aside in a trust to fund a Defined Benefit Plan, there are no individual accounts a Participant can call his own or withdraw. Bear in mind some plans will allow a party to withdraw the money previously contributed with certain restrictions. Think of a Defined Contribution Plan as a basket full of money and a Defined Benefit Plan as a basket full of promises.

L. Hybrid Plan

A Hybrid Plan is exactly what it sounds like—a mix of a Defined Benefit Plan and a Defined Contribution Plan. In dealing with a Hybrid Plan, you have to sort out its features and consider them separately as appropriate for a Defined Benefit Plan or a Defined Contribution Plan.

Hybrid Plans have names like the following:

Cash balance pension plan

Pension equity plan

Floor-offset plan

Age-weighted profit-sharing plan

New comparability profit-sharing plan

Target benefit plan or pension plan

Cash balance pension plans have been quite controversial since 1997 due to claims their funding mechanism discriminates against older workers.

M. Alternate Payee

An Alternate Payee is any spouse, former spouse, child, or "other dependent" of a Participant who is recognized by a Domestic Relations Order as having a right to receive all, or a portion of, the benefits payable under a plan with respect to such Participant. 29 U.S.C. § 1056(d)(3)(K).

Notice that an Alternate Payee may receive "all, or a portion of" the funds otherwise payable with respect to a Participant. This amount is not restricted by ERISA but may be subject to limits imposed by state domestic relations law and the terms of the Domestic Relations Order.

Section 1056(d)(3)(J) states "an Alternate Payee under a Qualified Domestic Relations Order shall be considered . . . a Beneficiary. . . ." By implication, an Alternate Payee under a Domestic Relations Order that has not yet been determined to be a Qualified Domestic Relations Order may not be able to claim full Beneficiary status. See the definition of "Beneficiary" in subsection 2.2E; *Brotman v. Molitch*, 1989 U.S. Dist. LEXIS 9157 (E.D. Pa. 1989). *See also Gabrielson v. Montgomery Ward & Co.*, 785 F.2d 762 (9th Cir. 1986).

It is important to recognize the statutory definition uses the term "child" and not "minor child." QDROs may be entered at *any* time, before or after the child attains the age of emancipation, to collect either current child support or even child support arrears accrued during the child's minority.

A party to an annulment stating that a marriage was void ab initio may still be considered a former spouse and a surviving spouse under ERISA. Department of Labor Advisory Opinion 92-17A.

Previously, the federal "Defense of Marriage Act," 1 U.S.C. § 7 (1996) (DOMA), caused potential issues in QDRO processing. This was because under DOMA, any ruling, regulation, or interpretation of the various administrative bureaus and agencies of the United States, the word "marriage" meant only a legal union between one man and one woman as husband and wife, and the word "spouse" referred only to a person of the opposite sex who is a husband or a wife. This led to issues in interpretation under the Code and ERISA as to what should and could be processed as to who was considered a "spouse" and whether it was recognized as a "marriage." However, in *U.S. v. Windsor*, the Supreme Court of the United States held that the definitions of "marriage" and "spouse" under DOMA excluded same-sex couples, and therefore violated the Equal Protection Clause of the Fifth Amendment. *U.S. v. Windsor*, 570 U.S. 744 (2013). DOMA effectively created differences in protections for divorced opposite-sex couples as opposed to same-sex couples, and *U.S. v. Windsor* cured these discrepancies.

In our experience, most Plan Administrators would divide private qualified plans if there was a court order. So long as a state court divorced the parties and issued a QDRO incident to that divorce, the Plan Administrator would process the QDRO without questioning the sex of the parties to the divorce and the implications of DOMA. It was not, however, until the ruling in *U.S. v.*

Windsor that the federal government would address and divide military and federal pensions. While outside the topics of discussion in this book, this decision also impacted and made available numerous other benefits for same-sex couples, including tax and immigration benefits.

N. Domestic Relations Order

A Domestic Relations Order (DRO) is any judgment, decree, or order (including judicial approval of a property settlement agreement) that

- Relates to the provision of child support, alimony payments, or marital property rights to an Alternate Payee of a Participant; and
- Is made pursuant to a state domestic relations law (including a community property law). 29 U.S.C. § 1056(d)(3)(B)(ii).

Although DROs are most commonly used in property divisions between divorcing spouses, note that this definition expressly allows them to be used for alimony and child support as well.

Note that an order is required; a separation agreement, private contract, or draft order that is not signed by a judge or other state official authorized to enter orders is not enough for a DRO. However, such private agreements may be transformed into a DRO if they are approved by a state court or a state agency authorized to issue child support orders. Department of Labor Employee Benefits Security Administration (EBSA) Booklet, *QDROs: The Division of Pensions through Qualified Domestic Relations Orders* (1997), Question 2-8; hereafter *EBSA Booklet.*

An order of a state probate court in an estate settlement proceeding dividing the plan benefit due a decedent (evidently in an effort to do some creative postmortem estate planning in order to minimize estate taxes) is not considered made pursuant to a domestic relations law and therefore cannot be a DRO. Department of Labor Advisory Opinion 90-46A.

O. Qualified Domestic Relations Order

A Qualified Domestic Relations Order (QDRO) is a DRO that

- Creates or recognizes the existence of an Alternate Payee's right to, or assigns to an Alternate Payee the right to, receive all or a portion of the benefits payable with respect to a Participant under a plan; and

- Meets the following seven additional requirements.

The DRO clearly specifies

1. The name and last known mailing address (if any) of the Participant and each Alternate Payee covered by the order;
2. The amount or percentage of the Participant's benefits to be paid by the plan to each such Alternate Payee, or the manner in which such amount or percentage is to be determined;
3. The number of payments or period to which such order applies; and
4. Each plan to which such order applies. *See Dial v. NFL Player Supplemental Disability Plan*, 174 F.3d 606 (5th Cir. 1999); *Guzy v. Ameritech Corp.*, 1999 U.S. Dist. LEXIS 8943 (E.D. Mich. 1999).

And the DRO

5. Does not require a plan to provide any type or form of benefit, or any option, not otherwise provided under the plan. *See Dickerson v. Dickerson*, 803 F. Supp. 127 (E.D. Tenn. 1992); *Stott v. Bunge Corp.*, 800 F. Supp. 567 (E.D. Tenn. 1992); *Custer v. Custer*, 776 S.W.2d 92 (Tenn. Ct. App. 1988), *cert. denied*, 493 U.S. 933 (1989). Federal cases arising in Tennessee holding that an order directing immediate payment to Alternate Payee before Participant reaches earliest retirement age violates this provision; state case holding to the contrary. *See also Hullett v. Towers, Perrin, Forster & Crosby, Inc.*, 1994 U.S. Dist. LEXIS 391 (E.D. Pa. 1994) (lump-sum vs. monthly payments), *rev'd on other grounds*, 38 F.3d 107 (3d Cir. 1994).
6. Does not require the plan to provide increased benefits (determined on the basis of actuarial value). *See Bailey v. Board of Trustees of the New Orleans Steamship Association/International Longshoremen's Association, AFL-CIO Pension Trust Fund*, 1996 U.S. Dist. LEXIS 231 (E.D. La. 1996).
7. Does not require the payment of benefits to an Alternate Payee that are required to be paid to another Alternate Payee under another order previously determined to be a QDRO. 29 U.S.C. § 1056(d)(3)(B), (C), and (D).

P. Actuarial Value

This concept is discussed in detail in Chapter 6.

Q. Written QDRO Procedures

ERISA requires each Employee Benefit Plan to establish "reasonable procedures" to determine the qualified status of DROs and to administer distributions under QDROs. Such procedures

1. Must be in writing;
2. Must provide for the notification of each person specified in a DRO as entitled to payment of benefits under the plan (at the address included in the DRO) of such procedures promptly upon receipt by the plan of the DRO; and
3. Must permit an Alternate Payee to designate a Representative for receipt of copies of notices that are sent by the plan to the Alternate Payee with respect to a DRO. 29 U.S.C. § 1056(d)(3)(G)(ii).

R. Representative

A Representative is someone designated in the DRO to receive copies of all notices sent by the plan to the Alternate Payee concerning the DRO (see part 3 of the definition of QDRO Procedures in subsection 2.2Q).

Representatives are usually lawyers, accountants, or other legal or financial advisors. In the case of a child support DRO, the appropriate state IV-D agency may be the Representative. Curiously, only Alternate Payees are allowed to appoint Representatives; Participants are not. Nonetheless, if the drafting attorney, whether representing the Participant or Alternate Payee or acting as a third-party drafting attorney, includes the name(s) of a Representative with the documents and correspondence, then virtually all plans will send copies to all listed and involved.

2.3 Key ERISA Concepts

A. Plan as Separate Legal Entity

ERISA requires that Employee Benefit Plans be separate legal entities from the company that funds them, the Plan Sponsor. This protects the plan from the claims of the employer's creditors and provides a separate vehicle to hold plan funds.

Although many companies have their own corporate legal or employee benefits departments to deal with QDROs, and these may be the people with whom you correspond, remember that the company and the plan are separate legal entities, particularly if you have to sue the plan. *Guzy v. Ameritech Corp.*, 1999 U.S. Dist. LEXIS 8943 (E.D. Mich. 1999); *Fortmann v. Avon Products, Inc.*, 1999 U.S. Dist. LEXIS 3451 (N.D. Ill. 1999).

B. Vested Pensions

A vested pension is one in which the Participant has earned certain rights to receive present or future benefits that cannot be taken away from him, even if he quits or is discharged. Vesting and its counterpart, forfeitures, are discussed in detail in Chapter 5.

C. Matured Pensions

A matured pension is one in which the Participant has attained an age, or a combination of age and years of service, or satisfied other conditions that are sufficient to entitle him to retire immediately and begin receiving benefits right away.

D. Pensions In Pay Status

A pension "In Pay Status" is one in which the Participant has already retired and is currently receiving benefits. *Mattox v. Mattox*, 734 P.2d 259 (N.M. Ct. App. 1987). The division of pensions is treated differently depending on whether the pension is In Pay Status or not, so it is critical to know whether the pension is already In Pay Status.

Divisions of pensions In Pay Status and not yet In Pay Status are discussed in detail in the model DRO in Chapter 8.

E. Fiduciary Duties

ERISA imposes on plan fiduciaries the duty to act "solely in the interest of the Participants and Beneficiaries, and for the exclusive purpose of providing benefits to Participants and their Beneficiaries." 29 U.S.C. § 1104(a)(1).

Every plan must name at least one fiduciary in its governing plan document. 29 U.S.C. § 1104. However, other persons involved in the administration and funding of the plan may also be found to be fiduciaries under ERISA, depending on the facts and circumstances of their involvement with the plan. Any person who

1. Exercises discretionary authority or discretionary control respecting management of a plan, or exercises any authority or control respecting management or disposition of its assets;
2. Renders investment advice to the plan; or
3. Has any discretionary authority or discretionary responsibility in the administration of the plan is a statutory fiduciary of that plan. 29 U.S.C. § 1002(21)(A).

The Plan Administrator and the Plan Sponsor are clearly fiduciaries; lawyers, accountants, actuaries, and consultants to the plan generally are not, although there may be exceptions. Individuals involved in making benefits determinations, including the qualification of DROs, probably are.

Fiduciaries are personally liable for breaches of their duties. ERISA forbids their employer to indemnify them against liability for breaches of their ERISA fiduciary duty. If you are having difficulty getting information from a plan or qualifying a DRO, it can help to casually indicate to the individual you are dealing with at the plan that you are aware of this provision. *See Schoonmaker v. Employee Savings Plan of Amoco Corp.*, 987 F.2d 410 (7th Cir. 1993) (participant's suit against plan and two individual fiduciaries for failure to follow plan's own QDRO Procedures).

F. Plan's Duties upon Receipt of a DRO

Plans are required to perform two important duties when they receive a DRO for qualification:

1. **First Duty**: *Notify the Parties of Receipt of a DRO and Determine Its Qualified Status within a Reasonable Time.* Upon the plan's receipt of a DRO,
   - (a) The Plan Administrator shall promptly notify the Participant and each Alternate Payee of the receipt of such order and the plan's QDRO Procedures for determining the qualified status of DROs; and
   - (b) Within a reasonable time after receipt of such order, the Plan Administrator shall determine whether such order is a QDRO and notify the Participant and each Alternate Payee of such determination. 29 U.S.C. § 1056(d)(3)(G)(i).

As a practical matter, the Participant and Alternate Payee, or their lawyers, have usually received a copy of the plan's QDRO Procedures much earlier in this process—almost always before the DRO is drafted, signed by the state court, and submitted to the plan.

2. **Second Duty**: *Segregate the Amount Payable to Alternate Payee While Determination Is Pending.*

   (a) During any period in which the issue of whether a DRO is a QDRO is determined (by the Plan Administrator, by a court of competent jurisdiction, or otherwise), the Plan Administrator shall separately account for the amounts (hereafter referred to as the "segregated amounts") that would have been payable to the Alternate Payee during such period if the order had been determined to be a QDRO.

   (b) If within the 18-month period described in clause (e) the order (or *modification thereof*) is determined to be a QDRO, the Plan Administrator shall pay the segregated amounts (including any interest thereon) to the person or persons entitled thereto.

   (c) If within the 18-month period described in clause (e),

      - It is determined that the order is not a QDRO or
      - The issue as to whether such order is a QDRO is not resolved,

      Then the Plan Administrator shall pay the segregated amount (including any interest thereon) to the person or persons who would have been entitled to such amounts if there had been no order.

   (d) Any determination that an order is a QDRO that is made after the close of the 18-month period described in clause (e) shall be applied prospectively only.

   (e) For the purposes of this subparagraph, the 18-month period described in this clause is the 18-month period *beginning with the date on which the first payment would be required to be made under the DRO.* 29 U.S.C. § 1056(d)(3)(H) (emphasis added).

Note that this definition contemplates that "a court of competent jurisdiction" has the power to determine that a DRO is a

QDRO, although as a practical matter this determination is almost always made by the plan (see Chapter 10).

Note also the italicized language in clause (b), which seems to suggest that the escrow (segregation) of funds should continue even after a DRO has been rejected by the Plan Administrator and while it is being modified during the qualification process.

Finally, note that under clause (e), the 18-month segregation period begins when the first payment under the DRO is due following receipt of the DRO by the plan, not when the order is received by the plan. *See EBSA Booklet,* Question 2-11.

Some Plan Administrators have argued unsuccessfully that the 18-month escrow period referred to here, 29 U.S.C. § 1056(d)(3)(H), should be an indication of the length of a "reasonable time" within which to determine the qualified status of a DRO under the preceding section, 29 U.S.C. § 1056(d)(3)(G)(ii). The courts and the Department of Labor have indicated that these two subsections are independent and that 18 months is much too long to be reasonable. *See EBSA Booklet,* Question 2-12.

G. Protection of Spouses and Former Spouses

Not all plans offer annuities as an optional form of benefit. Very few defined contribution plans do, but almost all defined benefit plans are required to do so by section 1055. Any qualified plan that *does* offer an annuity option is subject to significant restrictions under sections 1055 and 1056 if the Participant is married.

First, any plan that offers an annuity option must, in the case of a married Participant, pay the annuity in the form of a Qualified Joint and Survivor Annuity unless the Participant's spouse consents in writing at the time of retirement to a different form of payment. 29 U.S.C. § 1055(c)(2)(A), (d).

Second, any plan that offers an annuity option must also provide a Qualified Preretirement Survivor Annuity that will pay the surviving spouse of a Participant an annuity for her life if the Participant dies before actually retiring. 29 U.S.C. § 1055(a)(2), (e), (f).

The parties generally need to be married for at least one year for these protections to apply. 29 U.S.C. § 1055(f).

Third, if a Participant and his spouse divorce, then "to the extent provided in any QDRO" the Participant's former spouse may be designated as an Alternate Payee to be treated as his "surviving spouse" under section 1055, and she is thus eligible to insist that the Participant choose a Qualified Joint and Survivor Annuity with her on retirement and to insist that she be designated as the surviving spouse and beneficiary of a Qualified Preretirement Survivor Annuity as provided in section 1055 of title 29. 29 U.S.C. § 1056(d)(3)(F).

The monthly payments under a Qualified Joint and Survivor Annuity will always be less than the payments under a Single Life Annuity because by definition the joint and survivor payments will continue for longer than a payment continuing only for the life of one of the two parties. However, most people prefer annuities in a form that guarantees them some payment, even if it is somewhat smaller, that is guaranteed to last as long as they live.

Note that to provide surviving spousal benefits under a Qualified Joint and Survivor Annuity for an Alternate Payee, a QDRO providing it must be accepted by the plan before the Participant actually retires if he has remarried. Otherwise, the right to survivor's benefits "vests in the Participant's current spouse on the date the Participant retires." *Hopkins v. AT&T Global Information Solutions Co.*, 105 F.3d 153, 156 (4th Cir. 1997).

A party to an annulment stating that a marriage was void ab initio may still be considered a "former spouse" and a "surviving spouse" under ERISA. Department of Labor Advisory Opinion 92-17A.

H. ERISA Preemption of State Law

ERISA states that its provisions "shall supersede any and all State laws insofar as they may now or hereafter relate to any Employee Benefit Plan." 29 U.S.C. § 1144(a); *Boggs v. Boggs*, 520 U.S. 833 (1997).

The term "State laws," as used in section 1144(a), includes statutes as well as all laws, decisions, rules, regulations, or other state action having the effect of law; and it includes the laws of the District of Columbia and the political subdivisions, agencies, and institutions of any state. 29 U.S.C. § 1144(c); *AT&T Management Pension Plan v. Tucker*, 902 F. Supp. 1168 (C.D. Cal. 1995).

The QDRO provisions of ERISA, which create and expressly recognize a role for state courts and state domestic relations laws, carve out an exemption to this general rule of ERISA state law preemption. *In re Marriage of Nasca*, 1999 U.S. Dist. LEXIS 13140 (N.D. Cal. 1999) ("The common theme in cases that courts have declined to find subject to complete ERISA pre-emption is that they involve disputes only as to the ultimate ownership of ERISA benefits, not their quality, nature or existence.").

I. Qualified Plan

This is also known as a "tax-qualified plan" or "ERISA-qualified plan." It refers to an Employee Benefit Plan that meets the requirements of the Internal Revenue Code so that (1) contributions to the plan by the employer are deductible when they are made, (2) income and capital gains realized on plan assets are not taxed when they occur, and (3) the Participant pays no income tax until he actually receives a distribution of funds from the plan.

Note that even plans that do not meet the requirements of the Internal Revenue Code for these tax benefits are often subject to the other regulatory requirements of ERISA, including the provisions governing QDROs. See section 13.2; *Guzy v. Ameritech Corp.*, 1999 U.S. Dist. LEXIS 8943 (E.D. Mich. 1999).

J. QDRO Litigation

The topic of QDRO litigation generally is beyond the scope of this handbook. It is possible to litigate QDRO cases—concerning unreasonable refusals of a Plan Administrator to qualify a DRO, for example, or a wrongful qualification of a defective DRO—but such litigation is extremely rare. In the 20 years since REA was enacted, there have been fewer than 100 reported federal cases on QDRO issues. In almost every case it is possible to get a Plan Administrator to accept and honor a DRO as a QDRO after one or two rounds of correspondence, well short of litigation, and that is the central purpose of this handbook. Should litigation become necessary, I strongly recommend that you retain the services of expert ERISA counsel.

It is, however, worth briefly noting that plans may be sued, by either a Participant or a Beneficiary, to "[a] recover benefits due to him under the terms of his plan, [b] to enforce his rights under the terms of the plan, or [c] to clarify his rights to future benefits under the terms of the plan." 29 U.S.C. § 1132(a)(1)(B). A state or IV-D agency may also sue "to enforce compliance with a qualified medical child support order." 29 U.S.C. § 1132(a)(7). Suits of either of these two types may be filed in either a state court of competent jurisdiction or the appropriate federal District Court. 29 U.S.C. § 1132(e)(1). Any other type of litigation against a plan must be filed in federal court. 29 U.S.C. § 1032(e)(1). See Chapter 10 for a detailed discussion of QDRO and ERISA litigation.

3 Essential Information and How to Get It

3.1 Introduction

For every Qualified Domestic Relations Order (QDRO), you will need four items of basic information:

Name and current address of the Participant and the Alternate Payee. Although the legislative history of the Retirement Equity Act (REA) and several cases have indicated that Plan Administrators should not be too quick to disqualify a Domestic Relations Order (DRO) for not stating this information if it is otherwise known to the Plan Administrator or readily ascertainable, it is always preferable to include it. In our experience, as noted later with more sensitive personal information, most Plan Administrators are accepting of the inclusion of the current address of the Participant and the Alternate Payee in a separate submission that is not part of the public record. This can be through an addendum or a cover letter to the Plan Administrator that includes this personal information.

Social Security number and dates of birth for the Participant and the Alternate Payee. Plans often require the Social Security number of both the Participant and the Alternate Payee for identification purposes and if there are tax implications with the Order(s). In general, the easiest way to ascertain this necessary information is directly from the Participant and Alternate Payee. If you are one of the attorneys during the divorce, this information can likely be found through documents and information produced during the discovery process, notably the parties' federal and state income tax returns.

Additionally, many plans require the dates of birth of both the Participant and Alternate Payee. It is unlikely that a DRO will be rejected for not having this information, but it is certainly not uncommon for plans to delay or hold off processing or even pre-approval review without having all of this information submitted. The more prudent approach is to have all of this information included, so there will be no unnecessary delays.

Exact name of each plan to which the DRO will apply. It is not uncommon that companies will have multiple retirement plans. A company can have a defined benefit plan, a defined contribution plan, a stock option plan, or a combination of multiple plans. Further, the incorporation of new plans of the same variety may come into play, which can create significant issues as well. This is not as simple as it sounds. Many companies have more than one Employee Benefit Plan, and they usually have confusingly similar names. For example, there is the "Lockheed Martin Capital Accumulation Plan," the "Lockheed Martin Salaried Savings Plan," the "Lockheed Martin Salaried Pension Plan," the "Lockheed Martin Retirement Savings Program," and so on.

If an employer sponsors more than one plan, most Participants may be members of more than one of them or even all of them. *Make sure you list and identify each plan of which the Participant is a member.* Plan Administrators are sticklers for detail, and the plan will very likely disqualify or reject your order solely because of misidentification, even if the Participant is a member of only one plan. It is not uncommon to see a draft order rejected because the plan name was incorrectly written in the order. Certain Plan Administrators will be helpful and correct your error; however, others may simply inform you that the plan name is incorrect and essentially tell you to "try again."

Make sure you identify each plan separately by its *exact name.* Plan names can be confusingly similar, as the previous example shows. You must consider in what form plan benefits can be paid from each separate plan and word your QDRO accordingly.

As a practice point, keep in mind that many plans sponsored by the same employer often have different addresses, contact persons, and telephone numbers. Organization of this potential varying information is key to ensuring that you handle this process properly and efficiently. If you're handling a case where a Participant has multiple plans, it can help to open separate sub-files within the file for each separate plan. This helps to avoid confusion between where each order is to be submitted, and most importantly, information between each plan/order. For example, many people going through divorce who are long-time employees of a company may have a defined benefit plan AND a defined contribution plan with that employer. It is always easier to keep these two items separate from inception and avoid possible cross-contamination.

You will also need to know the amount of benefits available from each plan, the forms in which such benefits may be paid, and all options concerning the form and timing of payments. Be aware that each plan may have a different form of benefit. The same company can have multiple different plans: a pension plan providing benefits only in the form of annuities, a 401(k) plan providing benefits in the form of a lump-sum distribution, and an Employee Stock Option Plan (ESOP) providing distributions of the company stock. For example, the "Global MegaCorp Employee Pension Plan" may provide benefits only in the form of annuities, while the "Global MegaCorp Employee Savings Plan" may provide for lump-sum distributions of cash, and the "Global MegaCorp Employee Stock Option Plan" may provide distributions solely of Global MegaCorp stock.

Under section 1056(d)(3)(D)(i) of title 29, a QDRO cannot require a plan to "provide any type or form of benefit, or any option, not otherwise provided under the plan." Although this seems like it should be self-explanatory, it isn't uncommon to see attorneys who did not do their due diligence during the case to advise their clients that they'll be able to take a lump sum out of this pension plan that certainly does not allow it. This obviously results in significant issues down the road, including additional litigation and potential malpractice claims. It is important that all documents related to the division of retirement accounts and plans specifically fall into the categories of what is allowable under each different plan. This requires the attorney(s) involved to adequately educate themselves on the plan(s) subject to property division in the case and, in turn, properly explain and educate the client as to what allowable options may be available.

Plans often give Participants and Alternate Payees options allowing them to choose the timing and form of receipt of benefits. For example, an Alternate Payee who is the former spouse of a Participant in a Defined Benefit Plan may choose to receive fixed monthly payments under an annuity either (1) from the date the Participant chooses to retire until the date of the Participant's death (Shared Interest Approach); or, more likely, (2) the actuarial equivalent of that payment, but starting when the Alternate Payee chooses and ending only on the Alternate Payee's death, no matter when the Participant actually chooses to retire or dies (Separate Interest Approach). The plan might even provide for a lump-sum cash payment in lieu of this stream of monthly payments in an annuity, generally depending on the gross contribution level to the plan. It is always important to review the plan guidelines to determine what is allowable before drafting. Sometimes a choice of options will have to be made in the DRO itself at the time it is entered. Other plans may allow an Alternate Payee to take a "wait-and-see" approach and choose one of the available options at a later date, such as when the Alternate Payee is ready to retire.

Read the plan documents described next to make sure you understand all of the available options. The QDRO Procedures and Annual Benefits Statements may also spell them out. Plan Administrators or lawyers for the plan are usually willing to discuss the basic plan options and alternative forms of distribution if you have any questions.

3.2 The Three Key Plan Documents

Fortunately, ERISA requires plans to publish and make available at no cost to you or your client several useful documents containing all the information described in the previous section. These three documents contain nearly everything you need to properly draft a QDRO and get it approved.

The three key documents are

- The Summary Plan Description
- The Annual Benefits Statement
- The Plan's Written QDRO Procedures

Many attorneys also like to obtain the full text of the plan. It may seem paradoxical, but this is often the least useful document. ERISA-qualified plans are governed by long, complex, and tedious documents. Page after page is filled with detailed instructions on issues that have nothing to do with QDROs, such as plan funding mechanisms and reports to be filed with the U.S. Department of Labor (DOL) and the Pension Benefit Guaranty Corporation (PBGC). It is the governing document, however, and in the event of a conflict between the text of the plan and any booklets, brochures, or other employee handouts (but not the Summary Plan Description; see subsection 3.2A), the full text of the plan is the governing document. *Nachwalter v. Christie*, 805 F.2d 956, 960 (11th Cir. 1986); *Johnson v. Central States, Southeast and Southwest Areas Pension Funds*, 513 F.2d 1173, 1174–75 (10th Cir. 1975). It is useful to request a copy of the full text of the plan just in case one of the points governed by that text does arise in the course of drafting a DRO. Having a copy on file shows that you have done your homework for your client, and it is a handy reference source to have if the plan advises you that it cannot approve your QDRO because it conflicts with some paragraph in the text of the plan itself.

Go ahead and ask for the full text of the plan if you are so inclined. Skim the table of contents to get a basic familiarity with the nature of the plan. Read carefully any provisions relating to divorce or QDROs. Then put this document away in the file for future reference if necessary; it probably won't be.

A. The Summary Plan Description

The word "summary" is somewhat misleading here, since these documents can be hundreds of pages long. They are supposed to be accurate, condensed versions of the plan itself and easier to read and understand than the jargon-filled full text of the plan.

Summary Plan Descriptions are required to state, "in a manner calculated to be understood by the average plan Participant," an accurate and comprehensive description of the rights and duties of Participants and Beneficiaries. 29 U.S.C. § 1022(a). As in the case of the full text of the plan itself, the plan is obligated to give you a copy of this document for free.

Perhaps somewhat surprisingly, some courts have held (at least in cases where the Summary Plan Description does not contain an express disclaimer and refers to the text of the plan itself as authoritative) that in the event of a conflict between the terms of the plan text and the Summary Plan Description, the Summary Plan Description is the governing document. *Heidgerd v. Olin Corp.*, 906 F.2d 903 (2d Cir. 1990); *McKnight v. Southern Life & Health*

Ins. Co., 758 F.2d 1566 (11th Cir. 1985); *Everson v. Blue Cross & Blue Shield*, 898 F. Supp. 532 (N.D. Ohio 1994); *Thompson v. Federal Express Corp.*, 809 F. Supp. 950 (M.D. Ga. 1992).

Ask for the Summary Plan Description; skim it, paying particular attention to any provisions concerning divorces or QDROs; and file the original for future reference. If there is anything that strikes you as particularly relevant to your current case, make sure to look up the original language in the full text of the plan itself and compare it with the corresponding part of the Summary Plan Description. Oftentimes, the most use you will get out of a Summary Plan Description is the contact information for the Plan Administrator and very general QDRO information.

B. The Annual Benefits Statement

Unlike the full text of the plan and the Summary Plan Description, which are general documents applying to all Participants, the Annual Benefits Statement is an individualized record that shows a particular Participant his actual or projected benefits. The Annual Benefits Statement is like a statement from your bank, showing deposits, withdrawals, and how much is in your account. It is unique to the Participant's personal account and shows its current status.

Annual Benefits Statements, as the name suggests, are issued at least once a year. Some plans issue them more frequently, semiannually or quarterly, but ERISA requires only that they be issued to each Participant at least annually. It is important to note that each statement may contain valuable information, but this statement may not cover everything you need from the Participant. These statements typically contain the following information:

1. Name, plan name, account number, and current mailing address of the Participant.

2A. A statement, as of a certain recent date, of how many shares of stock, or how much cash, is on deposit in the plan for the Participant's benefit (in the case of defined contribution plans); or

2B. A statement, as of a certain recent date, of what lump-sum or monthly payment the Participant could expect to receive upon retirement, assuming certain normal and early retirement ages (in the case of defined benefit plans).

Be careful when reading part 2B of the Annual Benefits Statement. Often the amount shown as "what the Participant will receive at the normal retirement age of 65" is based on several assumptions about the Participant's future salary and increases that, as a matter of state law, may not be available for division between the Participant and the Alternate Payee (see Chapter 5). Also, the discussion in the Annual Benefits Statement of "what the Participant will receive at the early retirement age of 55" often does not disclose that part of this payment—often a very large part—is a subsidy for early retirement and thus not available to the Alternate Payee unless the Participant actually takes early retirement. See subsection 6.2M; *Fastner v. Fastner*, 427 N.W.2d 691 (Minn. Ct. App. 1988). As noted throughout this book, it is always advisable to consult with a financial expert for a valuation to obtain a clearer understanding of what expected values would be.

3. A statement of whether the Participant is "vested" or not in plan benefits, and, if vested, what percentage the Participant is vested (see Chapter 5).
4. Comparable information for the same date exactly one year earlier (this shows how vesting has changed in the past year and how rapidly the Participant's plan benefit is growing).

A Sample Annual Benefits Statement and a detailed explanation of how to read and analyze its entries are set forth in Appendix L.

While you should focus primarily on obtaining the most recent Annual Benefits Statement, it is very useful to also obtain the statements for the preceding two or three years. Together they will show an accurate picture of how rapidly the Participant's plan benefit is increasing and will reveal any changes in contribution levels or the exercise of investment options made by the Participant during this period. If the Participant is eligible to make preretirement withdrawals from the plan and has actually done so, you will need several years of Annual Benefits Statements to catch this. While the Annual Benefits Statements provide significant amounts of important information, if these are the only individualized statements utilized, it can limit the amount of current account balance information that may be necessary for division.

C. The Plan's Written QDRO Procedures

ERISA requires all plans to adopt "reasonable procedures to determine the qualified status of domestic relations orders and to administer distributions under such qualified orders." 29 U.S.C. § 1056(d)(3)(G)(ii). These QDRO Procedures

1. Must be in writing, 29 U.S.C. § 1056(d)(3)(G)(ii)(I);
2. Must provide for notification of each Participant and Alternate Payee about the Procedures promptly after the plan receives a DRO, 29 U.S.C. § 1056(d)(3)(G)(ii)(II); and
3. Must permit an Alternate Payee to designate a representative to whom copies of all notices concerning the DRO sent by the plan to the Alternate Payee must be sent by the plan, 29 U.S.C. § 1056(d)(3)(G)(ii)(III).

In addition to these minimal statutory requirements, the DOL requires QDRO Procedures to meet certain additional standards. These standards are contained in Department of Labor, Employee Benefits Security Administration, *QDROs: The Division of Retirement Benefits Through Qualified Domestic Relations Orders* (2020) (hereafter referred to as the *EBSA Booklet*). The *EBSA Booklet* can be downloaded from the DOL website at www.dol.gov (or a quick Google search for "dol.gov QDRO") and contains an overview of QDROs, QDRO administration standards, QDRO drafting standards, advisory opinions addressing various QDRO topics, and sample QDRO language. The *EBSA Booklet* is written in question-and-answer format with answers in bullet points. This makes it very digestible and easy to answer questions you may have. Its basic mandate to Plan Administrators is that their QDRO Procedures and their interaction with Participants, Alternate Payees, state IV-D agencies, lawyers, and state courts should be "user friendly" rather than adversarial.

The provisions of the *EBSA Booklet* require Plan Administrators to design and administer their QDRO Procedures in the following manner:

1. Provide information about plans, plan benefits, and Participants' actual benefit entitlements as early as possible to Alternate Payees and their lawyers (Question 2-1).
2. Design their QDRO Procedures so that they do not "unduly inhibit or hamper" the process of obtaining qualification

of a DRO or the making of payments under QDROs, and are made in a "timely, efficient and cost-effective manner" (Questions 2-4, 2-5, and 2-10).

3. Provide information in the QDRO Procedures concerning the plan and the benefits available under it; describe any time limits set by the Plan Administrator for making QDRO determinations; explain what steps the Plan Administrator will take to protect and preserve pension assets or benefits upon receipt of a DRO; and explain any internal appeal or review procedures for QDRO determinations (Question 2-5).
4. An administrator may assess reasonable expenses attributable to QDRO determination (Question 2-6).
5. Provide model QDRO forms to the parties, although the plan may not refuse to qualify a DRO that otherwise meets the requirements of ERISA solely because it does not follow any sample or model form provided by the plan (Question 2-7).
6. Not inquire into matters of state law (such as personal jurisdiction over the parties, subject matter jurisdiction, service of process, correct interpretation and application of state law, whether the Alternate Payee is in fact the former spouse or child of the Participant, etc.) if a DRO is regular on its face (Question 2-8).
7. Not reject a DRO for failure to specify certain factual information that is readily available to the Plan Administrator, such as the Participant's name and address (Question 2-9).
8. Provides that the Plan Administrator must determine whether a DRO is a QDRO "within a reasonable period of time after receiving the order" (Question 2-10).
9. Provide that the 18-month escrow period (described in Chapter 2) covers any short periods during the qualification process after a DRO has been rejected but before an amended DRO has been resubmitted to the plan to prevent Participants from making immediate requests for withdrawals of plan benefits during the amendment period (Question 2-12).
10. If a DRO is not accepted as a QDRO by the Plan Administrator, prompt written notice should be given to all concerned,

including the involved parties and attorneys. Oftentimes, these can be specified in the DRO or in the correspondence included with the preapproval submission. The notice should not simply state that the DRO is not a QDRO, but should

(a) Specify the reasons why the Plan Administrator believes the order is not a QDRO;

(b) Refer to specific provisions of the plan on which the Plan Administrator's decision was based;

(c) Explain any time limits that apply to the rights of the parties (such as the duration of any protective action the Plan Administrator will take to prevent withdrawal of the Alternate Payee's share by the Participant); and

(d) Describe any additional material, information, or modifications of the DRO required to make it a QDRO, and explain why *they are necessary* (*EBSA Booklet,* Question 2-14). *See also* 29 C.F.R. § 2560.503-1(f)(1)–(4) (similar requirement for Plan Administrators giving notice of denial of claimed benefit).

The Written QDRO Procedures are a most important document that should be obtained as early as possible in the divorce or support proceeding. It is recommended to make these QDRO Procedures your starting point. Following the QDRO Procedures from the outset is immensely helpful from a drafting and administration standpoint and can save you many headaches down the road.

Written QDRO Procedures provide such helpful information as how DROs are processed by the plan, who within the plan is responsible for processing them, and what steps the plan will (or may) take to safeguard the interests of potential Alternate Payees while the determination of qualified status is pending. Written QDRO Procedures also often contain helpful model QDROs, or model clauses, provisions, or other specific language for QDROs, that will be acceptable to the plan.

A good set of Written QDRO Procedures will provide

1. A complete checklist of all plan requirements for approving *DROs as QDROs*;
2. A roadmap of all procedural steps that will be taken by the Plan Administrator;
3. A description of any required or forbidden clause; and

4. A complete guide to the qualification process, including the plan's preferred method of preapproval and final submission, from the time the Plan Administrator first receives a DRO to the moment it makes the last payment due an Alternate Payee under a QDRO.

Obtain a copy of this document as soon as possible. It generally is not a difficult process to do so. A simple phone call or letter to the Plan Administrator is usually sufficient to get a copy if you identify yourself as representing either a Participant or an Alternate Payee, or as an attorney hired to draft the QDRO. Plan Administrators are generally quite happy to give out copies of their Written QDRO Procedures as they understand that more often than not it makes their jobs easier. The Written QDRO Procedures are generic plan-based information and do not include any personal or account-specific information about any particular Participant, so the Procedures cannot be withheld on privacy grounds. The Plan Administrator wants you to read, understand, and follow its Written QDRO Procedures. If the Plan Administrator is reluctant to provide you with a copy of its Written QDRO Procedures, point out that you are asking for them so that you can do a good job of drafting the DRO and thus minimize the time, effort, and energy the Plan Administrator and its officials and lawyers will have to put in to qualify your DRO. Offer any proof the plan asks for to confirm that you represent one of the parties and that there is a divorce or support action pending. This is oftentimes personal information about the Participant, including the Participant's name, date of birth, type of account, Social Security number, or address. Also, if all you are seeking is the Written QDRO Procedures, clarify that you are not seeking any personal information and simply are seeking general information for the plan.

Once you receive it, read and study this document carefully to learn what the plan will and will not accept. This is especially important during the pendency of the divorce; in settlement negotiations, including preparing for and conducting mediation; and in trial preparation. For example, if the Written QDRO Procedures contain a model QDRO or model clauses, use them whenever possible in drafting your DRO. But use extreme caution when using model language, as it may not be the most beneficial for your client. For example, the Written QDRO Procedures may allow for certain options from a death benefit standpoint, but the model QDRO limits those very options. Where acceptable, using the plan's own preapproved forms will save you a significant amount of time and effort and can make the qualification process much smoother. It is more important to make sure that all the agreed-upon or ordered provisions are included in the QDRO. Often, additional provisions need to be included to ensure these provisions are included.

Plans sometimes attempt to limit or abolish the substantive rights of the Participant or Alternate Payee by inserting provisions in their Written QDRO Procedures—for example, stating that an Alternate Payee is not entitled to receive her benefits in the form of a single-life annuity even though that form of benefit payment is an available option under the plan. This is improper, since any substantive limits must be contained in the text of the plan itself and the Summary Plan Description. Any issues like this can be avoided by reviewing the Procedures. Written QDRO Procedures govern only the process by which QDROs are evaluated, not the substance of what clauses they may contain.

While most plans will have model language, in the event it does not, an alternative method to avoid drafting issues is by requesting that the Plan Administrator send you a QDRO that was recently approved (with the names and any other identifying information blacked out) so that you can model your DRO on that form. You can also ask plan officials to give you the contact information of lawyers who have recently had QDROs approved by the plan, so that you might consult with them and ask them for copies of the approved orders.

There is the possibility you may encounter a plan that, in violation of ERISA, has not adopted Written QDRO Procedures. If you encounter difficulty in getting such a plan to accept your order as a QDRO, this can be a useful negotiating point in your efforts to persuade the plan to see things your way.

You should also ask for any informal booklets, pamphlets, or information sheets that the Plan Administrator or Plan Sponsor distributes to employees explaining the types of benefits payable by the plan, options or alternative forms of payments, how payments are calculated, when they may begin, and so on. These booklets often provide the clearest explanation of how the plan operates and because these booklets are not filled with legalese, are very generally helpful.

3.3 How Do You Obtain These Key Documents?

A. When You Represent the Participant

If your client is the Participant, simply ask him/her to obtain all these documents from his/her personal records or from the Plan

Administrator and forward them to you. In every state, evidence about pension rights and QDRO Procedures is relevant in divorce, property division, alimony, or child support proceedings. Sooner or later these documents will have to be gathered and turned over to the Alternate Payee's counsel. In a perfect world, all Participant clients would cooperate fully in this area. However, at times this may require some client control for the attorney(s) involved to avoid issues with the Court down the road. Refusing to turn them over voluntarily will only likely lead to sanctions of the type discussed later. We've all had clients who were essentially helpless in understanding what you were requesting of them. If this is your client, ask them for contact information for the Human Resources and/or benefits department of their employer, and communicate your request to them directly.

B. When You Represent the Alternate Payee

If your client is the Alternate Payee, there are several ways in which copies of these documents can be obtained:

1. *Self-help.* Often, if still in the same residence as the Participant, the Alternate Payee may also have access to these documents. However, if this is going to be more trouble than it is worth, potentially leading to more difficult litigation and/or issues between parties, then go through the legal channels to obtain these documents.
2. *From the Participant.* In an ideal world, attorneys will be able to informally exchange documents concerning the assets and financial situations of the parties, including the documents specified previously. In reality, though, reasonableness is not always readily available, thereby requiring going through discovery procedures to procure these documents. If cooperation is still not available, see the next step.
3. *From the Plan Administrator.* Most plans are anxious "not to get in the middle" of a divorce or other domestic dispute. More than this, plans are very much of the preference to have things "done their way." If a plan knows that a QDRO is coming in, they would prefer things to be as smooth as possible. This is generally accomplished by providing this information to the attorney(s) involved. That being said, with the proper information, all necessary documentation

can be obtained through the plan. Plans have three main goals in dealing with QDRO situations:

(a) To make sure that they do nothing to "disqualify" the plan (i.e., to injure its favorable tax status as an ERISA-qualified plan);

(b) To avoid paying out more than 100 percent of plan benefits attributable to the Participant; and

(c) To protect themselves from personal liability for breach of their fiduciary duty to the Participants and Beneficiaries of the plan.

The first goal is that the plan be cautious in following its own QDRO Procedures, that it not approve poorly drafted DROs, and that it carefully review DROs submitted to the plan for qualification (this also impacts point 3c above).

The second goal is that the plan's actuaries carefully review the form and amount of plan benefits payable to the Participant and the Alternate Payee under the DRO to make sure that the plan does not have to pay out any benefit twice.

The third goal is that the plan representatives strictly follow the plan procedures and requirements. ERISA expressly provides for personal liability for plan "fiduciaries." *See* 29 U.S.C. §§ 1002(21) and 1104. Plan officials have been sued for alleged violations of plan terms and plan QDRO Procedures. *See, e.g., Schoonmaker v. Employee Savings Plan of Amoco,* 987 F.2d 410 (7th Cir. 1993) (suit against plan and two plan officials individually for failure to follow plan's written QDRO Procedures).

As previously discussed, a copy of the plan, the Summary Plan Description, and the QDRO Procedures are non-participant-specific documents. Given that status, plans should have very little, if any, hesitation in distributing these documents. On the opposite end of the spectrum, participant-specific documents, such as the Annual Benefits Statement, would not be available without a subpoena or a written release for this information signed by the Participant, because it contains confidential and very personal salary and benefits information.

Unfortunately, some plan officials interpret the third goal as meaning they should "take sides" with the Participant and against the Alternate Payee, and they refuse to provide any documentation without a fight. This state of affairs can sometimes lead plan officials to (wrongly) consider that their fiduciary duty under ERISA is to protect *only* the interests of the Participant if necessary and at the same time disfavor the interests of the Alternate Payee. This may actually result in a refusal to voluntarily provide plan documents, especially Annual Benefits Statements, to the Alternate Payee or her representative. Often the refusal is claimed to be based on the need to protect the "confidentiality" or privacy interests of the Participant.

How can obstacles of this kind be overcome? There are five basic methods. At least one of them will eventually succeed. In increasing order of aggressiveness, they are as follows:

1. *Send the Plan Administrator a letter* like the one set forth in Appendix B. It includes a reminder that the plan's fiduciary duties extend to both Participants and Alternate Payees and of the plan's other ERISA duties as discussed previously.
2. *Ask the Participant to sign a Release of Information Form* like the one set forth in Appendix H covering the information you want. Send this to the plan. Additionally, both attorneys' consent is always helpful on this end. If the Participant refuses, see the next step.
3. *Get the state court to enter an order directing the Participant to sign the Release of Information Form* if he refuses to do so voluntarily. Most state courts, recognizing the well-established rule that pension and benefit plans are marital or community property, or potential sources of alimony or child support, will sign such orders as a matter of course. In the event that a matter relating to this—namely the refusal to produce this documentation—comes before a judge, it is certainly not uncommon to receive an award of attorney's fees or an order of contempt because the Participant has no legitimate reason to refuse to sign such a form. You can ask that the court implement sanctions against the Participant, including financial penalties or even incarceration, if the Participant continues to refuse to cooperate.

   A state court order directed against the Participant ordering him to sign the release is usually more effective than a state court order directed at the plan ordering it to provide the information to the Alternate Payee or her counsel for a variety of reasons. Such orders may not be effective unless the plan is a party to the divorce or support action, which is not possible in all states and may be prohibited by ERISA (see section 10.1). Court orders against Participants also help the plans to eliminate direct liability against the plan, causing plans to be more willing to comply.

4. *Notice the deposition of the Plan Administrator.* With the notice, enclose a subpoena duces tecum to require production of the documents listed previously and others (see Appendix D) at the deposition. Especially when simply requesting general plan information, it is difficult to believe that a plan would want to have to deal with something of this nature rather than produce said information.
5. *Sue the plan.* This is a last resort and should almost never be necessary just to get this kind of information. If it does become necessary, see Chapter 10 on QDRO litigation.

If you encounter much difficulty obtaining these documents from a Participant at this early stage of a case, there are a few different provisions that can be included in settlement agreements or court orders to address issues. First, you can have Participants agree to provide any and all necessary documentation to draft, process, and implement a QDRO. Additionally, you might want to consider adding in a "nondisclosure" clause providing that any assets that have not been disclosed by the Participant and listed in the agreement or order but are discovered at a later date shall be awarded a significant allocation such as 90 percent to 100 percent to the Alternate Payee. This approach often has the effect of encouraging candor and full disclosure.

4 Interim Relief

4.1 Introduction

Divorce litigants and child support obligors sometimes commit hostile, bizarre, and even self-destructive acts under the stress of domestic relations litigation. Among other irrational behaviors, they have been known to quit their jobs to avoid alimony or child support, withdraw funds from or otherwise liquidate bank accounts and retirement accounts, flee the country, and destroy property to avoid having to share it.

What can you do when your client, the Alternate Payee, calls you in great distress on an already hectic Friday afternoon when you are trying to get away for a long weekend (experienced divorce lawyers know that this sort of call comes only on hectic Friday afternoons, never on slow Tuesday mornings)? What do you say when she tells you that the Participant has just announced, "I'm putting in my retirement papers at 5 o'clock today, and you won't get a dime"; or "I'm withdrawing all the money out of the pension plan right away and moving to Mexico—you'll never get a penny of it"; or "I'm selling all the company stock in the retirement account and putting the money in North Korean junk bonds"?

Some of the things that you and your client should be wary of during the divorce or even in anticipation of divorce are the Participant withdrawing funds from a defined contribution plan or changing the beneficiary of a defined benefit retirement plan. The Participant might also take a loan against a retirement plan. In many cases, but not all, a Participant who is married must have the signed consent of his or her spouse in order to make such a withdrawal or plan change.

Even if the parties do act rationally, what can you do if you represent the Alternate Payee and the Participant threatens to make an irrevocable election under the plan or take other steps that may prejudice your client's rights before a final decision in the case? Or if the Parties reach an agreement and the Participant, just really not knowing, cashes out his 401(k) plan before the Qualified Domestic Relations Order (QDRO) is submitted?

4.2 Immediate Steps

There is little that counsel for an Alternate Payee can do about a Participant's plan benefits until you learn what plans are involved. Follow the steps set out in Chapter 3 to obtain this information as soon as possible. In many jurisdictions, when a divorce is filed, most courts immediately issue a standing order, restraining order, or injunction forbidding either party from making any changes to the marital estate except in the normal course of business. If you are in a jurisdiction that does not do this and you are concerned that the Participant is about to take an immediate action that is potentially harmful to your client's interests, consider taking one of the courses of action described in the subsections that follow.

A. Informal Request

One approach is to call the Plan Administrator and advise a responsible official there that you are representing an Alternate Payee in a divorce or support action. This call may need to be in addition to a call to the Participant's employer's Human Resources department or benefits department. Always follow this up with written correspondence regarding the representation. You can include a copy of the standing order with this correspondence. Ask the Plan Administrator not to make any distribution from any plan to the Participant, including a formal request for a "freeze," and to advise you in advance of any investment decisions the Participant may want to make. Please note that many qualified plans do not allow Participants the authority to start dictating specific investment decisions. There are certainly some that allow this kind of control (see Fidelity's BrokerageLink), which can create a new set of issues in the QDRO realm of a case. If you have had the opportunity to obtain plan information at this point, then you should be aware of whether specific investment decisions are a possibility. Most plans will allow a general investment approach of sorts, however, such as "aggressive" or "conservative" investment decisions.

Request that the Plan Administrator not honor any change of Beneficiary requested by the Participant if your Alternate Payee client is currently the named Beneficiary of any plan. Follow up your telephone call with a letter, which should be faxed and mailed (preferably certified, so it can be tracked). Faxing an unsigned draft Domestic Relations Order (DRO) may also be effective if you cannot get the state domestic relations court to enter an interim DRO as recommended in this chapter. In many instances, and depending on the Plan and the Plan Administrator, the Plan Administrator will freeze the asset for so long as the divorce is pending, or for a designated period of time, and until the Plan receives a QDRO. If the Plan Administrator will only hold for a certain period, such as six, 12, or 18 months, then make sure that you update the Plan Administrator as necessary to update the hold. Notification of a pending divorce action or preemptively submitting a proposed DRO for review will oftentimes trigger this freeze.

The Plan Administrator may turn your request down. Compliance with this kind of request is not authorized by ERISA, and it might subject the plan and its officials to personal liability to the Participant (see the discussion of *Schoonmaker v. Employee Savings Plan of Amoco Corp.*, 987 F.2d 410 (7th Cir. 1993) in Chapter 10). I would encourage you instead to consider requesting an interim DRO, as described in the next section.

However, not all plans are this adamant about such requests, and this informal approach may occasionally succeed. But even if it does work, I recommend that you pursue the courses described in the next sections as soon as possible before the Plan Administrator—perhaps under pressure from the Participant and his counsel—decides to stop honoring your informal request.

B. Interim DRO

If the Participant has indicated that there is a risk to the asset, potentially putting your client at a significant disadvantage for purposes of the division of property, ask the state domestic relations court to enter an immediate "emergency" DRO assigning all plan benefits (or a rough estimate of the Alternate Payee's ultimate share) to your Alternate Payee client. Do the best you can with the language of the DRO, but don't worry too much about its refinements. Take an hour or two to prepare a very rough draft, and then file it with the state court. Get the judge to sign the DRO as soon as possible. This is one of those situations, explained further in this book, where you need to be very familiar with the QDRO process in general and be sufficiently prepared to answer the judge's questions as to what you are requesting and why. Most judges are going to be apprehensive to address something of this nature, even on an interim basis, without good cause, and without a lot of specific authority to allow it. Do your research ahead of time to ensure that the judge has reliable law to support the entry of an interim DRO. As soon as the judge signs your DRO, fax it to the Plan Administrator and follow up by mail.

As soon as the plan receives any DRO, however flawed and hastily drafted, it must obey the "escrow" provisions of section 1056(d)(3)(H) of title 29 of the United States Code, which mandates that the plan, for a period of up to 18 months, may not pay out any benefits assigned to the Alternate Payee by the DRO while the determination whether the DRO is a QDRO is pending (see Chapter 2). This is precisely what you want to achieve, and ERISA makes it happen automatically as soon as the plan receives a DRO.

Note that the Participant might still attempt to designate a new Beneficiary because such designations are not frozen under the escrow provision. However, section 1055 of ERISA generally prohibits designating anyone other than a spouse (or former spouse designated to have the rights of a spouse in a QDRO) as a Beneficiary. This brings in the aforementioned submission of the standing order (or other similar document) to the plan.

At this point you can relax a bit and work out and carefully prepare a better-quality DRO, following the suggestions in this handbook, and substitute it for your earlier rough draft.

C. State Law Remedies

At the same time you request the state domestic relations court to enter your "emergency" DRO, you should ask for a specific order regarding assets, temporary restraining order, or injunction against the Participant to prevent any negative (toward the

Alternate Payee) actions pertaining to the plan. This order forbids him to make any elections concerning his plan benefits, or any changes of Beneficiaries, without giving written notice to the Alternate Payee and consent of the Alternate Payee or leave of the court. Send a copy of this order to the Plan Administrator. Such an order may not be technically effective against or binding on the plan, which is not a party to the litigation and probably immune from state court sanctions under ERISA, but there is a very good chance the Plan Administrator will try to thwart the Participant from violating this order. Most Plan Administrators do not want to be in the middle of the litigation of two divorcing parties and are likely to comply with the court order. At the very least, such an order enables you to seek appropriate sanctions against the Participant himself should he violate it.

4.3 Benefits Already In Pay Status

If the Participant has already retired and is receiving annuity payments from a Defined Benefit Plan, there is nothing he or anyone else can do to change the amount or form of payments, so interim relief should not usually be necessary. However, if the Participant has a Defined Contribution Plan from which he is making periodic withdrawals, he will still have the ability to make a sudden and complete withdrawal. In such a case, interim relief should be sought as described previously. Whether any action should be taken here is dependent on the plan and its terms. Do your research and review what is allowable under the plan, and take any necessary steps from there.

4.4 Investment Decisions

It is one thing to quickly draft a DRO and send it to the plan to freeze withdrawals and distributions from the plan. Be cautious, however, about asking the state court to give the Alternate Payee control over all investment decisions affecting the shares of both parties while the funds remain on deposit in the plan. As noted earlier, it is highly unlikely that the plan would even allow specific investment control to the plan participants themselves.

If the Participant has threatened to take negative action regarding the plan, the Alternate Payee has a legitimate concern that a serious dissipation of marital plan assets might occur. But does the Alternate Payee really want to take on responsibility for making investment decisions regarding the Participant's share of plan benefits? Even if your Alternate Payee client is the Wizard of Wall Street, her investment decisions may, in hindsight, turn out to be unwise and may provoke a claim by the Participant against the Alternate Payee for dissipation of his share of the marital property.

In addition, ERISA technically does not require a plan to follow an Alternate Payee's investment choices. Unless the plan itself requires it to allow an Alternate Payee named in a QDRO to make such decisions, ERISA does not require that this power be granted to anyone other than a Participant. Remember that under ERISA, all a plan must do to honor a QDRO is divert the payment of benefits from a Participant to an Alternate Payee—nothing more.

The smartest and safest option is to simply seek an interim DRO to block distributions or irrevocable decisions on the applicable plan. However, should specific investment decisions be a possibility that is allowable under the plan, then seek specific language allowing control over investment decisions only over 50 percent of the Participant's assets as a rough estimate of the Alternate Payee's ultimate share of plan benefits. The obvious drawback of allowing EITHER party specific control of the investment decisions is that you may not know the final division of property and debts in the divorce. There may be a number of other assets that could change *how* assets are allocated. The safest approach is that neither party has any specific control and the account is effectively frozen through the divorce process (or otherwise managed solely by the plan's financial advising representative(s) without input from either party).

4.5 If Your Application for Interim Relief Fails

If the application for interim relief fails in any respect, you can always argue at a later hearing that the Participant should be penalized (and the Alternate Payee rewarded) by the state court for any adverse consequences of the Participant's choices as a dissipation or diminution in value of the parties' joint property. If a dissipation occurs regarding this specific asset, hopefully there are additional assets that can make up that dissipation. In reality, most cases are not like that, though.

If your application fails, remember that not all choices made by a Participant are irrevocable. One interesting case from California, *In re Marriage of Allison*, 189 Cal. App. 3d 849 (Cal. Ct. App. 1987), held that a state divorce court may order a plan to undo an election made by the Participant. In that case the trial court bifurcated the proceedings by first granting the parties a divorce, reserving jurisdiction to hear property division and alimony claims at a later date. The Participant retired between the date the divorce was granted and the date of the property division hearing, electing a Single Life Annuity as he was entitled to do under 29 U.S.C. § 1055 as a single man. The Alternate Payee wanted a Qualified Joint and Survivor Annuity, which she would have been entitled to demand under ERISA if she were still married to the Participant. (It is not clear from the opinion whether the plan had notice of the divorce proceedings or not.) The plan was joined as a party to the divorce case under a California rule permitting such joinder (see section 10.1), and it argued that the election of form of benefits by the Participant was irrevocable under the terms of ERISA and the plan itself.

The California court held that it would be "fundamentally unfair" and inequitable to allow the Participant to make irrevocable elections while the divorce action was pending and before the pension plan had been divided by the trial court. The plan argued that because it had already begun making payments at the higher monthly level of a Single Life Annuity, it could not now change the annuity to a Qualified Joint and Survivor Annuity without violating the principle of "actuarial equivalence" required by ERISA (see Chapter 6). The court dismissed this argument, noting that the plan could either collect any previous overpayment from the Participant or the Alternate Payee, or both, or temporarily reduce their monthly Qualified Joint and Survivor Annuity payment until the plan recouped any excess payment it had already made under the Single Life Annuity, thus making the plan and both parties whole by restoring the status quo ante.

The *Allison* case is quite correct in principle and in its reasoning. It may assist you if the Participant makes unfavorable elections or decisions before you are able to obtain interim relief, or if your application for interim relief is denied.

In our experience, where someone has taken definitive steps resulting in a dissipation of marital assets and the intent was clear, judges are extremely receptive to alternative, and even creative, ideas for recompensing the Alternate Payee for the Participant's action(s).

5 Inclusion and Valuation

5.1 Introduction

Every Domestic Relations Order (DRO) and Qualified Domestic Relations Order (QDRO) is affected by both state and federal law. Although federal law governs the requirements for QDROs and is the central focus of this handbook, state law often places restrictions on what portion of a pension may be divided by a QDRO, establishes the proper valuation date for pension benefits, and governs many other aspects of the extent and value of the benefits to be divided between the parties by a QDRO.

5.2 Inclusion Dates

Although every state today considers pension rights acquired during the course of the marriage as marital or community property, each state will define how division of those pension rights is handled. In general, states consider property, including pension rights, acquired before the marriage exempt from division between the spouses, as it is premarital and separate property. In some states, only property acquired before separation is available for division between the spouses. The reasoning here is that a spouse should not take a share of those retirement contributions and rights that were not acquired "as a result of the marital efforts." In other states, all property acquired before the parties actually divorce, without regard to how long they have been separated, is considered joint property. State law thus decides the size of the "pie" available for division between the spouses. This will oftentimes fall within the discretion of the judge. Make sure that your representation takes your state statutory authority and case law into consideration when addressing this topic. *In re Marriage of Lehman*, 955 P.2d 451 (Cal. 1998); *White v. White*, 319 S.E.2d 447 (Ga. 1984); *Olivo v. Olivo*, 624 N.E.2d 151 (N.Y. 1993); *Workman v. Workman*, 418 S.E.2d 269 (N.C. Ct. App. 1992); *Murphy v. Murphy*, 461 S.E.2d 39 (S.C. 1995); *Ball v. Ball*, 445 S.E.2d 449 (S.C. 1994); *Long v. Long*, 1999 Va. App. LEXIS 566 (Va. Ct. App. 1999).

When pension rights have been earned partially during the marriage and partially during an exempt period (either before the marriage or after separation or divorce), state courts often use a fraction to define the marital portion of the pension. For example, let's assume the Participant worked for the Plan Sponsor (Employer) for a total period of 30 years before retirement. The Participant worked for the Plan Sponsor for a period of two years *before* the marriage, 24 years *during* the marriage, and four years *after* the divorce. For purposes of calculating the ***marital portion***, you would look at the marital versus nonmarital (premarital, separate) years as a portion of the total service (2 (separate) + 24 (marital) + 4 (separate) = 30 (total)). Here, we have six years of separate service (two years before the marriage PLUS four years after the divorce) that would not be applicable. You're only going to calculate the 24 years of service that accrued ***during*** the course of the marriage, divided by the total (30 years). Accordingly, the marital portion of the pension that is subject to division by the court is 24/30 = 0.80 (80.00%). The remaining 0.20 (20.00%) remains the Participant's separate property, not subject to division. *Jerry L. C. v. Lucille H. C.*, 448 A.2d 223 (Del. 1982).

Suppose, in this case with the numbers just referenced, the Participant is already retired and receiving $6,000 per month, and suppose further the state court has determined the Alternate Payee should receive 50 percent of the marital assets. As just noted, the ***marital portion*** of the pension is equivalent to 80.00 percent of the total pension. Here 80.00% × $6,000.00 = $4,800.00. This means that only $4,800.00 of the total $6,000.00 is subject to division, and that remaining 20.00 percent ($1,200.00) is the separate property of the Participant.

Accordingly, what the court may divide is the marital $4,800.00 benefit. As just noted, the court determined that the Alternate Payee would receive 50 percent of the *marital* assets. This means that the marital portion of $4,800.00 would be equally (50/50) divided, with each Party receiving 50 percent of the marital portion, equaling $2,400.00. In total, the Participant would receive $3,600.00 of the TOTAL pension ($1,200.00 *separate* funds + $2,400.00 *marital* funds) and the Alternate Payee would receive $2,400.00 in *marital* funds.

Although the Alternate Payee is not entitled to a direct share of the nonmarital (or separate) portion of the Participant's pension, it should not be ignored. Depending on the applicable state law, the trial court may be allowed to consider the extent and value of the separate assets of each of the parties in deciding how to divide and allocate the joint or marital property between them. *See* 13 Del. C. § 1513. The nonmarital portion of a pension plan may be a significant asset the Alternate Payee can argue justifies a higher-percentage award of marital assets to her. Also keep in mind the use of the nonmarital portion of a pension to satisfy alimony or child support orders is allowed.

The same rationale applies with equal force to the division of military and civil service pension plans.

For this, do not forget to allocate funds to the Alternate Payee when figuring out numbers as they may apply for property division and child support and/or alimony. If you forget to credit the Alternate Payee with her portion of the pension while calculating child support and/or alimony, it can create a significant financial windfall for the Alternate Payee. For example, if you fail to add the $2,400.00 earlier into the Alternate Payee's "column" and still account this for the Participant, then base the child support calculation on $6,000.00 for Participant versus $0.00 for Alternate Payee, rather than the proper $3,600.00 for the Participant versus $2,400.00 for the Alternate Payee, the calculation for support would be vastly different.

Even though a state statute or case law may seem to make post-divorce events irrelevant to defining what is available for division between the parties, the unique nature of pension rights means this is not always true, as discussed in detail in the following section.

5.3 Use and Misuse of Coverture Fractions

QDROs for defined benefit plans frequently divide a Participant's benefit into "marital" and "nonmarital" (or "community" and "separate") portions by using a "coverture fraction." The purpose of the coverture fraction is to determine what portion of the Participant's benefit is marital, community, or is otherwise subject to division. In most situations and under most state law, only the marital or community portion is divisible between the divorcing spouses, while the nonmarital or separate portion remains the exclusive property of the Participant. The numerator (top) of the coverture fraction is the period of time (generally determined by number of months or years) of qualifying service or employment by the Participant under the plan *that overlaps the marriage*, while the denominator (bottom) of the fraction is the total period of service (again determined by the same manner as numerator, whether months, years, etc.) by the Participant under the plan. A typical coverture fraction formula then awards the Alternate Payee a percentage of the Participant's benefit multiplied by the coverture fraction, numerator/denominator.

Here's a simple example: an Alternate Payee and Participant were married January 1, 1980. The Participant began working for his current employer on January 1, 1990. The parties were divorced on January 1, 2000. The Participant continued to work until January 1, 2010, when he retired and both parties began receiving payments from the plan. As part of the divorce, whether by agreement or ordered by the court, the Alternate Payee was awarded 50 percent of the *marital* portion of the Participant's benefit under the plan.

With these facts you can determine the numerator—the time period of marriage overlapping the Participant's employment and qualifying time under the plan—is from January 1, 1990 (date of first employment), to January 1, 2000 (date of divorce), for a total of ten years. Similarly, the denominator—the time period of employment and qualifying time under the plan—is from January 1, 1990, to January 1, 2010, for a total of 20 years. The coverture fraction here, ten years of marriage overlapping employment over 20 years of total employment, determines the marital or community portion is equivalent to one-half of the total benefit under the plan. The Alternate Payee's share is then determined by multiplying the 50 percent award in the divorce times the coverture fraction (10/20). It can then be determined the Alternate Payee is entitled to 25 percent of the total benefit under the plan.

A key point to remember in using coverture fractions in QDROs is larger numerators favor Alternate Payees, whereas larger denominators favor Participants.

At first glance, coverture fractions seem very simple. This is deceptive. Careful analysis of the factual situation and careful drafting of the words of the coverture fraction are required to properly allocate the Participant's benefit into marital and non-marital shares.

The key concept in writing a correct coverture fraction is *overlap*—the period of time the marriage of the parties overlaps the period of time the Participant is accruing benefits under the plan.

A. Beginning Date for the Numerator

The beginning date for the numerator is the later of the date of marriage or date of entry into the plan. Drafters often fail to realize the numerator of the coverture fraction should begin on the *later* of these two dates. If the parties were married before the commencement of the Participant's employment by the Plan Sponsor (as in the previous example), there is no *overlap* of the marriage and the employment during that early period, so the pre-employment years of marriage do not count and should not be included in the coverture fraction. By the same token, if the Participant began employment by the Plan Sponsor *before* the marriage, the later date (marriage) should be used in the numerator since the portion of the pension attributable to his premarital employment, while single, is separate, not marital, property.

B. Ending Date for the Numerator

The ending date for the numerator is the earlier of the date of last employment or the cutoff date for the acquisition of marital or community property under state law. The ending date of the numerator of the coverture fraction is the earlier of the date the Participant ceases to be employed by the Plan Sponsor or the cutoff date for the acquisition of marital or community property under state law. If the Participant ceases to accrue benefits under the plan (by quitting his employment, being fired, retiring, or achieving the maximum allowable benefit under the plan) at a time when the parties are still married, that date should be used as the ending date of the numerator. Additionally, in the event a Plan Sponsor modifies or terminates ongoing participation in a certain plan, then this would also be categorized into the examples of a cutoff date for the purposes of a coverture numerator. If the Participant is still accruing plan benefits when the parties separate or are divorced, then that date should be used. Each state proscribes a different ending date for calculation of the numerator. Some states use the date of separation of the parties, some the date of filing of the divorce action, and some the date of divorce. A court may order a specific date based upon the judge's discretion and/or state law, or the parties may agree to a date for the purposes of the division. Regardless, it is extremely important to follow the court's order, agreement, or state law to properly address and identify the date.

C. Commencement of Employment versus Entry into the Plan as Starting Point for the Numerator

As briefly touched on earlier, when you are first addressing coverture fractions and addressing the marital or community portions of interest in a plan, the period of employment does not always equate to participation in the plan. For purposes of determining the marital portion, it is imperative to determine what amount of service qualifies, and what does not. Some Plan Sponsors enroll Participants in their benefit plans immediately upon commencement of employment. However, ERISA permits Plan Sponsors to defer participation in their Plans until an employee is 21 years old or has worked for the Plan Sponsor for at least one year (two years in certain special cases), or both. *See* 29 U.S.C. §§ 1052(a)(1)(A) and (B). In other words, the Participant's benefit under the plan will not be increased by any employment before age 21 or before the first or second anniversary of employment. Additionally, depending on what is allowed under the plan, some plans will permit certain elections that could directly impact the period of participation, and ultimately, the total benefit. When this is applicable in drafting, be careful to exclude such employment, even if it occurred during the parties' marriage, from the numerator of the coverture fraction. This is especially true if you represent the Participant, as it could be allocating a greater percentage than what is actually marital to the Alternate Payee. The safest way to address this from a drafting and language standpoint is to use "years of credited service during the marriage" rather than "years of employment during the marriage" in the definition of the numerator.

D. Years of Employment versus Years of Credited Service in the Denominator

As in section 5.3C, years of employment do not always correspond to years of credited service. Years of credited service may be less than years of employment due to delayed entry into or participation in the plan. In addition, some defined benefit plans' benefit calculation formulas have a maximum number of years of credited service for benefit calculations. Prior to drafting a QDRO, negotiating a settlement, or trying this issue, ensure you have reviewed plan guidelines and documentation to address whether the Participant has a delayed entry or participation in a plan or even a credit for additional years for the purposes of calculating years of creditable service. An example of this is that certain doctors in the Commissioned Corps of the Public Health Service Corps receive a credit of four or five years of service when calculating their retired pay. When drafting a QDRO where this is applicable, and especially when representing the Alternate Payee, you must take care to use credited service rather than years of employment to avoid disadvantaging the Alternate Payee.

Several examples illustrate the application of these principles.

Example 1: If the parties were married January 1, 1980, and the Participant began working for the Plan Sponsor on the same day and began accruing credited service one year later (January 1, 1981) and the parties were divorced on January 1, 2000, the numerator of the coverture fraction is 20 years if years of employment are used, but only 19 years if years of credited service are used. Use of 19 years in the numerator favors the Participant, while use of 20 years in the numerator favors the Alternate Payee because the value of the fraction will be larger.

Example 2: Using the same facts as in Example 1, assume further the Participant continues to work until January 1, 2010 (30 years of employment), but the plan imposes a maximum of 25 years of credited service in its benefit formula. If the drafter of the QDRO uses 30 as the denominator, the Alternate Payee will be shortchanged (19/30 years, 63 percent marital). The correct allocation is to use the actual years of credited service at the maximum of 25 years in the denominator so the marital portion is 19/25, or 76 percent marital.

Example 3: The QDRO provides the Alternate Payee shall receive 50 percent of the marital portion of the pension, the numerator of the fraction shall be ten years, and the denominator shall be "the number of years the Participant

> accrues benefits under the plan prior to the divorce." The parties were married for ten years, exactly overlapping the Participant's employment by the Plan Sponsor. If the Participant continues to work for the employer, the denominator should increase every year so the value of the coverture fraction should decrease every year (10/11, 10/12, etc.). The language used here permanently freezes the coverture fraction at 10/10, to the Participant's disadvantage.

A quick test of a properly drafted coverture fraction is to verify the numerator is usually a fixed number, because it has fixed beginning and ending dates known at the time the QDRO is drafted. Conversely, the denominator is a variable number, since it can potentially continue to increase until the Participant retires or the Alternate Payee elects to commence receipt of his/her benefit—both unknown dates at the time the QDRO is drafted. The denominator will be a fixed number only if the Participant has already retired at the time the QDRO is drafted or ceased his employment before the date the QDRO is drafted, since under those circumstances he is no longer accruing benefits under the plan.

There is no need to use a coverture fraction if the Participant's employment was *entirely* marital in that it began *after* the date of the marriage and terminated *before* the date of divorce or separation. A flat and defined percentage without a coverture fraction may be used in such cases.

E. Do Not Use Coverture Fractions to Divide Defined Contribution Plans

Defined benefit plans pay out benefits on retirement that are proportional to the Participant's length of service and salary, so use of a coverture fraction to divide the benefit into marital and nonmarital portions is both logical and equitable. Defined contribution plans, on the other hand, have balances that fluctuate depending on the stock market value of invested funds, withdrawals, loans, elections to participate in the plan or not, and similar factors that have no relationship whatsoever to length of service during the marriage or before retirement. As such, a Defined Contribution Plan account should use a percentage or dollar amount as of the relevant date under state law (separation, filing of divorce action, divorce) or a mutually agreed date. This isn't to say time period language cannot apply to the division of a Defined Contribution

Plan. Oftentimes defined contribution plans will be divided based upon contributions during a specified time period (usually the length of the marriage). Coverture fractions, however, should not be used to divide these accounts.

5.4 Post-Divorce Events

In many states, certain post-divorce events will affect the amount available for division between the spouses. *In re Marriage of Lehman*, 955 P.2d 451 (Cal. 1998); *In re Marriage of Hunt*, 909 P.2d 525 (Colo. 1995); *Olivo v. Olivo*, 624 N.E.2d 151 (N.Y. 1993); *In re Marriage of Chavez*, 909 P.2d 314 (Wash. 1996). The three considerations discussed in the following subsections are hybrids of state and federal law; they are features of many ERISA-qualified plans that need to be looked at through a state law filter when dealing with QDROs.

Sample clauses dealing with the following four considerations are found in the model DRO in Chapter 8.

A. Post-Divorce Allocation of Interest, Dividends, and Capital Gains and Losses to Alternate Payee's Share

Often the payment of benefits to an Alternate Payee under a QDRO may be deferred for several years. If the plan is a Defined Contribution Plan, the Alternate Payee will usually be assigned a percentage or fraction of the balance in the Participant's plan account, or a fixed dollar amount, as of the date of divorce, date of hearing, or some other date fixed by the state court or the parties. Since the Alternate Payee's share may be held inside the plan for several years before being distributed to her, it is vitally important to specify in the QDRO:

1. Whether any interest, dividends, or capital gains (or losses) will be allocated to the Alternate Payee's share of plan benefits awarded by the QDRO between the effective date of the QDRO and the date the funds are actually paid to her by the plan; and
2. If so, precisely how these increases (or decreases) will be calculated (oftentimes this will be regulated or controlled by the plan).

Failure to specify the effective date of the QDRO or exactly how to calculate subsequent changes in the value of an Alternate

Payee's share while it remains within the plan is a common source of conflict and litigation. *Matassarin v. Lynch*, 174 F.3d 549 (5th Cir. 1999); *Nachwalter v. Christie*, 805 F.2d 956 (11th Cir. 1986); *McPherren v. McPherren*, 967 S.W.2d 485 (Tex. Ct. App. 1998); *Childs v. Kinder*, 1998 Ohio App. LEXIS 5543 (Ohio Ct. App. 1998). Plans generally will not approve a DRO that does not clearly specify these matters, but subsequent litigation over ambiguities may still occur even if the plan does accept a defective DRO. *See Hullett v. Towers, Perrin, Forster & Crosby, Inc.*, 1994 U.S. Dist. LEXIS 391 (E.D. Pa. 1994), *rev'd on other grounds*, 38 F.3d 107 (3d Cir. 1994).

B. Post-Divorce Contribution Dates and Proration

Many employers make contributions to their Employee Benefit Plans just once a year. The contribution is generally based on the employee's salary during the previous year. The employee must still be employed by the Plan Sponsor on the date of the contribution to receive anything at all. As mentioned numerous times throughout this book, it is important to review plan documents to know if these options and possible issues need to be addressed.

Suppose, for example, Mr. Holmes is employed by the Global MegaCorp, which on January 1 of each year contributes 10 percent of each employee's total salary earned during the previous year to a Defined Contribution Plan. During the entire year 2023, Mr. Holmes earned $90,000. If he is still employed on January 1, 2024, his employer will contribute $9,000 to his pension plan. However, if he is fired or quits his job before that date—even one day before that date—no contribution at all will be made.

Now suppose Mr. Holmes and his wife are divorced on August 31, 2023. Is Mrs. Holmes entitled to any share of the $9,000 to be deposited in Mr. Holmes's pension account on January 1, 2024? The funds won't be deposited until four months after the date of the divorce, so in some states they might not technically be marital property. However, Mr. Holmes performed 8/12 of the work and received 8/12 of the salary on which this contribution is based during the marriage of the parties. Mrs. Holmes has a compelling argument that contributions made after a marriage has terminated, but based on work performed and events occurring during the marriage, should be divisible between the spouses.

The best resolution is probably a pro rata entitlement. In other words, if Mr. and Mrs. Holmes were married for the first eight months of the year for which a $9,000 contribution is made at the very end of the year, the marital share should be 8/12 times $9,000, or $6,000. The remaining $3,000, attributable to Mr. Holmes's post-divorce earnings, remains his separate and nonmarital property.

Admittedly, this $6,000 portion of joint property is created partly by events occurring during the marriage (Mr. Holmes's employment and salary through the end of August) and partly by events occurring after the marriage has terminated (Mr. Holmes's continuing to work for Global MegaCorp from the end of August through January 1 of the following year). Had he quit before January 1, there would be nothing at all to divide between the parties, so the issue becomes moot.

Ideally, language can be drafted and included in the QDRO addressing the issues and providing clear direction as to the Alternate Payee's entitlement under the circumstances. However, often the best way to deal with this situation is to adopt a wait-and-see approach for subsequent events. Using this method, we can say Mrs. Holmes is entitled to a share of the pension contributions that are made with respect to the period of the marriage, through the end of August. Depending on a subsequent event (Mr. Holmes's employment status on January 1), that asset will be worth either $6,000 (if Mr. Holmes is still employed by Global MegaCorp) or $0 (if he is not). Whatever that figure might be, $6,000 or $0, it is what is available for division between the parties. This is the same approach state courts took when they first ruled pensions that were unvested on the date of divorce were nonetheless marital or community property and divisible between the parties (see the following subsection).

This approach requires waiting to see the outcome of future events, but rarely more than a year or two. This approach and all reasoning behind the waiting need to be fully explained to the parties, and the attorneys as well. It isn't often the parties understand the process, any delays, and especially delays that have a potential to last longer than a year. Even if state law defines marital property as what is acquired "during the marriage" or "prior to separation," this argument can still be made and should be accepted.

C. Vesting

ERISA allows employers to delay the "vesting" of certain benefits contributed by the employer for up to seven years to encourage employee loyalty. Once a part of the benefit is "vested," it belongs to the employee as an inalienable right; until it is vested, that part of the employee's benefit may be taken away as a consequence of certain events, such as the employee's quitting his or her job or being fired (see Chapter 2).

ERISA allows two vesting schedules, which are set forth in 29 U.S.C. § 1053(a)(2):

Number of Years Employed	Gradual Vesting	"Cliff" Vesting
1	0%	0%
2	20%	0%
3	40%	100%
4	60%	100%
5	80%	100%
6	100%	100%

Gradual vesting begins in the second year and rises at 20 percent per year until it reaches 100 percent in year six. "Cliff" vesting is so called because it happens all at once, like suddenly falling off a cliff, in year three. A slightly faster set of vesting schedules is used for plans classified as "top-heavy" under ERISA.

Three important points should be noted about these vesting schedules:

1. These schedules show the minimum percentage of vesting allowed by ERISA; some plans provide for a more rapid vesting schedule.
2. Vesting schedules apply *only* to the amount of *employer contributions* to the plan; if employees are allowed to make contributions from their own funds to the plan, they are always 100 percent vested in the amount of their own employee contributions no matter how many years they have worked for the employer. 29 U.S.C. § 1053(a)(1).
3. An employee who dies becomes immediately 100 percent vested in all plan benefits, no matter how many years he has worked for the employer. If the plan is terminated, every Participant also becomes immediately vested in 100 percent of the plan benefits.

Vesting has created two controversies in divorce cases. Very few states allow a division of only the vested portion of a Participant's pension. Since the decision in *In re Marriage of Brown*, 544 P.2d 561 (Cal. 1976), most states have allowed a division of all pension benefits, vested and unvested, with appropriate adjustments to be made if vesting does not occur. *Courtney v. Courtney*, 344 S.E.2d 421 (Ga. 1986); *Kuchta v. Kuchta*, 636 S.W.2d 663 (Mo. 1982). Some courts follow a wait-and-see approach similar to that described previously in the discussion of post-divorce contributions, revisiting the issue after the expiration of several more years to see whether the pension has by then become fully vested. *See Annotation, Pension or Retirement Benefits as Subject to Award or Division by Court in Settlement of Property Rights Between Spouses*, 94 A.L.R.3d 176. It is not uncommon to see courts use a coverture fraction for that portion, and if the Participant vests, then the Alternate Payee will receive a portion, and if the Participant does not vest, then the Alternate Payee receives nothing. This avoids the "wait-and-see" approach.

For example, assume Mr. Garcia's employer contributes $100 per year to a pension plan for his benefit. Mr. Garcia makes no contributions himself, and no interest or other income accrues on his individual account. The plan follows the six-year vesting schedule shown previously, and Mr. Garcia is married to Mrs. Garcia from the first year through the fourth year, when they divorce.

Mr. Garcia's pension rights look something like this:

Year	**Cumulative Contributions**	**Vested %**	**Vested Benefits**
(a)	**(b)**	**(c)**	**(b) times (c)**
1	$100	0%	$0
2	$200	20%	$40
3	$300	40%	$120

This is the status quo in year three. Mr. Garcia argues—and a few states might agree—that Mrs. Garcia is entitled to a share only of $120, the amount of his vested pension rights.

If he were to quit his job tomorrow, $160 is all Mr. Garcia would receive. But it is also possible Mr. Garcia will continue to work for that employer for at least three more years, in which case his pension rights will look like this:

4	$400	60%	$240
5	$500	80%	$400
6	$600	100%	$600

Mrs. Garcia is clearly not entitled to any part of the $300 contributed in years 4 through 6 after the divorce. Notice, however, the $300 that was on deposit in year 4 when the parties divorced is no longer only 40 percent vested and thus worth only $120. It is now 100 percent vested and thus worth $300. Mrs. Garcia will argue she is entitled to a share of this $300, not a share of $120. While the value of the amount available is to some extent influenced by post-divorce events, the entire amount was deposited in the retirement account during the marriage.

Some states may take a wait-and-see approach and look at these subsequent events to decide the amount available for division between the parties. If Mr. Garcia continues to work for the same employer for at least three more years (or dies, which triggers 100 percent vesting) after the divorce, the funds contributed during the marriage will go from 40 percent vested to 100 percent vested, and the amount divisible between the spouses will rise from $120 to $300. The unfortunate part about that approach is that it continues to keep people ultimately tied together post-divorce.

State law, not ERISA, determines how much is available for division between the parties. In fact, ERISA allows a Participant's entire benefit to be paid to an Alternate Payee if the QDRO so provides. If state law permits, counsel for the Alternate Payee should draft the clause dividing the pension rights of the Participant to take post-divorce vesting into account. Counsel for the Participant will, of course, argue for the contrary result. *See Hullett v. Towers, Perrin, Forster & Crosby, Inc.*, 1994 U.S. Dist. LEXIS 391 (E.D. Pa. 1994), *rev'd on other grounds*, 38 F.3d 107 (3d Cir. 1994).

D. Forfeitures

Forfeitures are simply the other side of the vesting coin. Let's return to the previous example, in which at the end of year 4 Mr. Garcia had $400 on deposit in his retirement fund and was 60 percent vested in it. We have already seen if Mr. Garcia had quit on that day, he would be entitled to receive only $240—the amount of his vested benefits. The doctrine of forfeiture answers the following question: What happens to the other $160 ($400 – $240) that was in Mr. Garcia's retirement account?

To start with, the $160 does not revert to his employer. The employer, as the Plan Sponsor, has already taken a tax deduction for the full $400 contributed to the plan, and ERISA prohibits reversion of such deposits to the employer. What almost always happens is the amount forfeited by Mr. Garcia is divided among the other Participants in the plan in proportions specified by the plan, usually in proportion to their salaries during the year.

Assume Mr. Garcia's pension plan has only two other Participants, Mr. Brown and Mr. Cardon. At the time Mr. Garcia quits his job and forfeits his $160, Mr. Brown earns $25,000 per year and Mr. Cardon earns $75,000 per year. On the next date forfeitures are allocated (probably the same date regular employer contributions are made to the plan), Mr. Brown will receive 25 percent of the forfeited $160, or $40, and Mr. Cardon will receive 75 percent of the forfeited $160, or $120. These sums will be taken away from Mr. Garcia's account and added to their plan accounts.

Forfeitures are usually allocated once a year, at the end of the plan's fiscal year, taking into account certain events that occurred during the preceding few years. ERISA requires plans to wait at least one year to see if an employee who left will return (if he does, his service to the company will be considered uninterrupted and no forfeitures will occur). Only then may the plan allocate any forfeitures arising out of his departure. This will occur at the end of the next plan year after the anniversary of his departure, which can sometimes postpone the allocation of forfeitures to the remaining participants in the plan for two or three years.

The precise details are a matter of plan design and should be available in the plan documents. What is important to note is the allocation of forfeitures to an account is usually delayed for at least a few years and should be treated like prorated year-end contributions as discussed in subsection 5.4B. If Mrs. Brown and Mrs. Cardon in this example are divorced sometime during the year, they would have a good argument the forfeitures allocated to their husbands' accounts a year or two later should be prorated into marital and nonmarital portions and divided accordingly.

5.5 Valuation Dates

States vary as to the date on which pension rights, as defined previously, should be valued. Some states prefer to use the cutoff date for the acquisition of marital property (the date of separation or divorce) as the valuation date. Other states use the date of trial or leave the matter to the discretion of the trial court. *Fastner v. Fastner,* 427 N.W.2d 691 (Minn. Ct. App. 1988). As always, the parties can agree to specify a valuation date.

Valuation dates should not be confused with the cutoff date for the acquisition of marital property. For example, the wife may have acquired 1,000 shares of Microsoft common stock between the date of the marriage and the date of divorce, which makes these shares joint marital property. The stock was worth $82 per share on the date of filing for divorce but $145 per share on the date of final trial. If the wife is to retain the stock in kind and the husband to receive 50 percent of the value of the stock, does he receive 50 percent of $82,000, the value of the shares on the date of divorce, or 50 percent of $145,000, the value of the shares on the date of trial? The answer is obviously vitally important. *Matassarin v. Lynch*, 174 F.3d 549 (5th Cir. 1999); *Nachwalter v. Christie*, 805 F.2d 956 (11th Cir. 1986); see subsection 6.2P. State law may place limits on the valuation dates and methods, and the exact wording of the QDRO will decide this issue. Most courts are going to find all of this is marital and the growth should be divided among the parties in a share pro rata to their interest in the plan.

The same reasoning applies to pensions. If the offset method discussed in section 5.6 is to be used, or is a possible alternative to be presented at trial, the accrued pension benefits of the parties must be valued as of the date state law mandates.

For example, assume a Participant has a right to receive a monthly pension payment of $1,000 starting at age 65. He is currently 62, and the mortality tables indicate he has a life expectancy of ten years. A discount rate of 5 percent is used. The Participant was 60 years old on the date of the divorce but is 62 on the date of trial. His pension rights would be valued at $55,130 on the date of divorce but at $64,032 on the date of trial (see subsection 6.2P).

A word of caution: pension valuations are notoriously difficult and vary tremendously depending on the assumptions used by the expert. *Dewan v. Dewan*, 566 N.E.2d 1132 (Mass. Ct. App. 1991) (a husband's pension was given six different values ranging from $96,970 to $730,067 by two different experts depending on assumptions as to future retirement date, interest rates, and future salary). Valuation is also expensive. It usually requires live expert testimony from an actuary or other pension expert unless the parties stipulate to admission into evidence of an expert's report.

The valuation date is not significant unless the offset method of dividing pension rights is to be used (see the following section) or the plan benefits are to be divided using the Separate Interest

Approach discussed in Chapter 6 and in clause 5 in the model DRO in Chapter 8.

5.6 Offset Method of Dividing Pensions

Most states hold it is not necessary to place a present value on future pension rights if they are to be divided in kind and paid to each spouse in the future rather than used as an "offset." *Fastner v. Fastner*, 427 N.W.2d 691 (Minn. Ct. App. 1988); *Elhajj v. Elhajj*, 605 A.2d 1268 (Pa. Super. Ct. 1992); *Annotation, Necessity that Divorce Court Value Property before Distribution*, 51 A.L.R.4th 11, section 20[c], "Valuation Required Unless Percentage of Future Benefits Awarded." However, if the Participant is to be awarded his entire pension and the Alternate Payee to be awarded an "offsetting" share of other marital assets, several difficulties arise. First, the pension rights must be valued by expert testimony as of the appropriate date. *Krafick v. Krafick*, 663 A.2d 365 (Conn. 1995); *Fastner v. Fastner*, 427 N.W.2d 691 (Minn. Ct. App. 1988); *Workman v. Workman*, 418 S.E.2d 269 (N.C. Ct. App. 1992). Second, the couple must have enough other sufficiently valuable assets to award to the Alternate Payee in return for her waiver of any rights in the Participant's pension. Parties often will go this route to avoid drafting multiple QDROs and dividing multiple accounts. Going this route with an offset and equalization with defined contribution plans, especially with defined values as of a certain date, is very simple. It is not with a Defined Benefit Plan. Oftentimes, it is easier to actually do multiple QDROs to avoid the uncertainty, disagreement, and potential issues the offsetting involves, including the valuations.

Despite these difficulties, many courts have recommended this approach because it enables the parties to make a "clean break" from each other and eliminates the risks of bankruptcy, flight by the Participant, and the like. These problems are largely illusory if the Separate Interest Approach (explained in Chapter 6) is used, since under that approach an Alternate Payee may be awarded a share of a Participant's pension in a fashion so nothing the Participant does will affect the Alternate Payee's receipt of benefits, and vice versa.

5.7 Alimony and Child Support

Plan benefits may be tapped to provide alimony or child support payments through QDROs. 29 U.S.C. § 1056(d)(3)(B)(ii)(I)

(QDROs may be used in connection with the "provision of *child support, alimony* payments, or marital property rights") (emphasis added); *Blue v. UAL Corp.*, 160 F.3d 383 (7th Cir. 1998) (QDROs used to collect over $200,000 in child support and counsel fees). QDROs may be used to collect these payments from the Participant's remaining share of the plan benefits even if a part of the Participant's plan benefits have already been assigned to an Alternate Payee by a prior QDRO as part of a property division. Keep in mind if using a QDRO to collect child support or alimony while still being subject to property division, some Plans cap the amount of the Participant or Member's interest to be paid to the Alternate Payee. For example, in the category of military retired pay, the maximum amount that can be paid by the Defense Finance and Accounting Service (DFAS) to a Former Spouse (Alternate Payee for military pension purposes) under the Uniformed Services Former Spouses' Protection Act (USFSPA) (10 U.S.C. § 1408) is 50 percent of the Member's (Participant) disposable income. For cases involving both a payment under USFSPA and an income withholding for child support or alimony obligation (42 U.S.C. § 659), DFAS will pay up to 65 percent of the Member's disposable income.

Alimony and child support have different characteristics from each other and from property divisions made under state domestic relations laws. For example, in most states court-ordered alimony automatically ends on the death of either party or the remarriage of the payee, and it is sometimes terminated or modified if the payee begins to cohabitate with another person or engage in a meretricious relationship. Property division payments, on the other hand, are not affected by the remarriage of the payee (or other applicable relationship status actions) and may not be affected by the deaths of the former spouses. In most states alimony orders are relatively easier to modify due to changes in the circumstances of either party than property division awards. Child support payments terminate or are modified on the occurrence of an entirely different set of contingencies (emancipation of the child, change in custody, and so on) and usually (although not always) end upon the death of the obligor. *See* J. Thomas Oldham, *What Does the U.S. System Regarding Inheritance Rights of Children Reveal About American Families?* 33 FAM. L.Q. 265 (1999), at 271. The federal and state income tax consequences of property division, alimony, and child support payments are also quite different. Child support is neither deductible to the payor nor taxable income to the payee.

Alimony was just the reverse prior to tax year 2019. The tax aspects of property division payments are covered in Chapters 8 and 10. In addition, alimony and child support payments generally are not dischargeable in bankruptcy proceedings, as they are in the nature of support, whereas property division payments often are.

QDROs drafted to collect alimony or child support need to take these different contingencies, and how the plan is to be officially notified of them, into account. QDROs can provide for automatic termination or modification of the payment levels upon the occurrence of any of these state law contingencies as long as they are properly drafted. Specific clauses for each type of payment are set forth in the model DRO in Chapter 8 and discussed in detail there.

Pensions already In Pay Status providing a monthly stream of annuity payments to a Participant may be subject to attachment or garnishment under applicable state law or the Uniform Interstate Family Support Act (UIFSA) rather than through a QDRO.

It is slightly awkward to try collecting current child support or alimony payments from defined contribution plans since such plans typically do not provide for monthly payments but rather lump sums. (They are, however, very suited to collecting arrears for this reason.) It is, however, possible to provide for annual withdrawals from a Defined Contribution Plan for current alimony or child support. As long as the Participant remains employed by the same employer, additional contributions will be made to his plan account at least once a year, and the new contributions can be withdrawn as soon as they are made. Where a plan will not allow for recurring payments from a Defined Contribution Plan, you will likely have to get creative for purposes of how this will be handled, which may result in you taking the steps for creating the aforementioned annual withdrawals.

6 How to Divide Deferred Payment Annuities

6.1 Introduction

Don't skip this chapter. We've pared down the math and the technical discussion to the bare minimum necessary for you to draft Domestic Relations Orders (DROs). But you cannot divide up pension benefits without having a basic understanding of the concepts discussed here.

Most pension plans provide benefits in the form of an "annuity," which is a stream of future monthly payments subject to certain contingencies. Annuities are a somewhat difficult subject, but you need to be familiar with them to draft DROs. Every Defined Benefit Plan pays its benefits in the form of an annuity. Some defined contribution plans also offer annuities as an option. Dealing with annuities is more difficult than dealing with any other form of payment option, but with a little effort you can master the vocabulary and basic concepts of annuities, select alternative approaches to their division, and put those approaches into practical use.

6.2 Definitions and Examples

A. Annuity

An annuity is a contract to pay a sum of money periodically (usually monthly) starting on a fixed date and continuing:

1. For a fixed period (such as ten years),
2. For the duration of the life of one person, or
3. For the joint lives of two persons.

Example: "The Global MegaCorp Employee Retirement Plan hereby promises to pay Mr. Alfred Williams $4,650 per month from the date of his retirement until the date of his death."

Annuities are not just something that you find in employer-offered retirement plans. Annuities are investment options that can be purchased by individuals. The purpose of an annuity is to have a guaranteed stream of income sometime in the future. In order to do that, individuals purchase an annuity for a certain amount of money up front. The amount that is required depends on the amount that is to be paid out, the length of period of the payments, and how soon the payments are to start. When annuities are based on a person's life span, private annuity companies will use actuarial tables to determine the estimated life span of that person.

B. Single Life Annuity

A Single Life Annuity is an annuity payable during the life of one person. This is the simplest form of annuity.

Example: "The Global MegaCorp Employee Retirement Plan hereby promises to pay Mr. Edward Heath $3,575, plus cost of living allowances calculated in accordance with section 17 of the plan, per month from the date of his retirement until the date of his death."

C. Joint and Survivor Annuity

A Joint and Survivor Annuity is an annuity payable during the joint lives of two persons, until the last of them (the survivor) dies. This is most commonly used for spouses.

Example 1: "The Global MegaCorp Employee Retirement Plan hereby promises to pay to Mr. Jeffrey Elson and his spouse, Mrs. Arlene Elson, $2,100 per month from the date of Mr. Elson's retirement until the last one of them to die does so."

Example 2: "The Global MegaCorp Employee Retirement Plan hereby promises to pay to Mr. Jeffrey Elson and his spouse, Mrs. Arlene Elson, $2,500 per month from the date of Mr. Elson's retirement until the death of the first of them to die, followed by payments to the survivor of $1,800 per month until the last one of them to die does so."

D. Qualified Joint and Survivor Annuity (QJSA)

A QJSA is a Joint and Survivor Annuity that meets the "qualifying" requirements of the Employee Retirement Income Security Act (ERISA) in that

1. The parties are spouses (or one of them is a former spouse of the Participant and is designated in a Qualified Domestic Relations Order (QDRO) to be eligible to elect a Qualified Joint and Survivor Annuity with the Participant, or to compel the Participant to make such an election); and
2. The amount payable after the death of the Participant is not less than 50 percent and not more than 100 percent of the amount payable while both parties are alive, 29 U.S.C. § 1055(d)(1)(A); and
3. The annuity is the "actuarial equivalent" of a Single Life Annuity for the life of the Participant. 29 U.S.C. § 1055 (d)(1)(B). (See subsections 6.2K and 6.2L for a discussion of the concept of "actuarial equivalence.")

Example: "The Global MegaCorp Employee Retirement Plan hereby promises to pay to Mr. Carson McElwee and to his spouse, Mrs. Genevieve McElwee, $6,200 per month from the date of Mr. McElwee's retirement during Mr. McElwee's life, and, in the event Mrs. McElwee survives him, to pay to her during her life [any amount between $3,100 and $6,200] per month until her death" (assuming that the amounts payable meet the "actuarial equivalence" test discussed later).

E. Preretirement Survivor Annuity

A Preretirement Survivor Annuity is an annuity paid to a Beneficiary if the Participant dies before he or she actually retires and begins to collect plan benefits.

Example: "The Global MegaCorp Employee Retirement Plan hereby promises to pay to Mrs. Eleanor Winslow $2,100 per month for her life from the date of the death of her husband, Mr. Robert Winslow, should he die before retiring."

F. Qualified Preretirement Survivor Annuity (QPSA)

A QPSA is a Qualified Preretirement Survivor Annuity that meets the "qualifying" requirements of ERISA that it be the actuarial equivalent of a Qualified Joint and Survivor Annuity that is payable

1. If the parties are spouses (or one of them is a former spouse of the Participant and is designated in a QDRO to be eligible to elect a QPSA with the Participant, or to compel the Participant to make such an election); and

2A. *(If the Participant dies before reaching the Earliest Retirement Age)* as if the Participant had survived until the Earliest Retirement Age, immediately retired, elected a QJSA, and then died the next day; or

2B. *(If the Participant survives beyond the Earliest Retirement Age)* as if the Participant had retired with a QJSA on the day immediately before his actual death. 29 U.S.C. § 1055(e).

Example: "The Global MegaCorp Employee Retirement Plan hereby promises to pay to Mrs. Gayle Staley $7,345 per month from either (a) the date her husband, Mr. Luke Staley, would have attained the Earliest Retirement Age allowed under the plan (should he die before retiring), or (b) the date of his death should he die after attaining the Earliest Retirement Age allowed under the plan, until she dies" [assuming that the $7,345 referred to meets the actuarial equivalence test described previously].

A Qualified Preretirement Survivor Annuity sounds like a nice benefit to have, and it is. But note that under ERISA the plan can deduct in advance the cost of funding this benefit from the regular Single Life Annuity payable to the Participant, or from the Qualified Joint and Survivor Annuity payable to the Participant and the Alternate Payee. Watch out for this cost, and make sure to provide for it in dividing the Participant's pension. To find the cost, you may have to ask the plan to tell you the monthly benefit payable under a QJSA or Single Life Annuity (a) if a QPSA is not provided, and (b) if one is, and then work out the difference in the monthly figures.

Note that a QDRO assigning an interest in "monthly pension benefits" was held not to cover payments under a QPSA where the

Participant died while still actively employed. *Dugan v. Clinton*, 8 EBC 2065 (N.D. Ill. 1987).

G. Marriage Requirements

Under ERISA, an employer may require that a Participant and his or her spouse be married for at least a year prior to providing a QJSA. The length of the marriage, under ERISA, is defined as one year beginning with the date of marriage and ending on the earlier of the Participant's receipt of the annuity or the Participant's death. 29 U.S.C. § 1055(f)(1). However, if the Participant marries within one year before the annuity starting date and the Participant and his or her spouse are married for at least one year at the time of the Participant's death, then they shall be treated as if they had been married for a one-year period ending on the Participant's annuity starting date. 29 U.S.C. § 1055(f)(2).

H. Fixed Term Annuity

A Fixed Term Annuity is an annuity payable for a fixed number of years.

Example: "The Global MegaCorp Employee Retirement Plan hereby promises to pay to the Division of Child Support Enforcement $886 per month effective immediately for 17 years and four months."

Fixed Term Annuities are quite rare in ERISA except in the child support context.

I. Hybrid Annuity

A Hybrid Annuity is an annuity blending one or more of the types of payments discussed previously. Some Single Life Annuities or Qualified Joint and Survivor Annuities have a hybrid minimum fixed term feature, which means that even if the payee or payees die, payments will continue to their heirs or estates for the fixed minimum term. *In re Marriage of Rich*, 73 Cal. App. 4th 419 (Cal. Ct. App. 1999) (payments for life of Participant with a 60-month minimum payout period).

J. Actuary

An actuary is a mathematician who specializes in the study and practical application of statistical calculations, especially those concerning life expectancies, the likelihood of future events (such as the percentage of employees predicted to take early retirement or to die before retiring), and interest rates. Actuaries often are employed by insurance companies, calculating the premiums an insurance company should charge today to fund death and other benefits that will become payable in the future. They are also employed by pension plans to calculate annuity values on the basis of predicted life expectancies, interest rates, projected disability, early retirements, and other contingencies.

K. Actuarial Value

An Actuarial Value is a mathematical calculation made by an actuary that includes interest rates, predicted life expectancies, and other future events to place a present-day value on a contingent future obligation or future stream of payments.

Example: An employee retires today at age 65 and will receive $1,000 per month until he dies. An actuary looks up the employee's life expectancy in the average mortality tables, looks at current interest rates, and calculates that the plan needs to have $181,663.73 on hand today to fully fund these payments from the date of retirement until the employee dies (see the discussion of Present Actuarial Value in subsection 6.2L).

Of course, not everyone dies at the exact moment the life expectancy tables predict, so unless this particular Participant dies on that specific day, the plan will either *overfund* or *underfund* his individual pension, depending on whether he dies earlier or later than predicted. However, if the plan has many employees, they will die *on average* as the mortality tables predict, and the actuary's calculations will inform the plan how much it needs to set aside for a group of employees and retirees as a whole. Actuaries are also involved in estimating what percentage of the employees in a large group will elect early retirement, their average salary increases between now and retirement, and other future events and financial matters for planning purposes.

This brief description is an oversimplification of actuaries' highly sophisticated mathematical work, as they will be sure to tell you if I don't. The good news is that you don't have to be an actuary, or even fully understand every aspect of actuarial calculations, to draft QDROs, so long as you have an understanding of these basic concepts and how they work.

L. Present Actuarial Value

Present Actuarial Value is the lump-sum value today of an amount of money on hand in the future, or a stream of payments to be made in the future.

Example 1: You have $1 on hand. A bank offers you 6 percent interest per year. You deposit $1 in the bank today. In a year, you will have $1.06. We cannot say that $1 is *equal* to $1.06, but we can say that the "present value" today of $1.06 to be received 365 days in the future is $1.

Example 2: Assume the same facts as in Example 1, except that now we will consider a bank with 100 depositors. All 100 of them deposit $1 in the bank, hoping to receive $1.06 in a year. However, under this bank's peculiar rules, you have to be alive one year from now to get $1.06; if you die before then, your estate will get your original $1 back but no interest at all.

The bank hires an actuary to study the demographic characteristics of its depositors. The actuary concludes that 50 percent of these 100 depositors will die in the next year, so the bank will not have to pay any interest on their accounts. This means that the bank does not have to have $106 on hand one year from today to pay off all 100 depositors or their estates but only $103. So we can say that the "actuarial value" of $100 on deposit in this bank today for this particular group of depositors is $103 one year from now.

Example 3: Just as a sum today and a single future sum can be compared as in Examples 1 and 2, a single sum today and a *stream of payments in the future* can be compared and valued. If interest rates are 5 percent and you want to make payments of $10 per month for 12 consecutive months, starting four years from today, how much do you need to have on hand today to fund that stream of future payments?

at 5 percent interest:	$100
one year later you will have:	$105
two years later you will have:	$110
three years later you will have:	$115
four years later you will have:	$120

So four years in the future you will have $120 on hand, and you can then make 12 monthly payments of $10 each. (This calculation is somewhat oversimplified because it ignores the compounding of interest, but the principle is valid.)

Using this example, we say the *present value* of a stream of 12 monthly payments of $10 each, starting four years from today, is $100. If you assume that no one will die during this period, we can also say that the value of $100 on hand today and the value of a stream of 12 monthly payments of $10 each commencing four years from today are *actuarially equivalent.*

Example 4: As in Example 3, just as a lump sum on hand today ($100) can be said to be the actuarial equivalent of one stream of future payments (12 payments of $10 each, commencing four years from today), *we can also compare two different streams of future payments.* We can say that one stream of payments is actuarially greater or lesser than the other or that the two future payment streams are equivalent.

Let's look at a couple, Mr. and Mrs. Kanefsky. Mr. Kanefsky is 55, and his wife is 40. Mr. Kanefsky plans to retire in ten years at age 65 and receive from his pension plan a stream of monthly payments of $1,000 each, starting on that date and lasting until he dies (a Single Life Annuity). An actuary estimates that Mr. Kanefsky will live to age 80, or 15 years after payments begin. Mrs. Kanefsky, who is 15 years younger than her husband, is divorcing him and wants to start receiving payments under a QDRO immediately. The actuary estimates that she will live to age 85. The trial judge has ordered that Mr. Kanefsky's pension rights be split 50/50 between the parties.

If the court awards Mrs. Kanefsky half of Mr. Kanefsky's accrued benefit, and he will receive $1,000 per month on retirement, should she get $500 per month as a 50/50 division?

Absolutely not! Consider these factors:

- Mrs. Kanefsky will start receiving her payments immediately, while Mr. Kanefsky will have to wait ten years to begin receiving his payments.
- Once payments start, Mrs. Kanefsky will receive payments for 45 years (from age 40 to death at 85) while Mr. Kanefsky will receive his payments for only 15 years (age 65 to age 80).

Because Mrs. Kanefsky will begin receiving payments earlier and will receive them for a longer period of time, the amount of her monthly payments must be lower than $500 to make them actuarially equivalent to one-half the value of Mr. Kanefsky's stream of future $1,000 monthly payments. (This is one of the most important statements in this handbook. If you don't grasp this example right away, it's worth reviewing the earlier material in this chapter a few times and then tackling this example again until you feel comfortable with it.)

In fact, assuming a 5 percent interest rate, Mrs. Kanefsky's actuarially equivalent payment would be $178.90 per month. If this seems too low to you, remember that she will start collecting her payments ten years before Mr. Kanefsky does, and she will receive them for 45 years—three times as long as the 15 years he is projected to receive benefits.

Bear in mind that once benefits are split between the parties, what one spouse does with his or her share generally has no effect on what the other spouse may do with his or her share, and vice versa. (This is true for defined contribution plans and defined benefit plans divided under the Separate Interest Approach described in subsection 6.2O and in Chapters 7 and 8.)

You do not have to be an actuary, or even be able to do actuarial calculations, to draft a DRO. All you need to know is the basic concept of actuarial equivalence, as explained previously, and how it relates to

1. Interest rates,
2. Time (How soon will payments begin? How long will payments continue once they begin?), and
3. Mortality rates.

M. Employer Subsidy for Early Retirement

An Employer Subsidy for Early Retirement is a supplemental payment provided by an employer to encourage early retirement that need not be taken into account in a QDRO unless the Participant actually takes early retirement. 29 U.S.C. § 1056(d)(3)(E)(i)(II); *Glassman v. Comm'r,* 1997 Tax Ct. Memo LEXIS 581 (1997); *In re Marriage of Lehman,* 955 P.2d 451 (Cal. 1998); *Fastner v. Fastner,* 427 N.W.2d 691 (Minn. Ct. App. 1988).

Example: Mr. Stewart is currently 53. A QDRO awards his former wife 50 percent of his retirement benefits. His Defined Benefit Plan provides Mr. Stewart with the right to retire at age 65 and receive $3,000 per month in a Single Life Annuity, or he can choose early retirement at age 55 and receive $1,800 per month in a Single Life Annuity. However, the *actuarial equivalent* of $3,000 per month starting at age 65 is only $1,346 per month starting at age 55. The difference between the $1,800 actually payable under the plan for retirement at age 55 and this $1,346 ($454 per month) is an extra payment, a subsidy, provided by the employer to encourage early retirement. *See Glassman v. Comm'r,* 1997 Tax Ct. Memo LEXIS 581 (1997).

If Mr. Stewart does not take early retirement, Mrs. Stewart is not entitled under ERISA to receive a share of the early retirement subsidy, so she will receive 50 percent of $1,346, not 50 percent of $1,800.

However, if Mr. Stewart *actually does take early retirement,* in some states Mrs. Stewart may be entitled to 50 percent of the full $1,800 that he receives if the state court so orders. *Halbert v. Halbert,* 469 S.E.2d 534 (Ga. Ct. App. 1996); *Gruber v. PPL Ret. Plan,* 520 F. App'x 112 (3rd Cir. 2013).

To understand why Mrs. Stewart might not get a share of this subsidy, think about the logic behind it. The employer is not legally obligated to offer Mr. Stewart an extra $454 per month at age 55. The employer makes this offer (over and above the benefit level that the employer is legally obligated by the terms of the plan to provide) only in the hope of persuading Mr. Stewart (and other employees) to retire early. If Mr. Stewart does not do so, his employer has not received what it bargained for. There is, therefore, no legal ground for forcing the employer to pay out to Mrs. Stewart any portion of what it offered Mr. Stewart when its offer was not accepted and it received nothing in return.

If, on the other hand, Mr. Stewart actually does retire early, the employer has received what it bargained for. In such a case, a QDRO *may* divide the early retirement subsidy between the parties. (Although if early retirement actually takes place, this subsidy may be divided without violating ERISA; whether the subsidy is joint property or not and subject to division between the parties is purely a matter of state law. The decision may therefore depend on whether the early retirement took place before or after the divorce and other state law principles; see Chapter 5.)

One of four things will happen in early retirement subsidy cases. First, the Participant may die before he actually retires, in which case the subsidy will disappear, leaving nothing to divide between the parties. Second, the Participant may not retire until on or after the Normal Retirement Age specified by the plan, in which case the subsidy will also disappear, leaving nothing to divide. Third, the Participant might actually take early retirement. In that case, ERISA no longer bars division of the subsidy between the parties, although some state laws may do so. Fourth, the Alternate Payee may elect to commence receiving her benefits (if the Separate Interest Approach is used) before the Participant actually retires, and in that case an award to her of a share of the early retirement subsidy is disallowed by ERISA, 29 U.S.C. § 1056(d)(3)(E)(i)(II). In other words, if state law permits division of the subsidy, it may be divided between the parties if it is actually received by the Participant; but it is not available to an Alternate Payee under ERISA unless it is actually received by the Participant.

See clause 5E in section 8.5 on how to divide an Employer Subsidy for Early Retirement when this is permitted by ERISA and state law.

Be careful when reading Annual Benefits Statements (see Chapter 3 and Appendix L). Often the amount shown as "what a Participant will receive at the early retirement age of 55" does not fully disclose that part of this payment—often a very large part—is a subsidy for early retirement and thus not available to the Alternate Payee unless the Participant actually elects to take early retirement.

N. Shared Interest Approach

The Shared Interest Approach is one method for dividing a Participant's interest in an Employee Benefit Plan. Under this approach the payments start when the Participant chooses, are paid in the form he chooses, and will terminate completely on his death unless a QJSA has been selected. The Alternate Payee "shares" in the Participant's pension. It is sometimes known as the "if, as, and when received" approach (see section 6.3 and the discussion of the alternative versions of clause 5 in the model DRO in Chapter 8).

O. Separate Interest Approach

The Separate Interest Approach is a second method for dividing a Participant's interest in an Employee Benefit Plan. Under this approach, the Participant's accrued benefit in the plan is valued as of a specified valuation date and split into two parts. The Alternate Payee may begin to receive her part when she chooses as allowed under the Plan, in any form she chooses as allowed under the Plan, and the payments need not terminate until her death even if the Participant dies before she does (see subsection 6.3E and the alternative versions of clause 5 in the model DRO in Chapter 8). Note, however, that some plans take the position that a Separate Interest is extinguished if the Participant dies before attaining the Earliest Retirement Age allowed by the plan, so it is always prudent to expressly provide (1) that death at that point will *not* extinguish the Alternate Payee's Separate Interest, and (2) for a QPSA for the Alternate Payee.

If a Participant has already retired and begun receiving benefit payments from the plan, the Separate Interest Approach is generally no longer available, and the Shared Interest Approach must be used.

P. Accrued Benefit

Accrued Benefit is the extent of plan benefits earned by a Participant's employment through a specified date. Note that the *accrual date* need not be the same as the *valuation date* (see sections 5.2, 5.3, and 5.4).

For example, a Participant might have accrued a certain entitlement to receive retirement benefits over the 20 years he was married to the Alternate Payee. If they divorce 15 years before the Participant is eligible to retire, the accrual of benefits will stop on the date of divorce or whatever different date is established by state law. However, the *value* of those benefits that were accrued during the marriage will change as time goes by (see Chapter 5). Just as a $100 U.S. Savings Bond may sell for $17 many years before its maturity date, and its price will increase with each passing day as the bond gets closer and closer to its maturity date, the same accrued benefit will have a different value on each different valuation date, and that value will grow higher and higher as actual retirement (or eligibility for retirement) draws nearer.

Q. Survivor Benefit Plan

A Survivor Benefit Plan is a Single Life Annuity for the life of a spouse or former spouse of a member of the military that provides payments to him or her after the death of the service member (see Chapter 11).

R. Former Spouse Survivor Annuity

Former Spouse Survivor Annuity is a Single Life Annuity for the life of a former spouse of a federal civil service employee that provides payments to him or her after the death of the federal employee (see Chapter 12).

6.3 Alternative Approaches to Dividing Annuities

Bear in mind that under all circumstances, whatever form of annuity is selected for payment of the Participant's pension rights, the stream of payments should all have the same Present Actuarial Value (see subsection 6.2L). There are usually only three ways in which ERISA pension annuities may be paid out: (1) as a Single Life Annuity for the Participant's life only, (2) as a Qualified Joint and Survivor Annuity for the lives of the Participant and the Alternate Payee, or (3) as a Qualified Joint and Survivor Annuity involving the Participant and his new spouse. Whichever payment method is chosen, the Present Actuarial Value for these different streams of payment is always the same, so *the total that is being divided is always the same.*

What *does* change, depending on the method of payment chosen, are the *duration* and the *level* of the monthly payment. The longer the duration, the lower the monthly payment level; the shorter the duration, on the other hand, the higher the monthly payment level. This is only logical: if you start with the same amount on hand to fund a stream of future monthly payments, you can pay someone either a lot of money for a fairly short time or a lesser amount of money for a longer period of time.

Because Single Life Annuities by definition have a shorter duration than a QJSA does, they will have a higher monthly payment level for the same accrued benefit. The payment level for such an annuity will depend on the ages of the two persons whose lives are used to measure its duration. The monthly payment level for (1) a QJSA for the Participant and the Alternative Payee may be higher or lower than the monthly payment level for (2) a QJSA for the same Participant and his new spouse, depending on the relative ages of the Alternate Payee and the new spouse. If the new spouse is younger than the Alternate Payee, the monthly payment level will be lower, but the payments will likely last longer. If the new spouse is older than the Alternate Payee, the monthly payment level will be higher, but the payments will not last as long.

If a Participant is entitled to receive an annuity from an ERISA-qualified plan, there are five ways (set forth in the subsections that follow) in which that annuity may be divided between him and an Alternate Payee who is his spouse or former spouse.

A. Pension Already In Pay Status

If the Participant has already retired and is receiving payments under the plan, it is almost always impossible to change the form or amount of benefits. The plan has begun making payments at a level based on the age of the Participant (and the age of any current spouse if a Joint and Survivor Annuity has been selected) and other actuarial factors and is entitled to rely on those previously elected choices. An Alternate Payee's choice is then narrowed to receiving a share of that stream of benefit payments for as long as the option already elected under the plan's terms will allow them to continue. *But see In re Marriage of Allison*, 189 Cal. App. 3d 849 (Cal. Ct. App. 1987) (plan ordered to undo election of form of benefit payments made by Participant for a rare exception to this principle). Usually, therefore, it is no longer possible to use the Separate Interest Approach once the pension is In Pay Status. However, it is still possible to place a present value on the future stream of payments and make an offsetting award of other marital assets even if the pension is already In Pay Status.

The annuity previously selected by the Participant will be in one of the forms discussed in the following subsections.

B. Shared Interest Approach: Single Life Annuity on Life of Participant

Payments will begin when the Participant chooses to retire and will end on his death. The state court simply divides this payment stream between the Participant and the Alternate Payee.

C. Shared Interest Approach: Qualified Joint and Survivor Annuity on Lives of Participant and Alternate Payee

This form of payment is available only if the Alternate Payee is designated by a QDRO as the spouse of the Participant for the purpose of electing a QJSA with him. 29 U.S.C. §§ 1055(a)(1), (d), and 1056(d)(3)(F). Payments will begin when the Participant chooses to retire and will continue until the death of the last to die of the Participant and the Alternate Payee.

D. Shared Interest Approach: Qualified Joint and Survivor Annuity on Lives of Participant and New Spouse (Other Than Alternate Payee)

If the Participant has remarried, he may choose—or be forced to choose, if his current spouse will not sign a waiver under 29 U.S.C. § 1055(c)(2)—a QJSA with his current spouse. Payments under such an annuity may still be divided between the Participant and an Alternate Payee who is not his current spouse, continuing until either the death of the Participant or the death of the Participant's current spouse.

My own view is that payments to an Alternate Payee may continue under a properly worded QDRO as long as either the Participant or his current spouse survives, since the benefits payable to them stem from the Participant's employment, not from any employment or efforts of the subsequent spouse, and are therefore "benefits payable *with respect to a* Participant under a plan," and not "benefits payable *to a* Participant" (emphases added). Section 1056(d)(3)(B)(i)(I) of ERISA says all benefits payable "with respect to" a Participant may be divided by a QDRO. If payments will continue to be made to the Alternate Payee following the Participant's death, this should be expressly and clearly stated in the DRO and this understanding confirmed in writing by the Plan Administrator. What is being divided is the Participant's accrued benefit as of a fixed date. The fact that the accrued benefit is being paid out over the joint lives of the Participant and his new spouse does not affect either the nature and source of the funds (Participant's accrued benefit) or the total amount that is being divided between the Participant and the Alternate Payee (see the discussion at the beginning of this section, 6.3, and the explanation of Present Actuarial Value in subsection 6.2L).

Some Plan Administrators do not agree that payments may continue after the Participant's death. If they don't, you will have to argue the point with them or have an actuary or other expert calculate the percentage of each monthly payment the Alternate Payee should receive during the Participant's life (but not after his death) in order to even things out.

Be particularly careful not to state "all payments to the Alternate Payee will end on the Participant's death" in a QDRO. If you use this wording (which is standard language in many plans' model orders), you will prematurely terminate the stream of payments to your Alternate Payee clients.

E. Separate Interest Approach: Single Life Annuity on Life of Alternate Payee

This is the choice most Alternate Payees prefer. It gives the Alternate Payee complete control over the timing of the commencement of the annuity payments, and they will not terminate until her death. Most people prefer not to run the risk of outliving their annuity payments.

IMPORTANT NOTE: Most plans and regulatory agencies agree that a Separate Interest is not affected by the death of the Participant. However, a few plans take the position that if the Participant dies prior to attaining the plan's Earliest Retirement Age, the Alternate Payee's Separate Interest is extinguished. It is therefore vitally important in drafting Separate Interest Approach QDROs to expressly provide that "payment to the Alternate Payee will not be affected by the death of the Participant at any time, either before or after attaining the Earliest Retirement Age." (The PBGC Model Separate Interest QDRO uses this clause in section 8, which states, "The Participant's death shall not affect payments under the Alternate Payee's separate interest.") If the Plan Administrator rejects this language and insists that the Alternate Payee's Separate Interest will be extinguished if the Participant dies prior to attaining the Earliest Retirement Age allowed by the plan, then it is essential to award a QPSA to the Alternate Payee in an equivalent amount so that she will receive her award if the Participant dies prior to attaining the Earliest Retirement Age allowed by the plan. See clause 7 in the model QDRO in section 8.5.

To implement this form of annuity, the Participant's accrued benefit must be valued as of an appropriate date (the later, the better from the Alternate Payee's perspective because the closer their payment date, the more valuable the pension benefits are) and an equivalent Single Life Annuity on the life of the Alternate Payee, calculated by the plan's actuaries, awarded to the Alternate Payee. Its biggest drawbacks are (1) the requirement for expert valuation of the Participant's accrued benefit, and (2) if the plan awards automatic periodic cost-of-living increases after a Participant retires, the DRO must include a separate clause awarding part of those increases to the Alternate Payee.

Single Life Annuities typically have higher monthly payments but do not last as long as QJSAs. To make a proper comparison, you will have to ask the plan's actuaries to advise you of the amounts of monthly payments that would be made with respect to the Participant under either approach and perhaps adjust any fraction in the pension division formula (see Chapter 7).

Bear in mind that these alternative approaches do not require an "all-or-nothing" election. It is possible, though usually too complicated to be desirable, to pay the Participant's plan benefits partially in one form and partially in another. So, for example, a Participant might end up dividing his plan benefit into a Single Life Annuity for the life of an Alternate Payee, with the remainder of his benefit payable in the form of a QJSA for the Participant and the Participant's current spouse.

Note that if you represent the Alternate Payee, whichever choice is made among the alternatives we have considered should always be supplemented with a QPSA for the Alternate Payee under 29 U.S.C. §§ 1055(a)(1) and (e). Otherwise, the Alternate Payee may get nothing if the Participant dies before achieving the Earliest Retirement Age (as defined in subsection 2.2I). To do so requires designating the Alternate Payee as the surviving spouse of the Participant in the QDRO for this purpose (see clause 7 in the model DRO in Chapter 8).

6.4 Which Alternative Is Best for Your Client?

This is sometimes an easy decision and sometimes a difficult one (see Chapter 7). Before you recommend to your client one of the alternatives set forth previously, you may have to ask the plan to do some actuarial calculations for you, or, if the plan refuses to do so, hire your own expert.

You need the plan to tell you,

- Based on the Participant's earnings to the date of divorce (or other date determined by state law), and
- Assuming that the Participant continues to work until either the Earliest Retirement Age or Normal Retirement Age (see subsections 2.2H and I), but receives no additional salary, or a nominal $1 per year,

what would be the monthly payment level for

1. A Single Life Annuity for the life of the Participant,
2. A QJSA for the lives of the Participant and the Alternate Payee, and
3. A Single Life Annuity for the life of the Alternate Payee (here you will have to give the plan a starting date and the Alternate Payee's current age).

If the Participant has remarried before the property division hearing in the divorce (possible in some states that allow "bifurcated" proceedings), you will also need to know the monthly payment level for

4. A QJSA on the lives of the Participant and his current spouse.

All of these monthly figures will be different, because of the different life expectancies involved, *but they should all be actuarially equivalent to each other under ERISA.*

Now you have some choices to make and to discuss with your client. Assuming you represent the Alternate Payee, you should usually select an option that makes sure the annuity payments to her will continue as long as any annuity payments are made to anyone else, or until the Alternate Payee dies.

If the plan says that it won't allow an Alternate Payee to receive payments after the Participant's death in case (4), you are going to have to persuade it that it is wrong, or you will need an actuary's help in calculating the proper increase in the fraction of each payment the Alternate Payee will receive during the Participant's life.

Example: Payments under a Single Life Annuity on the Participant's life only would be $1,000 per month and are expected to last for 18 years (his life expectancy). Payments under a QJSA covering the lives of the Participant and his new spouse would be $800 per month and are expected to last for 27 years. (These two income streams are, in fact, actuarially equivalent at a 5 percent interest rate.) The state divorce court has said that the Alternate Payee is entitled to "42 percent of the Participant's pension." How should the DRO read?

If the Participant elects a Single Life Annuity, the Alternate Payee gets $420 (42 percent of $1,000) per month until the Participant dies (estimated in 18 years).

If the Participant elects a QJSA with his new spouse, the Alternate Payee should get $336 (42 percent of $800) per month until the survivor of the Participant and his new spouse dies (estimated in 27 years).

However, if the Alternate Payee gets only $336 per month until the Participant dies (expected in 18 years) and nothing after that, *she is being substantially shortchanged.* In fact, she will receive 20 percent less than she should.

Why? If the decision is made by either the Plan Administrator or the state divorce court to terminate the Alternate Payee's payments when the Participant dies, *the correct level of payments to be made to her out of the $800 per month paid under the annuity is no longer 40 percent but 52.5 percent.* The mathematics involved may look complex, but common sense confirms this conclusion: 52.5 percent of $800 is $420, and the Alternate Payee will receive it for the Participant's life expectancy, 18 years, and nothing after that. This is exactly what she was scheduled to receive under a Single Life Annuity on the Participant's life ($420 per month for 18 years), and the two payment streams are by definition exactly equal to each other.

In short, the Alternate Payee is entitled to receive either

- $420 per month for 18 years, or
- $336 per month for 27 years.

Who decides which income stream she will receive? This is a matter for litigation or negotiation. Some Alternate Payees will prefer the risk of receiving a higher payment for a shorter period of time; others will prefer a lower payment for a longer period. The choice is not entirely up to the Alternate Payee, because the Participant (and perhaps his new spouse) may have very different goals and desires. In addition, the Plan Administrator may argue that certain alternative payment methods are not available from the plan.

There is no single right answer for every case. The important thing in this context is to make sure that the Alternate Payee does not get shortchanged—which will sometimes require you to persuade a trial judge that 42 percent should be rewritten as 52.5 percent in order to properly implement the court's decision that the Alternate Payee receive "42 percent of the Participant's pension."

The alternative methods of dividing up a Participant's accrued plan benefit are explored in more detail in the discussion of the alternative versions of clause 5 in the model DRO in Chapter 8. Remember the following:

1. For spouses and former spouses, a Single Life Annuity for the Alternate Payee's life, with the starting date to be

chosen by the Alternate Payee and coupled with a QPSA, is almost always the best choice.

2. For child support QDROs, the best choice is almost always a Fixed Term Annuity or a Single Life Annuity on the life of the child that begins payments immediately, or as soon as possible. Here the object is to get immediate funds into the hands of the child while they are needed, during childhood, not to provide a secure retirement in the distant future. (Joint and Survivor Annuities are not available under ERISA unless the parties are spouses or former spouses, so they cannot be used in child support cases.)
3. For Participants the best choice is a method that provides for any unpaid plan benefits to revert to them if the Alternate Payee dies (or otherwise ceases to be eligible to receive plan benefits) before the Participant dies. This is most easily accomplished using the Shared Interest Approach, but it may also be accomplished under the Separate Interest Approach with an appropriate reversion clause (see section 8.5, clause 8) *if the terms of the plan permit a reversion of a separate interest* to the Participant. *In re Marriage of Rich*, 73 Cal. App. 4th 419 (Cal. Ct. App. 1999) (shared interest automatically reverted to Participant on Alternate Payee's death under terms of the plan). It is important to clarify with the plan whether this is possible or not, and, if so, what language to use to make sure this reversion occurs.

Except for this reversion provision and any restrictions or problems created by the text of the plan itself, the Participant's rights and payments will not ordinarily be affected by any choices made by the Alternate Payee, regardless of whether the Shared Interest or Separate Interest Approach is used.

7 Assessing Your Client's Needs and Wishes: Formulating a Strategy

7.1 Introduction

Let's assume you have two cases in which you represent Alternate Payees. You have gathered all the information you need about the Participants' plan benefits using the techniques described in Chapter 3 and have analyzed the various alternatives for dividing the Participant's annuity using the techniques set forth in Chapter 6. By coincidence, the Participants' benefits in both cases are identical in value—each is entitled to receive a monthly pension payment of $4,000.

In the first case, your Alternate Payee client is 60 years old, poorly educated, and in declining health and has never worked outside the home. There are few other assets available to divide between the parties, and the Alternate Payee has no pension rights of her own. In the second case, on the other hand, your client is 25 and has an MBA from a prestigious business school, a good job as an investment banker, and a promising future. She is in excellent health. There are significant liquid assets (a home, a vacation home, stocks, bonds, and so on) available for division between the parties. The parties have no children, and each wants a "clean break" from the other.

Even though the Participants' pension benefits in both cases are identical in value, it is obvious that these two cases call for radically different treatment of those rights and different strategies on behalf of the Alternate Payee. In the first case, the Alternate Payee will almost certainly prefer monthly payments from her share of the Participant's benefits, starting whenever she elects to begin receiving them and continuing for the duration of her life. In the second case, the Alternate Payee may prefer a present-day award of cash or some other liquid asset of comparable value in lieu of a share of pension benefit payments to begin in 30 years or so. *See* Ira Mark Ellman, *The Maturing Law of Divorce Finances: Toward Rules and Guidelines,* 33 FAM. L.Q. 801, 801–02 (1999).

7.2 What Are the Realistic Alternatives?

The fundamental choice each Alternate Payee must make is between receiving her share of pension payments as a series of monthly payments later in life and receiving an offsetting award of other current liquid assets in exchange for waiving those rights.

In some cases the available options may be limited by the facts of the situation, or the choice may be obvious.

A. Other Assets

In most cases, through discovery, the attorneys should have a very thorough understanding of what the financial circumstances of the parties are. Under certain financial circumstances, it may be possible to otherwise "offset" or compensate an Alternate Payee for his/her interest in the Participant's account or plan. The first question then is, is there a sufficient amount of value in the other assets maintained by the parties, individually or collectively, to adequately offset the Alternate Payee's interest in the Participant's plan? If there is not, in the case of a pension, more likely than not, the Alternate Payee will have to wait for payments to begin per the plan, or as otherwise elected depending on the approach for the pension.

Courts may be reluctant to use the "present-day offset" or "immediate offset" method if it results in one party's receiving all of the current assets (house, cars, investments, etc.) while the other party receives nothing but pension rights that he may or may not live to receive. If the present value of the Participant's pension rights exceeds approximately 20 percent of the total assets available for division between the parties, this can be a problem that prevents this method from being used. *Krafick v. Krafick*, 663 A.2d 365 (Conn. 1995); *Fastner v. Fastner*, 427 N.W.2d 691 (Minn. Ct. App. 1988); *Workman v. Workman*, 418 S.E.2d 269 (N.C. Ct. App. 1992).

B. Need for Valuation

To use the present-day offset method, it is necessary to perform a present value calculation on the estimated total future benefit received from a defined benefit plan. *Erb v. Erb*, 661 N.E.2d 175 (Ohio 1996); *Bloomer v. Bloomer*, 267 N.W.2d 235 (Wis. 1978). A court cannot (or *should not*) award current assets sufficient to offset the value of a pension unless it knows the estimated total value equivalent of the pension. Unless the parties stipulate to a value for the pension rights, the parties will need to utilize the services of a financial professional to perform the necessary calculations to determine the present value of a pension. These calculations are difficult and extremely involved, and they are best left to a professional, such as a forensic accountant, who specializes in this area to perform the work. Additionally, in the event this area of litigation comes before the court, it will require an expert to testify as to the valuations and process of determining the value(s). Arrange for this valuation as early as possible so you can give your client good advice on the alternatives available and prepare for expert testimony at trial if necessary.

C. Defined Contribution Plans

When dealing with the division of defined contribution plans (401(k), 403(b), etc.), it almost always makes sense to divide the account and roll it over into an individual retirement account (IRA) in the Alternate Payee's name alone. This is a rather simple process that avoids adverse tax consequences for either party (see Chapters 8 and 10).

A common mistake by those using this approach, however, is to assume, when crafting a settlement or taking a position in litigation, that the Alternate Payee will have immediate access to funds in a Participant's Defined Contribution Plan. While many defined contribution plans will permit an Alternate Payee to make an immediate withdrawal, some refuse to permit any withdrawal by either party until the Participant has terminated his employment or attained the Earliest Retirement Age permitted by the plan. In any case dealing with division of retirement assets, always consult the plan to determine what, if any, allowable disbursement options will be and all factors regarding said disbursements, including timing. It is not uncommon for attorneys and parties to reach an agreement regarding the division of an account or form of division only to later find out that it is not possible under the plan. If your negotiation or litigation strategy is premised on the Alternate Payee's having immediate access to the funds in the Participant's plan, always verify with the plan that this is possible. Similarly, it is always going to be to your client's benefit to review the plan to know what is allowable when crafting your litigation strategy. Failure to do so can lead to unexpected, delayed, and potentially very difficult litigation.

D. Defined Benefit Plans

In dealing with defined benefit plans, there are five possible alternative methods for dividing a Participant's annuity rights. These methods are discussed in detail in Chapter 6 on annuities.

E. Terms of the Plan

Before addressing the division of a plan, always review the plan's guidelines and description to address possible payment options available under the plan. Whether this is in discussing terms of the divorce with the client or opposing counsel, preparing for mediation, or preparing for final trial, it is imperative to understand what is possible under the plan. Since a Qualified Domestic Relations Order (QDRO) cannot require a plan to provide "any type or form of benefit, or any option, not otherwise provided under the plan," 29 U.S.C. § 1056(d)(3)(D)(i), the distribution alternatives will be limited to what is allowed under the plan. Unfortunately, it is quite common that parties (and attorneys) reach out asking that a QDRO be prepared as part of an agreement, or even a division of retirement assets ordered by the court through a QDRO, only for that option to not be allowed under the plan. The most common occurrence in this area is an agreement that the Alternate Payee is to receive a lump-sum dollar amount from a Defined Benefit Plan that is already In Pay Status. A few minutes of verifying the terms of the plan can save a big headache down the road.

F. Tax Consequences

The tax effect on both parties of each alternative form of distribution should also be considered. For detailed information about tax consequences, see section 10.3.

G. What If a QDRO Is Not Available?

All ERISA-qualified plans are subject to QDROs, and similar orders are available to divide federal civil service and military retirement (for example, Court Orders Acceptable for Processing (COAPs), Military Pension Division Orders (MPDOs), or Qualified Court Orders (QCOs)). However, in certain cases, you may find that a QDRO-like order may not be available for a nonqualified corporate plan or a state or local government plan, or that the parties may be unable to meet the jurisdictional requirements for direct payment of a portion of disposable retired pay under the military retirement system due to length of marriage overlapping creditable military service (see Chapter 11). That does *not* mean your nonemployee client is without a remedy. While direct payment under a court order is most often the ideal and most practical outcome, alternative remedies do exist in the event they are necessary. As previously addressed, a frequently utilized alternative is determining a present value of the account/plan and offsetting the Alternate Payee's (for military and federal retirement plans: former spouse) portion against another asset. Should any alternatives be utilized, parties need to be extremely clear with the intent and language included in an agreement.

7.3 What Factors Should Be Considered?

The factors to be considered in deciding which form of distribution to pursue are essentially the same as those set forth in most state property division statutes. These include the following:

1. Ages of the parties.
2. Health of the parties.
3. Current income, employment history, occupational skills, education, training, and earning capacity of each party.
4. Duration of the marriage.
5. The Alternate Payee's own pension rights or other retirement plans, if any.

6. Availability of current liquid assets to be assigned to the Alternate Payee in the marital property divisions in lieu of a share in Participant's pension rights.
7. Separate, nonmarital property owned by either party.
8. Potential tax consequences to each party of the proposed method of property division. *See, e.g.*, 13 Del. C. § 1513.
9. Prospects for remarriage, if the client tells you that such prospects are specific and quite likely to occur in the near future. *Hullet v. Towers, Perrin, Foster & Crosby, Inc.*, 1994 U.S. Dist. LEXIS 391 (E.D. Pa. 1994); *Pospisil v. Pospisil*, 1999 Conn. Super. LEXIS 499 (Conn. Super. 1999). This factor is directly relevant for areas such as survivor benefits in military and federal plans, which can automatically terminate if the former spouse remarries before the age of 55.

   About two-thirds of divorced women, and a slightly higher percentage of divorced men, eventually remarry and their financial condition generally improves, sometimes significantly, in the second marriage. *See* Ira Mark Ellman, *The Maturing Law of Divorce Finances: Toward Rules and Guidelines*, 33 FAM. L.Q. 801, 801–02 (1999). Averages may be interesting, but they are never as useful as the kind of detailed professional analysis of their individual situations and prospects that each client needs and expects.
10. A "clean break" between the parties. It is not uncommon to hear parties going through a divorce talk about how they would like to sever ties with their soon-to-be-ex-spouse. Keep in mind that most private pension plans will allow for a Separate Interest Approach, which bases the pension payments on the life of the Alternate Payee rather than the Participant. Since the Alternate Payee's portion is based upon the Alternate Payee's life, it does not rely on the Participant's commencement of benefits, nor does it require addressing surviving spouse or other beneficiary consideration for the Alternate Payee. If a Separate Interest Approach is unavailable, and if the parties would otherwise have no lingering ties with each other (such as children) and desire to do so, it may be better to utilize an alternative by awarding the Alternate Payee assets to offset the Alternate Payee's interest in

the pension. This has even been addressed by courts. *Hoyt v. Hoyt*, 559 N.E.2d 1292 (Ohio 1990).

11. Financial needs of the parties (or namely, the Alternate Payee). Ideally, an Alternate Payee would never need to rely on a distribution from a QDRO. Unfortunately, in the real world of practice, this is a very common reality for some parties, and these circumstances need to be taken into consideration when discussing distribution options.

7.4 Which Alternative Should Your Client Pursue?

All the factors listed in section 7.3 should be discussed with your client as early in the case as possible, but especially during any discussions of settlement, in preparation of and during mediation, and in preparation of final trial. The earlier, the better. No client wants to learn the ins and outs of a pension *during* a mediation where a decision may need to be made relatively quickly. It is important to educate your clients on these topics ahead of time so they can make an informed decision. Note that Part B of the Client Questionnaire in Appendix I asks each client to express a preference on the timing and form of receipt of benefits from his or her spouse's pension. You must discuss with your client not only whether an offsetting award of other assets should be pursued but also, in case a QDRO will be used, the pros and cons of the Shared Interest and Separate Interest Approaches, and the pros and cons of seeking a share of (1) a Single Life Annuity on the Participant's life, (2) a Qualified Joint and Survivor Annuity (QJSA) on the lives of the Participant and the Alternate Payee, (3) a QJSA on the lives of the Participant and his current spouse (not the Alternate Payee), or (4) a Separate Interest Single Life Annuity on the life of the Alternate Payee, in each case coupled with a Qualified Preretirement Survivor Annuity (QPSA); see Chapters 6 and 8.

While lawyers can give sound, professional, and objective advice about these matters and can explain how they will affect the client's case, in the final analysis it is the client who must live with the consequences of the decision. Give your best professional advice, and make sure the client understands the range of choices and the pros and cons of each. Then let the client make the decision, and turn your professional skills to helping the client pursue the goal he or she has chosen.

7.5 QDROs for Child Support and Alimony

QDROs for child support or alimony by definition involve contingencies not usually relevant to property division QDROs. Alimony, for example, usually ends on the death of either the payor or the payee, or on the remarriage (and depending on the state, cohabitation) of the payee; property division awards generally are not dependent on remarriage. Alimony is also, in most states, modifiable due to certain changes in circumstances or events listed earlier. Generally, property division is *not* modifiable unless circumstances dictate such a division be set aside or reconsidered by the trial court. This is generally limited to limited situations, like fraud.

Child support (except for the collection of previously accrued arrearages) usually ends on the emancipation of the child(ren) but can also end upon the death of the payor (*see* J. Thomas Oldham, *What Does the U.S. System Regarding Inheritance Rights of Children Reveal about American Families?* 33 FAM. L.Q. 265, 271 (1999)) or on the death, marriage, or a change in custody of the child. These payments generally have a fixed monthly amount. Under most circumstances and in many states, a sum certain can be determined for purposes of both child support and alimony. However, uncertainty with potential modifications, emancipation issues, and potentially impacting provisions in Settlement Agreements or Final Judgments (among other matters) can make it extremely difficult to ascertain a present value. In light of this, oftentimes alimony and child support are better handled as monthly payments received under the pension plan rather than as a lump-sum offset. Like all other aspects of asset and retirement division, a conversation regarding the parties' circumstances will best guide how to approach and handle each situation.

The characterization of the payments under a QDRO as alimony, child support, or property division is also important for tax purposes. Child support payments received are not subject to any tax consideration; however, the Participant (payor) may be required to pay taxes on the sums distributed from the plan for purposes of their child support obligation. Property division between divorcing spouses generally avoids tax consequences; however, if the property is in a pension or Employee Benefit Plan, the party who ultimately withdraws the funds from the plan will have a tax liability.

In addition, alimony and child support obligations are not dischargeable in bankruptcy while certain property division awards may be.

If you decide to use QDROs for alimony or child support, remember that the goal is to meet the client's immediate needs—not to provide for a secure retirement many years from now. This ordinarily leads you to recommend, and your client to choose, whichever alternative starts the payments flowing the soonest.

7.6 Representing the Participant

While the discussion in this chapter has focused on representing Alternate Payees, the same considerations—age, health, availability of other assets for offsets, and the like—have an equal impact on Participants. When you are representing a Participant, just as any party going through a divorce, the first topic that needs to be addressed is realistic views of what the expected benefit value will be post-division. Oftentimes, the Participant, if already receiving the benefit, is reliant upon that amount and a full understanding of resulting benefit is necessary through this process. Additionally, it is important to ascertain his needs and goals as to the preferred method of dividing his pension rights; to consider how the factors listed previously come into play; to discuss these matters with the client and come to a mutually agreed strategy for pursuing the client's goals; and to document these decisions in writing, as discussed in the following section. An important consideration when representing the Participant is to provide, to the maximum extent possible, for the reversion of the Alternate Payee's share of plan benefits to the Participant if the Alternate Payee dies before the Participant. In fact, some plans actually do not allow for the Alternate Payee's designation of a beneficiary or to the Alternate Payee's estate and automatically revert to the Participant upon notification of the Alternate Payee's death.

7.7 Avoiding Malpractice Claims

The most important step in avoiding malpractice claims is to be thorough and communicative with your client, whether the Participant or Alternate Payee. In every divorce case, and any situation addressing asset division, one aspect, if not the most important, is communication with the client. When addressing retirement division, most clients will have very little knowledge as to the potential outcomes, possible alternatives, and what important factors should be addressed and weighed. It is the attorney's job to fully inform and discuss these areas with the clients so that the best and most educated choice for each situation can be made. This starts with the attorney adequately educating him- or herself on what is allowable under the plan and, in turn, educating the client on the same. Once these factors and alternatives have been reviewed with the client, it is important to send the client a letter summarizing the discussions you have had on all these topics, reviewing the recommendations you made and the reasons for them, and asking for the client's final decision on which alternative to pursue. In the modern era, an email can usually suffice for this purpose as well.

To ensure that you're protected from potential malpractice claims, you can have the client sign a copy of this letter acknowledging his/her understanding of the discussions and decisions. Similarly, an email response from the client can sufficiently represent his/her understanding of the final decision. Alternatively, clear language can be included in the correspondence to the client reflecting a lack of response or further communication acts as implied consent to a full understanding of the decision made. This is particularly important in situations where a client makes an unusual choice—for example, if an Alternate Payee declines to be covered by a Qualified Preretirement Survivor Annuity, or if a Participant wants to make an irrevocable commitment to retire early. This is an area of the law where there is a lot on the line that can significantly impact a person's livelihood potentially for the rest of his/her life. As a result, it is extremely important for any lawyer in such a situation to carefully document that sound advice was given to the client detailing all available options, and the client ultimately made the final decision with all the facts in front of him/her.

8 Drafting the DRO

8.1 Introduction

Now that you have obtained the information you need (Chapter 3), arranged for any necessary interim relief (Chapter 4), considered all the federal and state law factors affecting which employee benefits are available for division and how to value them (Chapter 5), analyzed the alternatives for dividing an annuity (Chapter 6), and worked with your client to identify his or her goals (Chapter 7), you are ready to draft a Domestic Relations Order (DRO). This chapter discusses who will draft the DRO and when it should be prepared. The heart of the discussion is section 8.5, which presents a model DRO with several alternate clauses for each of the issues discussed elsewhere in this handbook, along with detailed comments on each clause.

8.2 Who Will Draft the DRO?

There are only five possibilities regarding who drafts the DRO:

1. The trial judge. I have yet to meet a trial judge who is willing to take on the responsibility of drafting a DRO. Judges, especially those who hear domestic relations matters, are overburdened with other urgent concerns. It is unrealistic to expect them to even consider performing this task. Further, most trial judges and their staff attorneys do not have the knowledge or expertise to effectively draft a DRO. If they do, then it is likely not an efficient use of time considering the number of other matters they have to address.

In all likelihood, a judge who is asked to draft a DRO will direct counsel to submit a form of order in accordance with the judge's ruling on the percentage of pension rights awarded to each party or a DRO that reflects the terms of a settlement. The judge will usually be willing to sign such an order, but he or she won't draft it.

2. The plan. While many plans provide model DROs as part of their written Qualified Domestic Relations Orders (QDRO) Procedures, they will not draft individual DROs. Plans have enough fiduciary responsibilities to Participants and Beneficiaries without undertaking the unauthorized practice of law on behalf of either party. Plans will, of course, comment on the correctness of draft DROs and will list any objections they may have to particular clauses in the DRO. They may even suggest language for particular clauses in a DRO you submit to them. They will not, however, take out a blank sheet of paper and write the first draft.

3. Counsel for the Participant. The Participant stands to gain nothing—and to lose a lot—if a QDRO is entered. After all, the purpose of the QDRO is to deprive him of some of his plan benefits. Consequently, it theoretically makes no sense at all for a Participant or his counsel to do any of the drafting work on the DRO. Besides, if the lawyer for the Participant does the work, it will be at the Participant's expense—a double dip into his funds. Participants and their counsel will, of course, wish to comment on the draft DRO and suggest clauses favorable to the Participant, but Participants often hope that through neglect, a QDRO will never be entered. (Sometimes that wish comes true; see Chapters 10 and 14.) Now, that being said, certain Participants may want to be in control of the preparation process to ensure that everything is handled properly. As noted earlier, Participants stand to lose a lot following the entry of a QDRO. They can lose even more if that QDRO is poorly prepared.

4. Counsel for the Alternate Payee. Counsel for the Alternate Payee has the most to lose if a QDRO is not entered. Failure to draft a DRO and get it signed by the trial judge and then qualified by the plan will result in an angry client and probably a malpractice suit for the amount of benefits the Alternate Payee should have received under the QDRO.

Counsel for the Alternate Payee thus has the strongest financial and professional incentives to draft the DRO and to make sure that the qualification process is followed through to successful completion.

5. A neutral attorney. It is becoming more common for attorneys and parties to agree in settlement to hire a third-party neutral attorney who specializes in the drafting of QDROs to draft the QDRO. In settlement, the parties will agree on who that person will be, will agree on how his or her fees are to be paid, and ideally will have already reached out to that person to confirm that the neutral attorney is available and his or her requirements.

If a third-party neutral is hired to draft the QDRO, attorneys and parties must keep in mind that the role of the third-party neutral is to implement what has been agreed upon by the parties in the settlement agreement. It is not his or her role to advise the parties on how to divide the asset. If the settlement agreement is not clear on how the plan is to be divided, then expect the third-party neutral to come back to the attorneys asking for clarification. If you are a third-party neutral attorney in this position, be careful as to how your fee arrangements are structured for this purpose. If it is a very litigious divorce and the parties are inclined to argue about anything and everything, drawing you in, you may be losing money for your practice if you don't have a proper fee arrangement. Similarly, if the parties are woefully uninformed as to what anything related to a QDRO means or the process, the same applies.

8.3 Preliminary Considerations

A. Prepare Separate DROs for Each Plan

You will need a separate DRO (or at least a separate paragraph) for each separate plan. Different plans, even those sponsored by the same employer, often have very different features and very different forms of benefit payments. While some required information is common to all DROs (such as the names and current addresses of the Participant and the Alternate Payee), many provisions will have to be different to account for the differences from plan to plan. This is something that certain plans may allow depending on the structure of the retirement plans subject to division. This comes back to doing your homework regarding plans and the procedures for QDROs. If you're unable to obtain all the proper information, to avoid confusion, it is usually better to prepare a separate DRO for each separate plan.

B. Prepare the DRO as Soon as Possible

A great source of malpractice and protracted collateral litigation is the division of pension benefits by stipulation or after a hearing by the state court, followed by judicial instructions to the parties and their lawyers to "prepare and file a QDRO." It is the failure or unexcused delay in sending a DRO to a plan for qualification that lies at the heart of such malpractice claims and disciplinary proceedings. *Payne v. GM/UAW Pension Plan*, 1996 U.S. Dist. LEXIS 7966 (E.D. Mich. 1996); *Layton v. TDS Healthcare Systems Corp.*, 1994 U.S. Dist. LEXIS 6709 (N.D. Cal. 1994); *Cuyahoga Bar Ass'n v. Williamson*, 652 N.E.2d 972 (Ohio 1995); *In re Louderman*, 1999 Wis. LEXIS 117 (Wis. 1999) (public reprimand for six-year delay in preparing DRO); *Carter v. Carter*, 869 S.W.2d 822 (Mo. Ct. App. 1994); *Williams v. Cooch & Taylor*, 1994 Del. Super. LEXIS 211 (Del. Super. Ct. 1994); see section 10.4.

Another significant problem that arises out of deferred QDRO drafting is that it fosters disparities between what the trial court ordered at the property division hearing or the parties agreed to in their settlement negotiations, on the one hand, and the exact wording of the QDRO, on the other—differences that can lead to litigation. *Fortmann v. Avon Products, Inc.*, 1999 U.S. Dist. LEXIS 3451 (N.D. Ill. 1999) (property settlement agreement approved by state court divided all pension benefits payable at retirement; DRO divided all benefits "as of" the date of the DRO, ten years before retirement); *Layton v. TDS Healthcare Systems Corp.*, 1994 U.S. Dist. LEXIS 6709 (N.D. Cal. 1994); *Holloman v. Holloman*, 691 So. 2d 897 (Miss. 1996); *Carpenter v. Carpenter*, 1996 Tex. App. LEXIS 3210 (Tex. Ct. App. 1996) (DROs amended three times and litigated for three years on issue of which plans were intended to be covered by them); *Wilson v. Wilson*, 492 S.E.2d 495 (Va. Ct. App. 1997).

Frequently you will find that the parties are agreed on every clause and every aspect of the DRO to be entered in their case—except the percentage or dollar amount to be awarded to the Alternate Payee. Don't let this lack of finality seduce you into delaying your work. Draft all the other clauses of the DRO and submit it to the plan for preapproval, leaving just one blank space for the percentage or dollar amount for you to fill in at the hearing.

Your goal should be to walk into the courtroom with a clean draft of a DRO already approved by the plan (see subsection 8.3C and Chapter 10), perhaps, as just mentioned, with only the final amount or percentage to be awarded to your client left blank. You will impress the judge, blow away the opposition, and avoid malpractice claims.

C. Prequalify the DRO with the Plan

If you're drafting a DRO, send your draft to the plan for review as early as possible—preferably well before the property division hearing or the time of execution of the divorce decree. It is always better to be able to submit the DRO and divorce decree at the same time, rather than having to wait until well after the divorce to get that aspect handled. Although the DRO is not an "order" at this stage and the plan cannot formally qualify it, most plans are grateful for the opportunity to review and informally comment on draft DROs—it makes the plan's task easier. The Department of Labor (DOL) encourages plans to provide advice and guidance to counsel for the parties as early as possible in domestic relations proceedings. *EBSA Booklet* Questions 2-1, 2-5, and 2-7. It is easier and more efficient for all parties to have this kind of informal review early in the process, rather than waiting for the judge to sign the DRO after a hearing or chambers conference and then, and only then, send it to the plan for its initial review.

D. The "Dirty Dozen": 12 Good Reasons Why Your Clients (and Your Malpractice Insurance Carrier) Don't Want You to Just Fill in the Blanks in the Plan's Model Order

Many Employee Benefit Plans provide model QDROs to the divorce bar. When family law attorneys follow these models by simply filling in the blanks (entering names and Social Security numbers, percentage shares awarded to each, and so on), the Plan Administrator's task of reviewing and approving QDROs is made much easier, and the cost to the plan of QDRO processing decreases significantly. But never forget: the plan is providing you with model QDROs for one reason and one reason alone—to simplify its own work and hold down its administrative costs. Model orders of pension plans are not designed to obtain the best result for your client.

That's your job. Just "filling in the blanks" can result in financial disaster for your clients and malpractice litigation against you.

Plan administrators are required by the Employee Retirement Income Security Act (ERISA) to accept QDROs that do not follow their standard forms and that provide better protection for your clients. In most cases it is essential to modify the plan's standard clauses and add some of your own in order to preserve your clients' rights.

Plan Administrators review QDROs only to ensure that their terms are consistent with ERISA and the language of the plan. Always remember: when the Plan Administrator accepts your QDRO, this does *not* mean that

- The QDRO is consistent with the underlying terms of the divorce decree or separation agreement,
- The QDRO represents the best deal for your client, or
- You won't be sued for malpractice.

Consider the following "dirty dozen" critical issues that are frequently ignored or improperly dealt with in a plan's model QDRO.

1. Did you preserve your client's rights in the event of a Pension Benefit Guaranty Corporation (PBGC) takeover of the plan? At the end of 2016, more than 840,000 retirees in more than 4,700 insolvent pension plans were forced to rely on the PBGC for their monthly checks. These figures mean it is inevitable that some of your clients will eventually be involved as Alternate Payees in a PBGC takeover plan. And PBGC payments are subject to severe financial and legal limits that may drastically reduce your client's payments—or even eliminate them entirely—unless you add a PBGC takeover clause to your QDRO.

If the maximum amount payable by the PBGC ($5,962.50 per month for 2018 for a Participant age 65) is less than the total amount payable to both parties, whose share will be reduced by the shortfall? The Participant's? The Alternate Payee's? Or will both parties' shares be reduced pro rata? A well-prepared QDRO will expressly provide how the parties will share any shortfall created by a PBGC takeover. However, not many model orders account for the effect of a PBGC takeover (probably because Plan Administrators are replaced in such circumstances and consequently will not be around to deal with the issues resulting from a PBGC takeover). Use clause 10 in section 8.5 to deal with this issue.

2. Did you obtain both forms of survivorship benefit for your client? Some model QDROs omit any mention of the plan's survivorship benefits—Qualified Preretirement Survivor Annuities (QPSAs) and Qualified Joint and Survivor Annuities (QJSAs)—entirely. Others give them only cursory treatment, providing a simple clause that "the Alternate Payee [will]/[will not] (strike out one) be treated as the surviving spouse of the Participant pursuant to sections 1055 and 1056(d)(3) of ERISA." While this language is better than nothing, it greatly oversimplifies the choices available in this area.

For example, choosing the "will" option in this clause awards 100 percent of the Participant's survivorship benefits to the Alternate Payee, leaving nothing at all for a subsequent spouse of the Participant, even though the Alternate Payee was awarded only 50 percent of the Participant's benefits. It is possible to cure this situation by providing that the Alternate Payee will be treated as the Participant's surviving spouse under sections 1055 and 1056(d)(3), "but only to the extent of the share of benefits awarded to the Alternate Payee by this order." This hand-tailored clause fully protects the Alternate Payee's interests while leaving the Participant free to designate the Beneficiary of the Participant's share of plan benefits. This is a highly attractive option when you represent the Participant but one that is almost never included in plans' model QDROs.

A related problem arises in the fairly common situation in which (1) the Alternate Payee is awarded a Shared Interest in the Participant's benefits; (2) the Participant remarries; (3) the Participant retires, electing a QJSA with his new spouse; and (4) the Participant then dies and is survived by both the new spouse and the Alternate Payee. The correct treatment of this situation under ERISA is that the Alternate Payee should continue receiving payments until the death of the new spouse. But approximately half of the model orders I have examined treat this situation incorrectly and state that all payments to the Alternate Payee will end when the Participant dies. Following a plan's model language in this area could lead to your Alternate Payee client inadvertently waiving several years of continuing payments that ERISA clearly states the Alternate Payee should receive. See the discussion of this issue in subsection 6.3D and the model clauses in section 8.5 for effective ways to deal with this common problem.

3. Did you obtain the proper after-tax net share of plan assets for your client? Three types of contributions may be made to a Defined Contribution Plan: employer, employee pre-tax, and employee after-tax. Employee after-tax contributions are not deductible by the employee when made, but they generate a substantial tax advantage when contributions are withdrawn because the Participant is taxed only on the difference between the amount withdrawn and the "basis" of that amount. (A client whose asset sold for $100, but that originally cost $40, is not taxed on the entire $100 received but only on the difference between the sale price and the basis: $100 – $40 = $60.)

Employee after-tax contributions have a tax basis usually equal to the amount contributed by the Participant from his salary. It is important to include a clause in your QDROs allocating the tax basis of those contributions between the Participant and the Alternate Payee, usually in the same proportion as the overall allocation of plan assets. In other words, if an Alternate Payee is going to receive 50 percent of the assets in a plan, she should also be allocated 50 percent of the *tax basis* of those assets. Otherwise, the intended distribution of assets between the parties may be severely distorted.

Example: A Participant has accumulated $200,000 in a 401(k) plan during the marriage that is divided 50/50 between the parties. The Participant's tax basis in the plan assets is $40,000. Both parties are in the 20 percent tax bracket. The Alternate Payee's after-tax share of the plan assets, if the basis is not expressly allocated between the parties in a QDRO, is $80,000 ($100,000 gross amount received, less 20 percent tax on $100,000 = $80,000). The Participant, however, nets $88,000 ($100,000 less $40,000 basis = $60,000; 20 percent tax on $60,000 = $12,000; $100,000 – $12,000 = $88,000). A simple clause splitting the tax basis 50/50 between the parties would have given each of them $84,000 on an after-tax basis, not $88,000 to one party and $80,000 to the other. A client who should have received $84,000 will not be happy with the $4,000 shortfall caused by failure to properly allocate the tax basis of plan assets awarded to him or her.

Employers' model QDROs never include a tax basis allocation clause. Why? Because the plan is not concerned with the tax liabilities of the parties, only with the total amount the plan has to pay out. Yet this is an issue that is vitally important to both parties and should be addressed in every QDRO. See clause 13 in section 8.5, which deals with this issue.

4. Did you preserve your client's right to a share of future cost-of-living adjustments? Some model orders may not provide for adjustment of the Alternate Payee's share if and when the Participant receives a cost-of-living adjustment (COLA). This means that the Participant will receive all COLA increases on both parties' shares. Unless your QDRO provides otherwise, within the space of a very few years, the initial division of pension rights will rapidly erode, resulting in a very unfavorable position for the Alternate Payee. A simple clause can allocate COLAs between the parties in proportion to their initial award, but many model QDROs omit this clause. Make sure to refer to the procedures as to how the plan may handle this. It is also going to be dependent on shared interest versus separate interest.

In Military Pension Division Orders (MPDOs) dividing military retired pay (see Chapter 11) and Court Orders Acceptable for Processing (COAPs) dividing federal civil service benefits (see Chapter 12), COLAs form a particularly important part of the benefit. The basic clause allocating the benefits must be correctly worded and must be expressly mentioned in the order to be effectively shared between the parties. As noted in later chapters, certain award forms in the aforementioned orders will automatically include COLAs, whereas certain award forms will not. For example, if an MPDO provides that the Former Spouse is to receive 50 percent of the Servicemember's disposable military retired pay, then this will automatically trigger receipt of COLA for the Former Spouse, and COLA will apply each year to the Former Spouse's portion. Conversely, if the MPDO provides that the Former Spouse is to receive the sum of $2,000.00 per month from the Servicemember's disposable military retired pay, then COLA will not be included.

Plan Administrators often don't include such a clause in their model QDROs. They do not care which party receives COLA payments as long as they don't have to pay out more than 100 percent of the COLA.

5. Did you obtain an equitable share of the early retirement subsidy for your client? Some employers offer an "early retirement subsidy." This is an enhanced monthly payment offered to encourage older members of their workforce to retire early. Most ERISA plans specify both an "early retirement age" and a "normal retirement age." Participants who retire after the Early Retirement Age but before the Normal Retirement Age may receive an early retirement subsidy.

Under section 1056(d)(3)(E)(II) of ERISA, an Alternate Payee who elects to begin receiving monthly payments after the Participant attains the Early Retirement Age permitted by the plan, but before the Participant actually retires, may not receive a share of such an early retirement subsidy. The rationale is simple: the employer voluntarily offers the early retirement subsidy to encourage part of its workforce to retire ahead of schedule. Unless the Participant actually retires early, the employer has not received any part of what it bargained for, so there is no justification for forcing the employer to pay a portion of its offered early retirement subsidy to the Alternate Payee.

So far, so good. But what happens if the Alternate Payee elects to begin receiving monthly payments after the Participant attains the Early Retirement Age allowed by the plan, but before the Participant actually retires, and the Participant then retires before attaining the Normal Retirement Age specified in the plan? The Participant will receive an early retirement subsidy for having voluntarily retired before the plan's Normal Retirement Age. Section 1056(d)(3)(E)(II) therefore no longer applies, and the Alternate Payee's monthly payment may now be adjusted to award the Alternate Payee a portion of the early retirement subsidy actually being received by the Participant.

Plans' model orders almost never include clauses allowing for an automatic sharing between the Participant and the Alternate Payee of any early retirement subsidy actually received by the Participant. Ignoring this possibility by simply following the plan's model order may deprive your Alternate Payee clients of thousands of dollars in increased benefits. See subsection 6.2M for a discussion of this issue and clause 5E in section 8.5 for a clause that addresses it.

6. Did you make the Participant personally liable if the plan doesn't pay? It may take several months for a QDRO to be submitted and then reviewed and approved by a Plan Administrator. What happens to the payments received by the Participant in the interim? The QDROs I prepare for Alternate Payees all state that payment to the Alternate Payee is a personal obligation of the Participant and his or her estate that will be discharged, in whole or in part, by the payments actually received by the Alternate Payee from the plan, and that any payments assigned to the Alternate Payee that are received by the Participant shall be turned over to the Alternate Payee within five days after receipt. An appropriate tax adjustment clause is also included. (29 U.S.C. § 1056(d)(3)(H) of ERISA does call for escrow of payments to be made to an Alternate Payee pursuant to a QDRO under review by the Plan Administrator, but not all payments will be captured by this language.)

This can be problematic if you are not involved at the settlement or final trial stages of the case. Ensure that language of this nature is always provided for in the settlement documents and any agreement, in addition to the QDRO (or other order—MPDO, COAP). Similarly, if you're representing an Alternate Payee (or Former Spouse, as the case may be), ensure that language of this nature is also included in any proposed divorce decree that would be presented in court. This is something that can and should be stressed to a trial court judge, especially if the Participant is already In Pay Status and is receiving a monthly amount. This can be especially true when dealing with certain entities, like OPM, that normally have extremely long processing times.

There is no reason why an Alternate Payee should be deprived of payments assigned to him or her due to delays in QDRO processing by the Plan Administrator or for any other reason. Plan Administrators don't include this clause in their model QDROs because they are concerned only with the obligations the QDRO imposes on their plan—not with whether the Alternate Payee actually receives anything. Clause 9 in section 8.5 deals with this problem.

7. Did you inadvertently trigger the 10 percent penalty on premature distributions? A properly drafted QDRO calling for immediate distribution to an Alternate Payee who is a spouse or former spouse of the Participant can eliminate entirely the 10 percent penalty that is otherwise payable on distributions from an ERISA-qualified plan before the Participant reaches the age of 59. Yet the language in the model QDROs of many plans, calling for rollovers or direct transfers to an individual retirement account (IRA) established for the benefit of an Alternate Payee, needlessly destroys this substantial tax advantage by causing the 10 percent penalty to be re-imposed. Don't fall into this trap if your Alternate Payee client plans to take withdrawals in the near future. Provide for direct payment to her from the Participant's plan. Generally, the best approach is to include language that provides that the Alternate Payee is to be paid "in any form or permissible option otherwise available," thereby giving the Alternate Payee the autonomy to determine how to receive the award.

8. Did you avoid the incorrect tax treatment of child support in your QDRO? Many Plan Administrators are not aware that

QDROs may be used to collect both current child support and arrears. *See* sections 1056(d)(3)(B)(ii)(I) and (K), which expressly provide that QDROs may be used to collect child support. Since the vast majority of QDROs are used for marital property divisions or alimony, many plans' model orders state that the Alternate Payee will be liable for all federal and state income taxes on distributions made to the Alternate Payee and thus relieve the Participant from any liability for those taxes.

If your QDRO is used to collect child support, the exact opposite tax result is true. Section 402(e)(1)(A) of the Internal Revenue Code expressly provides that in the case of child support QDROs, the Participant is taxed on all withdrawals from the plan and the recipient of the child support payment is not taxed on his or her receipt. This is consistent with the general provisions of the Internal Revenue Code concerning the income tax consequences to the payor and the recipient when child support is paid—namely, that the payor receives no tax deduction for child support payments and the recipient realizes no taxable income on their receipt. *See also* IRS Publication 575, *Pension and Annuity*, at 2. Including in a plan's model order the standard provisions relating to income tax, which are designed for divorce cases and division of pension rights between spouses, will at best engender substantial confusion and the issuance of an incorrect Form 1099-R by the plan to the wrong party. At worst, blindly following the plan's standard tax clause may result in the imposition of federal and state income taxes on a child (or custodial parent) and the relief of the noncustodial parent from tax liability when the reverse should have been the case.

It is always desirable to do three things when you draft a QDRO for child support. First, remind the Plan Administrator in writing of the provisions of section 402(e)(1)(A) of the Internal Revenue Code as described previously. Second, expressly provide in your order that the Participant, not the Alternate Payee, will be taxable on all distributions (this will often require radical amendment of the model QDRO's standard clause on this issue). Finally, when you send an executed child support QDRO to a Plan Administrator for final acceptance, include a reminder in your cover letter that all Form 1099-Rs should be sent to the Participant, not to the Alternate Payee.

9. Did you obtain lifetime benefits for your client or allow the plan's standard language to cut them short? The model orders of many plans provide for the division of monthly payments only under the Shared Interest Approach. This means that the Participant retains exclusive control over the timing of the receipt of payments by both parties: under the Shared Interest Approach, payments of the main plan annuity will begin only when the Participant actually retires and will end as soon as the Participant dies (see subsection 6.2N).

There are obvious disadvantages to the Alternate Payee of using the Shared Interest Approach. The Alternate Payee may need to begin receiving payments many years before the Participant actually elects to retire. At the other end of the payment stream, the Alternate Payee may be left with no payments at all for several years if he or she outlives the Participant if there is no survivor benefit option available or selected.

Most Alternate Payees therefore prefer the use of the Separate Interest Approach, which is described in subsection 6.2O. Under this approach, the Alternate Payee gains complete control over the timing of her payments. Monthly payments will begin whenever the Alternate Payee elects them to, even if the Participant has not actually retired, subject only to the constraint that the Participant must have attained the Early Retirement Age provided by the plan, which is often as low as age 50. Payments then continue under the Separate Interest Approach for the duration of the Alternate Payee's life, even if the Participant dies first.

IMPORTANT NOTE: Most plans and regulatory agencies agree that a Separate Interest is not affected by the death of the Participant. However, a few plans take the position that if the Participant dies prior to attaining the plan's Earliest Retirement Age, the Alternate Payee's Separate Interest is extinguished. It is therefore vitally important in drafting Separate Interest Approach QDROs to expressly provide that "payment to the Alternate Payee will not be affected by the death of the Participant at any time, either before or after attaining the Earliest Retirement Age." (The PBGC Model Separate Interest QDRO uses this clause in section 8, which states, "The Participant's death shall not affect payments under the Alternate Payee's separate interest.") If the Plan Administrator rejects this language and insists that the Alternate Payee's Separate Interest will be extinguished if the Participant dies prior to attaining the Earliest Retirement Age allowed by the plan, then it is essential to award a QPSA to the Alternate Payee in an equivalent amount so that she will receive her award if the Participant dies prior to attaining the Earliest Retirement Age allowed by the plan. See clause 7. (For an excellent and detailed discussion of the Shared Interest and Separate Interest Approaches and sample language to use to implement them, *see IRS Notice* 97-11, IRB 1997-2 (January 13, 1997).)

Despite these obvious advantages of the Separate Interest Approach for an Alternate Payee, very few plan model orders contain Separate Interest Approach clauses, probably because the Shared Interest Approach is simpler and cheaper for a plan to administer and requires fewer actuarial calculations to be made. Simply filling in the blanks in such an order means you may have placed your Alternate Payee client at a severe disadvantage.

The exact language to be used in implementing the Separate Interest Approach will vary widely from plan to plan, depending on the type and form of benefit options provided by the plan, Early and Normal Retirement Ages, and so forth. Helpful ideas on Separate Interest Approach clauses are found in *IRS Notice* 97-11 and the PBGC's very helpful publication *Qualified Domestic Relations Orders & The PBGC* (Rev. 08/22; available at PBGC.gov); see also section 8.5, clauses 5 and 6.

10. Did you obtain a share of the participant's accrued benefits, not just vested benefits? Model QDROs often speak of dividing only the Participant's "vested" benefit, rather than his "accrued" benefit—often a larger figure. It is clear that accrued, but unvested, benefits are divisible marital or community property under the divorce laws of almost every state. If your client has been awarded "50 percent of Participant's account balance as of [date]" and you follow the plan's model QDRO language that awards Alternate Payees a share of vested benefits only, you may cost your client a small fortune.

Accrued but unvested benefits may be the subject of a QDRO. Make sure you use your own language, not the plan's, to cover them. See clause 5L in section 8.5 for a sample clause maximizing the amount awarded to your Alternate Payee clients. How this is handled may be problematic for the timing of the divorce and what the plan will allow (vested versus accrued). Depending on the vesting schedule, if applicable, this may require an agreement by the parties or an order of the court to revisit the issue later once that "marital" accrued portion vests. Alternatively, if there is a sufficient amount of other assets available, then this could potentially be offset value-wise to avoid continued post-litigation entanglement.

11. Did you allow the plan's automatic adjustment for investment experience clause to decrease your client's benefits? Many plans' model orders provide that the Alternate Payee shall receive "___ percent of the Participant's account balance as of [insert date] adjusted for all gains, losses, dividends, and interest from that date until the date of distribution to the Alternate Payee." This *may* be a desirable clause if the market has gone up in the meantime, but it can lead to financial disaster in a period of precipitous market declines. Remember that account balances may decline as well as increase—think about the Enron case. The problem may be particularly acute if several years have elapsed from the date of the divorce decree or separation agreement until the date the QDRO is entered.

If the state divorce court order or the parties' agreement simply calls for a division of the Participant's account balance in the plan "as of [date]," unthinking use of the plan's model language will distort the division. If your client is on the losing side of the investment experience because you simply copied the plan's adjustment for investment experience clause, malpractice litigation is almost inevitable. Instead of routinely copying this clause from the model into your orders, ask for account statements from the plan for the date of division and a recent date. Consult with your client as to whether they want this option selected and advise them to discuss with a financial professional if they are unsure. Unless you are a financial professional, making that decision yourself as the lawyer has the potential to create a significant issue. *See Austin v. Austin*, 2000 Me. LEXIS 61 (Me. 2000).

If you are a neutral attorney preparing the QDRO and an agreement has already been executed or a divorce decree signed, go by what is specifically included in the agreement or decree. If there is nothing about the inclusion of gains and losses (or market forces, investments, etc.), then note that they are not entitled to gains and losses. If that is provided for in the agreement or decree, draft that language accordingly. If you're in this position, when sending a draft to the attorneys and/or parties, specify that is why this was drafted in this fashion and inclusion of that language is entirely at their discretion.

12. Did you get your client a fair pro rata share of the plan's year-end contribution? Many plans make their employer contributions only once a year, at the end of a "plan year" (plan years often, but not always, end on December 31). If your Alternate Payee client divorces or is separated partway through the plan year, make sure you provide an appropriate adjustment.

Example: The XYZ, Inc. pension plan's year ends September 30. On that date XYZ, Inc. will contribute $12,000 to Mr. Black's account. This $12,000 contribution is made attributable to and in recognition of Mr. Black's services to XYZ, Inc. over the preceding 12 months. You represent Mrs. Black. The parties divorced (or separated, if that is the relevant event terminating the acquisition of marital or community property under the law of your state) on May 31, eight months into the plan year. Because Mrs. Black was married to Mr. Black for 8/12 of the period in which he earned the right to the year-end contribution, she should be entitled to a share of the additional $8,000 available for division (8/12 × $12,000 = $8,000). Yet the plan's model QDRO ignores this amount entirely.

Bear in mind that this subsequent contribution for the end of the year that spans the terminating event for the acquisition of joint property will not show up on any plan records until the very last day of the plan year (and bear in mind that some plan years end on dates other than December 31). Your client might get divorced on the day before the end of the plan year and be entitled to a share of 364/365 of that year's contributions, but you will miss that potentially valuable asset entirely if you follow the plan's model QDRO language!

* * * * *

"You have to follow our model order; we don't accept any other forms." Have you ever had a Plan Administrator reject your draft QDRO with these words? They are simply not true. Federal case law and the DOL (which has jurisdiction over ERISA) have made it very clear that any state divorce court order that meets all the requirements for QDROs set forth in ERISA and the written terms of the plan must be accepted by a Plan Administrator as a QDRO. In other words, the Plan Administrator *cannot* insist that you follow its model QDRO form. *See EBSA Booklet* Question 2-7 ("A plan may not condition its determination of QDRO status on the use of any particular form.").

Never accept such a statement from a Plan Administrator. Some plans will initially resist any attempt to depart from their model language. Sending them a reference to or copy of the relevant section of the DOL booklet cited here quickly changes their minds. Don't let the Plan Administrator browbeat you into leaving out clauses favorable to your client just because they are different from the model QDRO provided by the plan.

As lawyers, we learn very early that no legal instrument is truly neutral. Every clause necessarily favors one party at the expense of the other, and QDROs are no exception. Model QDRO clauses are always designed to simplify the Plan Administrator's job. In some cases they favor Participants (employees) at the expense of Alternate Payees. Always remember that a plan's model QDRO is drafted with these goals in mind, not with the intent of securing the most favorable result for your client, particularly if you represent the Alternate Payee. Clauses in the model QDRO almost always err in the direction of oversimplification or in favor of the Participant. Clauses missing from the model QDRO can be even more troublesome because they will often result in your overlooking important issues.

It's difficult to imagine defending a pension division malpractice case by protesting that you "got the plan's model order and filled in all the blanks"—or even worse, had your paralegal or secretary do so. This is not the sort of legal expertise your clients are paying you to provide, and it is extremely doubtful that any court would accept this level of effort as a defense to a charge of malpractice. But, that does mean that you need to start early. Most clients do not want to wait a long time after the divorce to get the assets or monies that are due to them, so submit the draft QDRO to the plan administrator early for preapproval, even if you don't have the exact percentage or amount to be transferred.

If you do use a plan's model order, make it your starting point, never the finished product. Modify the plan's suggested clauses as needed, and add your own to cover the issues discussed previously. Model QDROs are no substitute for knowing the substantive law in this area of ERISA and exercising your legal skills and judgment to hand-tailor a suitable QDRO in every case. Just "filling in the blanks" can do serious harm to both your clients' pocketbooks and your professional reputation.

8.4 QDROs Don't Have to Be Complex

Here's a short DRO:

[Normal State Court Caption]

Order

1. The names and mailing addresses of the Participant and the Alternate Payee are: Participant: John C. Burns, 123 Broad Street, Augusta, GA 30910, date of birth May 19, 1964, Social Security number 123-45-6789, and Alternate Payee: Mary J. Burns, 456 Peachtree Lane, Augusta, GA 30911, date of birth September 19, 1967, Social Security number 987-65-4321.

2. Alternate Payee is the former spouse of Participant. This order is made pursuant to the domestic relations law of the State of Georgia to assign to the Alternate Payee the right to receive part of the Participant's plan benefits as a division of marital property in this divorce action.

3. Alternate Payee shall receive directly from the Global MegaCorp Employee Stock Ownership Plan the sum of $75,812.15 as soon as the plan may legally distribute it to her.

/s/ John J. Equiter,
Judge

Is this a QDRO? Well, there are several things about this order that could be drafted much better, and I certainly don't recommend that you follow it as a model. However, this DRO does meet all the ERISA requirements for a QDRO. Assuming that the plan makes cash distributions (so that this order does not require the plan to pay benefits in a form not otherwise available) and that there is enough in the Participant's vested account balance on the withdrawal date to pay the designated amount, it would have to be accepted as a QDRO by the plan.

I've included this example just to emphasize that QDROs do not need to be long, complex, or confusing documents. Bear in mind that many refinements and improvements should be made to every DRO you draft, as discussed in the remainder of this chapter.

8.5 Model DRO with Alternative Clauses for a Defined Benefit Plan

Set forth in this section is a complete model DRO with alternative clauses covering the different types of plans, formulas for benefit divisions, starting and ending dates for payments, and similar issues.

Clauses 1–4 and 7–14 are fairly simple and have few variations. They should be used in every DRO with only minor modifications as the circumstances of the case require.

Clauses 5 and 6 are the heart of the DRO: How much does the Alternate Payee get? When can she start to receive it? And for how long will she receive it?

ERISA allows plans to offer many options and many alternative forms of benefit payments, which will govern the amount and timing of receipt of plan benefits by an Alternate Payee. The clauses covering these matters in a DRO must deal with all of these complexities. Consequently, there are many variations and options for clauses 5 and 6 that must be studied and evaluated to determine the most favorable arrangement for your client.

[Normal State Court or Agency Caption]

Order

This order is entered this ___ day of ___, 20__ [after a hearing] [by stipulation of the parties]. This order is intended to be a Qualified Domestic Relations Order as that term is used in ERISA, 29 U.S.C. § 1056(d)(3).

COMMENT: Under ERISA, only *an order* may be a DRO or a QDRO. ERISA requires a "judgment, decree or order (including approval of a property settlement agreement)." 29 U.S.C. § 1056(d)(3)(B)(ii). A state administrative agency that is authorized to issue child support orders may issue a DRO. *EBSA Booklet* Question 1-3.

1. *Parties.*

A. Participant:

Name:	John Smith
Address:	123 Main Street Augusta, Georgia 30911
Social Security Number:	Provided to the Plan Administrator under separate cover.
Date of Birth:	Provided to the Plan Administrator under separate cover.

B. Former Spouse:

Name:	Betty Smith
Address:	789 2nd Street Augusta, Georgia 30911
Social Security Number:	Provided to the Plan Administrator under separate cover.
Date of Birth:	Provided to the Plan Administrator under separate cover.

COMMENT: The names and last known mailing addresses of the Participant and the Alternate Payee are expressly required by ERISA, 29 U.S.C. § 1056(d)(3)(C)(i). If this information is known or readily ascertainable by the Plan Administrator, the order should still be accepted by the Plan Administrator. *Hawkins v. Comm'r*, 86 F.3d 982 (10th Cir. 1996); *In re Williams*, 1999 U.S. Dist. LEXIS 8650 (C.D. Cal. 1999); *EBSA Booklet* Question 2-9.

While ERISA does not require the date of birth or Social Security number for the Participant or the Alternate Payee, including them helps the Plan Administrator make sure it is dealing with the correct person and is a reasonable request. Always include them when submitting for processing. Dates of birth are required in dealing with defined benefit plans to compute actuarially equivalent benefits. If the QDRO is going to be a part of the public record, it is advisable that you do not put the complete Social Security numbers and dates of birth in the court order but rather indicate that the information will be provided under separate cover that is not part of the public record. Then include that information in the cover letter or an additional personal information addendum to the Plan Administrator when you submit the DRO/QDRO.

2. *Domestic Relations Law.* This order is entered pursuant to the domestic relations laws of the State of _____, in particular [State] Code Section _____ concerning [property division] [alimony] [child support] to recognize and assign to the Alternate Payee that portion of the plan benefits payable with respect to the Participant specified below.

COMMENT: Under ERISA, DROs may only be entered pursuant to a "State domestic relations law (including a community property law)." 29 U.S.C. § 1056(d)(3)(B)(ii)(II). An order of a state probate court in an estate administration proceeding dividing the plan benefit due a decedent (evidently in an effort to do some creative postmortem estate planning to minimize estate taxes) is not considered made pursuant to a "domestic relations law" and therefore cannot be a DRO. *DOL Advisory Opinion* 90-46A. ERISA also requires that a DRO "relates to the provision of child support, alimony payments or marital property rights." 29 U.S.C. § 1056(d)(3)(B)(ii)(I).

It is always desirable to state the nature of the payments in the DRO for four reasons:

1. To satisfy the plan that the DRO meets this requirement of ERISA;
2. To make sure that the proper and intended tax consequences are achieved by the DRO;
3. To establish the background for identifying the events (death, remarriage, emancipation, and so on) that may terminate the payments under the DRO (see clause 6);
4. To establish whether the payments are dischargeable in bankruptcy or not, a decision made under federal bankruptcy law but heavily influenced by the characterization of the payments under state law.

3. *Relationship of Alternate Payee to Participant.* The Alternate Payee is the [spouse] [former spouse] [child] [other dependent] of the Participant.

COMMENT: ERISA requires that an Alternate Payee have one of these relationships to the Participant. 29 U.S.C. §§ 1056(d)(3)(B)(ii)(I); 1056(d)(3)(K).

OPTIONAL ADDITIONAL CLAUSES

3A. *The Alternate Payee and the Participant were married on May 19, 19__; separated on June 14, 20__; and were divorced by this Court in this action on November 2, 20__.*

[or, in cases where the Alternate Payee is a child of the Participant:]

3B. *The Alternate Payee was born on September 1, 20__.*

COMMENT: While not required by ERISA, these clauses contain useful information that may be needed by the Plan Administrator. Clause 3A is essential if the Alternate Payee's share of plan benefits is determined by a coverture or "time rule" formula involving a fraction in which the numerator is the number of years the parties were married during the Participant's membership in the plan and the denominator is the Participant's total time accrued under the Plan. Clause 3B is essential if the QDRO is one for child support and the payments will automatically terminate on the Alternate Payee's reaching a certain age. If this information is not in the DRO itself, the plan will have to be notified of it in some reliable and acceptable fashion; it is easier simply to insert it in the DRO (see clause 6M).

COMMENT: Remember, where the Alternate Payee is a dependent, it may be contrary to law to include a minor child's full birthdate, so be cognizant of this. The safer approach is to submit any personal information of that nature under separate cover.

4. *Identity of Plan.* This order applies to the Global MegaCorp Employee Retirement Plan and any amended, successor, substitute, or replacement plan that subsequently takes the place of that plan, or into which the benefits payable to the Participant by that plan are transferred. The address of the plan is 222 West Corporate Drive, Santa Barbara, California 99099.

COMMENT 1: ERISA requires that QDROs "clearly specify . . . each plan to which the order applies." 29 U.S.C. § 1056(d)(3)(C)(iv). *See Dial v. NFL Player Supplemental Disability Plan*, 174 F.3d 606 (5th Cir. 1999); *Holloman v. Holloman*, 691 So. 2d 897 (Miss. 1996); *Carpenter v. Carpenter*, 1996 Tex. App. LEXIS 3210 (Tex. Ct. App. 1996) (DROs amended three times and litigated for three years on issue of which plans were intended to be covered by them). Many employers sponsor multiple plans with confusingly similar names, and it is vitally important to use the correct name in each DRO you draft. Failure to do so will cause immediate rejection of your DRO by the plan. It is also important to confirm the correct plan name with the Plan Administrator. If you have submitted for review and preapproval and have the wrong plan name, the Plan Administrator will let you know. Now, some will let you know *what* it needs to be corrected to, and some will just let you know that it is incorrect and offer no further assistance.

COMMENT 2: It is important to provide that the QDRO also applies to successor, substitute, or replacement plans. It is not unusual for Plan Sponsors to redesign their employee benefits packages every few years, and often this involves terminating one plan and substituting a new one in its place. A QDRO should automatically apply to such new plans, as it will if this language is used. *See McPherren v. McPherren*, 967 S.W.2d 485 (Tex. Ct. App. 1998).

COMMENT 3: The address of the plan is not required by ERISA, but it is useful to include it in the QDRO for convenience of future reference.

If you haven't read Chapter 6 yet, you should do so before reading the variations on clauses 5 and 6. Even if you have already read Chapter 6, this would be a good time to go back and briefly review its special technical vocabulary and principles.

---

5. *Division of Payments.* [The wording of clause 5 will vary greatly depending on whether the plan is a Defined Contribution or Defined Benefit Plan, and, in the case of a Defined Benefit Plan, whether a "Shared Interest" or "Separate Interest" is used.]

Part A: Division of a Defined Benefit Plan Already In Pay Status

INTRODUCTORY COMMENT: This is one of the easiest types of plan benefits to divide. Because the Participant has already retired and is collecting monthly payments from the plan, there are no options from which to choose and no decisions to be made about the timing of the beginning or ending dates of receipt of plan benefits by the Alternate Payee.

A Participant receiving monthly payments already will have elected either

1. A Single Life Annuity (in which case payments to the Alternate Payee must terminate, as all payments do, on the Participant's death), or
2. A QJSA with the Alternate Payee (in which case payments to the Alternate Payee at some level will continue until her death), or
3. A QJSA with the Participant's new spouse (in which case payments to the Alternate Payee may last as long as either the Participant or his current spouse survives).

Because the election of the form of annuity has already been made, it cannot normally be changed. *But see In re Marriage of Allison*, 189 Cal. App. 3d 849 (Cal. Ct. App. 1987), and section 4.5.

5A. The Alternate Payee shall be entitled to receive, effective immediately, . . .

1. $575.00 per month . . .
2. [40.875%] [12/19] of the gross monthly benefit payable with respect to the Participant as if he had elected a Single Life Annuity on the date of his retirement (including/not including disability payments payable under the plan). . . .
3. A fraction, the numerator of which is the number of months the parties were married during the Participant's employment by the Plan Sponsor, and the denominator of which is the total number of months the Participant was employed by the Plan Sponsor, of the gross monthly benefit payable with respect to the Participant as if he had elected a Single Life Annuity on the date of his retirement. . . .
4. Of all benefits payable with respect to the Participant, whether as a service pension for Normal or Early Retirement, or disability, or otherwise by the Plan. . . .

5B-1. *(for use where Participant and Alternate Payee have elected a QJSA on their joint lives)* In the event the Participant dies before the Alternate Payee, the Alternate Payee shall be entitled to receive the entire amount payable with respect to the Participant after the death of the Participant and until the death of the Alternate Payee as previously elected by the parties.

5B-2. *(for use where Participant has elected a QJSA with his current spouse who is not the Alternate Payee)* The Alternate Payee shall be entitled to receive 42.66 percent of the monthly amount payable with respect to the Participant as long as either the Participant or his current spouse survives, but payments to the Alternate Payee shall cease after the last to occur of (a) the death of the Participant or (b) the death of Participant's current spouse, Mrs. Althea Burns, Social Security number and date of birth provided under separate cover, and in any event shall cease upon the Alternate Payee's death.

5B-3. *(for use where Participant has elected a QJSA with his current spouse who is not the Alternate Payee)* The Alternate Payee shall be entitled to receive 42.66 percent of the monthly amount payable with respect to the Participant until the first to occur of (a) the death of the Participant or (b) the death of Participant's current spouse, Mrs. Althea Burns, Social Security number and date of birth provided under separate cover, and 58.775 percent of all payments made with respect to the Participant thereafter, until the death of the survivor of the Participant and his current spouse, but in any event all payments to the Alternate Payee shall terminate upon her death. [See comment 5.]

COMMENT 1: Using a fixed dollar figure as in subclause 5A-1 *generally* deprives the Alternate Payee of any cost-of-living or other increases that the Participant may receive in future years from the plan. Using a percentage or fraction as in subclauses 5A-2 and 5A-3 *generally* shares any such increase proportionately between the parties. Again, always make sure that the plan procedures and guidelines are reviewed in conjunction with the QDRO preparation to ensure that you're checking all the boxes necessary.

COMMENT 2: Clause 5A provides for payment to the Alternate Payee to begin immediately. There is no reason to delay payments, since the annuity is already In Pay Status and payments are being received. It can be included here or in a later separate paragraph about direct payments from the Participant to the Alternate Payee until such a time as the Alternate Payee begins receiving directly from the plan.

COMMENT 3: If the Participant has already elected a Single Life Annuity, payments will automatically cease when he dies. If the Participant has already elected a QJSA with the Alternate Payee, payments to the Alternate Payee will continue after the Participant's death if she outlives the Participant. Use clause 5B-1 or a variant in this situation. Either way, the election has already been made and cannot normally be undone.

COMMENT 4: Note that if the Participant has remarried and has elected a QJSA with his current spouse, the monthly payments will be lower than they would have been under a Single Life Annuity on the life of the Participant alone. This may require comparison of the two monthly payments and adjustment of the fraction by the state court. In such a case it is also important to verify with the plan whether payments to the Alternate Payee will stop on the death of the Participant, or only on the death of the survivor of the Participant and his current spouse, and the DRO should be drafted accordingly. The language "as if he had elected a Single Life Annuity on the date of retirement" is designed to prevent the payments to the Alternate Payee from being reduced by the election of a QJSA for the Participant and his current spouse as they otherwise would be. Use clause 5B-2 or a variant in this situation.

COMMENT 5: Some QJSAs will adjust the payment level upon the death of the first person. ERISA allows that the amount payable after the death of the Participant must be between 50 and 100 percent of the amount payable while both parties are alive. 29 U.S.C. § 1055(d)(1). If the payment level will change after the first death to occur, clause 5B-3 should be used.

COMMENT 6: Alimony and child support QDROs require special clauses concerning the termination of payments. These are discussed under clause 6.

COMMENT 7: If the DRO is intended to divide disability benefits, this should be expressly stated in the definition of what is being divided. Some states treat disability payments received by one spouse quite differently from ordinary service pension payments, even if payments are made by the same Employee Benefit Plan and even if disability payments are made in lieu of ordinary service pension payments.

Part B: Division of a Defined Benefit Plan Not Yet In Pay Status

INTRODUCTORY COMMENT: This is the most difficult type of plan benefit to divide because there are so many different ways to do so.

There are two alternative methods to divide such plan benefits: the Shared Interest Approach and the Separate Interest Approach. They are quite different in design and consequences to the Alternate Payee.

The Shared Interest Approach is the easiest one to draft, but it is rarely, if ever, the best option or even appropriate for an Alternate Payee. The main features of the Shared Interest Approach are that

- Payments to the Alternate Payee cannot begin until the Participant chooses to retire; and
- Payments must end on the Participant's death unless the Alternate Payee is designated in the QDRO as the spouse of the Participant for the purpose of electing a QJSA with the Participant under 29 U.S.C. § 1056(d)(3)(F), and such an election is actually made at the time of the Participant's retirement (unless an alternative survivor option is available directly through the plan).

These are gambles that most Alternate Payees don't want to take. Instead, Alternate Payees almost universally prefer to have their share of benefits paid (1) starting when they choose to begin receiving them and (2) usually ending when the Alternate Payee dies, no matter what retirement date the Participant elects or when he dies. This is the Separate Interest Approach, which is discussed in detail in subpart II.

Participants are usually indifferent as to which approach is used because the starting date and duration of the payments and the amount received by the Participant are generally the same under either method. However, the Participant will be better off if the Shared Interest Approach is used because typically the former spouse's portion of the benefit will revert back to the Participant if the Alternate Payee dies before he does. Some plans may permit this even under the Separate Interest Approach if the Alternate Payee dies before she begins to receive any plan benefits (see clause 8). Few plans permit a reversion if the Alternate Payee has already begun to receive benefits.

Whether the Shared Interest Approach or the Separate Interest Approach is used, it is always desirable to provide death benefits for the Alternate Payee under a Qualified Preretirement Survivor Annuity using clause 7.

Subpart I. Shared Interest Approach

INTRODUCTORY COMMENT: The Shared Interest Approach is almost identical to the division of a plan benefit already In Pay Status, as in part A. This is because once a pension is In Pay Status, it is not possible for the Plan Administrator to recalculate the pension into two pensions, and therefore, only a shared interest division can be used. The only difference is the timing of the beginning of the payments; the Shared Interest Approach is used before the Participant has retired and has begun to receive annuity payments.

Generally, the DRO will use the same language as in clauses 5A and B, except that the starting date for the receipt of payments by the Alternate Payee cannot be "immediately" but should rather be phrased as follows:

5C. . . . as soon as the Participant begins receiving benefits from the plan . . .

COMMENT: There is usually no reason to delay receipt of the Alternate Payee's payments under the Shared Interest Approach because nothing is gained by it. Be careful under the Shared Interest Approach to consider whether payments to the Alternate Payee will be made only during the life of the Participant (if he elects a Single Life Annuity) or whether they will continue until the death of the Alternate Payee even if the Participant dies first (if a QJSA for the Participant and the Alternate Payee is elected). Either alternative is possible under the Shared Interest Approach; see clauses 5A and 5B-1, 5B-2, and 5B-3.

A third possibility is that if the Participant has remarried before retiring, he will choose (or be forced to choose by the provisions of 29 U.S.C. § 1055) a QJSA with his current spouse. In such a case the fraction for payment to the Alternate Payee will probably need to be adjusted, and the plan should be asked whether payments to the Alternate Payee may continue even after the Participant dies if his current spouse survives him (see comments 4 and 5 to clauses 5B-1 through 5B-3 and subsection 6.3D). My own view is that in this situation, payments to an Alternate Payee may continue under a properly worded QDRO so long as either the Participant or his current spouse survives because the benefits payable to them stem from the Participant's employment by the Plan Sponsor and are therefore "benefits payable with respect to a Participant under a plan" that may be divided by a QDRO and assigned to an Alternate Payee under 29 U.S.C. § 1056(d)(3)(B)(i)(I).

Some Plan Administrators may not agree with this view. This issue should be explored in detail with the Plan Administrator, and written confirmation should be obtained from the plan to specify how long payments may continue in this situation.

Subpart II. Separate Interest Approach

INTRODUCTORY COMMENT: Under the Separate Interest Approach, the Alternate Payee controls all decisions about the timing of her receipt of the benefit payments. This is most desirable and is usually the first choice of Alternate Payees. The one major drawback to this approach is that it requires a fairly complex actuarial calculation of the value of the "accrued benefit" of a Participant as of a specified date in order to divide the total plan benefits between the parties (see subsection 6.2P).

This actuarial calculation can (and the vast majority of the time is to) be made by the plan itself. If the plan won't make the calculation for you, you can demand that it advise you of its actuarial assumptions and hire your own freelance actuary to do the math for you. You likely will not encounter this issue. In our experience, plans are going to handle all of the calculations for this rather than listen to an outside source not used by them explain how they should conduct their business.

Using the Separate Interest Approach also requires you to give some thought to increases in plan benefits payable with respect to the Participant after the Valuation Date (as specially defined in this section). If they are not properly dealt with, the Participant will receive all such increases and the Alternate Payee none of them. (This problem does not arise under the Shared Interest Approach if a percentage or fraction is used.)

To ensure the Plan Administrator clearly understands that you are using the Separate Interest Approach and to avoid any later argument, it is desirable to begin clause 5 with the phrase "Notwithstanding the death of the Participant at any time, whether before or after the Alternate Payee begins to receive plan benefits, the Alternate Payee shall receive, as a separate interest, . . .".

In drafting a DRO using the Separate Interest Approach, it is necessary to use four precisely defined terms for clarity and to avoid repetition. These terms are not defined in ERISA or elsewhere and have no commonly understood meaning for every plan, so their definitions must be set out in full at the beginning of clause 5:

5D. As used in this order, the following capitalized terms shall have the following meanings:

"Accrued Benefit" means the largest benefit that the Participant is entitled to receive from the plan in the form of monthly payments from a Single Life Annuity on the life of the Participant, commencing at the Normal Retirement Age specified by the plan.

"Valuation Date" means the date as of which the Participant's Accrued Benefit is to be calculated. If the Participant dies before the Alternate Payee begins to receive any benefits from the plan, the Valuation Date shall be the day before the date of the Participant's death.

COMMENT 1: Note that an earlier valuation date, such as the date of divorce, leads to a lower value for the Accrued Benefit. Regardless, though, a plan may very well require the date of divorce or something similar in order to process the QDRO. Additionally, a court may automatically include the date of divorce, or the Participant's attorney may refuse to include that date (whether because they don't understand or are just being difficult). This will likely, again, require you to take the steps to demonstrate why it should be as you're requesting for the Alternate Payee.

COMMENT 2: The "Valuation Date" should not be confused with the cutoff date for acquiring marital property under state law, as discussed in Chapter 5 and subsection 6.2P. State law prescribes the start and end dates for the acquisition of joint property (or, more often, as determined within the judge's discretion); the Valuation Date is the date on which the property determined to be joint is valued. This is like saying that all shares of Microsoft stock acquired by the Participant before the date of divorce are joint property, but the value of those shares will be determined on the date he writes the check to pay the Alternate Payee for her interest in them.

"Actuarial Equivalent" means any form of benefit available under the plan (such as a Single Life Annuity for the life of the Alternate Payee) that differs in duration or manner of payment from another form of benefit available under the plan (such as an annuity with a different starting date for the life of the Participant or a QJSA) but that is actuarially equivalent to the other form of benefit when calculated using the actuarial assumptions and factors used by the plan itself.

COMMENT: There is one form of benefit an Alternate Payee cannot be awarded in a QDRO, and that is "a Joint and Survivor Annuity with respect to the Alternate Payee and his or her subsequent spouse." 29 U.S.C. § 1056(d)(3)(E)(i)(III). Any other form of annuity offered by the plan to Participants may be chosen by an Alternate Payee.

"Supplemental Benefit" means any amount payable to the Participant by the plan in excess of his Accrued Benefit, whether as a Subsidy for Early Retirement or otherwise.

COMMENT: Inclusion of this definition favors the Alternate Payee. If you represent the Participant, try to keep it out. *See In re Marriage of Lehman*, 955 P.2d 451 (Cal. 1998); *Quade v. Quade*, 1999 Mich. App. LEXIS 283 (Mich. Ct. App. 1999) (Alternate Payee not entitled to early retirement benefits unless expressly mentioned by court; award of "50 percent of defendant's Ford Motor Company Pension with rights of survivorship" insufficient). Use of this definition will include in the division formula Supplemental Benefits that are in existence at the time of the Valuation Date. To make sure that subsequent cost-of-living increases are shared between the Participant and the Alternate Payee, you will have to use clause 5K.

After reciting these definitions:

5E. (a) Notwithstanding the death of the Participant at any time, whether before or after the Alternate Payee begins to receive plan benefits, the Alternate Payee shall be entitled to begin receiving, directly from the plan, at such time as she may elect on or after the date on which the Participant attains (or would have attained if he dies earlier) the Earliest Retirement Age (as that term is defined in 29 U.S.C. § 1056(d)(3)(E) and in the plan), or at any earlier time permitted by the plan, an amount equal to 50 percent of the Actuarial Equivalent of the Participant's Accrued Benefit [and the Participant's Supplemental Benefit] multiplied by the [fraction] [percentage] specified below.

(b) Payments to the Alternate Payee shall be made in the form of a Single Life Annuity for the life of the Alternate Payee, or in such other form as the Alternate Payee may elect from among the options then available from the plan (but not in the form of a Joint and Survivor Annuity for the Alternate Payee and his or her subsequent spouse, if any) at the time the Alternate Payee elects to begin receiving payments. The Valuation Date for determining the Accrued Benefit [and the Supplemental Benefit] of the Participant under this clause shall be [the date of divorce] [date of this order] [date Alternate Payee elects to begin receiving benefits from the plan] [day before the date the Participant died if he dies before the Alternate Payee has begun to receive any benefits from the plan].

(c) The fraction referred to above shall have a numerator equal to the number of years and months during the marriage while the Participant worked for the Plan Sponsor [which the court determines to be 20 years and three months]. *The denominator shall be equal to the total number of years and months the Participant works for the Plan Sponsor before the date payments to the Alternate Payee begin or the date of the Participant's death, whichever shall first occur.*

(d) In determining this fraction, any hypothetical, putative, or extra years of service taken into account by the plan in determining years of service during any period in order to calculate Participant's benefits shall not be included in either the numerator or the denominator of the fraction, but only Participant's actual years of service shall be counted. See *In re* Marriage of Lehman, 955 P.2d 451 (Cal. 1998).

COMMENT 1: This clause gives the Alternate Payee the maximum control over the timing of the payments she will receive. She may elect to begin receiving them at any time on or after the Earliest Retirement Age allowed by the plan (see subsection 2.21) or any earlier date if the plan allows one. The longer she waits to elect to begin receiving payments, the greater the amount of each monthly payment she will receive.

COMMENT 2: Note that the Valuation Date is not necessarily the date on which the Alternate Payee will begin receiving payments. It can be any date the QDRO specifies up until the day the Alternate Payee elects to begin receiving payments. (That is the last possible date because it becomes necessary at that time to calculate the monthly amount of the Alternate Payee's payments.) The later the Valuation Date, the greater the value of the Accrued Benefit and the higher the monthly payment to the Alternate Payee. This is going to depend upon what the plan will allow as far as the Valuation Date.

If allowable, the most appropriate date to use for the Valuation Date for the Alternate Payee's benefit is the date the Alternate Payee elects to begin receiving benefits from the plan. The fractional formula at the end of this clause automatically separates the Accrued Benefit into marital and nonmarital shares. Use of any earlier Valuation Date (such as the date of the divorce or date of the DRO) will shortchange the Alternate Payee and may significantly reduce the benefits payable to her. This is, again, why it is always important to review the plan guidelines to see what is allowable under the plan. If you have questions about valuations and how this may look with different valuation dates, then consult with a financial expert who can run these calculations for the Alternate Payee.

To deal with the contingency that the Participant might die before the Alternate Payee begins receiving any plan benefits, the Valuation Date for his Accrued Benefit in such a case is deemed to be the day before his death, the latest possible date. (This language should also forestall any argument by the plan that the Participant's death automatically reduces his Accrued Benefit to zero, so that the Alternate Payee is not entitled to receive any benefits under this formula. It may still be worthwhile to ask the plan to confirm this interpretation or to suggest other language if the plan does not agree.)

COMMENT 3: The fraction mentioned previously is preferable to a percentage because the fraction causes an automatic adjustment of the marital and nonmarital shares of the Accrued Benefit, while a percentage has to be fixed as of the date of the DRO and probably will not accurately reflect future events and contingencies.

Be careful not to subject the Alternate Payee to a double discount! Your DROs should either award "50 percent of the Participant's Accrued Benefit as of [date of separation or divorce]" or "50 percent of Participant's Accrued Benefit as of [date Alternate Payee commences receipt of benefit] times coverture fraction (number of years employed during marriage/total number of years employed until Alternate Payee commences receipt of benefit)." If you specify "50 percent of Participant's Accrued Benefit as of [date of separation or divorce] times number of years employed during marriage/total number of years employed until Alternate Payee commences receipt of benefit," you are applying two discounts to the Alternate Payee's share and reducing it substantially. Setting her benefit at 50 percent of the Accrued Benefit on the date of separation or divorce already automatically assigns all post-marital benefit accruals to the Participant. Using a coverture fraction applied to Accrued Benefit at the time Alternate Payee begins receiving benefits does the same thing. There is no need to discount the Alternate Payee's benefit twice. This is a common, and very expensive, error.

COMMENT 4: Even though this clause should, in theory, protect the Alternate Payee if the Participant dies before he reaches the Earliest Retirement Age or she begins receiving payments from the plan, it is still desirable to provide death benefits for the Alternate Payee using clause 7 to provide a Qualified Preretirement Survivor Annuity.

COMMENT 5: If the intent of the parties is that, if the Alternate Payee dies before beginning to receive benefits, her portion will revert to the Participant, some plans will require this clause to be rephrased as a "conditional assignment of benefits." This means that the assignment is conditional on the Alternate Payee actually beginning to receive benefits from the plan, so that if she dies before doing so, the benefits conditionally assigned to her revert to the Participant by adding this clause at the end of clause 5E:

5F. This assignment of benefits to the Alternate Payee is conditioned on her surviving until she begins to receive benefits from the plan. Should she die before doing so and while the Participant or any of his Beneficiaries is still alive and eligible to receive plan benefits, this assignment of plan benefits to her shall lapse and become null and void immediately upon her death, and all benefits previously assigned to her by this order shall revert to the Participant or his designated Beneficiaries.

COMMENT: This is something the Participant should bargain for. The only possible alternative is payment of the Alternate Payee's share to her beneficiaries or estate, by stating:

5G. Should the Alternate Payee die before beginning to receive any benefits from the plan, her share of plan benefits shall be paid as specified in clause 8 below.

COMMENT: See the discussion of clause 8.

5H. The Alternate Payee is the child of the Participant and was born September 1, 2006 (or provided under separate cover, if inclusion of a minor child's date of birth is prohibited in your jurisdiction). Payments under this order are for the benefit of the Alternate Payee as child support and shall be made until September 1, 2024.

COMMENT: Child support QDROs. If the QDRO is to be used to collect child support, payments to the Alternate Payee should begin immediately or as soon as possible. In addition, there is no need to divide the Participant's Accrued Benefit into "marital" and "nonmarital" shares (and no method for doing so).

The child support clause set forth here ensures that the payments will start *as soon as possible* and will be equal to either the monthly amount of child support determined by state law or the Participant's entire Accrued Benefit if that is less than the amount of monthly child support.

Clause 5H provides for termination on the child's eighteenth birthday. A more complex set of termination events may be used if the plan can do the necessary actuarial calculations as described in clauses 6L and 6M.

If there are (or will be) arrears at the time the Alternate Payee starts receiving payments under this clause, the arrears may be either estimated and included in the monthly payment or collected after this DRO lapses by the use of a second QDRO. The file on each child support Alternate Payee should be reviewed for arrears or increases every three to five years and one final time on the Alternate Payee's seventeenth birthday. Contact with the plan should be renewed at those times to discuss the availability of further Accrued Benefits from the Participant, so that the payment level under the QDRO currently in effect may be increased or a second DRO drafted and qualified by the plan before the first DRO expires on the Alternate Payee's eighteenth birthday. If the

Participant is still employed by the Plan Sponsor, his Accrued Benefit will increase every year and a higher level of payments will be available.

5I. Notwithstanding the death of the Participant at any time, whether before or after the Alternate Payee begins to receive plan benefits, the child Alternate Payee shall be entitled to begin receiving, directly from the plan, as soon as the plan may distribute any benefit to an Alternate Payee or as soon as possible after the date Participant attains (or would have attained if he dies earlier) the Earliest Retirement Age (as that term is defined in 29 U.S.C. § 1056(d)(3)(E)), whichever shall first occur, an amount equal to the lesser of:

1. $355 per month, or
2. The Actuarial Equivalent of 100 percent of the Participant's Accrued Benefit, payable to the Alternate Payee in the form of an annuity to pay all such plan benefits to the Alternate Payee from the date payments to her begin until the Alternate Payee's eighteenth birthday, and the Valuation Date for determining the Accrued Benefit of the Participant shall be the day before the Alternate Payee begins receiving benefits from the plan.

COMMENT: Here we are concerned with getting money for the child or IV-D agency as soon as possible, while he or she is growing up, and not with retirement security for a mature adult that might lead to the selection of a later Valuation Date.

COMMENT: *Alimony QDROs.* See clauses 6K and 6M for terminating events if the payments are characterized as alimony.

Some plans grant Participants an annual or more frequent cost-of-living increase after they retire. Such increases are not part of a Participant's Accrued Benefit at any time, and thus the Alternate Payee under a Separate Interest Approach will not receive any such increases unless clause 5J is used.

IMPORTANT NOTE: Most plans and regulatory agencies agree that a Separate Interest is not affected by the death of the Participant. However, a few plans take the position that if the Participant dies prior to attaining the plan's Earliest Retirement Age, the Alternate Payee's Separate Interest is extinguished. It is therefore vitally important in drafting Separate Interest Approach QDROs to expressly provide that "payment to the Alternate Payee will not be affected by the death of the Participant at any time, either before or after attaining the Earliest Retirement Age." (The PBGC Model Separate Interest QDRO uses this clause in section 8, which states, "The Participant's death shall not affect payments under the Alternate Payee's separate interest.") If the Plan Administrator rejects this language and insists that the Alternate Payee's Separate Interest will be extinguished if the Participant dies prior to attaining the Earliest Retirement Age allowed by the plan, then it is essential to award a QPSA to the Alternate Payee in an equivalent amount so that she will receive her award if the Participant dies prior to attaining the Earliest Retirement Age allowed by the plan. See clause 7.

5J. In the event the payments made by the plan to the Participant following his actual retirement are increased at any time for a cost-of-living adjustment, and such cost-of-living adjustments are not included in the Participant's Supplemental Benefit as that term is defined [in clause 5E] above, the Alternate Payee will receive [42.67 percent] [29/33] [pro rata share] of each such cost-of-living adjustment.

COMMENT: This clause creates a hybrid arrangement because it does not strictly speaking follow the Separate Interest Approach. It requires the Participant to be already retired for it to take effect, and payments under it will terminate when the Participant dies. However, there is no other way to grant an Alternate Payee a share of post-retirement cost-of-living adjustments under the Separate Interest Approach. Using this clause means the Alternate Payee will receive the greatest part of her payments (her share of the Participant's Accrued Benefit) under the Separate Interest Approach and may receive some supplemental cost-of-living adjustment payments on a different schedule and subject to different starting and termination dates under this clause.

This difficulty does not arise under the Shared Interest Approach if a fraction or percentage is used because the payments to the Alternate Payee automatically rise in proportion to any cost-of-living increase. This should not be an issue for the plan to accomplish; however, in the event that it is, or if there are concerns, you can always include a direct-payment provision for this portion. If you do this, you need to make sure that it is clear how the Supplemental Benefit is calculated to the Alternate Payee and how the Supplemental Benefit will be paid.

Part C: Division of a Defined Contribution Plan

INTRODUCTORY COMMENT: Defined contribution plans are generally easier to divide than defined benefit plans. They are similar to a sum of money in a bank account or shares of stock in a brokerage account. There is a present-day sum of money on hand, so there is no need to be concerned with Accrued Benefits, Actuarial Equivalence, Shared or Separate Interest Approaches, or similar concepts and procedures unique to defined benefit plans. However, not all defined contribution plans permit immediate distributions to Alternate Payees. Make sure you ascertain from the plan when such distributions may be made.

In dividing a Defined Contribution Plan, there are a number of key issues:

1. How will the marital (joint) share of the total plan account balance be defined?
2. How will the marital share of plan assets be valued? (See Chapter 5.)
3. Should the Alternate Payee leave her share of the funds on deposit in the plan or withdraw those funds and transfer them to her own IRA? If possible, always leave this election for the Alternate Payee, unless specifically required by a plan to happen in a certain way.
4. If the Alternate Payee's funds are left on deposit in the Participant's plan, what rights will the Alternate Payee have to direct the investment of those funds?
5. If the Alternate Payee's funds are left on deposit in the Participant's plan, what right will the Alternate Payee have to elect the time when she may withdraw those funds?

The first step is to define exactly what is being divided:

5K. For the purposes of this order, the marital [joint] [community] portion of the Participant's plan benefit that is divided by this order is composed of:

1. All vested [and unvested] benefits in the Participant's plan account as of the date of divorce [if date not specified earlier in clause 3, specify here]; plus
2. All employer contributions made to the Participant's plan account at any time that are attributable to Participant's

service to the Plan Sponsor during the period of time ending on the date of divorce, whether such contributions are actually made before or after the date of divorce or the date of this order; plus

3. All forfeitures allocated to the Participant's plan account attributable to Participant's service to the Plan Sponsor during the period of time ending on the date of divorce, whether such forfeitures are actually allocated to his plan account for the benefit of the Participant before or after the date of divorce or the date of this order; plus
4. All interest, dividends, gains, and losses on any of the foregoing amounts from the date of divorce until all benefits assigned to the Alternate Payee by this order have been paid to her by the plan (*see Austin v. Austin*, 2000 Me. LEXIS 61 (Me. 2000));
5. [Including][Not including] the amount of any loan outstanding against the Participant's account balance as of the date specified above.

COMMENT 1: This is a comprehensive clause including the most expansive definition of the extent of the marital or community assets to be divided. State law may require a less extensive definition. See Chapter 5; *Childs v. Kinder*, 1998 Ohio App. LEXIS 5543 (Ohio Ct. App. 1998) (failure to specify predisbursement interest).

COMMENT 2: The date of divorce is used as the key date for cutting off the accumulation of joint property. State law (and the discretion of the trial court judge) may require or permit the use of a different date, such as the date of separation, in which case an appropriate substitution should be made in the language of this clause.

COMMENT 3: Note that the treatment of loans against the Participant's account balance is a vitally important issue whose resolution is somewhat counterintuitive. From the plan's point of view, a loan is an asset with a positive value, not a liability with a negative value. *Example*: On the valuation date, the Participant's account consists of $80,000 in stocks and bonds and a $20,000 loan receivable from the Participant. If the Alternate Payee is awarded 50 percent *excluding* the loan amount, she will receive $40,000 (50 percent of $80,000); if the QDRO language states that the loan balance will be *included*, she will receive $50,000 (50 percent of $100,000). *Caution*: Some plans' Written QDRO Procedures contain presumptions—

that loans will be excluded or included from the total account balance—if the QDRO is silent on this issue.

5L. . . . less the Participant's account balance on [date of marriage] and less any contribution made [after date of separation].

COMMENT: This clause is necessary only in situations where the Participant worked for the Plan Sponsor prior to the marriage or after the state law cutoff date for the accumulation of joint property—that is, if state law focuses on the date of separation. Otherwise, if all of the Participant's service to the Plan Sponsor took place during the marriage, 100 percent of the account balances attributable to that service are included in the property to be divided.

This clause is an optional clause that may not be accepted by the Plan Administrator. In many instances, the Plan Administrator will only accept a fixed dollar amount or percentage but not a formula award that requires the Plan Administrator to do math. When seeking a division such as this, contact the Plan Administrator well beforehand to determine whether this is allowed by the plan rules.

A situation like this is likely better handled by having any premarital portion valued *with growth* (premarital employee contributions + premarital employer contributions + growth of both). If you are mathematically inclined and have all of the data available, this is possible. The safer route is to go with a financial expert, though. It is generally necessary that you have extremely good records to determine the growth portion of the account.

5M. Alternate Payee's share of Participant's plan benefits is:

1. $23,408.96.

COMMENT 1: Note that this approach places on the Participant all the risk (and all the reward) of increases and decreases in the plan's account balance. He will be entitled to any increase in the investments in his account, but he will bear all losses in that account since the amount payable to the Alternate Payee remains fixed no matter what gains or losses occur.

COMMENT 2: If a fixed dollar amount is stated, consider stating here whether the Alternate Payee should receive market gains and/or losses on her portion from the date of valuation until the date of segregation.

COMMENT 3: If a percentage (or fraction) formula is used, clauses 5L and 5M or variations of them should be used as part of the formula that defines the amount payable to the Alternate Payee.

COMMENT 4: *Child support and alimony QDROs.* It is slightly awkward to try to collect current child support or alimony payments from defined contribution plans, since typically they do not allow for monthly withdrawals or payments but rather for lump sums. (They are, however, very suited to the collection of arrears for that reason.) It is, however, possible to provide for annual withdrawals from a Defined Contribution Plan for current alimony or child support. If it is not, then you'll likely need to revisit this step multiple times. As long as the Participant remains employed by the same employer, additional contributions will be made to his plan account at least once a year, and the new contributions can be withdrawn as soon as they are made. If this is desired, the following clause may be used:

5N. . . . from the plan on January 1, 20__, and January 1 of each calendar year thereafter, the lesser of (a) $24,000, or (b) Participant's entire vested accrued plan benefit as of that date, until. . . .

COMMENT: So long as the Participant continues to work for the Plan Sponsor, more contributions will be made to his account every year so additional sums may be collected.

Appropriate termination events (see clause 6) should be added here.

5O. Alternate Payee may withdraw her share of plan benefits as determined hereunder from the plan at any time on or after the earliest date on which the plan permits an Alternate Payee to do so, or the Alternate Payee may direct that her share of plan benefits be transferred by the Plan Administrator directly to an IRA or other qualified plan.

COMMENT: It is usually desirable to make this withdrawal as soon as possible. The Alternate Payee should ordinarily roll her share over into an existing IRA (or a new one to be established) so that the parties' financial matters may be completely disentangled at the earliest possible moment. A rollover of this kind means the Alternate Payee will not have to pay any income tax when the rollover occurs but only when she begins making withdrawals from the IRA. If, on the other hand, a QDRO has not been entered, or the Alternate Payee is a child or other dependent of the Participant, payments made by the plan to the Alternate Payee are taxable to the Participant. *Hawkins v. Comm'r*, 86 F.3d 982 (10th Cir. 1996); *Brotman v. Comm'r*, 105 T.C. 141 (1995); *Darby v. Comm'r*, 97 T.C. 51, 58 (1991); 26 U.S.C. § 402(a)(9). If the Alternate Payee has her own Defined Contribution Plan, she can first roll over her share of the Participant's benefits into an IRA containing no other assets and then roll over the contents of the new IRA into a Defined Contribution Plan and not pay any federal income tax on either transaction.

5P. Until Alternate Payee has withdrawn her share of plan benefits from the plan, she shall have the same rights to receive information, to make elections and investment decisions, and to designate a Beneficiary or Beneficiaries for her share of plan benefits as any ordinary Participant in the plan, and the Plan Administrator shall furnish such information and election forms to her as if she were a Participant. The Plan Administrator shall segregate the interest assigned to the Alternate Payee by this order on the books and records of the plan and shall send the Alternate Payee periodic reports of the contents and value of her separate account.

COMMENT: Most defined contribution plans allow their Participants to select different investment options, offering them a bond fund, equity fund, international fund, company stock fund, and similar choices. If the Defined Contribution Plan permits Participants to make such investment choices, use this clause.

Note that these rights are not conferred by ERISA even if this order is a QDRO. ERISA requires plans to pay part or all of a Participant's plan benefits to an Alternate Payee only if the order is approved as a QDRO, not to enjoy any of these other rights of a Participant. An Alternate Payee under a QDRO will gain some rights because she will be considered a Beneficiary under 29 U.S.C. § 1056(d)(3)(J). Even so, you should still spell out all of the Alternate Payee's rights in the DRO. You cannot just say "she will be treated like any other Participant," because there are some rights—for example, the rights to be allocated a share of forfeitures (see Chapter 5) from departing participants, to make new contributions to the plan or receive matching employer contributions, or to take out loans against her account—that she cannot have under any circumstances under ERISA.

6. *Duration of payments.* The Alternate Payee shall receive payments pursuant to this order:

COMMENT: All QDROs for a Defined Contribution Plan will need a commencement date for payment to occur; however, be absolutely sure that a plan will allow for *payments* (emphasis on the plurality). Many plans will not allow for a duration of payments because they will only allow a single lump-sum payment, whether a distribution or rolling into a separate existing account.

(i) *Commencement date for payment(s):*

6A. . . . immediately. . . .

COMMENT: This is desirable if the terms of the plan permit it. It is particularly appropriate in dividing defined benefit plans already In Pay Status and defined contribution plans because it permits the Alternate Payee to withdraw her share and roll it over into an IRA to avoid any adverse tax consequences, and it immediately disentangles the financial matters of the parties. It is also appropriate for child support or alimony QDROs.

6B. . . . as soon as the Participant reaches, or would have reached, the Earliest Retirement Age permitted by the plan. . . .

COMMENT: This is also a desirable arrangement. However, the Alternate Payee and her lawyer should have some idea of what date this is, or what events will trigger it, before agreeing to accept it in lieu of a more specific definition of the commencement date.

6C. . . . as soon as the Participant attains, or would have attained, the Earliest Retirement Age permitted under the plan, or on such earlier date as the plan permits payments to be made to Alternate Payees, whichever occurs first. . . .

COMMENT: Often this will be the same date as in clause 6B. However, certain plans may permit payments to Alternate Payees even before the Participant reaches or would have reached the Earliest Retirement Age.

6D. . . . when the Participant begins to actually receive payments of plan benefits. . . .

COMMENT: This clause is not desirable and should rarely, if ever, be used. It leaves the timing of the payment of benefits to the Alternate Payee entirely to the whim of the Participant. Clauses 6A, 6B, 6E, or 6F provide better arrangements.

6E. . . . when the Alternate Payee attains age 55. . . .

COMMENT: This is a somewhat more favorable clause than 6D, but it is inferior to clause 6F, which gives the Alternate Payee much more flexibility. The Alternate Payee may today think she wants to start collecting her share of the pension at age 55; but circumstances may change, particularly if age 55 is many years distant, and a more flexible approach is desirable. If this clause is used, the terms of the plan should be reviewed to make sure that it permits payments to her when she reaches the specified age.

6F. . . . at a time to be elected by the Alternate Payee and notified to the plan on or after the earliest date on which the plan may legally pay or distribute any plan benefits to her. . . .

COMMENT: This is almost always the best clause to use. It permits the Alternate Payee to choose to begin receiving benefits as early as legally possible, yet it allows her to defer that distribution until she has had a chance to assess the circumstances of her life.

(ii) *Termination date for payment(s)*:

COMMENT: As noted earlier, plans may not allow for any sort of *duration* with payments, so review the plan literature ahead of time. Do not go into settlement negotiations with opposing counsel or into court arguing for something that the plan cannot, or will not, do.

6G. . . . until a total of $127,500 is paid to Alternate Payee.

COMMENT: This clause is most suited to dividing a Defined Contribution Plan with a specific account balance and is not generally suited to defined benefit plans. If the distribution is likely to take more than a year under this clause, it is desirable to state the amount payable as "$127,500 plus 6 percent per year simple interest on the unpaid balance due the Alternate Payee from time to time." Note that this clause may not adequately take into account post-divorce contributions or forfeitures, as discussed in Chapter 5.

6H. . . . until the Participant dies.

COMMENT: This is not desirable. It unduly limits the amount payable to the Alternate Payee and does not improve the Participant's financial position.

6I. . . . until the Alternate Payee remarries.

COMMENT: This clause should never be used. If the QDRO is for alimony, see clause 6K.

6J. . . . until the Alternate Payee dies.

COMMENT: This clause is redundant in cases involving a Defined Benefit Plan because payments to the Alternate Payee will stop automatically on her death. But see clause 8B.

6K. *(Alimony QDRO)* . . . until the first to occur of (a) the death of the Participant, (b) the death of the Alternate Payee, or (c) the remarriage of the Alternate Payee.

COMMENT: This clause may be used in alimony QDROs. It simply recites the standard events under the laws of most states that terminate alimony. If this clause is used, clause 6M should also be used.

6L. *(Child support QDRO)* . . . until the first to occur of (a) the death of the Participant or (b) the following events in the life of the Alternate Payee: (i) reaching her eighteenth birthday (or if, on her eighteenth birthday, she is enrolled in high school and likely to graduate, then on the earlier of (A) her nineteenth birthday or (B) her graduation from high school), (ii) dying, (iii) marrying, (iv) enlisting in the armed forces, (v) being otherwise emancipated, or (vi) being placed in the permanent custody of the Participant, whichever shall first occur, provided, however, that payments shall continue beyond the occurrence of any such event until any arrears of unpaid child support and interest thereon have been paid in full.

COMMENT: This clause is suitable for use in child support QDROs and recites the standard events that terminate child support under the laws of most states. In some states the courts may order child support to continue after the Participant's death. *See* J. Thomas Oldham, *What Does the U.S. System Regarding Inheritance Rights of Children Reveal about American Families?* 33 FAM. L.Q. 265 (1999), at 271. In those jurisdictions, subclause (a) may be omitted. The change of custody clause (vi) is often omitted because the custody of children often changes more than once before they attain their majority. The plan may also require a more specific statement of the amount of arrears, and any interest payable on arrears, in this clause.

If this clause is used, clause 6M should also be used.

6M. . . . but the plan shall not be considered to have received notice of any of the occurrence of any of these events until the plan receives (a) from the state court that entered the original DRO or another court of competent jurisdiction a further order declaring that such a terminating event has occurred and that the plan should cease making payments under the DRO, or (b) a certified copy of an official death or marriage certificate.

COMMENT 1: If clause 6K or 6L is used, the question arises as to how the plan is to be officially notified of the occurrence of one of the terminating events. Plans are reluctant to accept informal notice, or even sworn statements, from Participants, who have an obvious financial interest in terminating payments made under a QDRO. Requiring informal notice or a sworn statement from an Alternate Payee is equally troublesome because the Alternate Payee may have other quarrels with the Participant that might lead her to refuse to provide verification of the occurrence of a terminating event, even though she should. From the plan's perspective, the most satisfactory method of notice is a supplemental court order from the court that originally entered the DRO or another court of competent jurisdiction, or, in the case of marriage or death, a certified copy of the official certificate. Where a state IV-D agency is the Alternate Payee in a child support QDRO, the plan should be willing to accept official notification of the occurrence of any of these events from the agency, and this clause should be modified accordingly.

COMMENT 2: Some plans may insist that they cannot make the actuarial calculations required by ERISA for an annuity that is not a Single Life Annuity unless the order has a definite stop date, such as the child's eighteenth birthday. If so, the best practice is to delete all the other emancipating events from clause 6L. The order can always be amended later to curtail payments should one of the other emancipating events occur, or extended if state law permits child support through the nineteenth birthday if still in high school, or even into college years. In the case of child support QDROs, this clause might state that the plan may cease payments on the child's eighteenth (or later) birthday without further notice if the child's date of birth is stated in the original DRO (see clause 3B).

7. *Survivor Benefits for Alternate Payee.*

COMMENT: In the area of defined contribution plans, it is very common that survivor benefits for the Alternate Payee are put into place until such a time as the benefit is paid (or otherwise allocated) to the Alternate Payee.

The Alternate Payee

A. Shall be treated as the surviving spouse of the Participant for the purposes of 29 U.S.C. § 1055(a)(2) concerning Qualified Preretirement Survivor Annuities to the extent of all of Participant's plan benefits; or

B. Shall be treated as the surviving spouse of the Participant for the purposes of 29 U.S.C. § 1055(a)(2) concerning Qualified Preretirement Survivor Annuities, but only to the extent of the plan benefits assigned to her by this order; or

C. Shall be treated as the surviving spouse of the Participant for the purposes of 29 U.S.C. § 1055(a)(2) concerning Qualified Preretirement Survivor Annuities for a fractional part of the total benefits available thereunder, with the numerator being the total number of years the parties were married to each other during Participant's employment by the Plan Sponsor and the denominator being the total number of years the Participant was employed by the Plan Sponsor prior to his death; or

D. Shall not be treated as the surviving spouse of the Participant for the purposes of 29 U.S.C. § 1055(a)(2) concerning Qualified Preretirement Survivor Annuities; or

E. Shall be treated as the spouse of the Participant for the purposes of 29 U.S.C. § 1055(a)(1) concerning Qualified Joint and Survivor Annuities [but only to the extent of the plan benefits assigned to her by this order]; or

F. Shall not be treated as the spouse of the Participant for the purposes of 29 U.S.C. § 1055(a)(1) concerning Qualified Joint and Survivor Annuities; or

G. [The DRO does not mention these subjects at all].

COMMENT 1: ERISA allows certain Alternate Payees who are former spouses (but not children or other dependents of a Participant) two important rights:

1. The right to receive certain death benefits in the form of a QPSA if the Participant dies before the Alternate Payee begins receiving plan benefits.
2. The right to compel Participants to elect QJSA for the joint lives of the Alternate Payee and the Participant when the Participant retires.

Hopkins v. AT&T Global Information Solutions Co., 105 F.3d 153, 156 (4th Cir. 1997). A QDRO must be entered before the remarried Participant actually retires; otherwise, the Participant's new spouse is vested with survivorship rights under QJSA on the date of retirement. *See Roth v. Roth*, 506 N.W.2d 900 (Mich. Ct. App. 1993).

Survivorship rights must be expressly mentioned and specifically awarded to the Alternate Payee by a trial court to be included in a QDRO. These benefits are available only to Alternate Payees who are "spouses" or "former spouses." 29 U.S.C. § 1056(d)(3)(F)(i). *To obtain these important benefits for an Alternate Payee who is a former spouse, the QDRO must expressly mention them.*

Clauses 7A–C deal with the Alternate Payee's right to receive a QPSA should the Participant die before retiring. Clause 7D deals with the Alternate Payee's right to receive a QJSA with the Participant (see Chapter 6 for definitions and details of these types of annuities).

Clause 7A assigns to the Alternate Payee the entire preretirement death benefits of the Participant.

Clause 7B assigns a lesser amount, limited to the benefits payable to the Alternate Payee had the Participant survived, leaving the balance to be paid to the Participant's new spouse, children, or any other eligible Beneficiaries as the Participant may direct.

Clause 7C assigns a lesser amount, computed by the fraction-of-years method, leaving the balance to be paid to the Participant's new spouse, children, or any other eligible Beneficiary as the Participant may direct.

Clause 7D expressly denies the Alternate Payee any preretirement death benefit.

Clause 7E has no effect on preretirement death benefits but compels the Participant to receive retirement annuity payments in the form of a QJSA with the Alternate Payee.

Clause 7F expressly denies the Alternate Payee the right to compel the Participant to elect a QJSA with her.

Note that clause 7G, in which the DRO does not mention these subjects at all, has the same effect as clauses 7D and 7F, and the Alternate Payee will receive nothing. ERISA gives the right to receive a QPSA or a QJSA to an Alternate Payee only "to the extent provided in any qualified domestic relations order." 29 U.S.C. § 1056(d)(3)(F).

COMMENT 2: If QPSA coverage is to be granted to an Alternate Payee by a QDRO, it must be separately and specifically identified. A QDRO assigning an interest in "monthly pension benefits" was held not to cover payments under a QPSA where the Participant died while still actively employed. *Dugan v. Clinton*, 8 EBC 2065 (N.D. Ill. 1987).

COMMENT 3: To the extent that a former spouse Alternate Payee is given either of these rights in a QDRO, *they will not be available* *to any subsequent spouse of the Participant, and vice versa. Hopkins v. AT&T Global Information Solutions Co.*, 105 F.3d 153, 156 (4th Cir. 1997). If you represent the Participant, you should be very careful to point this out and negotiate and litigate the case accordingly, particularly if you know that the Participant plans to remarry. Clause 7B, clause 7C, and use of the clause in brackets in clause 7E are usually fair compromises protecting and allocating each party's appropriate interests. *See* 26 C.F.R. §§ 1.401(a)–13(g) on allocating payments between former and current spouses.

COMMENT 4: Note that under ERISA, the plan is permitted to deduct the cost of providing a QPSA from the regular Single Life Annuity payable to the Participant or the QJSA payable to the Participant and the Alternate Payee. Watch for this cost, and make sure to negotiate it and expressly provide in the QDRO for which party will bear it if the plan doesn't. To accurately determine the exact cost, you may have to ask the plan to tell you the monthly benefit payable under a QJSA or Single Life Annuity if a QPSA is not provided. If one is provided, use it to work out the actuarial difference.

COMMENT 5: Note that use of this clause concerning payment of a death benefit is completely independent from the ordinary share of benefits assigned to the Alternate Payee under the appropriate versions of clause 5. However, you should also note the following:

1. In the case of a Defined Contribution Plan, payments under clauses 5 and 6 may be worded to continue until the Alternate Payee has received her share in full, even if the Participant dies before this occurs.
2. In the case of a Defined Benefit Plan divided under the Shared Interest Approach, as soon as the Participant dies, if his death occurs before he begins receiving payments, the ordinary payments that would otherwise be made to the Alternate Payee under clause 5 will vanish; all the Alternate Payee will have, if anything, is the payments provided under clause 7. (The ordinary payments under clause 5 will also cease if the Participant dies even after beginning to receive payments unless a QJSA covering the Participant and the Alternate Payee, or a QJSA for the Participant and his new spouse, has been elected and the new spouse survives the Participant.)
3. In the case of a Defined Benefit Plan divided under a Separate Interest Approach under clause 5, payments of the

Alternate Payee's benefits should not be affected by the Participant's death at any time. However, make sure you check with the plan to confirm that this is the way you have worded the DRO; otherwise, all the Alternate Payee may receive is the death benefit provided by clause 7.

8. *Contingent Alternate Payees; Recomputation of Participant's Plan Benefits.*

INTRODUCTORY COMMENT: In clause 7 the focus was on what the Alternate Payee would receive if the Participant died before she did, or before she began to receive plan benefits. In clause 8 the focus is on what happens if the Alternate Payee predeceases the Participant.

8A. In the event the Alternate Payee dies before receiving [any] [all] of the plan benefits assigned to her by this order, the remaining plan benefits assigned to her shall be paid to [the Contingent Alternate Payee(s), whose name, address and Social Security number is _____, and whose relationship to the [Alternate Payee] [the Participant] is _____] [the estate of the Alternate Payee].

COMMENT: It is clear that a Contingent Alternate Payee may be named if

1. He or she is within the class of permissible Alternate Payees of the Participant (spouse, former spouse, child, or other dependent of the Participant); and
2. The Alternate Payee has not yet received any plan benefits.

This is clear because the same result could be obtained by entering two QDROs, one in favor of the Alternate Payee and one in favor of the Contingent Alternate Payee, with the first QDRO contingent on the Alternate Payee surviving to begin collecting plan benefits, and the second QDRO expressly deferring to the first one.

What is not clear under ERISA is whether:

3. If the Alternate Payee has received some, but not all, plan benefits, particularly under a Defined Benefit Plan, there is any duty on the part of the plan to pay anyone any sums at all after her death; and
4. A Contingent Alternate Payee named in a DRO can be a person who is a permissible Alternate Payee of the Alternate Payee (spouse, former spouse, child, or other dependent) but does not have such a relationship with the

Participant (for example, a child of an Alternate Payee by a previous marriage who is not a child of the Participant).

The answer to part (3) is that it depends on the type of plan. There is more likely to be something left to inherit under a Defined Contribution Plan than under a Defined Benefit Plan, although this depends on the plan's exact terms.

The answer to part (4) is that the Contingent Alternate Payee has to have one of the prescribed relationships *with the Participant, not with the Alternate Payee*, in order to be named in a QDRO. However, if there is anything to inherit under (3), the way to pass it to a Contingent Alternate Payee who is not related to the Participant is probably not in the QDRO itself but in a beneficiary election form filed with the plan or in the Alternate Payee's will.

This area of the law is somewhat unsettled. Some plans will tell you that you cannot designate any Contingent Alternate Payee in a QDRO, which is incorrect. Other plans will tell you that they will allow it, but only if the Contingent Alternate Payee is within the definition of a regular Alternate Payee of the Participant (that is, spouse, former spouse, child, or other dependent *of the Participant*, not of the Alternate Payee), which is correct. *In re Marriage of Shelstead*, 66 Cal. App. 4th 893 (Cal. Ct. App. 1998). Most plans will tell you that you cannot designate an Alternate Payee if the plan is already In Pay Status or you use the Shared Interest Approach to dividing a Defined Benefit Plan as described previously, which is probably correct unless there is a death benefit associated with the payment being received.

Unless you want to make new law by litigating the matter under ERISA, ask the plan whether and to what extent it permits the designation of Contingent Alternate Payees, and go along with what the plan advises you.

8B. In the event the Alternate Payee [and every Contingent Alternate Payee named in this order] predeceases the Participant, or for any other reason permanently ceases to be eligible to receive any further payments from the plan, the Participant may apply to the plan to increase the remaining benefits to be paid to him or to his other Beneficiaries if, and to the extent that, the terms of the plan permit him to apply for and receive such an adjustment.

COMMENT: This clause costs the Alternate Payee nothing and may allow the Participant to receive more from the plan. Not all plans allow for this kind of recalculation. Check with the plan to see if this sort of recomputation is permitted. If it is, this is an important clause that counsel for the Participant should bargain for in negotiations or argue for in the property division hearing. *In re Marriage of Rich*, 73 Cal. App. 4th 419 (Cal. Ct. App. 1999) (Alternate Payee's share of pension reverted to Participant after Alternate Payee's death).

9. *Participant Not to Interfere with Alternate Payee's Rights.* The Participant is hereby ordered not to do, or fail to do, any act, or to make any choice or election, or by inaction fail to make any choice or election under the plan, that would interfere in any way with the payment to the Alternate Payee of the share of his plan benefits assigned to the Alternate Payee by this order. In the event any payment assigned to the Alternate Payee by this order is paid to or received by the Participant, the Participant shall be deemed to have received such payments as trustee for the benefit of the Alternate Payee and shall immediately pay the same over to the Alternate Payee. The obligations set forth herein are personal obligations of the Participant and his estate that shall be satisfied and offset by all amounts received by the Alternate Payee directly from the Plan.

COMMENT: This clause is really directed at the Participant, not the plan, so arguably it does not belong in a QDRO but rather in the original divorce decree or child support order. It is a good idea to include it in the QDRO if only to put the Plan Administrator on notice of its terms and because most attorneys do not think to put it in the divorce decree or settlement agreement. The third sentence is particularly important if the Participant's benefits are already In Pay Status or he is close to retirement. It may take several months for the Plan Administrator to approve the order as a QDRO, and there is no reason why the Participant should keep the Alternate Payee's share of benefits as a windfall while that process drags on. Personal payments of this kind by the Participant to the Alternate Payee may be characterized as alimony to allow the Participant to deduct them.

The last sentence in clause 9 recognizes the dual nature of QDROs—as orders creating an obligation of both the Participant and the Plan. Participants frequently object to its inclusion. If necessary to appease the Plan Administrator, you can add a sentence at the end of the clause stating, "Nothing in this paragraph shall affect the Plan's obligations to either party in any way."

10. *Pension Benefit Guaranty Corporation Takeover.* In the event the Pension Benefit Guaranty Corporation (PBGC) becomes the

trustee of the plan and the total amount payable with respect to the Participant or the Alternate Payee or both is reduced by the PBGC, any necessary reduction will be applied by decreasing [each party's payments by the same percentage as the percentage by which the PBGC directs total payments with respect to both parties to be reduced] [by decreasing the Participant's payments first] [by decreasing the Alternate Payee's payments first].

COMMENT: Insolvent defined benefit plans may be taken over by the PBGC. However, the PBGC will not pay plan benefits above certain limits, so it is possible that the payments to one or both of the parties might have to be reduced.

The PBGC maximum payment for single-employer pension plans terminating in 2022 for a straight-line annuity at age 65 was $6,204.55 per month; this figure is adjusted annually to reflect changes in the Social Security taxable-wage base.

This clause does not need to be used in dividing a Defined Contribution Plan.

11. *Effect of Order.* This order shall not be construed or interpreted to

A. Require the plan to provide any type or form of benefit, or any option, not otherwise provided under the plan;
B. Require the plan to provide increased benefits (determined on the basis of actuarial value); or
C. Require the payment of benefits to the Alternate Payee that are required to be paid to another Alternate Payee under an order previously determined to be a QDRO.

COMMENT: This clause simply recites the "3 Don'ts" contained in ERISA, 29 U.S.C. § 1056(d)(3)(D) and is often referred to as a "savings clause." Including this clause casts the burden of determining whether there is any conflict in these areas on the plan, which is where it belongs. Counsel for the Participant or the Alternate Payee do not need to say more than this in their draft DRO to protect their respective clients' interests.

OPTIONAL ADDITIONAL CLAUSE

D. In the event of any conflict between this clause and any other clause of this order, the provisions of this clause shall prevail.

COMMENT: Plans often request this clause to ensure that they do not have to pay out more than they should or violate the existing payment options available from the plan.

12. *Representative for Alternate Payee.* Richard A. Green, Esquire, Green & Chanthol, 222-C West Ninth Street Plaza, Augusta, Georgia 39099, is hereby appointed the Representative of the Alternate Payee pursuant to section 1056(d)(3)(G)(ii)(III) of ERISA to receive copies of all notices sent to the Alternate Payee during the qualification of this order as a Qualified Domestic Relations Order.

13. *Tax Effect.* It is the intention of the court [and the parties] that federal and state income taxes on all payments received by the Alternate Payee under this order shall be borne . . .

13A. . . . by the Alternate Payee and not by the Participant, and the Alternate Payee is ordered to indemnify and hold the Participant harmless with respect to any federal or state income tax imposed on the Participant as a result of the Alternate Payee's receipt of her payments . . .

13B. . . . by the Participant and not by the Alternate Payee, and the Participant is ordered to indemnify and hold the Alternate Payee harmless with respect to any federal or state income tax imposed on the Alternate Payee as a result of the Alternate Payee's receipt of her payments . . . , *provided, however,* that the plan's obligations to any party shall not be affected in any way by this clause.

COMMENT: While not binding on the Internal Revenue Service or state tax authorities, this clause should always be included. First, it expressly states the intent of the trial court (and the parties, if the order is entered by stipulation) as to the tax effect of the payments to the Alternate Payee. Second, it requires the appropriate party to indemnify the other in case the intended tax consequences do not occur. Without such a written indemnity, there is no such obligation from either party to the other.

The general rule for federal income taxes is that Participants are taxable on all distributions from their plans. The only limited exception is for Alternate Payees who received payments under a QDRO—and even then the Alternate Payee must be a spouse or former spouse of the Participant. *See* 26 U.S.C. § 402(a)(9); *Hawkins v. Comm'r,* 86 F.3d 982 (10th Cir. 1996); *Brotman v. Comm'r,* 105 T.C. 141 (1995). Payments to an Alternate Payee who is a child of the Participant are ***always*** taxable income to the Participant and never to the Alternate Payee.

ERISA and the Internal Revenue Code expressly permit QDROs to be used to collect child support. However, under section 402(e)(1)(A) of the Code, "*an alternate payee who is the spouse or former spouse of the participant shall be treated as the distributee* of any distribution or payment made to the alternate payee under a QDRO" (emphasis added). Thus, if the custodial parent named as the Alternate Payee in a child support QDRO is either a spouse or former spouse of the Participant, the distribution will be taxable to the custodial parent even if the QDRO expressly characterizes the payment as one for child support. In other words, under section 402(e)(1)(A), the tax treatment of a distribution under a QDRO is governed by the identity of the distributee, not by the characterization of the nature of the payment in the QDRO as one for child support.

The only way to make a participant liable for the taxes on a child support payment under a QDRO is to designate the child(ren) themselves as the Alternate Payees, which is expressly permitted by ERISA and the Code. The custodial parent may then be appointed, in either the QDRO itself or a separate court order, as the agent or guardian for the child(ren) Alternate Payees for the purposes of endorsing and cashing the distribution check from the plan.

Since Plan Administrators rarely deal with child support QDROs, it is desirable to send them a cover letter when a child support QDRO is first submitted, advising them of the correct tax treatment of the distribution. Otherwise, the plan will send the custodial parent an incorrect Form 1099-R at the end of the calendar year, attempting to impose the tax liability on him or her—an error that takes an enormous amount of time, effort, and energy to subsequently correct with the IRS.

13C. The Alternate Payee's basis for income tax purposes in the assets assigned to her by this order shall be ___ percent of the Participant's basis in his account balance as of [date], and the Participant shall provide the Alternate Payee and her advisors with such information and documents as may reasonably be required to determine the Alternate Payee's basis as set forth herein.

COMMENT: *See* section 72(m)(10) of the Internal Revenue Code. This clause applies only to defined contribution plans. It is important for the Alternate Payee to be able to determine her tax basis in the amount awarded to her, so her tax liability can be minimized. Three types of contributions may be made to a Defined Contribution Plan: employer, employee pre-tax, and employee after-tax. Employee after-tax contributions are not deductible by the employee when made, but they generate a substantial tax advantage when contributions are withdrawn because the Participant is taxed only on the difference between the amount withdrawn and the "basis" of that amount. (An asset you sell for $100 that cost you $40 results in your being taxed not on the entire $100 received, but only on the difference between the sale price and the basis, $100 – $40 = $60.)

Employee after-tax contributions have a tax basis usually equal to the amount contributed by the Participant from his salary. It is important to include this clause in your QDROs allocating the tax basis of those contributions between the Participant and the Alternate Payee, usually in the same proportion as the overall allocation of plan assets. In other words, if an Alternate Payee is going to receive 50 percent of the assets in a plan, she should also be allocated 50 percent of the tax basis of those assets. Otherwise, the intended distribution of assets between the parties may be severely distorted. For example, assume the Participant has accumulated $200,000 in a 401(k) plan during the marriage that is divided 50/50 between the parties. The Participant's tax basis in the plan assets is $40,000. Both parties are in the 20 percent tax bracket. The Alternate Payee's after-tax share of the plan assets, if the basis is not expressly allocated between the parties in a QDRO, is $80,000 ($100,000 gross amount received, less 20 percent tax on $100,000 = $80,000). The Participant, however, nets $88,000 ($100,000 – $40,000 basis = $60,000; 20 percent tax on $60,000 = $12,000; $100,000 – $12,000 = $88,000). A simple clause splitting the tax basis 50/50 between the parties would have given each of them $84,000 on an after-tax basis, not $88,000 to one party and $80,000 to the other. A client who should have received $84,000 will not be happy with the $4,000 shortfall caused by failure to allocate the tax basis of plan assets awarded to him or her. It is equally important to require the Participant to furnish sufficient information and documents so the Alternate Payee can compute her tax basis in the assets assigned to her.

Employers' model QDROs never include this tax basis allocation clause. Why? Because the plan is not concerned with the tax liabilities of the parties, only with the total amount the plan has to pay out. From an Alternate Payee's standpoint, however, this issue is vitally important to both parties and should be addressed in every QDRO. Ensure, however, that you're not stepping outside of your area of expertise with the preparation and inclusion of a provision of this nature.

14. *Reservation of Jurisdiction.*

A. This court reserves jurisdiction to amend the provisions of this order in light of comments received from (a) the plan, (b) another court of competent jurisdiction, or (c) any other organization or party, during the process of deciding whether this order is a Qualified Domestic Relations Order.

B. This court also reserves jurisdiction to amend or modify the provisions of this order, even after it has been determined to be a Qualified Domestic Relations Order by the plan; to terminate or suspend the payment of benefits to the Alternate Payee as a result of remarriage, cohabitation, attainment of a certain age, emancipation, change of custody, or other events justifying a change in payments; or to modify this order (subject to clause 14) to deal with any unforeseen tax consequences or other effects of this order, and to enforce the tax indemnity and cooperation provisions of this order.

COMMENT: This is a vitally important clause. It is often necessary to revise a DRO several times during the qualification process, and it is vitally important that the state trial court retain jurisdiction under clause 14A to do so. In many states, the trial court loses jurisdiction over a divorce or support case once the final order in the case has been entered if an express reservation of jurisdiction like this is not made. *Edwards v. Edwards*, 838 S.W.2d 494 (Mo. Ct. App. 1992); *Rohrbeck v. Rohrbeck*, 566 A.2d 767 (Md. 1989). The result can be a nightmare of protracted litigation and malpractice claims.

Clause 14B is much broader. It is always desirable in alimony QDROs, and it is very desirable in case of future difficulties with the Internal Revenue Service about the intended and actual tax consequences of the DRO. *See Hawkins v. Comm'r*, 86 F.3d 982 (10th Cir. 1996) (failure of state trial court to reserve jurisdiction meant DRO could not be revised by trial court).

Use the broadest reservation of jurisdiction clause permitted by state law to deal with all these unforeseen contingencies. *Wilson v. Wilson*, 492 S.E.2d 495 (Va. Ct. App. 1997). Unfortunately, not all states permit this (*Johnson v. Johnson*, 1999 Tenn. App. LEXIS 625 (Tenn. Ct. App. 1999); *Woods v. Woods*, 1999 Tex. App. LEXIS 7538 (Texas Ct. App. 1999)); but to the extent you can reserve jurisdiction by using these clauses, it is always desirable.

If appropriate, add a clause indicating that each party has waived his or her right to appeal or move for a new trial.

SO ORDERED:

____

Judge

COMMENT: Under ERISA, only an order may be a DRO or a QDRO. Usually a judge will sign the order, but an authorized official of a state agency that can enter child support orders may also sign it.

[Signatures of counsel for both parties]

[Signatures of both parties]

COMMENT: While not required by ERISA, signature of counsel for both parties, or, better yet, signature of the parties themselves, helps to counter later claims that they had not approved, or at least read, the provisions of the order. Your client's signature on this order will also be very helpful in fending off any subsequent malpractice claims. Furthermore, it is extremely helpful to have party signatures on a proposed QDRO that is being submitted to a trial court, because it shows the court that the parties have consented to the entry of the QDRO, and the court does not have to take any further action or steps to ensure no later pushback on the execution of the QDRO.

8.6 Final Quality Control Check

Once you have drafted a DRO, following the guidelines and model clauses in this chapter, check your work. The best way to do this is to have someone else who has not been involved in your drafting read it for clarity. This may be another lawyer or paralegal in your office. Don't involve your client in this phase of the review.

Review your DRO for the following issues: Does your draft DRO contain all of the required information and clauses set forth in this chapter? Is it clear? What happens if the Alternate Payee dies before the Participant, and vice versa? What happens to each party's share of plan benefits after he or she dies? Rewrite the draft as necessary in light of the reviewer's comments. Use the checklist in the next section to make sure you have thought through and dealt with all issues. Then, and only then, should you review the DRO with your client to make sure it is consistent with his or her stated goals, and then send it to the plan for a preliminary and informal review.

8.7 DRO Checklist

___ 1. Order contains names, addresses, and Social Security numbers of Participant and all Alternate Payees (or references this information in a separate cover letter or addendum that is not part of the court's public record).

___ 2. Order identifies state domestic relations law section involved and specifies whether it is for property division, alimony, or child support.

___ 3. Order identifies Alternate Payee's relationship to Participant as spouse, former spouse, child, or other dependent (can further identify distributee for child support QDRO).

___ 4. Order states date of marriage and date of divorce (less important, and likely unnecessary, for QDROs for defined contribution plans), or date of birth for child for child support (likely going to be referenced in a separate cover letter or addendum that is not part of the court's public record).

___ 5. Order clearly specifics the ***exact*** name of each plan to which it applies.

___ 6. Order clearly specifies what plan benefits, or what fraction of plan benefits, it is dividing.

___ 7. *For defined contribution plans*: Order covers vesting, forfeitures, interest, and Alternate Payee's control over investments while funds remain in plan.

___ 8. *For defined benefit plans*: Order clearly follows Shared Interest Approach or Separate Interest Approach.

___ 9. If Shared Interest Approach is used, Alternate Payee has requested this and understands that (a) payments cannot begin until Participant retires, and (b) payments must end upon Participant's death unless a QJSA has been elected.

___ 10. Order clearly specifies starting and ending dates (or amounts or events) for receipt of payments by Alternate Payee.

___ 11. Order clearly specifies the amount of each payment or formula for calculating that amount.

___ 12. Order provides Alternate Payee is to be treated as surviving spouse of Participant for all of Participant's plan benefits or Alternate Payee's share to obtain QPSA.

___ 13. Order provides Alternate Payee is to be treated as spouse of Participant for purpose of obtaining QJSA for all of Participant's plan benefits or Alternate Payee's share.

___ 14. Order allows for recomputation of Participant's benefit if Alternate Payee does not collect entire share or ceases to be eligible to collect share (optional).

___ 15. Order appoints Representative (optional).

___ 16. Order directs Participant not to interfere with Alternate Payee's rights.

___ 17. Order contains appropriate PBGC takeover clause (Defined Benefit Plan only).

___ 18. Order specifies intended tax effect.

___ 19. Order contains appropriate reservation of jurisdiction clause allowing trial court to modify as needed during qualification and afterward.

___ 20. Order clearly specifies what happens if Alternate Payee dies before receiving any benefits from plan.

___ 21. Order clearly specifies what happens if Participant dies before receiving any benefits from plan.

___ 22. Order contains any special features unique to this case (specify):

____

____

____

____

From DRO to QDRO

9

9.1 Submission to the Court for Judge's Signature and Filing

Remember that under the Employee Retirement Income Security Act (ERISA), a separation agreement, settlement agreement, memorandum of understanding, or any other document reflecting an agreement and executed by parties is not enough for purposes of effectuating division of an applicable account. A court order is required (or, in child support cases, an administrative order of child support if state law permits). However, court orders under ERISA include any "judgment, order or decree (including approval of a property settlement agreement)." 29 U.S.C. § 1056(d)(3)(B)(ii). As a practice point, especially if an extended period of time has elapsed between the time of divorce and the Qualified Domestic Relations Order (QDRO) process occurring, it is a safe practice to include initial lines for the parties on each page and signature lines for both parties. In recent years, most judges have become increasingly agreeable to e-signatures, considering the frequent use beginning in 2020. Always do your homework, though, and make sure that the judge's office will approve this method and that the judge will not require original signatures. Ensure that you are doing everything to make this process as efficient as possible.

The act of each party initialing and signing helps reflect to the court that both parties knowingly reviewed and approved of the language of the order. Once the parties have both signed the order, submit to the judge for signing and filing. Once the Domestic Relations Order (DRO) is filed, get a certified copy to submit it to the Plan Administrator. Given the significant financial aspects of this area, most plans are quite stringent about the submission of court orders and will require certified copies, for good reason. Also, ensure that the plan does not require other documents from the divorce submitted contemporaneously with the DRO. Include these additional requirements, as applicable, in your organizational checklist to make sure that you're taking all necessary steps to properly handle this process. While rare, additional documentation can be required. The most common example of this is a court order reflecting the dates of marriage of parties or child-support-related documentation on Qualified Medical Child Support Orders (QMCSOs).

9.2 Send the DRO to the Plan as Soon as Possible

It is generally a smart practice to send the certified copy of the DRO (and any other necessary documentation) by certified mail. This allows the attorney(s), parties, and plan to track the documents. A brief cover letter indicating that you are enclosing a DRO for qualification and summarizing the key features of the DRO should be included. In this letter you may ask the plan to confirm your understanding and interpretation of the effect of the DRO and what happens in certain contingencies (a model letter is included in Appendix C). Given that most documents filed with courts are public record (unless otherwise specifically designated by the court), ensure that no specific identification numbers are included in the actual DRO, but include this information in the correspondence to the plan. This can include the parties' dates of birth, Social Security numbers, personal addresses, or specific account numbers, plan identification numbers, or plan contract numbers. Copies of the letter and the enclosed DRO should be sent to opposing counsel and to your client. It certainly does not hurt to notify the court of the same; however, limit the personal information to avoid the unintentional filing of the correspondence in public record.

Many plan administrators will now allow submission via email or via online portal. On the email side of things, always ensure that proper security protocols are taken, whether these are secured and encrypted messaging, password protection, or other similar steps, because of the sensitive nature of the information being submitted. Some Plan Administrators, if allowing submission via email, may open a secure email option. For submission via online portal, there may not be a "submission confirmation" or other similar communication regarding submission of the QDRO and personal information of the parties. If this is the case, screenshot the submission screen, if possible. Additionally, you can contact the plan regarding a submission confirmation, although this should be sent out later, regardless. Always keep the parties and counsel informed as to the status of submission, even if you do not have submission confirmation to send over.

9.3 Follow Up, Follow Up, Follow Up!

Plans do occasionally lose or mislay QDRO applications. *Fortmann v. Avon Products, Inc.*, 1999 U.S. Dist. LEXIS 3451 (N.D. Ill. 1999). It isn't common, but it can certainly happen. I have had a personal experience where the DRO was sent via certified mail, tracked, and delivered to the plan; however, the Plan Administrator insisted that it was never delivered or otherwise never received. In one particular matter, the DRO was confirmed delivered to the plan in less than one week, but we never received any sort of confirmation as to the submission on the end of the plan. The end result of this was that we had to request another certified copy of the DRO from the clerk of court and go through the same process again. It was a delay that was immensely frustrating to the parties and especially the Alternate Payee. As a practice point, whether using a checklist or electronic reminder or tickler, remember to follow up on these matters. If the DRO is never turned into a QDRO, the problem is going to be yours, not the plan's.

Generally, if you have submitted the DRO for review and preapproval (which is strongly, strongly recommended), the processing phase should (theoretically) go quicker because the DRO is already in the system and there is likely a file on it.

The key here is persistence. Sooner or later you will succeed in getting the DRO qualified, if you keep at it.

9.4 Rewrite the DRO as Necessary

Once it receives a DRO, the plan wants to qualify it with the minimum expenditure of time, effort, and energy by the Plan Administrator. This normally is a very quick process if you have previously submitted a draft DRO for review and preapproval and it was preapproved. A well-managed plan will take an educational approach to DROs, not an adversarial approach (see subsection 2.2Q and section 15.3), and will try to help you get the DRO qualified as expeditiously as possible.

Assuming that the plan follows the guidelines set forth in the *EBSA Booklet*, if it must reject your DRO, it will do the following:

1. Specify the reasons why the DRO is not a QDRO;
2. Refer to specific provisions of the plan on which the rejection was based;
3. Explain any time limits that apply to the rights of the parties (such as the duration of any protective action the plan will take to prevent withdrawal of the Alternate Payee's share by the Participant); and
4. Describe any additional material, information, or modifications of the DRO to make it a QDRO and explain why they are necessary. *EBSA Booklet* Question 2-14. *See also* 29 C.F.R. §§ 2560.503-1(f)(1)–(4) (similar requirement for Plan Administrators giving notice of denial of benefit by Participant or Beneficiary).

If the plan does not initially provide you with this information when it rejects your DRO, call or write the plan and ask for it.

Rewriting a DRO once is a fairly common experience, even if the Plan Administrator has given you preliminary informal approval of your draft. If the Plan Administrator provides an educational and comprehensive response, revisions and any need for rewriting should be relatively simple.

9.5 Get the Qualification Decision in Writing

Once the plan has accepted your DRO as a QDRO, make sure that you get written confirmation of the qualification from the plan. Although this is required, oftentimes it can slip through the cracks in larger plans. The written confirmation of qualification of the QDRO should go to all interested parties. This will generally be sent to any contacts included in the QDRO and/or cover letter submission. It is always a safe practice to include the parties' respective addresses as well as those of any attorneys involved. If this information is not included, a party or involved attorney will not receive the written qualification confirmation. Regardless, it is always a safe practice to circulate the written confirmation as soon as received to ensure that any interested party is informed of the status. Confirm that the written qualification either specifically identifies the DRO that is being qualified by date or attaches a copy of the DRO accepted as a QDRO to the certificate in order to avoid confusion. *Fortmann v. Avon Products, Inc.*, 1999 U.S. Dist. LEXIS 3451 (N.D. Ill. 1999) (plan's records did not indicate which of two conflicting DROs it had accepted as a QDRO). Make sure to request the plan to put the qualifying letter or certificate in the Participant's employee benefits file so that the plan doesn't inadvertently ignore the QDRO when the time comes to pay out plan benefits.

If the parties have not already received the document, send the original qualification letter or certificate to your client, and any attorneys involved, advising him or her that this is an important legal document and should be kept in a safe place. Keep a copy for your file.

9.6 Following Up with Parties

Even after you receive the qualification letter from the plan, there are still additional steps that are outside the abilities of the attorneys, including the transfer or disbursement of the funds. Being that this is solely for the parties, and, namely, Alternate Payee, often, attorneys will not be copied on these communications. This then requires the attorneys to make sure everything is squared away with the parties and that steps were correctly managed to ensure completeness, whether this is with one-time lump-sum transfers or regular benefits on pensions.

It is common that people will ask specific questions regarding transfer or disbursement of funds. Unless you are specifically certified or qualified to discuss the financial and/or tax implications, advise the Alternate Payee to consult with a financial professional to assist with those questions.

9.7 Review Old QDROs Every Three to Five Years

Circumstances may occur that require revisiting and reviewing old QDROs, including that plans can be terminated; Participants and Alternate Payees remarry or die; goals and circumstances change. The vast majority of the time, when circumstances change, the client will contact you. However, as a practice point that will be very well appreciated with the client, you should make a notation on the file to review it at least once every five years, or more frequently if circumstances warrant. Prepare a form letter to be sent to every client asking if he or she would like you to review the status of the QDRO to make sure no material changes have occurred and no problems have arisen. This work is separate from the original divorce or support proceeding and may be billed accordingly. This is also a graceful way to stay in touch with clients who may need additional legal services from you.

Child support QDROs, alimony QDROs (depending on duration), and Qualified Medical Child Support Orders (QMCSOs) should be reviewed every three years and on the child(ren)'s seventeenth birthday. Again, if there is any sort of change, odds are the client will be contacting you very quickly regarding the matter, but it is a strong practice to check in on these orders.

9.8 When You Reach an Impasse

Hopefully this never occurs. Even in the most difficult circumstances, it has ultimately been handled. Most plans will (even if it takes a substantial time waiting on hold) provide a representative to discuss outstanding issues with the DRO and potential remedies. To a degree, there is only so much that can be explained, though. As mentioned earlier, plans do not take an adversarial approach and will work with you to get matters resolved. Nonetheless, when you have exhausted your state court remedies and the plan's internal review and appeal procedures in an effort to qualify a DRO (*see* 29 U.S.C. § 1133(2); *Guzy v. Ameritech Corp.*, 1999 U.S. Dist. LEXIS 8943 (E.D. Mich. 1999)) but have still not achieved your client's goals, you will need to consider suing the plan or engaging in other QDRO litigation as discussed in the following chapter.

QDRO Litigation 10

10.1 Litigation against the Plan

What can you do if you represent an Alternate Payee and the plan has refused to accept your Domestic Relations Order (DRO) as a Qualified Domestic Relations Order (QDRO)? Or if you represent a Participant and your Employment Benefit Plan has qualified a defective DRO?

In my experience, it is extremely rare that the attempt to qualify a DRO as a QDRO will end in litigation. In most cases, any problems can be resolved by the Plan Administrator, counsel for both parties, and the state court that became involved during the DRO—usually requiring only a few revisions to the text of the order to comply with plan rules or to accomplish the intent of the court or parties regarding the division of the account.

On those extremely rare occasions when litigation is necessary, expert Employee Retirement Income Security Act (ERISA) counsel should be retained to conduct it. The ERISA is a complex and lengthy statute, and a full review of all aspects of ERISA litigation is beyond the scope of this handbook. The material set forth in this section provides only a brief overview of different types of QDRO litigation with a few citations on each topic as a starting point for further research should litigation become necessary.

Litigation should rarely be necessary. There are two key ERISA provisions governing QDRO litigation. The first is a passing and rather cryptic reference in 29 U.S.C. § 1056(d)(H) to the "period in which the issue of whether a DRO is a QDRO is being determined (by the Plan Administrator, by a court of competent jurisdiction, or otherwise)" during which the Plan Administrator must segregate the amount payable to the Alternate Payee. No other reference to court proceedings is found in the QDRO provisions of sections 1055 or 1056, and no one is quite sure what the phrase "or otherwise" means in the quoted language. The courts have interpreted this language and other general provisions of ERISA as authorizing both state and federal courts to determine whether a DRO is a QDRO, as discussed in this chapter.

The second fundamental QDRO litigation provision is 29 U.S.C. § 1132, which covers all ERISA litigation. Section 1132(a)(1)(B) authorizes a Participant or a Beneficiary to bring a civil action "to recover benefits due him under the terms of the plan, to enforce his rights under the terms of the plan, or to clarify his rights to future benefits under the terms of the plan." 29 U.S.C. § 1132(a)(1)(B). This provision has been interpreted as authorizing civil suits to determine the qualified status of DROs and for other relief against employee benefit plans.

The following is a review of the significant issues surrounding QDROs that have been dealt with in federal and state court litigation since QDROs were created by the Retirement Equity Act in 1984.

A. Concurrent Jurisdiction

Section 1132(e)(1) expressly provides that "state courts of competent jurisdiction and district courts of the United States shall have concurrent jurisdiction of actions under [Section 1132(a)(1)(B)]." *In re Marriage of Oddino*, 939 P.2d 1266 (Cal. 1997), *cert. denied*, 523 U.S. 1021 (1998); *In re Marriage of Levingston*, 16 Cal. Rptr. 2d 100 (Cal. Ct. App. 1993); *Board of Trustees of Laborers Pension Trust v. Levingston*, 816 F. Supp. 1496 (N.D. Cal. 1993). The Department of Labor has taken the position that state courts have no jurisdiction to determine whether a DRO is a QDRO and that the federal courts have exclusive jurisdiction over determining this *EBSA QDRO Booklet* Question 1-13. However, once the issue has been litigated and decided in a court of competent jurisdiction, that should be the end of it. In *Jones v. American Airlines, Inc.*, 1999 U.S. Dist. LEXIS 11507 (D. Wyo. 1999), the federal court deferred to a prior ruling by a Texas state court that its own order was a QDRO on Full Faith and Credit grounds.

B. Federal Venue Provisions

If an ERISA action of the type described in the previous section is brought in federal court, the venue for the suit is the district where the plan is administered; where the breach took place; or where a defendant resides or may be found, and nationwide service of process is permitted. 29 U.S.C. § 1132(e)(2). There is no requirement for diversity of citizenship or for any minimum amount in controversy in such federal ERISA actions. 29 U.S.C. § 1132(f).

C. State Jurisdiction and Venue

Proceedings in state courts must meet ordinary state jurisdictional and venue requirements.

D. Removal to Federal Court

Cases filed against Employee Benefit Plans in state courts may be removed by the defendant under 28 U.S.C. § 1441(b), which provides that state court cases may be removed if they are "founded on a claim or right arising under the Constitution, treaties or laws of the United States [such as ERISA] . . . without regard to the citizenship or residence of the parties. . . ." *Samaroo v. Samaroo*, 743 F. Supp. 309 (D.N.J. 1990) (*Samaroo I*).

However, in *In re Marriage of Nasca*, 87 F. Supp. 2d 967 (N.D. Cal. 1999), a previously removed action was remanded to state divorce court. The Participant's pension plan had been joined as a party defendant to a state court divorce case before the division of his pension as required by California law. California Family Code, section 2337(c)(6)(A). The defendant plan removed the case to federal court, claiming federal jurisdiction over the claim against it under ERISA. After some procedural wrangling involving an appeal to the Ninth Circuit and remand to the U.S. District Court, the entire case was remanded to state divorce court.

The U.S. District Court found that no federal ERISA issues had yet arisen in the case because a DRO had not even been entered. The federal court distinguished cases like this one where there was no dispute about the "quality, nature or existence" of benefits payable under the plan, only their "ultimate ownership" that could, and should, be decided by a state court ("Here there is no dispute about the amount or nature of the benefits due under the plan; the state court is asked to decide only which party will receive them"). *See also Mackey v. Lanier Collection Agency & Serv. Inc.*, 486 U.S. 825 (1986).

In addition, the U.S. District Court in *Nasca* found that since the action should never have been removed in the first place and its removal conferred no benefit on the divorce litigants (in fact, it delayed their divorce action for five years), the plan was ordered to pay the divorcing couple's legal fees of $65,000 under the fee-shifting provisions of the general federal removal statute. 28 U.S.C. § 1447(c).

E. Remand to State Court

In *Samaroo I*, the U.S. District Court remanded that portion of the case that involved the plaintiff's efforts to obtain a DRO nunc pro tunc. The parties had divorced in 1984, and the state divorce court ordered the Participant (not the plan) to pay a fixed amount to the plaintiff upon his retirement. However, the Participant died in 1987, before he was eligible to retire. The plaintiff then moved for an amended DRO in the state court divorce action and joined the plan as a party to that case to compel it to honor any amended DRO. The plan removed the divorce case to federal court under 28 U.S.C. § 1441(b). The federal court held that the case before it involved "two separate cases masquerading as one": one action to amend the DRO, and the other to force the plan to accept the DRO as amended as a QDRO. Finding that the first claim for relief was exclusively within the jurisdiction of the state courts as a domestic relations matter (*Solomon v. Solomon*, 516 F.2d 1018, 1025 (3d Cir. 1975)), the federal court remanded that portion of the case to the state divorce court and retained jurisdiction over the second claim, but stayed all proceedings on the second claim pending action on the first claim by the state court.

See also the discussion of *In re Marriage of Nasca*, 87 F. Supp. 2d 967 (N.D. Cal. 1999), in subsection 10.1D.

F. Remand to Plan Administrator

Although such an action is not technically a "remand," some courts have sent cases to Plan Administrators for reconsideration or redetermination of benefits if there have been procedural irregularities or other violations in determining whether a Participant or Beneficiary was entitled to receive benefits, including improper QDRO determinations by the Plan Administrator. *See Counts v. American General Life & Acc. Ins. Co.*, 111 F.3d 105 (11th Cir. 1997); *Weaver v. Phoenix Home Life Mut. Ins. Co.*, 990 F.2d 154 (4th Cir. 1993); *Jones v. American Airlines, Inc.*, 1999 U.S. Dist. LEXIS 11507 (D. Wyo. 1999); *Rutledge v. American Gen'l Life & Acc. Ins. Co.*, 871 F. Supp. 272 (N.D. Miss. 1994).

G. Exhaustion of Administrative Remedies

When the litigation claim is a statute-based claim under ERISA, a plaintiff may be required to exhaust his or her administrative remedies prior to filing a lawsuit in federal court. The Seventh and Eleventh Circuits require the plaintiff to exhaust his or her administrative remedies. *See Robyns v. Reliance Standard Life Ins. Co.*, 130 F.3d 1231, 1235 (7th Cir. 1997); *Counts v. American Gen. Life and Accident Ins. Co.*, 111 F.3d 105, 109 (11th Cir. 1997). The remaining circuits do not require exhaustion of administrative remedies. The Second Circuit reasoned that while the Plan Administrator has expertise in interpreting and applying the plan rules, the courts have the expertise in statutory construction. *See Campanella v. Mason Tenders' Dist. Council Pension Plan*, 299 F. Supp. 2d 274 (S.D.N.Y. 2004).

However, the federal courts have the discretion to waive the requirement for the plaintiff to exhaust his or her administrative remedies if doing so would be futile or there is no administrative remedy. *See Counts v. American Gen. Life and Accident Ins. Co.*, 111 F.3d 105, 109 (11th Cir. 1997). *See also Edwards v. Briggs & Stratton Retirement Plan*, 639 F.3d 355, 365 n.5 (7th Cir. 2011) ("We have never treated the requirement of exhaustion of administrative remedies in ERISA cases as being jurisdictional and instead . . . we consistently have held that the decision to require exhaustion in a given case is committed to a district court's discretion."); *Mack v. Kuckenmeister*, 619 F.3d 1010, 1020 (9th Cir. 2010) ("Because the exhaustion requirement is a creation of the federal courts . . . and is not written into the statute, it is a prudential rather than jurisdictional requirement."); *Crowell v. Shell Oil Co.*, 541 F.3d 295, 308–09 (5th Cir. 2008) ("We have never construed the ERISA exhaustion doctrine strictly as a jurisdictional bar and have referred to it as a defense. Other circuits have expressly held that ERISA exhaustion is not jurisdictional, and we agree."); *Metro. Life Ins. Co. v. Price*, 501

F.3d 271, 280 (3d Cir. 2007) ("ERISA's exhaustion doctrine places no limits on a federal court's subject matter jurisdiction.").

H. Federal Court Qualifies Order

In several cases, federal courts have examined and decided the issue of whether a DRO was a QDRO. *See In re Williams,* 1999 U.S. Dist. LEXIS 8650 (C.D. Cal. 1999) (bankruptcy proceeding); *Bass v. Mid-America Co., Inc.,* 1995 U.S. Dist. LEXIS 15719 (N.D. Ill. 1995) (court found parties' divorce decree a QDRO even though parties evidently never complied with provision in it that "if necessary, the parties further agree that such allocation shall be carried out pursuant to a stipulated QDRO"); *Layton v. TDS Healthcare Systems Corp.,* 1994 U.S. Dist. LEXIS 6709 (N.D. Cal. 1994) (divorce decree not a QDRO). *See also Hawkins v. Comm'r,* 86 F.3d 982 (10th Cir. 1996), *rev'g Hawkins v. Comm'r,* 102 T.C. 61 (1994), which is discussed in detail in section 10.3.

While the federal court in *Guzy v. Ameritech Corp.,* 1999 U.S. Dist. LEXIS 8943 (E.D. Mich. 1999), reviewed and upheld a Plan Administrator's interpretation of a QDRO, it also commented that the Participant should have addressed his complaint to the state court that entered the DRO and sought a modification of it there.

I. State Court Qualifies Order

A few state courts have taken the position that they can qualify a DRO as a QDRO. In *Mack v. Estate of Mack,* 125 Nev. 80 (2009), the Nevada Supreme Court held that a state court could find that a DRO was a QDRO. This finding was reinforced by the Ninth Circuit in *Mack v. Kuckenmeister,* 619 F.3d 1010 (9th Cir. 2010) when it deferred to the Nevada Supreme Court on the basis of Full Faith and Credit, holding that "whether a DRO constitutes a QDRO under ERISA is a question of law which a state court can determine in the first instance by looking to the statutory requirements and underlying order." In *Jones v. American Airlines, Inc.,* 1999 U.S. Dist. LEXIS 11507 (D. Wyo. 1999), the federal court deferred to a prior finding by a Texas state court that its own order was a QDRO on Full Faith and Credit grounds. In *Custer v. Custer,* 776 S.W.2d 92 (Tenn. Ct. App. 1988), *cert. denied,* 493 U.S. 933 (1989), the state court qualified its own order as a QDRO and ordered immediate payment of benefits to the Alternate Payee over the plan's protests that immediate payments were not an option authorized under the terms of the plan.

J. QDROs Based on "Sham" Divorces

The Fifth Circuit held that a Plan Administrator could not look beyond a DRO at the underlying marriage. In *Brown v. Continental Airlines, Inc.*, 647 F.3d 221 (5th Cir. 2011), Continental Airlines sued nine pilots and their spouses, alleging that the pilots obtained "sham" divorces in order to receive lump-sum distributions from the plan that they would not otherwise be able to receive until retirement. Continental Airlines sought restitution of the pension benefits that it paid out pursuant to DROs issued pursuant to these "sham" divorces. The Fifth Circuit held that the Plan Administrator only has the authority to determine if a DRO is a QDRO based upon whether it satisfies all the statutory requirements, "and the participants' good faith in obtaining a divorce is not among those criteria." Brown at 226.

K. Plan as Party to Divorce Action

Several states permit joinder of the plan as a party to the divorce action itself in order to afford complete relief to the parties. California Family Code section 2337(d)(1): "Prior to entry of judgment a party's retirement or pension plan *shall* be joined as a party to the proceeding for dissolution, unless joinder is precluded or made unnecessary by Title 1 of the federal Employee Retirement Income Security Act of 1974 (29 U.S.C. Sec. 1001 et seq.), as amended (ERISA), or any other applicable law" (emphasis added); *Dickerson v. Dickerson*, 803 F. Supp. 127 (E.D. Tenn. 1992); *Stott v. Bunge Corp.*, 800 F. Supp. 567 (E.D. Tenn. 1992); *Cleveland v. Board of Trustees, Police and Fireman's Retirement System*, 550 A.2d 1287 (N.J. App. Div. 1988); *Erb v. Erb*, 661 N.E.2d 175 (Ohio 1996); *Custer v. Custer*, 776 S.W.2d 92 (Tenn. Ct. App. 1988), *cert. denied*, 493 U.S. 933 (1989); *In re Marriage of Allison*, 189 Cal. App. 3d 849 (Cal. Ct. App. 1987); *Payne v. GM/UAW Pension Plan*, 1996 U.S. Dist. LEXIS 7966 (E.D. Mich. 1996).

This kind of joinder has been disapproved by the Department of Labor (DOL) as contrary to ERISA and is highly questionable in light of the decision in *AT&T Management Pension Plan v. Tucker*, 902 F. Supp. 1168 (C.D. Cal. 1995). In *Tucker*, the plan was joined as a party in the Tuckers' divorce action, forced to litigate various ERISA and QDRO issues for four years, and finally ordered to pay the divorcing couple more than $60,000 in lawyers' fees in connection with those state court divorce proceedings.

The plan, not surprisingly, filed an action in federal court for injunctive and declaratory relief to prevent further mandatory participation in the divorce case and to declare void the judgment for lawyers' fees. The plan prevailed on the ground that ERISA's state law preemption sections (29 U.S.C. §§ 1144(a) and (c)(1)) and the fiduciary duty section requiring that plans be managed "for the exclusive purpose of providing benefits to participants and their beneficiaries" (29 U.S.C. § 1104(a)(1)(A)(i)) barred such an award against a plan by a state court in divorce proceedings. The federal court also held that an award of lawyers' fees against the plan would violate the anti-alienation and anti-assignment rules for ERISA-qualified plans (29 U.S.C. § 1056(d)(1)) because lawyers' fees cannot be the subject of a QDRO, even assuming the state court order to be a QDRO.

The federal court in *Tucker* came very close to declaring the entire California statute enabling plans to be joined as parties to divorce actions void in violation of ERISA, which the DOL as amicus curiae urged it to do. It refrained only because the plan had not raised this issue at any time during the four years it participated in the state court divorce proceeding and went on to decide the case in favor of the plan on "narrower grounds." *Tucker*, at 1175 n.5.

See also the discussion of *In re Marriage of Nasca*, 1999 U.S. Dist. LEXIS 13140 (N.D. Cal. 1999), in subsection 10.1D (plan joined as defendant in divorce action under California law removed case to federal court; case remanded to state court and plan ordered to pay the divorcing couple's total lawyers' fees of $65,000 under 28 U.S.C. § 1447(c)).

L. Failure to Follow Plan's Own QDRO Procedures

Failure of the plan to follow its own written QDRO Procedures usually results in liability to the injured Participant or Alternate Payee. *Schoonmaker v. Employee Savings Plan of Amoco Corp.*, 987 F.2d 410 (7th Cir. 1993); *Fortmann v. Avon Products, Inc.*, 1999 U.S. Dist. LEXIS 3451 (N.D. Ill. 1999). In *Barnes v. Maytag Corp.*, 799 F. Supp. 926 (S.D. Ill. 1992), however, the court seemed to adopt a "no harm, no foul" rule, holding that even though the plan concededly had violated ERISA by not adopting the required QDRO Procedures, the plaintiff had to show a causal connection between any denial of benefits and the failure to adopt or follow written QDRO Procedures.

The *Schoonmaker* and *Fortmann* cases are discussed in more detail in Chapter 15.

M. Lawyers' Fees

Legal fees are available in actions under ERISA by a Participant or Beneficiary against a plan. 29 U.S.C. § 1132(g). Such awards are not automatic but are within the discretion of the court.

The courts have over the years evolved a set of criteria for fee awards in ERISA actions under 29 U.S.C. § 1132(g). These are

1. The degree of the opposing party's culpability or bad faith;
2. The ability of the opposing party to satisfy an award of lawyers' fees;
3. Whether an award of lawyers' fees against the opposing party would deter other persons acting under similar circumstances;
4. Whether the party requesting lawyers' fees sought to benefit all Participants or Beneficiaries of an ERISA plan or to resolve a significant legal question regarding ERISA itself; and
5. The relative merits of the parties' positions. *Iron Workers Local No. 272 v. Bowen*, 624 F.2d 1255 (5th Cir. 1980); *Smith v. CMTA-IAAM Pension Trust*, 746 F.2d 587 (9th Cir. 1984); *Hummell v. S.E. Rykoff & Co.*, 634 F.2d 446 (9th Cir. 1980).

An additional criterion has been added to these five: the prevailing party. Federal courts recognize a strong presumption that the court will award costs to the prevailing party. *Sheets v. Yamaha Motors Corp., U.S.A.*, 891 F.2d 533, 539 (5th Cir. 1990). Nevertheless, Federal Rules of Civil Procedure 54(d) permits the court to exercise its discretion and withhold an award of costs to the prevailing party, which will be reviewed for an abuse of discretion. *See Salley v. E.I. Du Pont de Nemours & Co.*, 966 F.2d 1011 (5th Cir 1992); *Hall v. State Farm Fire & Cas. Co.*, 937 F.2d 210, 216–17 (5th Cir. 1991).

An Alternate Payee who prevails in QDRO litigation will become a Beneficiary (29 U.S.C. § 1056(d)(3)(J)) and thus is eligible for an award of lawyers' fees against the plan. *Bailey v. Board of Trustees of the New Orleans Steamship Association/International Longshoremen's Ass'n, AFL-CIO Pension Trust Fund*, 1996 U.S. Dist. LEXIS 2422 (E.D. La. 1996) (award of lawyers' fees to prevailing Alternate Payee). Note, however, that if a federal court finds that a DRO is not a QDRO, the person named in it as an "alternate payee" is not considered to actually be an Alternate Payee under ERISA and therefore cannot be a Beneficiary. 29 U.S.C. §§ 1056(d)(3)(J), (K).

Since this party is not a Beneficiary, a federal court has no subject matter jurisdiction over the case and thus no jurisdiction to award lawyers' fees. *Brotman v. Molitch*, 1989 U.S. Dist. LEXIS 9157 (E.D. Pa. 1989). *See also Gabrielson v. Montgomery Ward & Co.*, 785 F.2d 762 (9th Cir. 1986) (widow who was not Beneficiary had no right to notice and hearing under 29 U.S.C. § 1133 and plan's internal procedures).

Although lawyers' fees are available in ERISA litigation under 29 U.S.C. § 1132(g), it is now doubtful that they are available against a plan under any state fee award or fee-shifting statutes. *AT&T Management Pension Plan v. Tucker*, 902 F. Supp. 1168 (C.D. Cal. 1995). *But see Blue v. UAL Corp.*, 160 F.3d 383 (7th Cir. 1998) (plan must make payments pursuant to QDRO even though state court may have erroneously included lawyers' fees in DRO).

See also the discussion of *In re Marriage of Nasca*, 1999 U.S. Dist. LEXIS 13140 (N.D. Cal. 1999), in subsection 10.1D (plan joined as defendant in divorce action under California law removed case to federal court; case remanded to state court and plan ordered to pay the divorcing couple's total lawyers' fees of $65,000 under 28 U.S.C. § 1447(c), the general fee-shifting provisions of the federal removal statute).

Lawyers' fees incurred in connection with QDRO litigation may be deductible by the taxpayer, subject to the 2 percent of adjusted gross income floor under 26 U.S.C. § 67(a). *Glassman v. Comm'r*, 1997 Tax Ct. Memo LEXIS 581 (1997).

N. Sanctions for Failure to Provide Information

Under 29 U.S.C. § 1132(c)(1)(B), any Plan Administrator who fails or refuses to comply with a request for any information that ERISA requires to be furnished to a Participant or Beneficiary within 30 days after the request may be fined $100 per day from the date of such failure or refusal and be subjected to other sanctions or relief imposed by the court. Whether to impose the fine or not is within the discretion of the court. *Bouteiller v. Vulcan Iron Works, Inc.*, 834 F. Supp. 207, 215 (E.D. Mich. 1993). And the request for information must be sent to the Plan Administrator, not any other party, such as the Plan Sponsor. *Guzy v. Ameritech Corp.*, 1999 U.S. Dist. LEXIS 8943 (E.D. Mich. 1999) (request sent to Plan Sponsor's manager of pension plans, not Plan Administrator). Some showing of harm caused by a failure to supply the information or delay in supplying it may also be required. *See Bouteiller*, above.

O. Standard of Review of Plan Administrator's Decision

"[A] denial of benefits [presumably including wrongful qualification or refusal to qualify a DRO] is reviewed [by the courts] under a de novo standard *unless* the plan gives the administrator or fiduciary discretionary authority to determine eligibility for benefits or to construe the terms of the plan." *Firestone Tire & Rubber Co. v. Bruch*, 489 U.S. 101, 115 (1989) (emphasis added). If the Plan Administrator is given discretion to determine eligibility for benefits or to construe the terms of the plan, the standard on review is whether the administrator's decision was reasonable and not arbitrary or capricious. *Firestone*; *Rizzo v. Caterpillar, Inc.*, 914 F.2d 1003, 1008 (7th Cir. 1990). This means that in any subsequent litigation the courts will have to review the Plan Administrator's factual and plan interpretation decisions under an "arbitrary or capricious" or "abuse of discretion" standard and not decide the issue de novo, although the plan's statutory and legal construction and conclusions may be reviewed de novo. *Firestone*, at 115; *Dial v. NFL Player Supplemental Disability Plan*, 174 F.3d 606 (5th Cir. 1999); *Sweatman v. Commercial Union Ins. Co.*, 39 F.3d 594, 597 (5th Cir. 1994); *Rizzo*, at 1008.

In small plans, the Plan Administrator is sometimes the Participant and one of the divorce litigants. In such cases, the courts, quite rightly, will give heightened scrutiny to QDRO determinations they make that are unfavorable to the Alternate Payee. *Fox v. Fox*, 167 F.3d 880 (4th Cir. 1999); *Lynn v. Lynn*, 25 F.3d 280 (5th Cir. 1994); *In re Lowenschuss*, 1996 Bankr. LEXIS 1416 (D. Nev. 1996); *In re Williams*, 1999 U.S. Dist. LEXIS 8650 (C.D. Cal. 1999).

P. Appointment of Alternate Payee as Plan Administrator

In *In re Williams*, 1999 U.S. Dist. LEXIS 8650 (C.D. Cal. 1999), the court appointed the Alternate Payee to serve as the Plan Administrator after the Participant had been automatically removed from that post by his filing for bankruptcy. *See also Lynn v. Lynn*, 25 F.3d 280 (5th Cir. 1994).

Q. Application to Qualify DRO after Death of Participant

Compare Payne v. GM/UAW Pension Plan, 1996 U.S. Dist. LEXIS 7966 (E.D. Mich. 1996) (ordering plan to pay benefits), *with Samaroo I* and *AT&T Management Pension Plan v. Robichaud*, 1998 U.S. Dist. LEXIS 21117 (D.N.J. 1998) (*Samaroo II*), *aff'd*, 193 F.3d 185 (3d Cir.

1999) (2-1), *cert. denied,* 529 U.S. 1062 (2000) (no benefits payable because DRO not accepted as QDRO prior to Participant's death). *See also Bailey v. Board of Trustees of the New Orleans Steamship Association/International Longshoremen's Ass'n, AFL-CIO Pension Trust Fund,* 1996 U.S. Dist. LEXIS 231 (E.D. La. 1996); *Hopkins v. AT&T Global Info. Solutions Co.,* 105 F.3d 153 (4th Cir. 1997).

In *Samaroo II* the Participant had died before retiring, and the initial DRO did not provide for survivorship benefits to be granted to the Alternate Payee. The plaintiff sought an amended DRO in the state divorce court (see section 10.1E) and it was granted, nunc pro tunc, as of a date before the Participant's death. The plaintiff then asked the plan to qualify the new DRO, but the plan refused on the ground that a QDRO covering a Defined Benefit Plan could not be entered after a Participant's death.

The plaintiff returned to federal court to seek an order compelling the plan to accept the amended DRO as a QDRO. The federal court declined to do so, finding that under the terms of the plan, all benefits lapsed on the death of the Participant unless a QDRO had been entered by a state court before that date, so the amended DRO required the plan to provide a type or form of benefit not otherwise provided under the plan and would require the plan to provide increased benefits in violation of sections 1056(d)(3)(D)(i) and (ii) of ERISA.

The district court in *Samaroo II* indicated, as the plan itself suggested, that the result would be different in a case involving a Defined Contribution Plan because "in that instance there is a fixed amount being held [by the Plan Administrator] on behalf of the Participant and the only issue is the proper beneficiary of the account funds, not whether the benefits should be paid at all." *Samaroo II,* n.4 at 9. *Compare Smith v. Estate of Smith,* No. 99-5973 (D.N.J. 2003) (DRO entered prior to Participant's death but not sent to Plan Administrator for qualification until after his death distinguished from nunc pro tunc order in *Samaroo II* and held to be a QDRO).

The *Samaroo II* case was the leading authority on postmortem qualification attempts until the decision of the Tenth Circuit in *Patton v. Denver Post Corp.,* 326 F.3d 1148 (10th Cir. 2003), which held to the contrary. In the *Patton* case, the employer had advised the parties of the existence of one plan, which had no survivorship benefits, but had negligently failed to advise them of the existence of a second plan, which did have survivorship benefits. The parties prepared a QDRO dividing only the first plan. Eleven years later, the Participant died. He had not remarried and consequently left no surviving spouse. In the meantime, the two formerly separate plans had merged. After the Participant's death, the Alternate Payee obtained a nunc pro tunc QDRO from the state divorce court and presented it to the plan for qualification. The Plan Administrator declined to accept the QDRO, relying on the reasoning in *Samaroo II*; but the Alternate Payee prevailed in the District Court (*Patton v. Denver Post Corp.*, 179 F. Supp. 1232 (D. Colo. 2002)), a decision that was upheld in the Court of Appeals. There the Tenth Circuit held that ERISA contains no express time limit for the presentation of a DRO to a plan for qualification; that the plan's liability to the Alternate Payee was no greater than its liability would have been had an unknown spouse of the Participant surfaced after his death; and that nunc pro tunc orders were useful legal fictions that should be honored by Plan Administrators in cases like this. The Tenth Circuit's opinion noted the merger of the two plans before the death of the Participant and heavily relied on the negligence of the employer in failing to disclose the second plan's existence to the parties, making it impossible for them to enter a QDRO with survivorship benefits before the Participant's death. In addition, because the Participant died leaving no surviving spouse, there were no competing claims to the plan's survivorship interests, so there was no possibility the plan would have to make duplicate payments. The result may well be different where there are such competing claims, as in *Davenport v. Estate of Davenport,* 146 F. Supp. 2d 770 (M.D.N.C. 2001) (DRO entered after Participant's death in favor of children of first marriage not effective against survivorship rights of subsequent surviving spouse).

The net effect of the *Samaroo II* and *Patton* cases is to make postmortem QDRO qualification attempts one of those troublesome legal questions to which the answer depends on which federal circuit hears the case—at least until the Supreme Court definitively resolves this issue.

See the discussion of the effect of the Pension Protection Act of 2006 and its implementing regulation on this issue in section 18.7.

R. QDROs for Employee Welfare Benefit Plans

While it is clear that QDROs may be used to divide an Employee Pension Benefit Plan, QDROs may also be used to direct the payment of benefits under an Employee Welfare Benefit Plan. Both are separate categories of Employee Benefit Plans, and both are regulated by ERISA; see subsections 2.2A–C. *Metro. Life Ins. Co. v. Fowler*, 922 F. Supp. 8 (E.D. Mich. 1996); *Carland v. Metro. Life Ins. Co.*, 935 F.2d 1114 (10th Cir. 1991).

S. Named Beneficiary in Plan File

Several courts have held that plans are entitled to rely on documents, including beneficiary designations, on file with them and not on divorce decrees that they may never have seen. *Melton v. Melton*, 324 F.3d 941 (7th Cir. 2003); *Brown v. Connecticut General Life Ins. Co.*, 934 F.2d 1193 (11th Cir. 1991); *McMillan v. Parrott*, 913 F.2d 310 (6th Cir. 1990); *Metro. Life Ins. Co. v. Marsh*, 119 F.3d 415 (6th Cir. 1997); *Kuhn v. Metro. Life Ins. Co.*, 1999 U.S. Dist. LEXIS 9964 (W.D. Mich. 1999). Cases on this issue often arise after Participants have died and current spouses are contesting with former spouses or children over who will receive the benefits now payable. *Silber v. Silber*, 99 N.Y.2d 395 (N.Y. 2003). A QDRO that has been filed with and accepted by the plan is, of course, the governing document—another reason to make sure that DROs are filed with the plan promptly after they are entered and that the qualification process is followed through to a successful conclusion.

The U.S. Supreme Court held in *Egelhoff v. Egelhoff*, 532 U.S. 141 (2000), that a beneficiary designation concerning a life insurance policy made pursuant to ERISA and on file with the plan would, under ERISA section 1144(a)'s preemption language, trump a Washington State statute providing that a beneficiary designation by a decedent was automatically revoked by a divorce because the Washington statute was held to conflict with section 1144(a)'s preemption language.

10.2 Bankruptcy

Several federal courts have been required to determine how to treat QDROs in bankruptcy filings by Participants. Filing for bankruptcy has been a traditional method for divorced spouses to try to free themselves from obligations to pay state court property division awards. While alimony and child support obligations are, as a matter of federal bankruptcy law, not dischargeable in bankruptcy proceedings, debts owed to a former spouse and property division awards may in some circumstances be dischargeable. In addition, since a debtor's beneficial interest in an ERISA-qualified plan is excluded from the bankruptcy estate under 11 U.S.C. § 541(c)(2) (*Patterson v. Shumate*, 504 U.S. 753 (1992)), if the debtor can discharge a debt to his or her former spouse, he or she will have achieved the best of both worlds—retaining the asset but voiding the related debt.

Bankruptcy courts have thus often been called upon to determine whether a DRO is a QDRO. *In re Williams*, 1999 U.S. Dist. LEXIS 8650 (C.D. Cal. 1999) (examining plan and terms of DRO and concluding that DRO is a QDRO). Some cases have reasoned that if a QDRO does exist, the Participant who has filed for bankruptcy no longer owes any debt to the Alternate Payee. The Employee Benefit Plan, not the Participant, is considered to be the debtor and, since the plan has not filed for bankruptcy, the Alternate Payee will continue to receive uninterrupted payments from the plan. If, on the other hand, the order in question is determined not to be a QDRO, the obligation to pay funds to the Alternate Payee is an obligation not of the plan but of the Participant, which might be dischargeable in his bankruptcy proceeding.

In re Gendreau, 122 F.3d 815 (9th Cir. 1997), involved a situation where an Alternate Payee had been granted an interest in the Participant's pension plan. In January 1993, the state court entered a DRO, but the Plan Administrator rejected it in May and asked the Alternate Payee to have the DRO amended. In November of that year, before the DRO was amended and resubmitted to the plan, the Participant filed for bankruptcy and listed the share of his pension plan assigned to the Alternate Payee as a dischargeable debt.

The Ninth Circuit held that even though no QDRO had yet been accepted by the plan, from the moment the state court assigned an interest in the Participant's pension rights to the Alternate Payee, subject to later implementation by a QDRO, the Alternate Payee had a claim only against the plan, not against the Participant. Because there was no debt owed by the Participant to the Alternate Payee, there was nothing for the bankruptcy court to discharge, so the Alternate Payee's claim against the plan was not affected at all by the bankruptcy of the Participant.

Note that the state court characterization of payments made pursuant to a QDRO may affect their dischargeability in bankruptcy. Alimony and child support are generally not dischargeable, while property division payments may be. The characterization of the nature of payments is a matter of federal bankruptcy law, and the bankruptcy courts are free to make their own determinations of the true nature of the payments de novo; but such determinations are, of course, heavily influenced by the state court's characterization of them.

10.3 Tax Litigation with the IRS

The issue of whether a QDRO has been entered also arises in the context of tax litigation with the Internal Revenue Service (IRS). As a general rule, all distributions from a pension or Employee Benefit Plan, no matter who receives them, are considered taxable income to the Participant. *Darby v. Comm'r,* 97 T.C. 51, 58 (1991). There is one important exception to this general rule: if (1) the payments are made pursuant to a QDRO, and (2) the Alternate Payee is a former spouse of the Participant, then payments to the Alternate Payee from the plan are taxable to her. 26 U.S.C. § 402(a)(9). If, on the other hand, a QDRO has not been entered, or the Alternate Payee is a child or other dependent of the Participant, payments made by the plan to the Alternate Payee are taxable to the Participant.

The IRS is usually indifferent as to whether the Alternate Payee or the Participant is responsible for the tax payments on the distributions from the plan. It has been known to assess both the spouse and the former spouse with a deficiency and let them slug it out. The leading case in which the IRS did just that is *Hawkins v. Comm'r,* 86 F.3d 982 (10th Cir. 1996), *rev'g Hawkins v. Comm'r,* 102 T.C. 61 (1994). The parties in this case were divorced in New Mexico in 1987. The husband was a dentist whose practice maintained a pension plan in which he had the largest single account. The divorce decree divided his pension plan, awarding $1 million in cash to the wife, which the plan paid to her in 1987 in the form of several checks written from the plan bank account. She did not roll the proceeds over into an individual retirement account (IRA) within the 60-day grace period allowed by 26 U.S.C. § 402(a)(5), which would have avoided current taxation of either party. Neither party reported the $1 million as income on their separate 1987 tax returns.

In 1989, concerned about his potential tax liability, the husband asked the state divorce court for entry of a QDRO nunc pro tunc so that his former wife, not he, would be liable for any taxes on the distribution. The state court denied his petition, holding that because it had not retained jurisdiction over the divorce case after entry of the decree, under New Mexico law it had lost jurisdiction over the matter and could not enter any nunc pro tunc orders.

The IRS assessed a deficiency against both taxpayers and let them fight it out, which they did in Tax Court. The Tax Court examined the language of the parties' divorce decree, ruled that it was not a QDRO, and assessed the deficiency against the husband. On appeal, the Tenth Circuit reviewed the language of the parties' original divorce decree and concluded, contrary to the finding of the Tax Court, that the language was sufficient to establish that the DRO was a QDRO. The wife was therefore an Alternate Payee and was liable for the tax on the entire distribution.

In *Karem v. Comm'r*, 100 T.C. 521 (1993), the Tax Court held that payments made from an ERISA-qualified plan more than one year before a QDRO was actually entered by the state court could not qualify for the special treatment afforded by 26 U.S.C. § 402(a)(9).

In *Brotman v. Comm'r*, 105 T.C. 141 (1995), the Alternate Payee, who had lost earlier litigation against her former husband in the U.S. District Court for the Eastern District of Pennsylvania (*Brotman v. Molitch*, 1989 U.S. Dist. LEXIS 9157 (E.D. Pa. 1989)) on the issue of whether a DRO was a QDRO, was held to be collaterally estopped from relitigating that issue in the Tax Court. She was, however, entitled to litigate the ERISA-qualified status of the plan to which the QDRO had been addressed because the issue of the plan's qualified status had not been litigated in the earlier action.

The characterization of the payments under a QDRO as alimony, child support, or property division is also important for tax purposes. Prior to 2018, alimony was generally deductible by the obligor and taxable income to the recipient. The payment of alimony is now no longer a taxable event between former spouses. Child support, on the other hand, is not and has never been deductible for tax purposes by the obligor and taxable income to the recipient. Property division between divorcing spouses is generally tax free, though if the property is in a pension or Employee Benefit Plan, the party who ultimately withdraws the funds from the plan will have a tax liability.

10.4 Malpractice

Malpractice litigation is separate from other types of ERISA litigation. It is usually brought as a separate action several years after a

QDRO was (or should have been) entered and normally involves only an angry client and his or her former lawyer, not the plan. *Annotation, Attorney's Liability for Negligence in Cases Involving Domestic Relations*, 78 A.L.R.3d 255.

The three most common causes of malpractice litigation in QDRO situations are as follows:

1. Failure to discover or seek division of pension and other employee benefits. *Smith v. Lewis*, 530 P.2d 589 (Cal. 1975); *Helmbrecht v. St. Paul Ins. Co.*, 362 N.W.2d 118 (Wis. 1985); *Krusesky v. Baugh*, 138 Cal. App. 562 (Cal. Ct. App. 1992); *Raudebaugh v. Young*, 87 Cal. App. 364 (Cal. Ct. App. 1978); *Hutchinson v. Divorce & Custody Law Center*, 449 S.E.2d 866 (Ga. Ct. App. 1994) (failure to seek interest in military pension); *Bross v. Denny*, 791 S.W.2d 46 (Mo. Ct. App. 1990).
2. Failure or unexcused delay in sending DRO to a plan for qualification. *Payne v. GM/UAW Pension Plan*, 1996 U.S. Dist. LEXIS 7966 (E.D. Mich. 1996) (problems arising from Participant's death between property division hearing and entry of QDRO); *Layton v. TDS Healthcare Systems Corp.*, 1994 U.S. Dist. LEXIS 6709 (N.D. Cal. 1994); *Zito v. Zito*, 969 P.2d 1144 (Alaska 1998) (eight-year delay); *In re Nomura*, 1996 Ariz. LEXIS 8 (Ariz. 1996); *Cuyahoga Bar Association v. Williamson*, 652 N.E.2d 972 (Ohio 1995); *In re Louderman*, 1999 Wis. LEXIS 117 (Wis. 1999) (public reprimand for six-year delay in preparing DRO); *Carter v. Carter*, 869 S.W.2d 822 (Mo. Ct. App. 1994); *Williams v. Cooch & Taylor*, 1994 Del. Super. LEXIS 211 (Del. Super. Ct. 1994) (failure to present DRO to court).
3. Significant disparities between what the trial court ordered at the property division hearing or the parties agreed to in their settlement and the wording of the QDRO. *Fortmann v. Avon Products, Inc.*, 1999 U.S. Dist. LEXIS 3451 (N.D. Ill. 1999) (property settlement agreement approved by state court divided all pension benefits payable on Participant's retirement; DRO divided all benefits "as of" the date of the DRO, ten years before retirement); *Layton v. TDS Healthcare Systems Corp.*, 1994 U.S. Dist. LEXIS 6709 (N.D. Cal. 1994); *Holloman v. Holloman*, 691 So. 2d 897 (Miss. 1996); *Quade v. Quade*, 1999 Mich. App. LEXIS 283 (Mich. Ct. App. 1999); *Carpenter v. Carpenter*, 1996 Tex. App. LEXIS 3210 (Tex. Ct.

App. 1996) (DROs amended three times and litigated for three years on issue of which plans were intended to be covered by them); *Wilson v. Wilson*, 492 S.E.2d 495 (Va. Ct. App. 1997).

Most, but not all, lawyers today are well aware that pensions and employee benefits are marital (joint) assets and are divisible between the parties. It is rare for these assets to be ignored or completely forgotten in domestic relations cases. Failure to send a DRO to a plan for qualification, or undue delay in sending a DRO, are today's most common causes of malpractice claims (see Chapter 14).

In one malpractice case, *Templeman v. Dahlgren*, 1990 U.S. Dist. LEXIS 10183 (D. Or. 1990), the defendant lawyer brought the pension plan into the case as a third-party defendant. The plaintiff, who had been represented by the defendant lawyer in her divorce action, had been assured by the defendant that she would receive $666.73 per month from her husband's pension plan. When he died suddenly, the plan paid her only $280 per month. She sued the lawyer for malpractice. The lawyer brought in the plan as a third-party defendant, stating that she had been assured of the $666.73 amount by the plan, pleading estoppel, and claiming a right to indemnification for any damages awarded in the malpractice action.

The Alternate Payee used a similar tactic in *Payne v. GM/UAW Pension Plan*, 1996 U.S. Dist. LEXIS 7966 (E.D. Mich. 1996), joining her former lawyer as a defendant in litigation against the plan but seeking relief from him only if she lost her case against the plan.

See Chapters 7, 10, and 14 for tips on how to avoid malpractice claims.

Military Retired Pay

11

11.1 Background

In 1981, the Supreme Court decided as a matter of federal statutory construction that military retired pay was not marital or community property subject to division between divorcing spouses by state courts. *See McCarty v. McCarty*, 453 U.S. 210 (1981). In response to the prompting by the Supreme Court in *McCarty*, Congress promptly enacted remedial legislation known as the Uniformed Services Former Spouses' Protection Act (USFSPA) in 1982 to overturn the holding in *McCarty*. USFSPA is presently codified at 10 U.S.C. § 1408. The act permits—but does not require—state courts to divide the Disposable Retired Pay of military officers and enlisted personnel. It is important to note that military retired pay and its division is not governed by ERISA but is instead governed by its own federal statutes under title 10 of the U.S. Code.

There are major differences between Employee Retirement Income Security Act (ERISA) plans and military retired pay. First, the Defense Finance and Accounting Service (DFAS) and Coast Guard Pay Center, which are the pay centers or "Plan Administrators," if you will, of military retired pay, will not review and comment on draft orders in advance, as most ERISA Plan Administrators will do. Second, a spouse or former spouse will not begin receiving payments from DFAS until the service member actually retires and begins receiving retired pay—unlike ERISA plans, where payments to an Alternate Payee may begin earlier even though the Participant remains employed by the Plan Sponsor. Third, survivor benefits awarded to a former spouse will be suspended if the former spouse remarries before age 55, subject to reinstatement only if the former spouse's subsequent marriage terminates by death, divorce, or annulment. Finally, strict statutory definitions and jurisdictional requirements, discussed in detail in this chapter, must be met for DFAS or the Coast Guard Pay Center to accept an order dividing military retired pay.

The military pension (also referred to interchangeably in this chapter as "military retired pay") is a "cliff vesting" pension, meaning a service member must serve at least 20 years to receive military retired pay. If the service member leaves the service prior to 20 years, then he or she will not receive a pension. This also means for the former spouse that even if there was a military pension division order, if the service member left service prior to the completion of 20 years, neither the service member nor the former spouse would receive military retired pay.

An indispensable resource in this area is Mark E. Sullivan's excellent book, *The Military Divorce Handbook: A Practical Guide to Representing Military Personnel and Their Families*, 3rd edition, American Bar Association, 2019. The annual *Retired Military Almanac* (Uniformed Services Almanac, Inc.) provides updated information on pay, benefits, and developments in military benefits. DFAS also publishes a helpful guide on its website at http://www.dfas.mil/garnishment.html.

11.2 Blended Retirement System

In 2018, the military rolled out its Modernized Military Retirement System, also referred to as the Blended Retirement System (BRS). Under the old retirement system, a military retiree would receive military retired pay upon his or her retirement and also had the option to participate in a Thrift Savings Plan. These two retirement plans—one a defined benefit plan and one a defined contribution plan—composed the military retirement system.

Under the old retirement system, to calculate the service member's military retired pay, you take the service member's average of his highest 36 months of pay (known as "high-36" and generally the last 36 months of service) multiplied by his months of creditable service multiplied by a multiplier of 2.5 percent. For those service members who entered service prior to 1980, their military retired pay was calculated using their final pay at the time of their retirement rather than the average of their highest 36 months of pay. For those service members serving in the reserve component (Reserves or National Guard), their retirement accrual is tracked in retirement points rather than months or years of service. When calculating the retired pay, the retirement points are converted to years of service by dividing the retirement points by 360.

Further, under the "old" system, the service member was also offered the opportunity to participate in a Thrift Savings Plan (TSP) administered by the TSP board. This plan is similar to the TSP offered to federal employees under the Federal Employee Retirement System (FERS), but with no government matching.

Beginning in 2018, service members who were then serving and had less than 12 years of service were required to make an election on whether to stay under the old retirement system or to opt into the new Blended Retirement System. Those service members who had more than 12 years of service (or 4,320 retirement points for reserve component service members) on December 31, 2017, were not given a choice and had to remain enrolled in the old system. For those service members who entered the service after December 31, 2017, they were automatically enrolled in the new blended retirement system.

So, what is this new blended retirement system? The new blended retirement system has four components, whereas the old retirement system had just the military retired pay and an optional TSP without government contributions. The first component of the new system is still the military retired pay (or pension); however, in the new system the multiplier is reduced from 2.5 percent to 2.0 percent.

The second component of the new system is the TSP but with automatic enrollment after 60 days and government contributions. Under the BRS TSP, the service automatically contributes 1 percent of the service member's base pay each pay period, even if the service member is not making any contributions. For those service members who were enrolled in the BRS TSP on October 1, 2020, or after, they are automatically enrolled at a 5 percent contribution of their base salary each pay period unless they opt for a different level. For those service members who were enrolled from January 1, 2018, to September 30, 2020, they were enrolled at a 3 percent contribution of their base salary each pay period unless they opted for a different level. For those service members who opted into the BRS TSP during the election period in 2017, they were not automatically enrolled at a contributing level. The service matches the first 3 percent of the service member's contributions dollar for dollar. The next 2 percent is matched at a rate of 50 cents per dollar. *See* tsp.gov. See also Chapter 12, section 12.9, regarding the division of Thrift Savings Plans.

The third component of the new retirement system is a mid-career bonus paid between a service member's eighth and twelfth year of service, the amount and timing of which is determined by the respective branch secretary. The mid-career bonus can be anywhere from two times to 13 times the service member's monthly base pay. The branch secretaries can use this to "shape the force," encouraging needed service members with certain military occupational specialties (MOS) to stay in. In most cases, the service member's receipt of the mid-career bonus will incur a further service obligation.

The fourth component of the new retirement system is the option of taking a portion of the military retired pay as a lump sum at the time of retirement. Upon retirement, a service member can elect to receive a lump sum equal to 25 percent or 50 percent of the present value of their military retired pay. The service member will receive the lump sum within 60 days of beginning receipt of military retired pay, and their monthly annuity will be reduced to 50 percent of their full monthly retired pay if they took a 50 percent lump-sum amount or 75 percent of their full monthly retired pay if they took a 25 percent lump-sum amount. Their monthly military retired pay will be restored to the full monthly amount once the retired service member attains his or her retirement age as defined by the Social Security Act. 10 U.S.C. § 1415.

Because the new system is being phased in, one will need to continue to understand and be prepared to deal with both retirement systems.

11.3 "Disposable Retired Pay"

Under 10 U.S.C. § 1408(a)(4), "Disposable Retired Pay" is the total monthly retirement pay to which a service member is entitled by law based on the service member's current rank and years of service, less deductions for

1. Previous overpayments of retired pay,
2. Forfeitures ordered by a court martial,
3. Disability retirement payments under 10 U.S.C. §§ 1201–1221 and Veterans Administration disability retirement payments (*Mansell v. Mansell*, 453 U.S. 210 (1989)), and
4. The amount deducted to provide a "Survivor Benefit Plan" annuity for a spouse or former spouse pursuant to a court order (see section 11.12).

When submitting a military pension division order to DFAS or the Coast Guard Pay Center, the pay centers will only divide the Disposable Retired Pay as defined here. A military pension division order that divides the disposable retired pay will divide both the monthly retired pay and any lump-sum payment elected by the service member at the time of retirement pursuant to 10 U.S.C. § 1415.

Prior to December 23, 2016, military pensions were often divided by courts using a simple time rule or coverture method. A time rule formula divides the pension based on a portion of the marital portion, where the marital portion is a fraction, the numerator of which is the number of months of service during the marriage and the denominator the number of months of total service (which was then filled in by the pay center upon the service member's retirement). An example of how this division would be written is "the former spouse shall receive 50 percent of the marital portion of the service member's disposable retired pay. The marital portion is a fraction, the numerator of which is 200 months (representing the number of months of service during the marriage) and the denominator of which is the total months of creditable service." This formula gave the former spouse 50 percent of what was earned during the marriage and is commonly used in private pensions. This formula was acceptable to the pay centers, but this formula also gave the former spouse or Alternate Payee the benefit of future years of service, active duty pay increases, and promotions.

The National Defenses Authorization Act of 2017, effective December 23, 2016, changed this. The NDAA 2017 changed the definition of disposable retired pay so that the division of the military pension is capped at the service member's current rank and years of creditable service at the time of the divorce. This "freezes" the former spouse's portion, and she does not get the benefit of any future years of service or promotions. However, the former spouse's portion will be adjusted each year based on the retired pay cost-of-living adjustments. This new rule is known as the frozen benefit rule.

11.4 Timing of Payments

Military retired pay is, in several respects, simpler to divide than ERISA pensions. Unlike the Separate Interest Approach for defined benefit plans, Subsidies for Early Retirement, Actuarial Equivalence, and other complex ERISA doctrines that allow, under certain circumstances, control over the timing of payments received by an Alternate Payee (see clause 5 in the model DRO in section 8.5), a military former spouse may *not* begin receiving her share of a service member's Disposable Retired Pay directly from the pay center until the service member actually retires and begins receiving retired pay, and no court order can affect the timing of the service member's decision to retire. 10 U.S.C. § 1408(c)(3). It is important to note that active duty service members begin receiving retired pay immediately upon their retirement, whereas reserve component service members do not begin to receive their retired pay until approximately the age of 60, even though they may retire much earlier than that.

Former spouses must wait until the service member actually retires and begins receiving retired pay and then begin collecting their shares on an "if, as, and when received" basis. A state court may, however, place a present value on a service member's Disposable Retired Pay rights and award a former spouse other marital assets as an offset under the general principles discussed in section 5.6. *Dewan v. Dewan*, 506 N.E.2d 879 (Mass. 1987).

Survivorship benefits for former spouses and children of a service member in the form of a separate annuity are available as an option under the military retirement system. Survivor benefits are discussed in section 11.12.

11.5 Divisibility of Disposable Retired Pay as Property by State Courts

USFSPA permits—but does not require—state courts to treat a service member's Disposable Retired Pay like any other pension rights in divorce or support proceedings. Title 10 U.S.C. § 1408(c)(1) provides that, subject to the limitations set forth elsewhere in this chapter, state courts "may treat Disposable Retired Pay payable to a [service] member . . . either as property solely of the member or as property of the member and his spouse in accordance with the law of the jurisdiction of such court."

Section 1408(c)(2) limits the type of interest that may be assigned to a former spouse to one that may not be "sold, assigned, transferred, or otherwise disposed of (including by inheritance) by a spouse or former spouse." In other words, benefits received by a former spouse under this section are personal to that individual and must cease on her death. Section 1408(c)(3) makes it clear that a state court may not order a service member to apply for retirement or to retire at any particular time. Finally, section 1408(c)(4) places certain limitations on the jurisdiction of state courts to divide military retired pay. The state court must have jurisdiction over the service member's retired pay rights by reason of

- Residence in the state, other than because of military assignment;
- Domicile in the territorial jurisdiction of the court; or
- Consent to the jurisdiction of the court. 10 U.S.C. § 1408(c)(4).

These jurisdictional rules are somewhat complex and confusing and are discussed in detail in section 11.9. If all of these requirements are met, a state court may divide a service member's Disposable Retired Pay between him and his spouse or former spouse.

11.6 State Law Division Factors

The pay centers allow for three different methods of dividing military retired pay. The first method of division is a flat dollar amount. The military pension division order dividing military retired pay can order that the former spouse receive a flat dollar amount from the service member's military retired pay. This is typically not a good option for the former spouse because when the award is a flat dollar amount, the former spouse will receive no cost-of-living adjustments on his or her portion, even if you write in the order that there shall be cost-of-living adjustments applied.

The second method of division is a flat percentage. When the award is expressed as a percentage, the former spouse will receive cost-of-living adjustments on his or her portion. Just remember, for any divorces after December 23, 2016, any percentage you specify will be capped at the service member's current rank and years of service at the time of the divorce, if the service member is still serving. Also, if the service member is in the reserve component and is retired but is not yet receiving retired pay, the award must still be capped under the frozen benefit rule.

The third method that is allowed by the pay centers is a formula award. The award can be expressed in the form of a time rule formula, as discussed previously, or as a "hypothetical" division. The hypothetical division is now required for the division of any military pension in which the service member is still serving; see the discussion regarding the frozen benefit rule in section 11.3. Several states required this type of division before the passage of the NDAA 2017, which now requires it.

Every state will have its own rules on the division of military pensions. Some states require the parties to be married for ten years overlapping ten years of service in order for any retirement plan to be divisible. Yet, other states require that the military pension be vested, meaning the service member is retired, before it can be divided.

11.7 Direct Payment for Property Division to Former Spouse

A second and separate set of requirements must be satisfied for the former spouse to receive direct payments from the military pay office—known as the "Designated Agent"—rather than receiving payments from the service member. (A list of the names and addresses of the Designated Agents for each branch of service is set forth on the DD Form 2293—see section 11.10.) The statutory requirements for direct payment to the former spouse from the Designated Agent are set forth in 10 U.S.C. § 1408(d).

1. The amount that all former spouses may receive directly from the Designated Agent is limited to 50 percent of the member's Disposable Retired Pay for the purposes of property division. 10 U.S.C. § 1408(e)(1). Note that this is not a limit on the percentage of Disposable Retired Pay that a

state court may award a former spouse—a state court might award 100 percent if it so chooses. *Fortney v. Minard*, 849 P.2d 724 (Wyo. 1993). Section 1408(e)(1) limits only the amount that a former spouse may receive directly from the Designated Agent.

2. The total directly paid by the Designated Agent for all court orders (for property division, alimony, and child support) may not exceed 65 percent of the amount of his Disposable Retired Pay as adjusted by certain requirements of the Social Security Act. 10 U.S.C. § 1408(e)(4)(B). This means the former spouse may receive 50 percent of the military retired pay for the purposes of the division of the pension but up to another 15 percent for the purposes of alimony and child support.
3. A former spouse may not receive direct payments from the Designated Agent unless she was "married to the [service] member for a period of ten years or more during which the member performed at least ten years of service creditable in determining the member's eligibility for retired pay." 10 U.S.C. § 1408(d)(2). This is often referred to as the "10/10" rule. Like the 50 percent ceiling on direct payments, this ten-year requirement is not a limit on a state court's power to divide military retired pay between divorcing spouses. A state court may divide military retired pay if the parties were married for a year, or a single day, or even not married at all during the member's military service if state law so permits. The ten-year requirement applies only to direct payment to the former spouse from the Designated Agent. *LeVine v. Spickelmier*, 707 P.2d 452 (Idaho 1985); *Oxelgren v. Oxelgren*, 670 S.W.2d 411 (Tex. Civ. App. 1984). If the parties marry, divorce, and remarry, the total years of marriage and military service during both marriages may be added together to determine whether the ten-year rule is satisfied. *Anderson v. Anderson*, 468 N.E.2d 784 (Ohio App. 1984).
4. Finally, section 1408 makes it expressly clear that service members remain personally liable for any amount ordered by a state court that exceeds the amount payable directly to the former spouse by the Designated Agent. 10 U.S.C. § 1408(e)(6).

11.8 Direct Payment for Child Support and Alimony Orders

Direct payment of alimony and child support orders by a Designated Agent is authorized by 10 U.S.C. §§ 1408(d) and (e). Alimony and child support payments are not subject to the restrictions discussed previously on property division payments to former spouses but only to the maximum of 65 percent of Disposable Retired Pay. Service members remain personally liable for any amount ordered by a state court in excess of the amount directly payable by the Designated Agent for alimony or support. 10 U.S.C. § 1408(e)(6).

11.9 State Court Jurisdiction

For alimony or child support payments, normal state court jurisdictional rules apply, and no special requirements are imposed by 10 U.S.C. § 1408. However, as noted previously, for a state court to treat a member's Disposable Retired Pay as marital, joint, or community property, certain special jurisdictional requirements must be met. The state court must have jurisdiction over the service member by reason of

A. Residence in the state, other than because of military assignment;

B. Domicile in the territorial jurisdiction of the court; or

C. Consent to the jurisdiction of the court. 10 U.S.C. §§ 1408(c)(4)(A)–(C). The courts have construed section 1408(c)(4) as affecting the subject matter jurisdiction of the state courts, not personal jurisdiction over the service member. *Steele v. United States*, 813 F.2d 1545 (9th Cir. 1987); *Lewis v. Lewis*, 695 F. Supp. 1089 (D. Nev. 1988); *Hodgson v. Hodgson*, 1999 Ohio App. LEXIS 4760 (Ohio Ct. App. 1999); *Seeley v. Seeley*, 690 S.W.2d 626 (Tex. Ct. App. 1985).

The meaning of subsection (A) is unclear. It seems to mean that, for example, a soldier stationed at Ft. Gordon, Georgia, who comes to live in Georgia because of that assignment is not subject to the jurisdiction of the Georgia courts. However, if that soldier chooses to live a few miles away in South Carolina, subsection (A) suggests that he might be subject to the South Carolina courts' jurisdiction.

Subsection (B) presents other difficulties of interpretation due to the use of the word "domicile." This is ordinarily a question of fact involving both physical presence (except for temporary absences) coupled with an intent to remain or return; and it is usually evinced by voter registration, driver's license and motor vehicle registration, payment of state income and property taxes, maintenance of bank accounts, ownership of a home, and similar indicia of connection with a state. *See, e.g., Andris v. Andris*, 309 S.E.2d 570 (N.C. Ct. App. 1983). "Domicile" should not be confused with "home of record," a technical military term denoting only the state from which a member enters or reenlists in the service; however, a service member may change his or her home of record. Many service members will claim states that have no income tax as their domiciles, even though they may not have any other connection with that state sufficient to support a bona fide claim of domicile.

Most cases that have arisen under section 1408(c)(4) have determined jurisdiction under subsection (C), based on the service member's implied consent to the jurisdiction of the state court by filing an answer or a general appearance in the divorce action. *Allen v. Allen*, 484 So. 2d 269 (La. App. 1986), *cert. denied*, 488 So. 2d 199 (La. 1986), *cert. denied*, 479 U.S. 850 (1986); *Gowins v. Gowins*, 466 So. 2d 32 (La. 1985); *Seeley, supra.* Other cases have held that a general appearance is insufficient to confer jurisdiction and that specific consent to the jurisdiction of the state court to divide a member's Disposable Retired Pay is required. *Flora v. Flora*, 603 A.2d 723 (R.I. 1992); *Tucker v. Tucker*, 277 Cal. Rptr. 403 (Cal. Ct. App. 1991); *Barrett v. Barrett*, 715 S.W.2d 110 (Tex. Ct. App. 1986). *See also Kovacich v. Kovacich*, 705 S.W.2d 281 (Tex. Civ. App. 1986) (no jurisdiction where husband never resided or was domiciled in Texas even though husband was petitioner in Texas divorce action).

The result of these special requirements for jurisdiction may require a bifurcation of divorce proceedings. If the court granting the divorce does not have jurisdiction over the service member in order to divide his or her military retired pay, then it is essential that the attorney for the former spouse request and ensure that there is language in the divorce decree that reserves the issue of the division of the military retired pay for a court that has jurisdiction. If this is not done, and the divorce decree is silent on the division of military retired pay, then the former spouse will have lost her interest in the military retired pay forever.

The military pay centers also will only honor court orders from

> (A) any court of competent jurisdiction of any State, the District of Columbia, the Commonwealth of Puerto Rico, Guam,

American Samoa, the Virgin Islands, the Northern Mariana Islands, and the Trust Territory of the Pacific Islands;

(B) any court of the United States (as defined in section 451 of title 28) having competent jurisdiction;

(C) any court of competent jurisdiction of a foreign country with which the United States has an agreement requiring the United States to honor any court order of such country; and

(D) any administrative or judicial tribunal of a State competent to enter orders for support or maintenance (including a State agency administering a program under a State plan approved under part D of title IV of the Social Security Act [42 U.S.C.S. §§ 651 *et seq.*]), and, for purposes of this subparagraph, the term "State" includes the District of Columbia, the Commonwealth of Puerto Rico, the Virgin Islands, Guam, and American Samoa.

10 U.S.C. § 1408(a)(1). What this means is that the pay centers will not honor a court order dividing military retired pay issued by a foreign country. It is not uncommon for service members who are deployed overseas to get divorced in a foreign country. If, just as before, the issue of division of the military pension is not reserved for a court of competent jurisdiction, the former spouse may lose her interest in the military pension.

11.10 Procedure for Obtaining Direct Payment

To be eligible to apply for direct payment of a share of a service member's Disposable Retired Pay as property division, the former spouse must have been married to the service member for at least ten years during which the service member performed creditable service of ten years or more. However, there is no such limit in the case of alimony or child support orders.

To apply for direct payment, the former spouse must submit Department of Defense (DD) Form 2293. The DD Form 2293 or written statement required by the Designated Agent for direct payment must

1. Contain an express notice or request to make direct payments.
2. Include a certified copy of the court order and other relevant documents.
3. Contain a statement by the former spouse that the court order has not been amended, superseded, or set aside.

4. Identify the service member's full name, Social Security number, and branch of service or other information sufficient to identify him.
5. State the full name, address, and Social Security number of the former spouse.
6. Before receiving the first payment, the former spouse must personally agree that any future overpayments to her are recoverable and are subject to involuntary collection from her or her estate.
7. Contain a statement that the former spouse personally agrees to promptly notify the Designated Agent:
    a. If the court order on which the payments are based is vacated, modified, or set aside;
    b. Of the former spouse's remarriage, if all or any part of the payment is for alimony; and
    c. Of any change in eligibility for child support payments (if the child dies, is emancipated, is adopted, or attains the age of majority, and so on), if all or part of the payment is for child support. If the state court order is for property division and does not expressly state that the former spouse satisfied the ten-year marriage eligibility rule for direct payment, the former spouse's application must include sufficient independent evidence that this requirement has been met.

Service of this paperwork must be made on the appropriate Designated Agent by certified or registered mail or by personal service (see Appendix N for their addresses).

As soon as possible, but in no event more than 30 days after service of the application for direct payment, the Designated Agent must send a written notice to the service member concerning this application. This notice must include

1. A copy of the state court order and accompanying documents.
2. An explanation of the statutory limits on direct payment to former spouses from the member's Disposable Retired Pay.
3. A request that the service member send to the Designated Agent a certified or authenticated copy of any court order amending, superseding, or setting aside the state court order enclosed with the former spouse's application.

4. A statement of the amount or percentage that will be deducted from his Disposable Retired Pay if the service member fails to respond.
5. The date on which direct payments to the former spouse are tentatively scheduled to begin.
6. Notice that the service member's failure to respond within 30 days after the notice is mailed to him may result in payment as described in the notice.
7. A statement that any information submitted by the service member in response to the notice may be disclosed to the former spouse or her agent in connection with the decision on the former spouse's application.

The Designated Agent will then examine the state court order submitted with the former spouse's request for direct payment together with any response submitted by the service member. The Designated Agent will review the state court order to make sure it satisfies the following requirements:

1. It must be regular on its face, meaning that it is issued by a court of competent jurisdiction in accordance with that jurisdiction's laws.
2. It must be legal in form and include nothing on its face that provides reasonable notice that it is issued without authority of law.
3. It must be a final decree.
4. If it was issued while the service member was on active duty and he was not represented in court by counsel, the order or other documents must show that the service member's rights under the Servicemembers' Civil Relief Act, 50 U.S.C. § 3901 *et seq.*, were waived or protected.
5. It must contain sufficient information to identify the service member (name, branch of service, rank, Social Security number).
6. If it is a property division order:

    a. The court must have jurisdiction over the service member by reason of (i) his residence, other than because of military assignment, (ii) his domicile in the territorial jurisdiction of the court, or (iii) his consent to the jurisdiction of the court as discussed in section 11.9.

b. The treatment of retired pay as property of the member and his former spouse must be in accordance with the laws of the state in which the court is located.
c. The order or other accompanying documents must show satisfaction of the ten-year rule for direct payment.

Within 90 days after service of the former spouse's paperwork on the Designated Agent, the Designated Agent must notify the former spouse whether the court order will be honored and in what amount; or, if it will not be honored, of the specific reasons it has been rejected. Designated Agents must honor stays of execution of state court orders that are issued by a court of competent jurisdiction. Applications for direct payment may be submitted to the Designated Agent at any time, even long before the service member is due to retire, and they may be approved by the Designated Agent for payment at a later date. However, if the application is approved more than 90 days before the service member begins receiving Disposable Retired Pay, the service member will be given a second notice and an opportunity to object (if, for example, a state court order has been set aside, or his former spouse has remarried before age 55) at the time he actually retires.

See the helpful website at https://www.dfas.mil for further information.

11.11 Military Retired Pay and Waiver for VA Disability

If a retired service member receives Veterans' Administration (VA) disability compensation, that service member may be required to waive an equal amount from his or her military retired pay. When this happens, the amount waived from the military retired pay will be taken out by the pay center prior to the division of the military retired pay pursuant to a court order. This means that it will have the effect of reducing the former spouse's portion of the military retired pay. Prior to 2017, smart attorneys would draft orders with an indemnification clause, requiring the retired service member to pay to his or her former spouse the difference between what the former spouse received and what the former spouse would have received. However, in the case of *Howell v. Howell*, 137 S. Ct. 1400 (2017), the U.S. Supreme Court held that state courts could not order a service member to indemnify his or her former spouse for any amounts waived for the receipt of VA disability compensation. Since *Howell*, a few states have held that if the service member agrees to indemnification in a divorce agreement and does not later appeal the order, the order will stand. *See Jones v. Jones*, 505 P.3d 224 (Alaska 2022); *Foster v. Foster*, 983 N.W.2d 373 (Mich. 2022); *Martin v. Martin*, 520 P.3d 813 (Nev. 2022); *Rudolph v. Jamieson*, No. 03-17-00693-CV, 2018 Tex. App. LEXIS 3983 (June 5, 2018); *In re Marriage of Kaufman*, 17 Wis. App. 2d 497 (2021).

11.12 Survivor Benefit Plan

The military Survivor Benefit Plan (SBP) is an optional annuity that provides post-death income to current or former spouses or children who survive a service member. Payments for SBP are deducted from the service member's monthly Disposable Retired Pay on a pre-tax basis. The SBP program is governed by 10 U.S.C. §§ 1447–1455. If SBP coverage is not elected, all payments to the former spouse automatically cease upon the service member's death.

SBP coverage is usually elective by the service member but may be ordered by a state court. 10 U.S.C. § 1450(f). SBP coverage must be elected at or before the time the service member actually retires, and SBP coverage for former spouses must be requested within one year after their divorce from the service member becomes final.

The service member himself may elect former spouse coverage, if the service member is still serving. If he does, he must notify DFAS of the court order or separation agreement requiring SBP coverage within one year after the divorce becomes final. If the service member does not do so, his former spouse may do so by filing a written request for SBP coverage from DFAS and providing a certified copy of the divorce decree or agreement within the same year after the divorce becomes final. This is what is referred to as a "deemed election." *King v. King*, 483 S.E.2d 379 (Ga. Ct. App. 1997) (second wife of service member, not first wife, entitled to SBP as neither service member nor first wife had notified government of state court order within one year after divorce decree granting first wife SBP as required by USFSPA).

SBP coverage automatically ends if the former spouse remarries before she reaches age 55, but it may be reinstated if that remarriage ends in divorce or annulment. Remarriage after age 55 has no effect on SBP coverage.

SBP coverage for a former spouse may not be combined with SBP coverage for a current spouse—it is one or the other. Obviously, this is a source of great potential conflict. However, service members may request a change in SBP coverage should they remarry or acquire a dependent child after SBP coverage for a former spouse has been elected. The service member must apply for a change in SBP coverage within one year after the remarriage or the child's birth. 10 U.S.C. §§ 1447–1455.

It is vitally important to remember that even if you have sent an order dividing a service member's military retired pay to DFAS and received its approval of that order, you must separately apply to DFAS for an award of SBP coverage (a "deemed election") or provide in your order that the service member must do so (a "voluntary election") for the award of SBP coverage to be effective. Correspondence concerning SBP awards must be sent to DFAS, U.S. Military Retired Pay, 8899 E. 56th Street, Indianapolis, Indiana 46249-1200.

11.13 Medical Coverage

Military medical care for former spouses of service members is a matter of automatic entitlement by statute if they meet certain requirements concerning the length of their marriage to the service member. Specifically, a former spouse that was married to a service member that served at least 20 years where there was 20 years of marriage and 20 years of overlap between marriage and military service, will be eligible for military medical care for that former spouse's life. This is referred to as a "20/20/20" former spouse—20 years of military service, 20 years of marriage, 20 years of overlap. A former spouse who is "20/20/15"—20 years of military service, 20 years of marriage, 15 years of overlap—will be eligible for military medical care for one year after the divorce. 10 U.S.C. §§ 1062 and 1072(2). No state court order or consent of the service member is required or permitted to affect this coverage.

11.14 Discovery

Pretrial discovery in military retired pay cases should generally follow the parameters of discovery in private pension cases. Use the model interrogatories and deposition questions in Appendices E–G with appropriate modifications for the military context. You cannot compel the pay center or the military service branch to provide information regarding the service member's military service and pay; therefore, you will need to request the information from the service member or have the court compel the service member to request the information from the pay center. The model release of information form in Appendix H may be used. Make sure to ask for the service member's most recent Leave and Earnings Statements (LESs), which show all elements of the service member's compensation. Because some of the components of service members' pay and allowances are tax-free, they will not appear on the service member's federal income tax returns.

The scope of pretrial discovery in military retired pay cases is somewhat narrower than in ERISA pension cases. The armed forces provide one and only one form of retirement plan, and there are far fewer options and choices to deal with. The focus of pretrial discovery in military retired pay cases should be on establishing years of service (or retirement points, if in the reserve component) while married, future prospects for promotion and retirement, and, in appropriate cases, National Guard or reserve component service. Any decision or election by the service member that might affect the amount of Disposable Retired Pay under section 11.3 should also be explored.

11.15 Model Order Dividing Military Retired Pay

[Normal State Court Caption]

Order

This order is entered this ___ day of ___, 20__ [after a hearing] [by stipulation of the parties]. This order is intended to divide the service member's Military Disposable Retired Pay as that term is used in the Uniformed Services Former Spouses Protection Act, 10 U.S.C. § 1408, and further defined in this order, [and to grant the service member's former spouse a survivor benefit plan].

1. *Parties.* The names and last known mailing addresses of the parties are: Service Member: COL John C. Burns, United States Army, 123 Broad Street, Augusta, GA 30910, Social Security Number xxx-xx-6789 ("Service Member"). Former Spouse: Mary J. Burns, 456 Peachtree Lane, Augusta, GA 30911, Social Security Number xxx-xx-4321 ("Former Spouse"). Complete Social Security numbers and dates of birth are provided under separate cover that is not a part of the public record.

2. *Jurisdiction.* This court has jurisdiction over the Service Member sufficient to divide his military retired pay due to [his residence, other than because of military assignment] [his domicile in the territorial jurisdiction of the court] [his consent to the jurisdiction of the court].

COMMENT: 10 U.S.C. §§ 1408(c)(4)(A)–(C) requires an affirmative showing on the face of the state court order of one of these jurisdictional bases for the division of Disposable Retired Pay as part of a property division. This showing is not required for alimony or child support orders, where normal state jurisdictional requirements apply (see section 11.8).

3. *Servicemembers' Civil Relief Act.* The Service Member's rights under the Servicemembers' Civil Relief Act, 50 U.S.C. § 3901 *et seq.*, have been observed and honored.

COMMENT: 10 U.S.C. § 1408(c) requires an affirmative showing, on the face of the state court order, of this waiver or protection. *See* 50 U.S.C. §§ 501–593; *Hawkins v. Hawkins*, 999 S.W.2d 171 (Tex. Ct. App. 1999).

4. *Relationship of Former Spouse to Service Member.* The Former Spouse is the former spouse of the Service Member.

OPTIONAL ADDITIONAL CLAUSE

4A. The Former Spouse and the Service Member were married on May 19, 19__; separated on June 14, 20__; and were divorced by this Court in this action on November 2, 20__. The Service Member entered active duty on June 3, 19__, and is still on active duty on the date of this order.

COMMENT: While not strictly required by USFSPA, this clause contains useful information that may be needed by the Designated Agent. First, it may be needed to calculate the former spouse's share of payments if they are determined by the common arrangement involving a fraction whose numerator is the number of years the parties were married during the service member's years on active duty. Second, these dates may be needed to establish that the former spouse is entitled to receive direct payments from the Designated Agent (which requires ten years of marriage or more during a period when the service member was on active duty for ten years or more; see item 3 in subsection 11.7) or entitlement to medical care, commissary privileges, and the like (see section 11.13). If this information does not appear on the face of the order, it must be supplied on DD Form 2293 or its equivalent by the former spouse to the Designated Agent. Further, the pay center will require proof of the date of marriage. If the date of marriage is not in the military pension division order or final decree of divorce, then the former spouse will have to provide a certified copy of the parties' marriage certificate.

5. *Method of Division.*

5A. *Fixed dollar amount.* Former Spouse shall receive $412.27 per month from the Service Member's Disposable Retired Pay.

COMMENT: This is a simple clause, but it has its drawbacks. The service member will receive all cost-of-living adjustments and increases, while the former spouse is restricted to a fixed amount unless the modification in brackets is used. *This is true even if the drafter of the Qualified Court Order attempts to provide for the application of COLAs to a fixed dollar amount; DFAS will simply ignore such a COLA provision.*

5B. *Fraction.* Former Spouse shall receive a fraction of the Service Member's total Disposable Retired Pay [including any cost-of-living or other postretirement increases], the numerator of which is the number of months [use retirement points if the service member is a reservist] the parties were married while Service Member served on active duty before retirement (200 months), and the denominator of which shall be the total number of months [again, use retirement points if the service member is a reservist] Service Member served on active duty before retirement. This fraction should then be multiplied by *X* percent [usually 50 percent, but this figure can be bigger or smaller]. [This is the time rule formula as discussed in sections 11.5 and 11.6.]

In determining this fraction, any hypothetical, putative, or extra years of service taken into account by the armed forces in determining years of service during any period in order to calculate the Service Member's benefits shall not be included in either the numerator or the denominator of the fraction, but only the Service Member's actual years of service. *In re Marriage of Lehman*, 955 P.2d 451 (Cal. 1998).

COMMENT: Since the passage of the NDAA 2017, the time rule formula can only be used for service members who are no longer serving. Further, because the service member is no longer serving, the number of years of service will be known, reducing the time rule formula to a flat percentage. Using the fractional method should automatically pick up any cost-of-living or other adjustments made to the service member's Disposable Retired Pay after retirement, but the better practice is to expressly state that they are included, as in the phrase in brackets. Reserve or National Guard service may also be included in the determination of the fraction.

5C. *Clause required with the new Frozen Benefit Rule.* In computing the Service Member's Disposable Retired Pay for the purpose of calculating the amount due to be paid to the Former Spouse under this order, the Service Member shall be deemed to have retired as of the date of the divorce as a [present rank] with [number of years of military service to date of divorce] years of creditable military service with a "high-36" of $xxxx.xx.

COMMENT: For a reserve component service member, the frozen benefit rule language would read as follows: "In computing the Service Member's Disposable Retired Pay for the purpose of calculating the amount due to the Former Spouse under this order, the Service Member shall be deemed to have retired as of the date of the divorce as a [present rank] with [number of retirement points up to the date of divorce] retirement points and a 'high-36' (or retired pay base) of $xxxx.xx."

5D. *This amount shall be paid directly to the Former Spouse by the Designated Agent.* To the extent the Designated Agent is prohibited by law or regulation from paying the entire amount required by this order to the Former Spouse, the Service Member shall personally pay any shortfall to the Former Spouse.

6. *Duration of Payments.* The Former Spouse shall receive payments commencing on the date the Service Member begins to receive his Disposable Retired Pay and ending (except for the Survivor Benefit Plan payments provided below) on his death.

COMMENT: This clause is not strictly necessary because under USFSPA these are the times when payments automatically begin and stop, no matter what the order says. If the service member is already retired, the order should state that payments should begin "immediately." If it is desired to provide payments to the former spouse after the death of the service member, clause 7 must be used.

7. *Survivor Benefit Plan.* Former Spouse shall be covered by the Survivor Benefit Plan, 10 U.S.C. §§ 1447 *et seq.*, and shall receive the maximum annuity allowed by law under the Survivor Benefit Plan.

COMMENT: The maximum allowable amount is 55 percent of the service member's regular annuity.

8. *Service Member Not to Interfere with Former Spouse's Rights.* The Service Member is hereby ordered not to do, or fail to do, any act; or to make any choice or election; or by inaction fail to make any choice or election, with respect to his Disposable Retired Pay or other aspects of his retirement; that would interfere in any way with the payment to the Former Spouse of the share of his Disposable Retired Pay and her Survivor Benefit Plan assigned to the Former Spouse by this order. In the event any payment assigned to the Former Spouse by this order is paid to or received by Service Member, Service Member shall be deemed to have received such payments as trustee for the benefit of Former Spouse and shall immediately pay the same to Former Spouse.

COMMENT: This clause is really directed at the service member, not the Designated Agent, so arguably it does not belong in this order, but rather in the original divorce decree. It is good to have it in this type of order if only to put the Designated Agent on notice of it.

9. *Recomputation of Service Member's Benefits.* In the event the Former Spouse predeceases the Service Member, the Former Spouse's portion shall immediately revert back to the Service Member.

COMMENT: This occurs by operation of law because, as discussed earlier in this chapter, a military pension is divided using a shared interest division. This clause costs the former spouse nothing and may allow the service member to receive more. *See In re Marriage of Rich*, 73 Cal. App. 4th 419 (Cal. Ct. App. 1999) (Alternate Payee's share of ERISA pension reverted to Participant after Alternate Payee's death).

10. *Tax Effect.* It is the intention of the court [and the parties] that federal and state income taxes on all payments received by the Former Spouse under this order shall be borne by the Former Spouse and not by the Service Member, and the Former Spouse is ordered to indemnify and hold the Service Member harmless with respect to any federal or state income tax imposed on the Service Member as a result of the Former Spouse's receipt of her payments.

11. *Reservation of Jurisdiction.*

A. This court reserves jurisdiction to amend or modify the provisions of this order in light of comments received from (a) the Designated Agent, (b) another court of competent jurisdiction, or (c) any other organization or party, during the process of deciding whether this order will be accepted and honored by the Designated Agent.

B. This court also reserves jurisdiction to amend or modify the provisions of this order, even after it has been accepted and approved by the Designated Agent, to terminate or suspend the payment of benefits to the Former Spouse as a result of remarriage, cohabitation, attainment of a certain age, emancipation, change of custody, or other events justifying a change in payments, or to modify this order to deal with any unforeseen tax consequences or other effects of this order.

COMMENT: This is a vitally important clause. It is often necessary to revise an order several times in dialogue with the Designated Agent, and it is vitally important that the state trial court retain jurisdiction under clause 11A to do so. In many states, the trial court loses jurisdiction over a divorce or support case once the final order in the case has been entered if an express reservation of jurisdiction like this is not made. *Edwards v. Edwards*, 838 S.W.2d 494 (Mo. Ct. App. 1992); *Rohrbeck v. Rohrbeck*, 566 A.2d 767 (Md. 1989). The result can be a nightmare of protracted litigation and malpractice claims.

If appropriate, add a clause indicating that each party has waived his or her right to appeal.

Use the broadest reservation of jurisdiction clause permitted by state law to deal with all of these unforeseen contingencies. *Wilson v. Wilson*, 492 S.E.2d 495 (Va. Ct. App. 1997).

SO ORDERED:

____

Judge

CERTIFIED A TRUE AND CORRECT COPY:

____

Clerk

[Signatures of counsel for both parties]

[Signatures of both parties]

COMMENT: While not required by the USFSPA, signatures of counsel for both parties, or, better yet, signatures of the parties themselves, help to counter later claims that they had not approved—or at least read—the provisions of the order. Your client's signature on this order may be very helpful in fending off any subsequent malpractice claims.

11.16 DD Form 2293

USFSPA also requires that when the state court order mandating direct payment is submitted to the Designated Agent, it must be accompanied by a DD Form 2293 or equivalent written statement that:

1. Contains an express notice or request to make direct payments.
2. Includes a certified copy of the court order and other relevant documents.
3. Identifies the service member's full name, Social Security number, and branch of service, or other information sufficient to identify him.
4. States the full name, address, and Social Security number of the former spouse.
5. Contains an agreement with the former spouse that any future overpayments are recoverable and are subject to involuntary collection from her or her estate.
6. Contains a statement that the former spouse personally agrees to notify the Designated Agent promptly (a) if the court order is vacated, modified, or set aside, and (b) of the former spouse's remarriage if all or a part of the payment is for alimony, and (c) of a change in eligibility for child support payments if the child dies, is emancipated, is adopted, or attains the age of majority if all or part of the payment is for child support.

11.17 Checklist for Order Dividing Military Retired Pay as Property

___ 1. Order contains names, addresses, and Social Security numbers of service member and former spouse.

___ 2. Order expressly states court has jurisdiction to divide service member's Disposable Retired Pay due to (a) residence in the state, other than because of military assignment, (b) domicile in the territorial jurisdiction of the court, or (c) consent to the jurisdiction of the court.

___ 3. Order expressly states waiver or inapplicability of service member's rights under Servicemembers' Civil Relief Act.

___ 4. Order expressly identifies former spouse as former spouse of the service member.

___ 5. Order states date of marriage and date of divorce.

___ 6. Order clearly specifies starting and ending dates (or amounts or events) for receipt of payments by former spouse.

___ 7. Order clearly specifies amount of each payment, or formula for calculating amount, to be paid to former spouse.

___ 8. Order provides deemed rank, date of retirement, and high-36 for service members still serving to be used in calculating amount payable irrespective of actual rank at retirement and years of service at retirement (frozen benefit rule language).

___ 9. Order provides Survivor Benefit Plan for former spouse (optional).

___ 10. Order directs service member not to interfere with former spouse's rights.

___ 11. Order specifies intended tax effect.

___ 12. Order contains appropriate reservation of jurisdiction clause allowing trial court to modify as needed during qualification process and afterward.

___ 13. Order contains any special features unique to this case (specify): ______________________________

___ 14. DD Form 2293 and attachments prepared and ready to file.

___ 15. DD Form 2656-1 or DD Form 2656-10 prepared and ready to file for SBP.

11.18 Thrift Savings Plan

Like federal civilian employees, service members are entitled to participate in the federal Thrift Savings Plan (TSP) program.

When representing the spouse of a service member, be sure to inquire if the service member participates in the TSP. See section 11.18 for details on the TSP program.

Section 12.9 contains detailed guidance on how to divide a TSP account through a Retirement Benefits Court Order.

Federal Civil Service Pension Plans

12

12.1 Federal Pension Plans

Federal government employees (other than military personnel) are covered by either the Federal Employees Retirement System (FERS) or the Civil Service Retirement System (CSRS). Participants in either system are subject to federal laws stating that their retirement benefits

> shall be paid (in whole or in part) by the Office [of Personnel Management] to another person if, and to the extent, expressly provided for in the terms of any court decree of divorce, annulment, or legal separation, or the terms of any court order or court approved property settlement agreement incident to any court decree of divorce, separation, annulment or legal separation. 5 U.S.C. § 8467.

These statutory provisions are implemented by a comprehensive set of regulations set forth at 5 C.F.R. §§ 838.101–1018 and the appendices to these regulations. A state court order accepted by the Office of Personnel Management (OPM) as complying with all statutory and regulatory requirements is known as a Court Order Acceptable for Processing, or COAP.

There are major differences between the Employee Retirement Income Security Act (ERISA) plans and CSRS/FERS benefits. First, unlike most ERISA Plan Administrators, OPM administrators will not review and comment on draft orders in advance. Second, a spouse or former spouse may not begin receiving payments from OPM until the federal employee actually retires—unlike ERISA plans, where payments to an Alternate Payee may begin even though the Participant remains employed by the Plan Sponsor. Third, survivor benefits awarded to a former spouse will be lost if the former spouse remarries before age 55. Finally, OPM's regulations contain a series of default presumptions that can be a trap for the unwary. For example, which of the following is higher: "self-only annuity," "gross annuity," or "net annuity"? The answer, which surprises many lawyers, is that self-only annuity represents the highest figure. The OPM default presumption is gross annuity if your COAP simply speaks of dividing an "annuity" without specifying which of these three levels you mean. Similar default interpretations and presumptions govern the amount of survivor benefits and which party pays for them, disposition of a former spouse's share of payments on his or her death, division of post-retirement cost-of-living adjustments, and similar matters that are discussed in detail in this chapter.

OPM publishes two handbooks on dividing retirement benefits in divorce. The first, *Court-ordered Benefits for Former Spouses* (RI 84-1 July 2014), is very brief and covers CSRS/FERS pension divisions as well as Federal Employees' Group Life Insurance (FEGLI) and Federal Employees Health Benefits (FEHB) in the context of divorce. OPM's *A Handbook for Attorneys on Court-ordered Retirement, Health Benefits, and Life Insurance under the CSRS, FERS, FEHB and FEGLI* (RI 38-116 July 1997) is a lengthy and comprehensive guide to drafting orders covering all of these topics. It is available from the U.S. Government Printing Office or may be downloaded from OPM's website at http://www.opm.gov. Both of these publications are extremely useful, if not necessary, if you intend to draft COAPs. In addition to being extremely useful for purposes of drafting and preparation of COAPs, these publications are great references in the litigation setting as well. The publications can be very helpful to explain certain provisions to a judge or even to opposing counsel. It is a good idea to have one printed copy to keep in your office and bring to court with you if necessary.

Neither the statute nor the regulations mention alimony or child support; both are concerned exclusively with a division of pension rights as property between former spouses. FERS or CSRS pensions that are In Pay Status may, of course, be garnished for child support or alimony under normal federal and state law garnishment procedures. Nor do these laws and regulations place any limit on the state court's discretion to treat FERS and CSRS pensions as marital or community property. As in the case of military pensions, 5 U.S.C. §§ 8345(j) and 8467 and their implementing regulations cover only what is required for a former spouse to collect pension payments directly from OPM. A state court order directing payments to be made from the federal employee to a spouse, former spouse, child, or other dependent is subject only to the general law concerning family obligations of the state involved.

Three separate types of FERS or CSRS benefits are subject to division in domestic relations cases and assignment, in whole or in part, to a former spouse. These are

- Employee annuities,
- Refunds of employee contributions, and
- Former Spouse Survivor Annuities.

A. Employee Annuities

Employee annuities are Single Life Annuities received or to be received by the employee, former employee, or retiree. Federal civil service employee annuities are Single Life Annuities for the life of the employee; they begin to make payments only when the employee actually retires, and all payments under the annuity terminate upon his death. Joint and Survivor Annuities are not available under CSRS or FERS; protection for surviving spouses or former spouses may be implemented only through a Former Spouse Survivor Annuity as discussed in subsection 12.1C.

Each employee annuity has three levels that may be divided by a COAP. These levels are defined in 5 C.F.R. § 838.103 as follows.

1. Self-Only Annuity

The self-only annuity is the highest figure. It is the total amount of the monthly payment to the employee on retirement as a Single Life Annuity on his life with no deductions or reductions of any kind. Synonyms recognized by OPM are "life rate annuity," "unreduced annuity," and "annuity without survivor benefits." 5 C.F.R. § 838.625(b). Nonetheless, the different forms can be confusing enough for most attorneys, and it is generally easier to not stray from the normal three.

2. Gross Annuity

Despite its name, the gross annuity is actually lower than the self-only annuity because there is a deduction of any amount deducted from the monthly annuity payment to provide a Former Spouse Survivor Annuity.

3. Net Annuity

Net annuity is the lowest figure, and it allows deductions for health insurance premiums, life insurance, Medicare, federal and state withholding taxes, and payments made under another COAP. Synonyms for "net annuity" recognized by OPM are "disposable annuity" and "retirement check." 5 C.F.R. § 838.625(a).

B. Refunds of Employee Contributions

To the extent they are not used to purchase retirement annuities, previous contributions to the FERS or CSRS by the employee during his employment will be refunded to him upon separation from service. This refund is divisible between the parties. This figure can be ascertained from the employee's statements and records.

C. Former Spouse Survivor Annuity

Although Joint and Survivor Annuities are not available from federal civil service pension plans, essentially the same protection for former spouses may be achieved by electing a Former Spouse Survivor Annuity (FSSA), which will pay monthly benefits to a former spouse in the event the employee predeceases her. Such annuities are funded by monthly deductions from the employee's annuity receipts and automatically end on the death of the former spouse. To be eligible for an FSSA, the former spouse must have been married for at least nine months (unless the marriage was terminated by the death of the employee) to an employee who had at least 18 months of creditable service under CSRS or FERS. 5 C.F.R. § 838.103.

The maximum amount of an FSSA is 55 percent of a self-only annuity for the employee under CSRS and 50 percent under FERS. 5 C.F.R. §§ 831.641, 838.921, and 842.613.

Divisions of these three separate types of benefits have some common features but many differences.

12.2 Common Features

Dividing any type of federal pension requires not a QDRO but a COAP. 5 C.F.R. § 838.103. In determining whether a state court order is a COAP, OPM follows the procedures and guidelines set forth in 5 C.F.R. § 838, as discussed next.

A. OPM Responsibilities

OPM states that it is "responsible for authorizing payments in accordance with clear, specific and express provisions of COAPs." 5 C.F.R. § 838.121.

B. State Court Responsibilities

OPM regulations assign to state courts the responsibility for

1. Providing due process to the employee or retiree;
2. Issuing clear, specific, and express instructions consistent with [federal law and these regulations];
3. Using the terminology defined in the regulations only in their specially defined meaning;
4. Determining when court orders are invalid; and
5. Settling all disputes between the employee or retiree and the former spouse. 5 C.F.R. § 838.122.

C. Former Spouses' Responsibilities

Former spouses, or "claimants," are responsible for

1. Filing certified copies of state court orders and other supporting documents with OPM;
2. Keeping OPM advised of their current mailing address;
3. Notifying OPM of any change in circumstances that could affect their entitlement to benefits; and
4. Submitting all disputes they may have with the employee or retiree to the appropriate state court for resolution. 5 C.F.R. § 838.123.

D. Employees' and Retirees' Responsibilities

Employees or retirees must raise any objections to the validity of state court orders in the appropriate state court and resolve all disputes with their former spouses in those courts, not in proceedings before OPM. 5 C.F.R. § 838.124(b).

E. Application for a COAP

The former spouse must apply in writing, either personally or through a representative, for payment of a portion of the employee's annuity, a refund of employee contributions, or an FSSA. 5 C.F.R. §§ 838.221, .421, and .721. No special form is required. However, the application letter must be accompanied by:

- A certified copy of the COAP.
- A certification from the former spouse or her representative that the COAP is currently in force and has not been amended, superseded, or set aside.
- Information sufficient for OPM to identify the employee or retiree, such as his full name, CSRS or FERS number, date of birth, and Social Security number.
- The current mailing address of the former spouse. It is always a good idea to include personal information for the former spouse as well (DOB, SSN).
- If the employee has not already retired or died, his mailing address. 5 C.F.R. §§ 838.221(b), .421(b), and .721(b).

F. OPM Notice Procedures

Upon receiving an application for a COAP, OPM uses the following procedure.

1. Notice to Former Spouse

1. OPM will first decide whether the state court order is a COAP.
2. If OPM decides that the state court order is not a COAP, it must provide the former spouse with its specific reason or reasons for reaching this decision and disapproving the application. 5 C.F.R. §§ 838.223, .424, and .723.
3. If OPM decides that the state court order is a COAP, it will advise the former spouse of the date OPM received the

application and the date payments to the former spouse will commence, the amount of payments, and the formula used by OPM to calculate the payments. 5 C.F.R. §§ 838.222(ii) and (iii), .423(ii)–(v), .722(ii) and (iii).

4. OPM must notify the former spouse that if she disagrees with the amount payable to her as calculated by OPM, she must obtain and submit to OPM an amended state court order clarifying the amount payable. 5 C.F.R. §§ 838.222(a)(1), .423(a)(1), and .722(a)(1).

2. Notice to Employee, Former Employee, or Retiree

Upon determining that a state court order is a COAP, OPM notifies the federal employee, former employee, or retiree:

1. That the former spouse has applied for benefits.
2. That the state court order is a COAP and that OPM must comply with it.
3. The date on which OPM received the COAP.
4. The formula that OPM will use to determine the amount payable to the former spouse.
5. That if the employee, former employee, or retiree contests the validity of the COAP or disagrees with the formula or amount of benefits OPM proposes to pay to the former spouse, he must obtain an amended state court order and submit it to OPM. 5 C.F.R. §§ 838.222(a)(2), .423(a)(2), and .722(a)(2).

3. Contesting Validity of COAP

If the employee, former employee, or retiree contests the validity of the COAP, he must submit to OPM a state court order that declares the COAP invalid or sets it aside. 5 C.F.R. §§ 838.224(a), .425(a), and .724(a). OPM is required to honor COAPs that are regular on their face and that are certified to be currently in force by the former spouse unless the employee, former employee, or retiree can submit a superseding court order. 5 C.F.R. §§ 838.224(b), .425(b), and .724(b).

Following a settlement of the parties, it is prudent, in order to avoid issues with the COAP, to have both sides (and counsel) review the COAP, initial each page, and sign the final page of the COAP. Similarly, even if ordered by the court, to avoid these issues, it is generally easier to consult with the other parties (or counsel, depending on the situation) prior to submitting to the court.

4. Conflicting COAPs

Conflicting COAPs affecting the same employee or retiree and providing for payments to be made to two or more individuals are honored in the order in which they were received by OPM. 5 C.F.R. § 838.134(a)(1). If conflicting COAPs relate to the same individual recipient, the COAP with the most recent date will be honored. 5 C.F.R. § 838.134(a)(2). If there are conflicting COAPs, OPM will rule as follows:

1. If the orders are from the same jurisdiction, OPM will honor the most recent order.
2. If the COAPs are from different jurisdictions, OPM will honor the COAP from the state indicated as the employee's, former employee's, or retiree's address in OPM's records.
3. If none of the COAPs is from the state indicated as the employee's, former employee's, or retiree's address in OPM's records, OPM will honor the most recent COAP. 5 C.F.R. §§ 838.134(a), (c).

Other general provisions concerning OPM's review processes and interpretation of COAPs are set forth at 5 C.F.R. §§ 838.1001–1018 and in appendices A and B to subpart J of part 838.

12.3 Division of Employee Annuity

Subject to the general requirements and procedures set forth in section 12.2, the following regulatory requirements must be followed to create a COAP to divide an employee's annuity.

A. Forbidden and Required Language

COAPs must not use ERISA terminology or the phrase "Qualified Domestic Relations Order" unless the state court order expressly states that the provisions of the order concerning CSRS or FERS benefits are "governed by Part 838, Title 5, Code of Federal Regulations," and must state that the provisions of the COAP concerning CSRS or FERS benefits are "drafted in accordance with the terminology used [in Part 838]." 5 C.F.R. § 838.302(a).

B. Express Division

To qualify as a COAP, the state court order must "expressly divide an employee annuity" (5 C.F.R. § 838.303(a)), which means that the order must

1. Sufficiently identify the retirement system in question (by mentioning CSRS, FERS, OPM, or federal government benefits, or "benefits payable based on service with the U.S. Department of Agriculture" or other agencies). 5 C.F.R. §§ 838.303(b)(1), .611; and
2. Expressly state that "the former spouse is entitled to a portion of the employee annuity" (by mentioning "annuities," "pensions," "retirement benefits," or similar terms). 5 C.F.R. §§ 838.303(b), .611, and .612(a).

C. Direct Payment

To qualify as a COAP, the state court order must also provide for OPM to pay directly to the former spouse a portion of the employee annuity. 5 C.F.R. § 838.304(a). To meet this requirement, the state court order must

1. Expressly direct OPM to pay the former spouse directly;
2. Direct the retiree to arrange or execute forms for OPM to pay the former spouse directly; or
3. "[B]e silent as to who is to pay the portion of the employee annuity awarded to the former spouse." 5 C.F.R. § 838.304(b).

OPM prefers that state court orders use the wording in clause 1 and will not accept state court orders that direct the retiree to pay a portion of his annuity to the former spouse unless the wording in clause 2 is used. 5 C.F.R. §§ 838.304(c) and (d).

D. Computation of Benefits

To be accepted as a COAP, a state court order must provide sufficient detailed instructions and information for OPM to compute the amount payable to the former spouse. 5 C.F.R. § 838.305(a). OPM requires that the amount payable to the former spouse be stated as

- A fixed amount;
- A percentage or fraction of the employee annuity;
- A formula that does not contain any variables whose values are not readily apparent from the face of the state court order or normal OPM files. 5 C.F.R. § 838.305(b)(1); or
- A pro rata share.
    - Pro rata share is expressly defined in 5 C.F.R. § 838.621 as "one-half the fraction whose numerator is the number

of months of federal civilian and military service that the employee performed during the marriage and whose denominator is the total number of months of federal civilian and military service performed by the employee [before retirement]."

- A state court order using this phrase will be construed accordingly and must specify the date of the parties' marriage.
- Additionally, unless the court order specifies a different ending date, the marriage ends for "pro rata computation purposes" on the date that the court order is *filed* with the clerk of court. 5 C.F.R. § 838.621(b). *See also* 5 C.F.R. § 838.623.

Information that OPM will consider as qualified under clause 3 includes the dates of employment and rates of pay of the employee, cost-of-living adjustments (COLAs), standard federal income tax withholding tables, and similar matters. 5 C.F.R. § 838.305(b)(2). *See also* 5 C.F.R. § 838.623 for detailed instructions on defining lengths of service.

E. COLAs

1. Fixed Monthly Amount:

   OPM will not apply COLAs to a fixed monthly amount awarded to a former spouse unless the COAP expressly directs OPM to apply COLAs. To include, use language such as: "When COLAs are applied to the Employee's retirement benefits, the same COLA applies to the Former Spouse's share."

2. Percentage:

   Unless the COAP provides otherwise, former spouses receive the same percentage of COLAs as the retiree does. 5 C.F.R. § 838.241.

   To not include COLAs for a percentage, include language such as: "The United States Office of Personnel Management is directed to not apply COLAs to the Former Spouse's share."

3. Fraction:

   Similar to percentage, OPM will automatically include COLAs in the former spouse's share "at the stated percentage," which means the percentage figure from the fraction.

To not include COLAs for a fraction, the COAP needs to specifically state that this is the intent, as just noted with percentages.

4. Pro Rata Share:

   Where an award is a "pro rata share" as explained more fully next, unless the COAP expressly states that COLAs are not added to the former spouse's share, then OPM will automatically add COLAs to the former spouse's percentage.

F. Pro Rata Share

Pro rata share is expressly defined in 5 C.F.R. § 838.621 as "one-half the fraction whose numerator is the number of months of federal civilian and military service that the employee performed during the marriage and whose denominator is the total number of months of federal civilian and military service performed by the employee [before retirement]." A state court order using this phrase will be construed accordingly and must specify the date of the parties' marriage. 5 C.F.R. § 838.621(b). *See also* 5 C.F.R. § 838.623.

G. Forbidden References

A state court order is not a COAP if OPM would have to examine a state statute or court decision (in a different case) to understand, establish, or evaluate the formula for computing the former spouse's share of the annuity, or if it awards an unspecified "community property fraction" or refers only to the "present value" of an annuity without specifying a dollar amount. 5 C.F.R. §§ 838.305(c) and (d).

H. Level of Annuity to which Formula, Fraction, or Percentage Is Applied

Unless the COAP expressly provides otherwise, OPM will apply any fraction, formula, or percentage set forth in the COAP to the "gross annuity" payable to the employee. 5 C.F.R. §§ 838.306(b), .625(c). However, a COAP specifying that the formula, fraction, or percentage should be applied to a "net annuity" or a "self-only annuity" will be applied to those levels of payment. 5 C.F.R. § 838.306(b). These terms are defined in 5 C.F.R. §§ 838.103 and .625 (see subsection 12.1A).

I. Payments after Death of Employee Not Allowed

A state court order directing that a former spouse's portion of an employee annuity may continue after his death is not a COAP. 5 C.F.R. § 838.302(b). However, an FSSA may be ordered (see subsection 12.1C).

J. Payments after Death of Former Spouse Allowed

Unless the COAP expressly provides otherwise, the former spouse's share of an employee annuity terminates upon his death, and his share reverts to the employee. 5 C.F.R. § 838.237(a). However, the COAP may allow the former spouse to designate that payments be made after his death (until the death of the employee) to (1) the state court, (2) an officer of the court acting as a fiduciary, (3) her estate, or (4) one or more of the employee's children. 5 C.F.R. § 838.237(b).

12.4 Division of Refunds of Employee Contributions

In addition to the general requirements set forth in section 12.2, to divide refunds of employee contributions, certain special requirements must be met.

A. Separation from Service and Entitlement

The federal employee must have separated from service, must have applied for a refund of his employee contributions, and must be entitled to receive such a refund. 5 C.F.R. § 838.411(a)(1). Employee contributions that may be payable at some indefinite future date may not be the subject of a COAP. 5 C.F.R. § 838.411(a)(2).

B. Time of Application

The application for payment by the former spouse must be received on or before "the last day of the second month before payment of the refund." 5 C.F.R. § 838.422(a)(1).

C. Required and Forbidden Language and References

The COAP must expressly divide the funds to be refunded; must expressly provide for direct payment to the former spouse; must properly identify the retirement system to which the COAP is directed; and must clearly specify the amount to be paid or any formula, fraction, or percentage of payment to be made in a manner similar to the requirements for dividing an employee annuity as discussed in subsection 12.1A. 5 C.F.R. §§ 838.502, .503, .504, .611, and .612(b)(1). If the state court order refers to "contributions," "deductions," "deposits," "retirement accounts," "retirement fund," or similar terms, they will be construed to refer to employee contributions subject to refund. 5 C.F.R. § 838.612(b)(1).

D. Order Barring Payment of Refunds (5 C.F.R. § 838.505)

OPM will not recognize a state court order that bars the payment of employee contributions to the employee as a COAP unless it meets three requirements:

1. The state court order expressly directs OPM not to pay a refund of employee contributions to the employee.
2. The state court order, or a prior COAP, awards the former spouse either a portion of the employee annuity or an FSSA.
3. Refund of his contributions to the employee would prevent payment to the former spouse under the court order described in (2). 5 C.F.R. §§ 838.432 and .505.

12.5 Provision of a Former Spouse Survivor Annuity

An FSSA provides continuing payments to a former spouse of a federal employee if he predeceases the former spouse. Payment to fund a Former Spouse Survivor Annuity will be deducted either from the employee's annuity (see the definitions of "self-only" and "gross" annuities in 5 C.F.R. § 838.103) or from the former spouse's share of an employee annuity. 5 C.F.R. § 838.933.

To obtain an FSSA, the same basic requirements as obtaining direct payment of a portion of the employee's annuity as specified in section 12.3 should be followed. The following additional requirements and conditions apply.

A. Remarriage

The application submitted to OPM by the former spouse must contain a statement in the form prescribed by OPM that

1. The former spouse has not remarried before age 55;
2. The former spouse will notify OPM within 15 calendar days of any remarriage before age 55; and

3. The former spouse will be personally liable to OPM for any overpayment resulting from a remarriage before age 55. 5 C.F.R. §§ 838.721(b)(1)(vi)(A)–(C).

OPM may require periodic recertification of these matters from the former spouse. 5 C.F.R. § 838.721(b)(2). These requirements exist because FERS and CSRS FSSAs automatically terminate on remarriage of the former spouse if the remarriage occurs before she reaches age 55. It is not uncommon to see former spouses delay remarriage so as to avoid disrupting their FSSA payments.

B. Required and Forbidden Language

In addition to the general requirements discussed in section 12.2 and subsection 12.3A, a COAP providing an FSSA may not use the phrases "will continue to receive payments after the death of," "will continue to receive benefits for her lifetime," or "benefits will continue after the death of [the employee]," and must use phrases such as "survivor annuity," "death benefits," "former spouse annuity," or "former spouse survivor annuity." 5 C.F.R. § 838.803(b).

C. Express Award of Former Spouse Survivor Annuity

The COAP must expressly award an FSSA or expressly direct an employee or retiree to provide an FSSA. 5 C.F.R. § 838.804. To do so, the COAP must properly identify the retirement system (*see* 5 C.F.R. § 838.911 and subsection 12.3B(1)) and contain language such as "survivor annuity," "death benefits," or "former spouse survivor annuity under 5 U.S.C. § 8341(h)," or similar terms. 5 C.F.R. § 838.912(a). If an FSSA is awarded in the COAP, when it is transmitted to OPM for approval it must be accompanied by a letter signed by the former spouse confirming (1) that the COAP and divorce decree are currently in force and have not been amended, superseded, or set aside; (2) that the former spouse has not remarried before age 55; (3) that the former spouse will notify OPM of any remarriage before age 55; and (4) that the former spouse will be personally liable to OPM for any overpayment to him or her under the FSSA provisions of the COAP resulting from his or her remarriage before age 55.

D. Specification of Type of Survivor Annuity

Under CSRS and FERS there are two types of survivor annuities: "former spouse survivor annuities" under 5 U.S.C. §§ 8341(h) and

8445, and "insurable interest annuities" under 5 U.S.C. §§ 8339(k) and 8444. 5 C.F.R. § 838.912(c).

FSSAs are less expensive and have fewer restrictions than insurable interest annuities, but they automatically terminate if the former spouse remarries before age 55. 5 C.F.R. § 838.912(c)(1). OPM will enforce COAPs requiring FSSAs (5 C.F.R. § 838.912(c)(1)) but cannot enforce court orders requiring the provision of an insurable interest annuity. The latter annuity is available only if it is voluntarily elected by the employee, or elected by an employee under compulsion of a state court order directed at him personally, not a COAP directed at OPM. 5 C.F.R. § 838.912(c)(2).

E. Computation of Formulas

If the FSSA amount is determined by a fraction, formula, or percentage, the state court order must expressly provide sufficient instructions and information for OPM to compute the amount payable to the former spouse. 5 C.F.R. § 838.805. (See subsection 12.3D.)

F. Time of Order

A state court order requiring the provision of an FSSA may not be issued after the retirement or death of the employee if it modifies an earlier order. 5 C.F.R. § 838.806(a). Such an order must be issued before the employee dies or retires. However, if the COAP is the "first order dividing marital property," it may be issued after the date of retirement or death. 5 C.F.R. §§ 838.806(b)(2), (c), (f). The "first order dividing marital property" does not include amendments, clarifications, explanations, interpretations, or supplemental orders issued under reserved jurisdiction of earlier orders, even if they purport to be effective on or "as of" an earlier date or nunc pro tunc. 5 C.F.R. § 838.806(f).

Section 838.806 is designed to cover the case where, as the first order is about to be entered, the employee dies or retires. However, it is also designed to prevent former spouses from having a "second bite of the apple" if the first order has already been accepted as a COAP but then the employee dies or retires.

G. Cost of FSSA Must Be Paid by Annuity Reduction

An FSSA may be funded only by withholding a reduction from either the employee's annuity or the former spouse's share of his annuity paid to her under a COAP, or both. 5 C.F.R. § 838.807. The state court order should specify from which source the funds are to be collected (5 C.F.R. § 838.807(b)), but unless the state court order provides otherwise, the deduction will be made from the employee's annuity. 5 C.F.R. § 838.807(c).

If the COAP requires the former spouse to pay for the FSSA, its cost will be deducted from her share of the employee annuity if such a share is awarded to her. 5 C.F.R. § 838.933(a). If the state court order conditions her award of an FSSA on her payment of the cost thereof, the order must also award her a portion of the employee annuity sufficient to cover that cost, or the order will not be considered to be a COAP. 5 C.F.R. § 838.933(c).

H. Amount

If the amount of the FSSA is not specifically stated in the COAP, OPM will pay the maximum amount available by law. 5 C.F.R. § 838.921. This is one of the very few areas where CSRS and FERS benefits differ. Under FERS, the maximum amount of a Former Spouse Survivor Annuity is 50 percent of the amount of a self-only annuity for the employee; under CSRS, the maximum is 55 percent. 5 C.F.R. §§ 831.641 (CSRS) and 842.613 (FERS).

I. Pro Rata Share

Under 5 C.F.R. § 838.922, the pro rata share is defined for FSSAs as it is for partitioning employee annuities: the fraction of married years over total years of service by the employee (see subsection 12.3F). A COAP that awards

1. A former spouse a pro rata share of a survivor annuity and states the date of the marriage; or
2. A former spouse a portion of a survivor annuity "as of a specified date before the employee's retirement"; or
3. A former spouse the "value" of a survivor annuity as of a specified date before retirement, without specifying what that value is,

will be deemed to award that former spouse a pro rata share of the maximum amount. 5 C.F.R. § 838.922.

J. Automatic COLA

A COAP awarding an FSSA is deemed to order automatic COLAs through the date of death of the employee unless the COAP expressly provides otherwise. 5 C.F.R. § 838.923. Expressly disclaiming these COLAs will result in a lower deduction to fund the FSSA but also results in lower payments under that annuity. Use of a fixed dollar amount will be interpreted to exclude COLA increases and should not be used unless that is the intended effect.

After the employee has died and the FSSA payments begin, COLAs are automatic and may not be disclaimed by the former spouse or prevented by the COAP. 5 C.F.R. § 838.735.

K. Temporary Annuity Order

The COAP may provide that the FSSA is to be awarded only for a limited time. However, such an order will become permanent on the date of retirement or death of the employee, or, in the case of a postretirement divorce, on the date of the initial court order. 5 C.F.R. § 838.923.

L. Election and Disclaimer

A COAP may provide that the former spouse will have the right to elect to receive an FSSA at a later date. 5 C.F.R. § 838.932(a). However, the former spouse may subsequently disclaim that right by filing a written election with OPM not to receive such an annuity. Once filed with OPM, such an election is irrevocable. 5 C.F.R. §§ 838.932(b) and (c).

M. Special Notice Requirements

In addition to the normal notice requirements to the former spouse and the employee discussed in subsection 12.2F, OPM must give notice of an application for an FSSA by the former spouse to "anyone whom OPM knows will be adversely affected by the COAP." 5 C.F.R. § 838.722(b)(2). The notice must state

1. That the former spouse has applied for an FSSA;
2. That the state court order is a COAP and that OPM must comply with it;

3. The date on which OPM received the state court order;
4. How the state court order may adversely affect the person to whom the notice is being given; and
5. If that person contests the validity of the state court order, he or she must obtain, and submit to OPM, a court order invalidating the state court order submitted by the former spouse. 5 C.F.R. §§ 838.722(b)(2)(i)–(v).

Persons to whom such additional notice must be given include current spouses of the employee or other former spouses under earlier COAPs because the award of an FSSA to a former spouse prevents OPM from paying a survivor option elected by the employee to his widow, or to another former spouse, if the elected benefit is inconsistent with the terms of the new COAP. 5 C.F.R. § 838.725(b).

12.6 Discovery

Pretrial discovery in civil service pension cases should generally follow the parameters of discovery in private pension cases. Use the model letter requesting information from the plan in Appendix B, and the model interrogatories and deposition questions in Appendices E–G with appropriate modifications for the civil service context. The model release of information form in Appendix H may also be used.

The scope of pretrial discovery in civil service pension cases is somewhat narrower than in ERISA pension cases. CSRS and FERS provide one and only one form of retirement plan, and there are far fewer options and choices to deal with. The focus of pretrial discovery in civil service pension cases should be on establishing years of service while married; future prospects for promotion and retirement; and, in appropriate cases, military service that may be counted toward years of service in the CSRS or FERS systems. Any decision or election by the employee that might affect the amount of the employee annuity, refunds of employee contributions, or the provision of an FSSA as discussed previously should also be explored.

12.7 Model COAP

Set forth in this section is a model COAP based on the matters discussed in the earlier sections of this chapter.

A significant difference between ERISA-qualified pensions and federal civil service pensions is that in the latter there are default assumptions that will be made by OPM unless the COAP, as discussed previously, specifically provides otherwise. Follow the model clauses carefully, and always be aware that silence on a particular point will result in OPM's using the default position spelled out in 5 C.F.R.

It is useful to review the general discussion of the model QDRO in section 8.5 before using this model COAP.

[Normal State Court Caption]

Order

This order is entered this ___ day of ___, 20__ [after a hearing] [by stipulation/agreement/settlement of the parties]. This order is intended to be a court order acceptable for processing, and the provisions of this order concerning Civil Service Retirement System (CSRS) or Federal Employees Retirement System (FERS) benefits are governed by part 838, title 5, Code of Federal Regulations. The provisions of this order concerning CSRS or FERS benefits are drafted in accordance with the terminology used in 5 C.F.R. part 838.

1. *Parties.* The names and last known mailing addresses of the parties are:

A. Participant:

Name:	John Smith
Address:	123 Main Street Augusta, Georgia 30911
Social Security Number:	Provided to the Plan Administrator under separate cover.
Date of Birth:	Provided to the Plan Administrator under separate cover.

B. Former Spouse:

Name:	Betty Smith
Address:	789 2nd Street Augusta, Georgia 30911

Social Security Number: Provided to the Plan Administrator under separate cover.

Date of Birth: Provided to the Plan Administrator under separate cover.

1A. The Employee and the Former Spouse were married on May 19, 19__; separated on June 14, 20__; and were divorced by this Court in this action on November 2, 20__.

COMMENT: If a formula based on the length of the marriage is to be used to apportion any payments, this information must appear on the face of the order.

2. *Identity of Plan.* This order applies to all of the Employee's CSRS or FERS retirement benefits arising out of all of his creditable civilian [and military] service and awards Former Spouse a share thereof as [property division] [alimony] [child support] under Section _____ of the domestic relations law of the State of _____.

COMMENT 1: Military service can in some circumstances be counted toward years of civilian federal service. This may result in higher benefits, but depending on whether the parties were married during the military service period, it may result in the former spouse receiving a higher or lower pro rata share. The calculation should be made both ways and the method most favorable to the client chosen.

COMMENT 2: The second part of this clause, identifying the nature of the payments under state law, is not necessary as far as OPM is concerned, but it is useful in determining the terminating events for the payments and the federal income tax consequences of payments made under the COAP.

Part A: Division of Employee Annuity

3. *Division of Employee Annuity.* The Former Spouse is entitled to receive a portion of the Employee's annuity as specified below. OPM is directed to pay directly to the Former Spouse her share of the Employee's annuity.

3A. *Fixed Dollar Amount.* The Employee is (or will be) eligible for retirement benefits under the [CSRS or FERS] based on employment with the United States Government. The Former Spouse is entitled to $[insert a number] per month from Employee's civil service retirement benefits. The United States Office of Personnel Management is directed to pay Former Spouse's share directly to Former Spouse.

3B. *Percentage.* The Employee is (or will be) eligible for retirement benefits under the [CSRS or FERS] based on employment with the United States Government. The Former Spouse is entitled to [insert a number] percentage of Employee's [insert "gross," "net," or "self-only"] monthly annuity under the [CSRS or FERS]. The United States Office of Personnel Management is directed to pay Former Spouse's share directly to Former Spouse.

3C. *Fraction.* The Employee is (or will be) eligible for retirement benefits under the [CSRS or FERS] based on employment with the United States Government. The Former Spouse is entitled to [insert fraction]ths of Employee's [insert "gross," "net," or "self-only"] monthly annuity under the [CSRS or FERS]. The United States Office of Personnel Management is directed to pay Former Spouse's share directly to Former Spouse.

3D. *Pro Rata Share.* The Employee is (or will be) eligible for retirement benefits under the [CSRS or FERS] based on employment with the United States Government. The Former Spouse is entitled to a pro rata share of Employee's [insert "gross," "net," or "self-only"] monthly annuity under the [CSRS or FERS]. The marriage began on [insert date of marriage]. The United States Office of Personnel Management is directed to pay Former Spouse's share directly to Former Spouse.

3E. *Based on Stated Formula.* The Employee is (or will be) eligible for retirement benefits under the [CSRS or FERS] based on employment with the United States Government. The Former Spouse is entitled to a share of Employee's [insert "gross," "net," or "self-only"] monthly annuity under the [CSRS or FERS]. Former Spouse shall receive a fraction of the monthly [gross] [net] [self-only] annuity payable to Employee, the numerator of which is the number of years the parties were married while Employee performed creditable military or civilian service (23 years and 4 months), and the denominator of which shall be the total number of years and months of Employee's creditable civilian [and military] service. This fraction shall then be multiplied by (a) *X* percent, and further multiplied by (b) the [gross] [net] [self-only] monthly annuity amount payable to Employee.

In determining this fraction, any hypothetical, putative, or extra years of service taken into account by OPM in determining years of service during any period in order to calculate Employee's benefits shall not be included in either the numerator or the denominator of the fraction, but only Employee's actual years of service. *In re Marriage of Lehman*, 955 P.2d 451 (Cal. 1998).

4. *Duration of Payments.* The Former Spouse shall receive payments pursuant to the preceding paragraph from the time Employee begins to receive annuity payments until Employee's death.

COMMENT 1: This clause is not strictly necessary because under CSRS and FERS, these are the times when payments automatically begin and stop.

COMMENT 2: If the state court considers these payments to be for alimony or child support, copy an appropriate variation of clause 6, the termination of payments clause, from the model QDRO in section 8.5.

5. *Cost-of-Living Adjustments.* Former Spouse [shall/shall] not be entitled to receive any cost-of-living adjustments to the amount paid to her under the preceding paragraph.

COMMENT: The former spouse will automatically receive COLAs if the order is silent. To deny them to her (and have them paid to the employee), this clause should be used. Use of a fixed dollar amount might be also interpreted to exclude COLA increases and should not be used unless that is the desired effect.

6. *Payment after Former Spouse's Death.* Upon the death of the Former Spouse, the amount of the Employee's annuity payable to her under the preceding paragraphs shall be paid to [the court] [an officer of the court acting as a fiduciary] [her estate] [one or more of the Employee's children].

COMMENT: Unless this clause is used, the former spouse's share of an employee annuity terminates upon her death, and her share reverts to the employee. Only payees of post-death benefits listed in the categories set forth in brackets in clause 6 may be designated by the former spouse to receive payments.

Part B: Division of Refund of Employee Contributions

7. *Division of Refund of Employee Contributions.* The Former Spouse is awarded a portion of any refund of the Employee's contributions

as set forth below. OPM is directed to pay directly to the Former Spouse her share of any refund of the Employee's contributions.

7A. *Fixed Dollar Amount.* The Former Spouse shall receive $____ from the Employee's refunded contributions.

7B. *Percentage.* The Former Spouse shall receive fifty percent (50%) from the Employee's refunded contributions.

7C. *Fraction.* The Former Spouse shall receive one-half (1/2) from the Employee's refunded contributions.

7D. *Formula.* The Former Spouse shall receive a fraction of the Employee's refunded contributions, the numerator of which is the number of years the parties were married while Employee performed creditable civilian [and military] service (23 years and 4 months) and the denominator of which shall be the total number of years and months of Employee's creditable military and civilian service. This fraction shall then be multiplied by (a) *X* percent and further multiplied by (b) the total amount of refunded contributions to determine the Former Spouse's share.

In determining this fraction, any hypothetical, putative, or extra years of service taken into account by OPM in determining years of service during any period in order to calculate Employee's benefits shall not be included in either the numerator or the denominator of the fraction, but only Employee's actual years of service. *In re Marriage of Lehman*, 955 P.2d 451 (Cal. 1998).

7E. *Pro Rata Share.* The Former Spouse shall receive a pro rata share of the Employee's refunded contributions, the numerator of which is the number of years the parties were married while Employee performed creditable civilian [and military] service (23 years and 4 months) and the denominator of which shall be the total number of years and months of Employee's creditable military and civilian service.

Part C: Provision of Former Spouse Survivor Annuity

8. *Provision of Former Spouse Survivor Annuity.* The Former Spouse is awarded a Former Spouse Survivor Annuity with respect to Employee's [CSRS] [FERS] benefits. OPM shall pay the annuity directly to her.

COMMENT 1: Although not part of the COAP itself, the application submitted to OPM by the former spouse must contain a statement in the form prescribed by OPM that

1. The former spouse has not remarried before age 55;
2. The former spouse will notify OPM within 15 calendar days of any remarriage before age 55; and
3. The former spouse will be personally liable to OPM for any overpayment resulting from a remarriage before age 55. 5 C.F.R. §§ 838.721(b)(1)(vi)(A)–(C).

OPM may require periodic recertification of these matters from the former spouse. 5 C.F.R. § 838.721(b)(2).

COMMENT 2: A state court order requiring the provision of an FSSA may not be issued after the retirement or death of the employee if it modifies an earlier order. 5 C.F.R. § 838.806(a). Such an order must be issued before the employee dies or retires. If, however, the COAP is the "first order dividing marital property," it may be issued after the date of retirement or death. 5 C.F.R. §§ 838.806(b)(2), (c), (f). The "first order dividing marital property" does not include amendments, clarifications, explanations, interpretations, or supplemental orders issued under reserved jurisdiction of earlier orders, even if they purport to be effective on or "as of" an earlier date or nunc pro tunc. 5 C.F.R. § 838.806(f).

COMMENT 3: The COAP may provide that the former spouse will have the right to make an election at a later date to receive an FSSA. 5 C.F.R. § 838.932. However, once the former spouse files a written election with OPM to receive such an annuity, the election is irrevocable. 5 C.F.R. §§ 838.932(b) and (c).

9. *Amount.* The Former Spouse's Survivor Annuity shall be in the amount of:

9A. *Fixed Dollar Amount.* Under section 8341(h)(1) of title 5, United States Code, [Former Spouse] is awarded a Former Spouse Survivor Annuity under the Civil Service Retirement System. The amount of the Former Spouse Survivor Annuity will be equal to $[insert a number] per month. The Office of Personnel Management is ordered not to increase this amount by COLAs occurring before the death of [Employee or retiree].

9B. *Pro Rata Share.* The pro rata share of the maximum amount permitted under 5 C.F.R. § 831.641 or 842.613. Under section 8341(h)(1) of title 5, United States Code, [Former Spouse] is awarded a Former Spouse Survivor Annuity under the Civil Service Retirement System. The amount of the Former Spouse Survivor Annuity will be equal to a pro rata share. The marriage began on [insert date].

9C. *Percentage or Fraction.* Under section 8341(h)(1) of title 5, United States Code, [Former Spouse] is awarded a Former Spouse Survivor Annuity under the Civil Service Retirement System. The amount of the Former Spouse Survivor Annuity will be equal to [insert a percentage or fraction] of [Employee]'s employee annuity.

9D. *Stated Formula.* "Under section 8341(h)(1) of title 5, United States Code, [former spouse] is awarded a former spouse survivor annuity under the Civil Service Retirement System. The amount of the former spouse survivor annuity will be the portion of [employee]'s employee annuity computed as follows:

[Insert formula.]

COMMENT 1: The amount of the Former Spouse Survivor Annuity may not exceed 55 percent of the employee annuity under CSRS or 50 percent under FERS.

COMMENT 2: The formula must be stated in the court order (including a court-approved property settlement agreement). The formula may not be incorporated by reference to a statutory provision or a court decision in another case. If the court order uses a formula, the court order must include any data that is necessary for OPM to evaluate the formula unless the necessary data is contained in normal OPM files.

9E. *Maximum.* The maximum amount permitted under 5 C.F.R. § 831.641 or 842.613. Under section 8341(h)(1) of title 5, United States Code, [Former Spouse] is awarded the maximum possible Former Spouse Survivor Annuity under the Civil Service Retirement System.

COMMENT: If not otherwise specified in the COAP, the amount of the Former Spouse's Survivor Annuity will be the maximum allowed by law as in clause 9E (see section 12.5).

GENERAL COMMENT: Be very careful of using other clauses to state the amount of the Former Spouse Survivor Annuity value because certain phrases may unwittingly trigger the pro rata provisions of 5 C.F.R. § 838.922 (see subsection 12.3F).

10. *Cost to be Paid by Annuity Reduction.* The Former Spouse's Survivor Annuity shall be funded by withholding a reduction in the appropriate amount from [that portion of the Employee's annuity that will be received by the Employee] [that portion of the Employee's annuity that is awarded to the Former Spouse by this order] [that portion of the Employee's annuity that will be received

by the Employee and that portion of the Employee's annuity that will be received by the Former Spouse in equal shares].

COMMENT: Payment for a Former Spouse Survivor Annuity must be deducted from one of these two sources. If not specified in the COAP, payment for the Former Spouse's Survivor Annuity will be deducted by OPM from the employee's share of his annuity. Division of the employee's "gross annuity" or "net annuity" automatically divides the cost of the FSSA between the parties by deducting it "off the top."

11. *Cost-of-Living Adjustments.* Former Spouse shall not be entitled to receive any COLAs made before the death of the Employee to the amount paid to her under her Former Spouse Survivor Annuity.

COMMENT: The former spouse will automatically receive COLAs to her FSSA if the order is silent on this point. 5 C.F.R. § 838.923. To deny them to her (which will reduce the cost of the deduction to fund the annuity but provide lower benefits), this clause must be used. Use of a fixed dollar amount might be interpreted to exclude COLA increases and should not be used unless that is the intended effect.

Once the FSSA is In Pay Status following the death of the employee, COLAs are automatic and may not be disclaimed by the former spouse or by a COAP.

Part D: General Provisions

12. *Recomputation of Employee's Benefits.* In the event the Former Spouse predeceases the Employee, or for any other reason permanently ceases to be eligible to receive payments from OPM before the full amount assigned to her by this order has been paid, the Employee may apply to the plan to increase the remaining benefits to be paid to him or his beneficiaries if, and to the extent that, OPM permits him to apply for and receive such an adjustment.

COMMENT: This clause costs the former spouse nothing and may allow the employee to receive more from OPM. This kind of recalculation will not always be available, but this is an important clause that counsel for the employee may bargain for in negotiations with the former spouse or argue for in court. *See In re Marriage of Rich,* 73 Cal. App. 4th 419 (Cal. Ct. App. 1999) (Alternate Payee's share of ERISA pension reverted to Participant after Alternate Payee's death).

13. *Employee Not to Interfere with Former Spouse's Rights.* The Employee is hereby ordered not to do, or fail to do, any act, or to make any choice or election, or by inaction fail to make any choice or election under the plan, that would interfere in any way with the payment to the Former Spouse of the benefits assigned to the Former Spouse by this order. In the event any payment assigned to the Former Spouse by this order is paid to or received by Employee, Employee shall be deemed to have received such payments as trustee for the benefit of Former Spouse and shall immediately pay the same to Former Spouse.

COMMENT: This clause is really directed at the employee, not at OPM, so arguably it does not belong in a COAP, but in the original divorce decree. It is good to include it in the COAP, however, if only to put OPM on notice of it.

14. *Tax Effect.* It is the intention of the court [and the parties] that federal and state income taxes on all payments received by the Former Spouse under this order shall be borne by the [Employee] [Former Spouse] and not by the [Former Spouse] [Employee], and the [Employee] [Former Spouse] is ordered to indemnify and hold the [Former Spouse] [Employee] harmless with respect to any federal or state income tax imposed on the [Former Spouse] [Employee] as a result of the Former Spouse's receipt of her payments, *provided, however,* that OPM's obligations to any party shall not be affected in any way by this clause.

COMMENT: While not binding on the Internal Revenue Service or state tax authorities, this clause should always be included. First, it expressly states the intent of the trial court (and the parties, if the order is entered by stipulation) as to the tax effect of the payments to the former spouse. Second, it requires the appropriate party to indemnify the other in case the intended tax consequences do not occur.

15. *Reservation of Jurisdiction.*

A. This court reserves jurisdiction to amend or modify the provisions of this order in light of comments received from (1) OPM, (2) a court of competent jurisdiction, or (3) any other organization or party, during the process of deciding whether this order is a COAP.

B. This court also reserves jurisdiction to amend or modify the provisions of this order, even after it has been determined to be a COAP, to terminate or suspend the payment of benefits to the Former Spouse as a result of attainment of a certain age, emancipation, change of custody, or other events justifying a change in payments, or to modify this order to deal with any unforeseen tax consequences or other effects of this order.

COMMENT: This is a vitally important clause. It is often necessary to revise an order intended to be a COAP several times during the qualification process, and it is vitally important that the state trial court retain jurisdiction under clause 15A to do so. In many states, the trial court loses jurisdiction over a divorce or support case once the final order in the case has been entered if an express reservation of jurisdiction like this is not made. *Edwards v. Edwards*, 838 S.W.2d 494 (Mo. Ct. App. 1992); *Rohrbeck v. Rohrbeck*, 566 A.2d 767 (Md. 1989). The result can be a nightmare of protracted litigation and malpractice claims.

Clause 15B is much broader. It is always desirable in alimony orders, and it is very desirable in case of future difficulties with the Internal Revenue Service about the intended and actual tax consequences of the Domestic Relations Order (DRO). *See Hawkins v. Comm'r*, 86 F.3d 982 (10th Cir. 1996) (failure of trial court to reserve jurisdiction meant DRO could not be revised).

Use the broadest reservation of jurisdiction clause permitted by state law to deal with all these unforeseen contingencies. *Wilson v. Wilson*, 492 S.E.2d 495 (Va. Ct. App. 1997).

If appropriate, add a clause indicating that each party has waived his or her right to appeal.

SO ORDERED:

____

Judge

CERTIFIED TO BE A TRUE AND CORRECT COPY:

____

Clerk

COMMENT: The order should be certified within the 90-day period immediately before its submission to OPM.

[Signatures of counsel for both parties]
[Signatures of both parties]

COMMENT: While not required by law, signatures of counsel for both parties—or, better yet, signatures of the parties themselves—help to counter later claims that they had not approved, or at least read, the provisions of the order.

12.8 Checklist for COAP

___ 1. Order contains names, addresses, and Social Security numbers of employee and former spouse.

___ 2. Order identifies state domestic relations law section involved and specifies whether it is for property division, alimony, or child support.

___ 3. Order identifies former spouse as former spouse of the employee.

___ 4. Order states date of marriage and date of divorce.

___ 5. Order clearly states that it is dividing the employee's annuity and ordering direct payment from OPM to former spouse.

___ 6. Order clearly specifies amount or formula to calculate amount payable to former spouse.

___ 7. Order clearly specifies starting and ending dates (or amounts or events) for receipt of payments by former spouse.

___ 8. Order specifies whether annuity payments to former spouse will include COLAs or not.

___ 9. Order clearly states that it is dividing a refund of the employee's contributions and ordering direct payment from OPM to former spouse.

___ 10. Order clearly specifies amount or formula to calculate amount payable to former spouse.

___ 11. Order clearly states that it is providing a Former Spouse Survivor Annuity to former spouse.

___ 12. Order clearly specifies amount or formula to calculate FSSA amount payable to former spouse.

___ 13. Order clearly specifies that cost of FSSA is to be deducted from annuity payment to employee, former spouse, or both.

___ 14. Order specifies whether FSSA payments to former spouse will include COLAs or not.

___ 15. Order allows for recomputation of employee's benefit if former spouse does not collect entire share of benefits.

___ 16. Order directs employee not to interfere with former spouse's rights.

___ 17. Order specifies its intended tax effect.

___ 18. Order contains appropriate reservation of jurisdiction clause allowing trial court to modify as needed during qualification and afterward.

___ 19. Order contains any special features unique to this case (specify): ______________________________

COAPs should be sent to Office of Personnel Management, Court Ordered Benefits Branch, P.O. Box 17, Washington, D.C. 20044-0017, together with a certified copy of the parties' divorce decree and the COAP and a letter in the form set forth in section 12.5C if an FSSA has been awarded.

12.9 Thrift Savings Plan

Since federal Thrift Savings Plan (TSP) accounts were created in 1986, many federal employees, both civilian and military, have participated in the TSP program, which is essentially equivalent to a civilian 401(k) Defined Contribution Plan. TSPs may be divided between divorcing spouses by an order known as a Retirement Benefits Court Order (RBCO). TSPs are administered by the Federal Retirement Thrift Investment Board (FRTIB), specifically the TSP Court Order Center in Newark, New Jersey, not by OPM in Washington, D.C. FRTIB publishes a helpful booklet, *Court Orders and Powers of Attorney* (TSPBK11 (Dec. 2023)). This is available at TSP.gov. It is extremely helpful to download this PDF and keep it in a designated folder on your computer. Similarly, it is also helpful to have a printed copy in an easily accessible location in your workspace for quick reference.

Acceptable forms for an RBCO are set forth in this booklet. The statutory requirements for the order are set forth at 5 U.S.C. §§ 8435(d)(1) and (2) and 8467, and the FRTIB regulations at 5 C.F.R. part 1653, subpart A. Generally, the same form used for an ERISA Defined Contribution Plan (see section 8.5) may be used for an RBCO with the following changes. The order must be captioned a "Retirement Benefits Court Order" and not a "Qualified Domestic Relations Order" or "QDRO." It may award the payee a fixed dollar amount or a percentage, a fraction linked to a specific date, or a time-based formula interest in the Participant's vested account balance. The payee of an RBCO may be the Participant's current or former spouse, dependent child, other dependent, or—unlike ERISA plans—the lawyer for a current or former spouse, dependent child, or other dependent. Payments under an RBCO will generally be made immediately after it is accepted by FRTIB, which will make only one payment, not a series of payments, regardless of what the RBCO may call for. If the RBCO names a current or former spouse as the payee, payment may be made directly to an individual retirement account (IRA) or other qualified plan for the benefit of the payee. Payments under an RBCO to a current or former spouse are taxable to that person; payments under an RBCO to a child or other dependent of a Participant are taxable to the Participant. It needs to be clearly specified whether gains and losses are included, similar to a QDRO, because if not specifically stated, the default is to not include. Finally, payments under an RBCO, like payments under a QDRO, are exempt from the 10 percent penalty for withdrawals before age 59.

TSP now allows users to create and submit court orders and powers of attorney, request spouse account information, and obtain model language to use in an order at TSP.gov/lifeevents. This is a very helpful and efficient way to submit orders and has been our preferred method of submission since it became available.

In order to submit a hard copy of a divorce decree, Retirement Benefits Court Order, and/or Child Support Court Order, send to The TSP Court Order Center, c/o Broadridge Processing, P.O. Box 120, Newark, NJ 07101-0120.

12.10 Railroad Retirement Act Pensions

Railroad Retirement Act pensions are governed by 45 U.S.C. § 231m *et seq.* and have several components. They cover certain railroad employees but not employees of private railroads who may be covered by ERISA pensions. The major components are Tier I benefits, Tier II benefits, and a Divorced Spouse Annuity. In *Hisquerdo v. Hisquerdo*, 439 U.S. 572 (1979), the U.S. Supreme Court held, as a matter of federal statutory construction, that Railroad Retirement Act benefits were not divisible between divorcing spouses. In response, in 1993 Congress amended section 14 of the Railroad Retirement Act to make Tier II benefits (but not Tier I benefits, which are analogous to Social Security benefits) divisible as property in divorce actions, and to create a Divorced Spouse Annuity. A detailed explanation of how to divide Tier II benefits is found on the Railroad Retirement Board's website, https://www.rrb.gov/Benefits/G-177D, under the heading "Attorney's Guide to the Partition of Railroad Retirement Annuities." Information on the website includes an explanation of the law and a model clause for orders dividing Tier II benefits.

Orders dividing Tier II benefits must be final decrees or orders for divorce or legal separation and must expressly provide for the division of Tier II benefits between an employee and a spouse or former spouse. 20 C.F.R. §§ 295.2, 295.3(a)(1). They must be for marital or community property divisions, not alimony or spousal support. 20 C.F.R. § 295.2. The Railroad Retirement Board must be ordered to make direct payments to the spouse or former spouse. 20 C.F.R. § 295.3(a). The award may be stated as a fixed dollar amount, fraction, percentage, or formula share of the employee's benefits. If you attempt to divide Tier I benefits in a court order, the Railroad Retirement Board will simply ignore those provisions. Disability annuities paid under the Railroad Retirement Act are divisible in the same fashion as ordinary retirement annuities unless the court order expressly provides otherwise. If the award to the spouse or former spouse is phrased as a fraction, percentage, or formula, the former spouse will automatically receive a pro rata share of postretirement cost-of-living adjustments. However, if the award to the spouse or former spouse is stated as a fixed dollar amount, or as a percentage awarded as of a particular point in time, in which case it will be converted into a fixed dollar award as of that date, the spouse or former spouse will not receive any share of postretirement COLAs.

The Railroad Retirement Board also accepts garnishment orders for child and spousal support under 20 C.F.R. chapter 11, part 350, including orders garnishing Tier I benefits for those obligations.

Orders dividing Tier II benefits as property or garnishing Railroad Retirement benefits for alimony or child support should not be referred to as "QDROs" but rather "Qualifying Court Orders Dividing Railroad Retirement Benefits." However, they may generally follow the QDRO form set forth in section 8.5, as modified by the contents of this section and the information and model clauses set forth in the Attorney's Handbook (Railroad Retirement Board's website, https://www .rrb.gov/Benefits/G-177D, under the heading "Attorney's Guide to the Partition of Railroad Retirement Annuities.") at the website given previously. Note, however, that unlike ERISA plans—but like CSRS/FERS and military plans—a divorced spouse may not begin to receive payments until the employee actually retires.

Divorced Spouse Annuities are automatically awarded by the Railroad Retirement Board to certain divorced spouses if they meet the statutory requirements. *See* 20 C.F.R. § 295.1(b). The requirements for a Divorced Spouse Annuity include marriage to an eligible railroad employee for at least ten consecutive years immediately before the divorce. Eligibility is lost if the divorced spouse is entitled to a Social Security benefit, based on her own earnings, that is greater than the divorced spouse annuity payable by the Railroad Retirement Board. If the divorced spouse remarries at any age, her eligibility for a Divorced Spouse Annuity is suspended, subject to being reinstated if that subsequent marriage terminates by death or divorce. No state court order is necessary to provide a Divorced Spouse Annuity, and no state court order may affect the provision of one.

The Railroad Retirement Board, unlike the Office of Personnel Management or the Defense Finance and Accounting Service, will review orders in draft form. Drafts submitted for review should be mailed to Railroad Retirement Board, Office of the General Counsel, 844 North Rush Street, Chicago, Illinois 60611-2092, or faxed to (312) 751-7102. Certified copies of final orders should be mailed to the same address.

12.11 Federal Reserve Employee Benefits System

While the Federal Reserve is technically not part of the U.S. Department of the Treasury, it was created by an act of Congress and is oftentimes included when referenced with federal civilian employment. Division for retirement plans under the Federal Reserve is much more similar to that of private retirement plans than the other federal government retirement divisions addressed in this chapter.

A division order for retirement plans of the Federal Reserve is designated as a QDRO rather than a specific designation like we discussed earlier for a COAP or Retirement Benefits Court Order. Similarly, administration of the QDROs for Federal Reserve retirement division is handled in the private sector. As of the time of preparing this book, the Office of Employee Benefits of the Federal Reserve System, acting as agent for the Committee on Plan Administration, is the Plan Administrator for the employee benefit plans. The Office of Employee Benefits of the Federal Reserve System has contracted with Alight Solutions LLC to establish procedures and administer QDROs.

The Federal Reserve offers two different retirement plans:

1. A defined benefit plan: the "Retirement Plan for Employees of the Federal Reserve System"
2. A defined contribution plan: the "Thrift Plan for Employees of the Federal Reserve System"

Much like many other private employer-sponsored retirement plans, the Federal Reserve includes both a defined benefit plan and a defined contribution plan. Fortunately, administration for both is handled in the same office, unlike a federal employee who has a TSP and a FERS pension, where submission will be to the TSP Court Order Center and OPM, respectively.

Please do not confuse the "Thrift Plan for Employees of the Federal Reserve System" with the "Thrift Savings Plan." Our office has encountered situations where neither the attorney(s) representing the Federal Reserve employee nor the Federal Reserve employee him- or herself understood which plan he or she fell under. This caused a significant amount of unnecessary back and forth regarding proper steps that needed to be taken and the appropriate order(s) to be submitted.

12.12 Other Federal Plans

A few federal agencies—the Department of State, the Federal Reserve System, the Central Intelligence Agency, and National Security Agency—are not covered by the FERS/CSRS system but have their own retirement plans. Should you ever have a case involving such an employee, write to his or her agency for guidance on dividing their pension rights and acceptable forms for court orders dividing their pension plans.

Miscellaneous Plans: IRAs, Nonqualified Plans, State and Local Pension Plans, and QMCSOs

13

13.1 IRAs

Individual retirement accounts (IRAs) are simple to divide between divorcing spouses, though not to tap for child support. IRAs (and SEPs, or simplified employee plans, which are large IRAs sponsored and partially or wholly funded by an employer) are not subject to the Employee Retirement Income Security Act (ERISA) but do have a special divorce division mechanism provided by federal law. Under 26 U.S.C. § 408(d)(6) of the Internal Revenue Code, a simple written agreement between the parties or state court order, with no special formalities, is all that is needed to effect a tax-free transfer of an IRA. The only requirements of section 408(d)(6) are that the transfer be "incident to a divorce," and there must be a "written instrument" or state court order directing the transfer in effect before it takes place.

The "written instrument" may be (1) a decree of divorce or separate maintenance or a written instrument incident to such a decree, (2) a written separation agreement, or (3) a decree requiring a spouse to make payments for the support or maintenance of the other spouse or former spouse. 26 U.S.C. § 121(d)(3)(C). Surprisingly, a number of attorneys are unaware of the process required with an IRA and that it differs from a Qualified Domestic Relations Order (QDRO). As a result, some paragraphs addressing this division will call for a QDRO, only leading to confusion regarding the necessary steps, confusion regarding intent of the parties, and uncertainty regarding the nature of the account to be divided. Likewise, some attorneys are not certain of the type of retirement account and will use IRA language regarding a 401(k) or QDRO language regarding an IRA. As a practice point, to avoid unnecessary delays, ensure that the provisions related to the IRA transfer specifically state the proper information.

Transfers of property are considered "incident to a divorce" if they occur (1) not more than one year after the date on which the marriage ceases, or (2) if later, so long as the transfer is related to the cessation of the marriage. 26 C.F.R. § 1.1041–1T, Q&A 6. To be considered "related to the cessation of the marriage," the transfer must be made pursuant to a written instrument as defined in 26 U.S.C. § 121(d)(3)(C) and must occur within six years after the date the marriage ceases. Transfers more than six years after the cessation of the marriage are presumed not to be related to the cessation of the marriage, but this presumption may be overcome by appropriate evidence. 26 C.F.R. § 1.1041–1T, Q&A 7. As a practice point, if you have a client dividing an IRA, to avoid any future complications, it is always better to handle these matters sooner rather than later. The vast majority of major financial institutions will have the forms necessary to complete this transfer, along with instructions on the company website.

Compared to the formalities required under ERISA or to divide a military or federal civil service pension, these requirements are easy to meet. A simple paragraph in a court order directing the division of one spouse's IRA is sufficient if the transfer is made reasonably promptly. The distribution may be taken directly by the other spouse, in which case it will be taxable income in the year received. Alternatively, it may be rolled over into an IRA, or paid directly into an IRA in the spouse's name, within 60 days, in which case there will be no immediate tax payable by either party. 26 U.S.C. §§ 402(a)(5)(A)–(C); *Hawkins v. Comm'r,* 86 F.3d 982 (10th Cir. 1996). *See Czepiel v. Comm'r,* T.C. Memo 1999-289 (Tax Ct. 1999) (husband taxable on receipt of funds he withdrew from his

IRA to make payment ordered by state court to compensate wife for division of other marital property as state court order did not direct division or transfer of IRA; husband's claim that withdrawal was involuntary, as he was compelled to do so by state court order due to lack of other assets, does not affect taxable nature of withdrawal under Internal Revenue Code; whether withdrawal is voluntary or involuntary is irrelevant for federal income tax purposes).

The most difficult feature of dividing IRAs is that section 408(d)(6) speaks of the "transfer" of an IRA, not its "division." The correct approach when a partial transfer is desired is first to divide the transferor's IRA into two new IRAs (a tax-free transaction), funding the second IRA with the amount to be transferred to the other spouse. The second IRA may then be transferred in its entirety to the other spouse under section 408(d)(6). We recommend this approach, as most financial institutions will not transfer an IRA or portion of an IRA to an account at another institution in another party's name. By way of example, if husband is ordered to transfer 50 percent of his IRA with Fidelity to wife, and wife wants to roll her portion of husband's IRA into her IRA with Vanguard, the parties can effect the transfer in one of two ways. The first way is that the husband can set up an IRA with Vanguard, transfer 50 percent of his IRA into his Vanguard IRA, and then transfer that IRA to the wife's IRA. Alternatively, the wife can set up an IRA with Fidelity, the husband can transfer 50 percent of his IRA into the wife's Fidelity IRA, and then the wife can transfer her Fidelity IRA to her Vanguard IRA. It is important to contemplate these mechanics with the parties because it can head off post-divorce litigation.

It is a mistake simply to fill out the IRA custodian's standard paperwork for transfer of an IRA, which often does not deal adequately with this point. A properly drafted transfer incident to a divorce clause will also include provisions allocating each party a fair share of the tax basis of the assets transferred, spelling out the intended tax consequences of the transfer, obligating each party to turn over payments received in error, a suitable retention of jurisdiction provision, and similar clauses from the Model QDRO provisions set forth in section 8.5 of this book.

13.2 Nonqualified Plans

Many companies have adopted benefit plans that are not "qualified" for the tax benefits provided by the Internal Revenue Code for their senior executives. These plans are usually supplements to, rather than substitutes for, the company's qualified plans that cover all employees. They are adopted because the Internal Revenue Code imposes significant restrictions on the benefits payable to "highly compensated" individuals and imposes significant penalties on "top heavy" plans. In light of these restrictions, many companies choose to provide the limited benefits acceptable under the Internal Revenue Code to their entire workforce through a qualified plan (and enjoy the tax advantage of being able to deduct the entire amount of the contributions made to that plan). Such companies then go on to pay a small group of senior executives' benefits under a nonqualified plan, which provides none of the tax advantages for either the employer or the employee available under a qualified plan. *See Guzy v. Ameritech Corp.*, 1999 U.S. Dist. LEXIS 8943 (E.D. Mich. 1999) (holding that QDRO applied to both qualified plan and nonqualified "Supplemental Plan"). Even without the tax benefits offered by the Internal Revenue Code, such plans may be a significant asset or source of revenue to be divided in a divorce or tapped for child support in a support action. They are commonly known as "excess benefit plans," "top hat plans," "golden handcuffs," or "golden handshakes." *See* Allen, Melone, Rosenbloom, & VanDerhei, *Pension Planning*, ch. 19 (8th ed. 1997), for a good general discussion of nonqualified plans.

If you are representing the spouse or child of a senior executive, investigate the possible existence of such plans. You can divide them as marital property, use them as a source of alimony, or tap them for child support through either a QDRO or a comparable state court order. Even though such plans are not "qualified" for the favorable tax treatment under the Internal Revenue Code, they are still usually subject to the reporting and regulatory provisions of ERISA and may be divided by a QDRO (see Chapter 2).

How can you tell whether a plan is ERISA qualified? The plan itself will tell you what it thinks its status is—but that may not be the end of the story. Being subject to ERISA is not a matter of voluntary election by the plan. ERISA regulates any plan that "provides retirement income to employees, or results in a deferral of income by employees for periods extending to the termination of covered employment or beyond." 29 U.S.C. § 1002(2)(A). There are only a very few specific and narrow statutory exemptions for "excess benefit plans that are unfunded." 29 U.S.C. §§ 1003(b)(5), 1002(36), and 1051(2). The burden of proof that a plan is exempt from ERISA (and thus does not need to honor a QDRO) seems to be on the plan. *Healy v. Rich Products,* 981 F.2d 68 (2d Cir. 1992); *Bass v. Mid America Co., Inc.,* 1995 U.S. Dist. LEXIS 15719 (N.D. Ill. 1995) (plan subject to ERISA and must honor QDRO despite claim of exemption by plan).

In practice, this means that if you encounter a plan that "provides retirement income . . . or results in a deferral of income" and refuses to accept a QDRO on the grounds that it is not subject to ERISA, the claim of exemption need not be accepted at face value. Litigation may be necessary if the lawyer for one or both of the parties and the plan reach an impasse on this issue. However, most plans, even if they are not qualified plans under ERISA, will honor a QDRO and divide the plan incident to divorce so long as the plan rules allow for such division. Thus, it is critical when one of the parties has a plan that is not readily identifiable, such as a 401(k), to request the plan rules to ascertain whether the plan is qualified and, whether it is or not, the plan administrator will accept a QDRO incident to a divorce.

13.3 State and Local Government Pension Plans

More than 16 million Americans participate in about 2,500 separate state, county, municipal, and local government pension plans. In contrast to ERISA plans and military and federal civil service plans, there are no uniform requirements for administration, funding, or disclosure in such state and local government plans. Allen et al., *Pension Planning* (8th ed. 1997), Appendix 3 at 504. Many of these plans simply do not have any procedure comparable to QDROs that could allow direct payments to the nonemployee spouse in a divorce (*Erb v. Erb,* 661 N.E.2d 175 (Ohio 1996)), even though state law might recognize the pension as a marital asset, and even though the plan might be joined as a party in the divorce proceeding. *Erb,* above; *Hoyt v. Hoyt,* 559 N.E.2d 1292 (Ohio 1990). Other states provide special statutory procedures for dividing state and local government pensions in divorce or for collecting alimony or child support from them. *See Smith v. South Carolina Retirement System,* 1999 S.C. App. LEXIS 116 (S.C. Ct. App. 1999) and S.C. Code § 9-18-20; *Woods v. Woods,* 1999 Tex. App. LEXIS 7538 (Tex. Ct. App. 1999); *Long v. Long,* 1999 Va. App. LEXIS 566 (Va. Ct. App. 1999). Some plans like this are not divisible in any capacity under state or local law. For example, in Georgia the Teachers

Retirement System is not a divisible plan. This oftentimes requires an offsetting of other assets to account for the value of this asset as previously addressed.

Each state and local government retirement plan must be dealt with in accordance with its own unique procedures. If the plan provides no mechanism comparable to a QDRO for separating the parties' interests in the pension, it may still be effectively divided between them by the "offset" method, or jurisdiction may be reserved to follow the "if, as, and when" approach used in the private pension field before the enactment of the Retirement Equity Act in 1984. See Chapter 5; *Krafick v. Krafick*, 663 A.2d 365 (Conn. 1995); *Jerry L. C. v. Lucille H. C.*, 448 A.2d 223 (Del. 1982); *Fastner v. Fastner*, 427 N.W.2d 691 (Minn. Ct. App. 1988); *Workman v. Workman*, 418 S.E.2d 269 (N.C. Ct. App. 1992). As discussed with nonqualified plans earlier, it is important here as well to get the plan rules for such local or state plans to know whether the plan can be divided and whether the plan will accept a QDRO-like order. In some cases, there are not plan rules but rather the state or local statute defines the benefit and whether it can be divided.

If a QDRO-like order is not available for a state or local plan, it does not mean your nonemployee client is without a remedy. While direct payment under a QDRO-like order is usually the best possible remedy, alternative remedies include placing a present value on the Participant's rights and awarding the Alternate Payee an offsetting share of other marital assets or ordering the Participant to directly pay a share of his or her pension payments if, as, and when received to the Alternate Payee as permanently nonmodifiable alimony that will not terminate on the remarriage or cohabitation of the Alternate Payee (see section 7.2). Payment of this obligation as alimony ensures that the tax consequences of the payment will be identical to those under a QDRO for both the Participant and the Alternate Payee.

13.4 Qualified Medical Child Support Orders

Although technically part of ERISA, these orders are not addressed to pension or other financial benefits but rather to continuing to provide health care coverage for the children of persons who are covered by group health plans.

Qualified Medical Child Support Orders (QMCSOs) were created by an amendment to ERISA in 1993 and are covered by

29 U.S.C. § 1169. The terms and procedures covering QMCSOs are quite similar to those covering QDROs in 29 U.S.C. §§ 1055 and 1056, as described in detail in earlier chapters. However, there are material differences between QDROs and QMCSOs, which are discussed in this section.

QMCSOs deal with "group health plans," not pension plans. An important factor to keep in mind when handling QMCSOs is that the only eligible beneficiary or recipient of this order is the child of the Participant in the group health plan, known as the "Alternate Recipient." Spouses and former spouses are not eligible to apply for benefits; 29 U.S.C. §§ 1169(a)(2)(C), (D). There is no restriction on the age of the child of the Participant for coverage under the statute, except that an adopted child or a child placed with the Participant for adoption must be under 18 at the time of adoption or placement for adoption in order to be an Alternate Recipient. 29 U.S.C. §§ 1169(c)(3)(A), (B). Given the allowable timeframe for medical coverage, and depending on what the parties can agree to, be mindful of duration provisions included in the order.

A Medical Child Support Order (MCSO), like a Domestic Relations Order (DRO), is an order of a state court (or state administrative agency with the power to enter child support orders) that (1) provides for health care coverage for a child of a Participant, (2) is made pursuant to a state domestic relations law (including a community property law), and (3) relates to benefits provided by a group health plan. 29 U.S.C. § 1169(a)(2)(B).

A QMCSO is an MCSO that, like a QDRO, "clearly specifies" the following:

- The names and addresses of the Participant and the Alternate Recipient (or IV-D agency);
- A reasonable description of the type of coverage to be provided to the Alternate Recipient; and
- The period of time to which the MCSO applies. 29 U.S.C. §§ 1169(a)(3)(A)–(C).

Just like a QDRO, a QMCSO may not require the group health plan to provide any type or form of benefit, or any option, not otherwise provided under the plan. 29 U.S.C. § 1169(a)(4). However, it may override certain plan provisions to conform with the requirement of 42 U.S.C. § 1396g-1 concerning coverage of illegitimate children, coverage for children not residing with the Participant or not residing in the Participant's state, and coverage for children not claimed as a dependent on the Participant's federal income tax return. 42 U.S.C. § 1396g-1(a)(1).

Group health plans are required to adopt reasonable written procedures for determining whether an MCSO is a QMCSO (29 U.S.C. § 1169(a)(5)), and to process MCSOs in a fashion similar to that specified for QDROs (29 U.S.C. § 1169(a)(5)), including providing notice of receipt of an MCSO to all interested parties. A National Medical Support Notice issued under section 401(b) of the Child Support Performance and Incentive Act of 1998 (42 U.S.C. § 651) is automatically a QMCSO as long as it meets the requirements of identifying the Alternate Recipient, Participant, plan, and period of coverage and does not require any type or form of benefit, or any option, not otherwise provided under the plan. 29 U.S.C. § 169(a)(5)(C). Recent federal legislation will require medical plans to accept QMCSOs submitted by state IV-D agencies on a standardized national form (when "appropriately completed"; that is, filled in with the names, addresses, and Social Security numbers of the Participant and Alternate Recipient, and identifying information about the employer and the scope of medical coverage awarded by the court). These standardized national forms will be promulgated jointly by the Departments of Labor and Health and Human Services. Although not expressly authorized for use by private parties, this form, when promulgated, should serve as a good model for private orders.

13.5 Model QMCSO

This form generally follows the form of the model DRO in section 8.5. No detailed comments have been provided here because they would generally reproduce the comments to the corresponding clauses found in section 8.5, which should be referred to as necessary.

[Normal State Court Caption]

Order

This order is entered this ___ day of ___, 20__ [after a hearing] [by stipulation of the parties]. This order is intended to be a Qualified Medical Child Support Order ("QMCSO") as that term is used in ERISA, 29 U.S.C. § 1169.

1. *Parties.* The names and last known mailing addresses of the parties are:

A. *Participant:* John C. Burns; 123 Broad Street, Augusta, GA 30010; Social Security Number XXX-XX-6789; Year of Birth: 1970. (Complete SSN and DOB provided under separate cover not filed with the Court.)

B. *Alternate Recipient:* Alyssa S. Burns; 456 Peachtree Lane, Augusta, GA 30911; Social Security Number XXX-XX-9999.

COMMENT: For a QMCSO, the Alternate Recipient must be a child of the Participant. Former spouses are not eligible.

2. *Domestic Relations Law.* This order is entered pursuant to the domestic relations laws of the State of ____, in particular [State] Code Section _____, to provide medical child support with respect to the Alternate Recipient and provide health benefit coverage to the Alternate Recipient and relates to the provision of benefits under such a plan.

3. *Relationship of Alternate Recipient to Participant.* The Alternate Recipient is the child of the Participant. The Alternate Recipient was born in 20___. (Make sure to be mindful of state law with identifying personal information. You can always include any personal information including dates of birth and Social Security numbers in the correspondence to the plan when submitting for processing.)

4. *Plan Name.* This order applies to the Global MegaCorp Employee Major Medical & Dental Coverage Plan and any amended, successor, substitute, or replacement plan that subsequently takes the place of that plan. The address of the plan is 222 West Corporate Drive, Santa Barbara, California 99099.

5. *Coverage.* The Alternate Recipient shall be entitled to receive the following coverage provided by the plan:

A. "Major medical and dental Option A, deductible $500" as set forth in the description of the plan; or

B. The maximum coverage available under the plan with the minimum deductible available under the plan.

The plan shall notify the Alternate Recipient and the Representative of any amendment or modification to the plan, or any termination or merger of the plan, that would result in this coverage becoming unavailable to the Alternate Recipient and shall allow the Alternate Recipient a reasonable period in which to make a new election of coverage at that time.

6. *Duration of Coverage.* The Alternate Recipient shall receive coverage pursuant to this order as soon as the plan accepts this order as a QMCSO. Coverage of the Alternate Recipients shall continue until the first to occur of (a) the death of the Participant, or (b) the following events in the life of the Alternate Payee: (i) reaching her eighteenth birthday (or if, on her eighteenth birthday, she is enrolled in high school and likely to graduate, then on the earlier of (A) her nineteenth birthday or (B) her graduation from high school), (ii) dying, (iii) marrying, (iv) enlisting in the armed forces, (v) being otherwise emancipated, or (vi) being placed in the permanent custody of the Participant, whichever shall first occur. The plan shall not be considered to have received notice of the occurrence of any of these events, and shall continue to make payments under this order, until the state court that entered the original QMCSO [or another court of competent jurisdiction] [or the IV-D agency identified in clause 8 below] sends a further order or official notice to the plan stating that such a terminating event has occurred and that the plan may cease making coverage available under this order [or receipt by the plan of a certified official death or marriage certificate]. [It is important to adjust this paragraph according to state law, or the agreement of the parties.]

7. *Effect of Order.* This order shall not be construed or interpreted to require the plan to provide any type or form of benefit or coverage, or any option, not otherwise provided under the plan. . . .

OPTIONAL ADDITIONAL CLAUSE

7A. . . . and in the event of any conflict between this clause and any other clause of this order, the provisions of this clause shall prevail.

8. *Role of IV-D Agency.* The payments to be made for the medical expenses for the Alternate Recipient hereunder shall be made to the "Division of Child Support Enforcement," and mailed to P.O. Box 5340, Augusta, GA 39099, as the entity designated by law to receive and disburse such payments for the Alternate Recipient pursuant to [state or federal law citation]. The Division of Child Support Enforcement is also designated as the Representative of the Alternate Recipient pursuant to section 1169(a)(5)(B)(iii) of

ERISA to receive copies of all notices sent to the Alternate Recipient during the qualification of this order as a QMCSO.

9. *Participant Not to Interfere with Alternate Recipient's Rights.* The Participant is hereby ordered not to do, or fail to do, any act, or to make any choice or election, or by inaction fail to make any choice or election under the plan, that would interfere in any way with the payment to the Alternate Recipient of the share of his plan benefits assigned to the Alternate Recipient by this order.

10. *Reservation of Jurisdiction.*

A. This court reserves jurisdiction to amend or modify the provisions of this order in light of comments received from (1) the plan, (2) a court of competent jurisdiction, or (3) any other organization or party, during the process of deciding whether this order is a Qualified Medical Child Support Order.

B. This court also reserves jurisdiction to amend or modify the provisions of this order, even after it has been determined to be a Qualified Medical Child Support Order by the plan, to terminate or suspend coverage of the Alternate Recipient as a result of attainment of a certain age, emancipation, change of custody, or other events justifying a change in payments, or to modify this order (subject to clause 7) to deal with any unforeseen tax consequences or other effects of this order.

SO ORDERED:

____

Judge

COMMENT: Under ERISA, only an order may be an MCSO or a QMCSO. A state agency authorized to issue child support orders may also issue an MCSO.

[Signature of counsel for Participant and IV-D agency]

[Signature of Participant]

14 QDROs: From Headache to Profit Center for Your Law Practice

14.1 Introduction

Many lawyers in private practice have come to regard Qualified Domestic Relations Orders (QDROs) as something out of a horror movie that should be avoided at all costs or a nagging headache that lingers on long after a case should have been closed and a constant source of friction and frustration about uncertainty, delay, and expense for their clients. It doesn't have to be that way. This chapter offers some practical tips and techniques for managing the QDRO aspects of a private law practice. These techniques will help you streamline and systematize your QDRO practice whether you are a solo practitioner or a member of a large firm. The ideas in this chapter will help you put the substantive law and model clauses presented earlier in this handbook to practical use in your daily practice. QDROs can, and should, be a source of additional revenues for your domestic relations practice and a source of client satisfaction, repeat business, and referrals, not malpractice litigation.

14.2 Know the Law

There's no substitute and no shortcut. You can't serve your clients well unless you know the law. Fortunately, you will rarely (if ever) need to use any source other than this handbook and your own knowledge of state divorce law.

I recommend that the first time you use this handbook, you read it from cover to cover, even the parts that you think don't apply to you. This will give you a broad overview of the law of QDROs and how that law works in practice. (For example, read the next chapter addressed to Plan Administrators and their lawyers in order to understand their needs and concerns. You'll gain a better understanding of how to deal with them in your next case.) Subsequently, you can use this handbook as a reference work, rereading those portions that apply to the QDRO that you are working on at the time.

If your practice involves a significant amount of QDRO work, attend Continuing Legal Education seminars on the subject. Join the Family Law Sections of the American Bar Association and your state and local bar associations to make sure that your knowledge is always current. Knowing what the law was five years ago is not much use.

14.3 Make Sure Your Clients Participate in All QDRO Decisions

Your clients are the ones who are going to have to live with the consequences of an erroneous or poorly drafted QDRO. An essential element of ensuring client satisfaction is educating your clients and making sure they feel in control of the major decisions made in the course of litigation or negotiation. You need to know the substantive law of QDROs and the payment options and other provisions of the plan in each case well enough to discuss the realistic alternatives with all of your clients, to answer any questions they may have about QDROs, and to help them make intelligent choices. It is important that these conversations occur early and often. Don't wait until after the settlement agreement is signed to discuss what a QDRO is with your client and what that means for him or her. Review all the factors in Chapter 7 with your clients and come up with a mutually agreed-upon set of goals.

It's vitally important that you *document these discussions and decisions in writing*. Part B of the Client Questionnaire in Appendix I calls for the client to express, in writing, his or her desired arrangement concerning the form and timing of receipt of benefits from the opposing spouse's pension. While the discussions are important regarding a defined contribution plan, they are less critical as there are fewer decisions to make; that is, there is no survivor annuity associated with a defined contribution plan. You should also discuss these issues with each client until you are sure that the client understands and feels comfortable with pursuing the strategy you both select. The best practice is to dictate a short letter or email to the client, reviewing the discussion you had on QDROs and tactics, as soon as possible after the client leaves your office. Send it to the client promptly, and ask him or her to countersign a copy and return it to you (or, in the case of an email, respond acknowledging that he or she understands and concurs). The few minutes it will take you to draft and send this letter are insignificant compared to the time, effort, expense, and loss of reputation involved in even one malpractice suit or complaint to the bar association that you "didn't get me what I wanted." When you draft the QDRO, have the client sign the QDRO itself as an added protection from such claims.

14.4 Keep Your Clients Informed

In private practice, there is one ironclad rule.

That ironclad rule is to keep your clients informed through the duration of the case. Tell the client what to expect from the beginning of the case and each step of the way. My clients got a copy of every piece of paper that came into or went out of my law practice that was related to the client's case. Pleadings, letters, documents received from the plan, experts' reports, discovery requests and responses, transcripts of depositions and hearings, court orders—everything. If you or your staff send out copies as a matter of course, no client will ever be able to claim that you didn't keep him or her informed about what was happening in his or her case. One of the most common complaints clients have about their lawyers is that they feel they do not know what is going on in their case. Clients appreciate being kept informed in this way and feel more in control—a key ingredient of client satisfaction.

Some clients make excellent amateur paralegals and will pore over every document you send them, often coming up with helpful ideas and evidence. Always listen to their ideas and encourage their active participation in their own cases.

Clients who are kept well informed about the progress of their case tend to be happier with your representation. They are less skeptical of hourly bills when they regularly see the tangible results of the time you spent on their case. Well-informed clients will send you lots of referrals; clients who feel they are being kept in the dark will complain to the bar association or sue you for malpractice.

14.5 Draft the DRO as Early as Possible, and Ask the Plan to Review It Early

Review Chapters 8 and 10 to familiarize yourself with the serious problems that arise if the Domestic Relations Order (DRO) is not drafted until late in the state court proceedings.

Many lawyers put off drafting the DRO until after the property division hearing or final settlement. In fact, many attorneys not only put off drafting the DRO until after settlement but also send it out to another attorney (this might be you) to interpret their agreed-upon language in the settlement agreement and draft and submit the DRO. Waiting until after final settlement or the final hearing is the wrong approach. If you represent the Alternate Payee, the correct approach is to draft the DRO as soon as possible. Leave the amount or percentage blank if necessary, but draft everything else. Ask the plan for an informal review of your draft DRO. You can usually do this before the trial judge or opposing counsel sees your work, but in some circumstances you might want to keep them involved at this early stage. Do this as many times as necessary until the plan gives tentative approval to your draft.

If you do this, you will be sure that you walk into the property division hearing or settlement conference ready to deal with all the issues that arise in QDROs, and that the DRO won't somehow "slip through the cracks" after the hearing or settlement and never get approved as a QDRO.

If you are an attorney who does not do your own QDROs, then involve the attorney that will be drafting the DRO early in the process. The DRO drafting attorney can give you settlement agreement language or language for the judge regarding the division of the retirement account. Further, the drafting attorney can submit a draft of the DRO to the plan for preapproval. We have had many cases where we were contacted by a party (not the attorney) post-divorce to draft the DRO, and the settlement agreement language was ambiguous, leading to further litigation to clarify the intent of the parties regarding the division of a retirement asset.

14.6 Come to Court Prepared

Get your draft DRO approved by the plan, as recommended in section 14.5. If you can, you should also get it "approved as to form" by opposing counsel. Bring it to court with as few blank spaces as possible; ideally, only the final amount should be left blank.

Why is it so important to do this? At trial, everyone—you, opposing counsel, both parties, and the trial judge—is focused on whether your client will get 40 percent, 50 percent, or 60 percent of the Participant's benefits. In the process, other important QDRO issues are often forgotten or neglected. Will the DRO use the Shared Interest or the Separate Interest Approach? Will the Alternate Payee receive a Qualified Preretirement Survivor Annuity? Is the starting date for the Alternate Payee's payments to be fixed in the DRO or elected by her later? Are Contingent Alternate Payees permitted? What happens to the Alternate Payee's share of plan benefits if she dies before receiving all of them? What is the intended tax effect of the DRO?

What frequently happens is that the trial court simply specifies a percentage and directs counsel to draft a DRO reflecting this. Counsel, or the parties, then either move on to other cases or get bogged down in arguing about these issues. This often results in at least one more hearing being required to resolve a case everyone thought was finished. It also results in collateral litigation over conflicts between the divorce decree and the DRO prepared in its aftermath. *See Fortmann v. Avon Products, Inc.*, 1999 U.S. Dist. LEXIS 3451 (N.D. Ill. 1999) (property settlement agreement approved by state court divided all pension benefits payable at retirement; DRO divided all benefits "as of" the date of the DRO, ten years before retirement); *Carpenter v. Carpenter*, 1996 Tex. App. LEXIS 3210 (Tex. Ct. App. 1996) (DROs amended three times and litigated for three years on issue of which plans were intended to be covered by them); *Holloman v. Holloman*, 691 So. 2d 897 (Miss. 1996); *Roth v. Roth*, 506 N.W.2d 900 (Mich. Ct. App. 1993) (trial court's order must expressly mention survivorship benefits for them to be included in DRO); *Wilson v. Wilson*, 492 S.E.2d 495 (Va. Ct. App. 1997).

The better practice, and the way to avoid all of these problems, is to come to court with a draft DRO covering all of these issues. You will blow the opposition away, impress your client, and get the task completely finished in one hearing. The dialogue might go something like this:

THE COURT: All right, it is my decision that Mrs. Brooks will receive 40 percent of the marital part of Mr. Brooks' pension rights, this decision to be implemented by a QDRO to be presented at a later date. . . . Let's see, is 60 days enough time for counsel to prepare and submit one?

COUNSEL FOR PARTICIPANT: All right, Your Honor.

COUNSEL FOR ALTERNATE PAYEE: Just a moment, Judge. If the Court pleases, there's no need for any delay at all. I hand the Court and opposing counsel a draft of the DRO. I have just filled in by hand the one blank space in it, so that it now shows 40 percent going to Mrs. Brooks as Your Honor just ordered. And here's a letter from the Plan Administrator saying that a QDRO in this form is acceptable to the plan, showing any amount between zero and 100 percent going to my client, and will be qualified by the plan. There's no need to delay; the Court can sign the order right now.

THE COURT: Any objections?

COUNSEL FOR PARTICIPANT: Er . . .

Some state courts have rules requiring that draft DROs be submitted before the final hearing. This can be a mutually agreed-upon form submitted by stipulation (perhaps with some final amounts left blank, as in the previous example); or, if the parties are very far apart on several QDRO issues, each party will be required to submit a proposed DRO well in advance of the hearing. This enables the trial judge to note the QDRO issues that must be resolved. It also forces the parties to come to the hearing fully prepared to deal with all aspects of the pension plan division. If your state does not have such a blanket requirement, ask the trial judge to enter an order requiring this procedure in every one of your QDRO cases.

14.7 Charge by the Hour, or Outsource Your QDRO Work

QDROs can be difficult and time consuming to prepare and qualify. To do the job properly, you have to identify all plans from which your client and the opposing party may be entitled to receive a benefit; obtain the relevant plan documents and information; read and analyze them; discuss the alternative methods of dividing plan benefits with your client; draft a DRO reflecting the client's goals; present it to the court; arrange for expert testimony in some cases; correspond with the plan; and revise the DRO as necessary until it is accepted as a QDRO. Charging a flat fee for this work just doesn't make sense.

If you are charging a flat fee for "routine" divorce or child support cases, you are going to be tempted to shortcut the QDRO process if it drags on for too long and to turn your attention to newer and more profitable cases. If you charge a flat fee, following through to make sure the DRO has been accepted by the plan (see Chapter 9) may take a lot of time for which you will not earn any extra fee.

Flat fees in QDRO cases are a sure recipe for trouble. It is impossible to estimate how long it will take in any particular case to draft and qualify a DRO, so charging a flat fee for QDRO work means that in any given case you will be charging the client either far too much or far too little for your professional services. Even if you normally charge a flat fee for uncontested divorces or child support hearings, I strongly recommend that you charge by the hour for your QDRO work. This ensures that you will have a proper financial incentive to do the job properly.

Many lawyers in private practice prefer to outsource their QDRO work by turning it over to a QDRO consultant or expert. If you are considering outsourcing some or all of your QDRO work, find a good consulting firm to work with you either on a confidential basis with no direct contact with your clients, or on a "turnkey" basis in which the consulting firm deals directly with your clients and does all the QDRO work. Under either arrangement, you may bill the consultant's fees through to your client as a disbursement. You should supervise and evaluate every consultant's work as necessary, and you can charge your clients for the time you spend working with the consultant or reviewing the consultant's work.

14.8 Working with a QDRO Expert

QDROs are the bane of many divorce lawyers' existence. They require an understanding of two completely separate and often conflicting sets of laws: matrimonial law on property division, alimony, and child support; and the federal and state laws affecting pensions, including the Employee Retirement Income Security Act (ERISA) and the comparable laws governing military retired pay (the Uniformed Services Former Spouses' Protection Act) and federal employee retirement systems. ERISA and other pension laws are full of arcane jargon, complex language, and pitfalls for family law attorneys. In coping with these difficulties, a QDRO expert can be an extremely valuable member of your team.

This section covers three important matters:

1. The scope of assistance you should expect from a QDRO expert and the unique role he or she can play whether your case is litigated or settled.
2. The more than 50 substantive QDRO issues that arise in divorce cases and how a QDRO expert can help you deal with them.
3. Finally, why in most cases only a lawyer, not an actuary or accountant, is properly qualified to serve as a QDRO expert.

A. The Unique Role of the QDRO Expert

Like experts in other fields, a QDRO expert can assist you in pretrial discovery on such issues as the nature and extent of the opposing party's employee benefits, pension plan features (including when payment will become available), survivorship rights, and a host of similar issues. Knowing the extent of each party's employee benefits and when and how they can be divided is an essential component of your legal services in any divorce case. The QDRO expert can also assist you by analyzing and commenting on reports prepared by any QDRO experts retained by the other side. You should retain your QDRO expert as early in the case as possible to assist you in understanding the retirement plans revealed in discovery and in your settlement and litigation strategies. You may find that you do not need a QDRO expert in a defined contribution plan, but we recommend that for defined benefit plans (or pensions), you at least consult with a QDRO expert.

Unlike experts in other fields, whose services are usually terminated as soon as a case is settled, even when cases are settled, QDROs must be drafted to implement the agreed division of the parties' pensions. A skilled QDRO expert can transform the provisions of your separation agreement into a QDRO that will be accepted by the plan as well as accurately implement the provisions of your agreement and, where the agreement is silent or ambiguous, draft the QDRO in the manner most favorable to your client. Unlike experts in other areas, whose services will no longer be needed if the case is settled, the QDRO expert is likely to continue to be involved in the case to assist you in drafting a proper QDRO that accurately reflects the terms of the agreed settlement.

B. Substantive QDRO Issues Requiring Expert Analysis

When cases are litigated, you may need a QDRO expert to testify to the many issues that arise in pension division cases—and there are more than 50 of them! These issues are listed next, broken down by categories of plans.

1. General Pension Issues

(A) Advantages and drawbacks of the use of a QDRO or comparable order versus present valuation calculation and immediate offset award method, including allocation of risk of nonsurvival

(B) Nature and extent of pensions and employee benefits in the case

(C) Availability and cost of survivor benefits

(D) Effect of QDRO award to former spouse Alternate Payee on rights and financial position of current or future spouse of Participant

(E) Personal obligation of the Participant to pay the Alternate Payee's assigned share of benefits to the Alternate Payee during the qualification process or if plan makes erroneous payments

(F) Consistency and correlation of QDRO provisions with the express provisions of the underlying separation agreement or divorce decree

(G) Propriety of QDRO clauses addressing issues not expressly addressed in the underlying separation agreement or divorce decree

(H) Why the terms and conditions of your proposed QDRO are superior to the other side's proposed QDRO

(I) Tax aspects of QDRO division

(J) Use of QDRO to collect alimony or child support in addition to QDROs for property division

(K) Legal malpractice in failure to draft or present QDRO to plan or errors in QDRO language

2. ERISA (Corporate) Defined Contribution Plans

(A) Division of vested and unvested benefits

(B) Division by dollar amount or percentage

(C) Adjustment of Alternate Payee's assigned benefit for investment experience (interest, dividends, gains and losses) from the date of division (i.e., separation or divorce) to the date of payment by the plan of the award to the Alternate Payee

(D) Treatment of employee loans secured by Participant's account balance in dividing the plan account

(E) Inclusion or exclusion of pro rata share of year-end employer contribution

(F) Allocation of tax basis between the parties

(G) Ability of the Alternate Payee to take a cash distribution and the tax impact thereof

3. ERISA (Corporate) Defined Benefit Plans

(A) Allocation of nonmarital benefits to Participant by either division of entire accrued benefit at date of separation or divorce or use of the coverture fraction method; pros and cons of each approach

(B) Commencement of payments to Alternate Payee before Participant's retirement

(C) Termination of Alternate Payee's payments on Participant's death or Alternate Payee's death

(D) Survivor benefits for Alternate Payee in the event Participant predeceases Alternate Payee

(E) Reversion of Alternate Payee's award to Participant if Alternate Payee predeceases Participant

(F) Effect of plan insolvency and Pension Benefit Guaranty Corporation takeover of plan on the rights of each party

(G) Division of early retirement subsidy between parties

(H) Existence and division of "nonqualified" plans

(I) Shared interest division versus separate interest division

4. Military Retired Pay

(A) Special federal jurisdictional issues (ten-year marriage overlap with creditable service, jurisdiction of state divorce court)

(B) Broad and narrow definitions of "disposable retired pay"

(C) Automatic reduction of former spouse's award if service member elects to receive disability payments

(D) Freezing rank and years of service at date of separation or divorce to determine disposable retired pay under the frozen benefit rule

(E) Survivor Benefit Plan (SBP)

- (i) Preclusion of award of SBP to current spouse if awarded to former spouse
- (ii) Cost and allocation of responsibility for payment of cost of SBP
- (iii) Termination of eligibility for SBP by remarriage of former spouse before age 55

(F) Allocation of postretirement cost-of-living adjustments (COLAs) between the parties

(G) Alternative methods of dividing military retired pay where marriage overlapped creditable military service by less than ten years

(H) Difference between active duty pensions and National Guard or reserve pensions

- (i) Time payments commence
- (ii) Calculation of marital and nonmarital shares by points, rather than years of creditable service

5. Federal Civil Service (FERS/CSRS) Plans

(A) Division of "self-only," "gross," or "net" annuity in Court Order Acceptable for Processing (COAP)

(B) Former Spouse Survivor Annuity (FSSA)

- (i) Cost and allocation of responsibility for payment of cost of FSSA
- (ii) Termination of eligibility for FSSA if former spouse remarries before age 55

(C) Barring or dividing refunds of employee contributions

(D) If former spouse predeceases federal employee, do former spouse's payments revert to employee, or are they paid to employee's children?

(E) Allocation of postretirement cost-of-living adjustments (COLAs) between the parties

(F) FERS/CSRS presumptions and standard interpretation of certain COAP terminology

6. Thrift Savings Plans (TSPs)

(A) Division of vested and unvested benefits

(B) Division by dollar amount or percentage

(C) Adjustment of former spouse's assigned benefit for investment experience (interest, dividends, gains and losses) from the date of division (i.e., separation or divorce) to the date of payment by the TSP of the award to the former spouse

(D) Treatment of employee loans secured by Participant's account balance in dividing the plan account

(E) Allocation of tax basis between the parties

7. Railroad Retirement Act Benefits

(A) Division of non-Tier I benefits

(B) Phrasing the order to include or exclude postretirement COLAs on former spouse's award

(C) Eligibility of former spouse for divorced spouse survivor annuity, and termination of eligibility by remarriage

8. State, County, and Municipal Plans

(A) Are QDRO-like orders available for the plan under relevant state law? If not, what alternative division mechanisms are available?

(B) Particular features of the state, county, or municipal plan at issue

(C) Allocation of COLAs

(D) Effect of postretirement deferred receipt programs—known as deferred retirement option plans (DROPs)—or Teacher and Employee Retention Initiatives (TERI) programs on the rights of former spouse and the timing of receipt of his or her benefits

9. Other Pension and Retirement Plans

(A) Special plans for certain federal employees (Department of State, Central Intelligence Agency, National Security Agency, etc.)

(B) Multinational organizations' pension plans (i.e., United Nations, World Bank, International Monetary Fund, etc.)

(C) Foreign pensions, governmental and private

C. Lawyer, Accountant, or Actuary?

In most cases, an accountant or actuary is not a proper expert witness or consultant on QDROs. A common misconception in the QDRO field is that the expert you need to testify must be an accountant or actuary (an expert on numbers) rather than a fellow lawyer (an expert on the legal aspects of pensions and the drafting and interpretation of legal documents). Remember that a QDRO is a "Qualified Domestic Relations *Order*." As a court order, a QDRO is a sophisticated legal document that may be drafted or interpreted only by someone skilled and educated in the law and the drafting and interpretation of legal documents—in other words, a lawyer with experience in pension law. You wouldn't hire a CPA to draft a motion or retain an actuary to advise you on jurisdictional issues. Accountants and actuaries have mathematical skills and training that are useful in many contexts, but drafting or testifying about QDROs is not one of them.

There is only one situation in which you should consider retaining an accountant or actuary as an expert. If the employee is going to "cash out" the nonemployee spouse's interest in the employee's pension, you will need an accountant or actuary to testify as to the "present value" of the future pension rights. This is a fairly simple mathematical calculation, involving future monthly benefits to be paid by the plan, life expectancies of the parties, interest rates, and the expected retirement age. However, this method *does not involve the use of a QDRO*—since the nonemployee spouse's interest will be bought out by the employee, by definition no QDRO will be necessary. In this situation, an actuary is a more credible expert than an accountant. The main difference between an actuary and an accountant is that while both deal with financial issues, an actuary deals with the probability of the occurrence of certain future events, while accountants usually deal with the accurate recording of past financial transactions. Actuaries' skills and formal training thus lie in the realm of economics, statistics, probability, and other branches of mathematics.

An accountant or actuary may testify as to his or her estimate of the *present value* of a stream of future pension payments because that is a purely mathematical issue. In these circumstances, a QDRO is not required at all, but in most cases, the most valuable and qualified QDRO expert will be a lawyer. Since QDROs are legal documents, only a qualified lawyer may properly serve as a QDRO expert. Actuaries and accountants have no formal training in the law or in the drafting or interpretation of legal documents like QDROs. While actuaries may be involved in pension plan design and administration, the plan's significant legal documents—such as the text of the plan itself, the Summary Plan Description, the Written QDRO Procedures required by section 206(d)(3) of ERISA, and the plan's model QDROs—*are drafted and interpreted by employee benefits lawyers, not actuaries.* Actuaries themselves recognize that their role in the QDRO process is extremely limited and cannot take the place of a lawyer's expert testimony. Actuarial Standard of Practice No. 34 (September 1999), promulgated by the Actuarial Standards Board (the national professional association and regulatory body for actuaries), states:

> The actuary should be familiar with the rules regulating the practice of law in the jurisdiction where the actuary will be rendering the services and *should avoid the unauthorized practice of law. For example, normally it would be inappropriate for the actuary to advise a non-attorney whether a draft court order meets applicable procedural requirements to be a valid order in the jurisdiction.* It would, however, be appropriate for the actuary to advise whether . . . each party's benefit is definitely determinable from the order. . . . *The question of whether the proposed order meets the state's procedural requirements is a legal one and is beyond the qualifications of actuaries who are not also attorneys.* The actuary's opinion as to whether a DRO is a QDRO or satisfies such other requirements as may apply to the specific type of court order and retirement plan should clearly state the scope of such opinion. For example, if the opinion is limited to an examination of the technical content of the order and does not extend to the legal form of the order, the opinion should so state. *If the actuary's opinion is intended to cover both the technical content and the legal form of the order, the actuary should beware of possible unauthorized practice of law.* Sections 3.2.4 and 3.7.1 (emphasis added).

If you are ever confronted with an actuary as a "QDRO expert" retained by the other side, it's very effective to confront him or her with the language quoted here.

Actuaries and accountants who either draft QDROs or offer expert testimony on their drafting or interpretation violate the prohibition against the unauthorized practice of law. While the definition of "unauthorized practice of law" varies from state to state as noted in Rule 5.5 of the ABA's *Model Rules of Professional Conduct*, typical definitions include the following:

> The "practice of law" means the *preparation of a pleading or other document incident to an action* . . . on behalf of a client before a judge in court as well as a service rendered out of court, including the giving of advice or the rendering of any service requiring *the use of legal skill or knowledge, such as preparing* a will, contract, or *other instrument, the legal effect of which under the facts and conclusions involved must be carefully determined.* Texas Government Code, section 81.101(a) (emphasis added).

and

> [T]he practice of law includes preparing any document in any medium intended to *affect or secure legal rights for a specific person* or entity . . . preparing any document through any medium for filing in any court [as a QDRO must be], administrative agency or tribunal for a specific person or entity; or negotiating legal rights or responsibilities for a specific person or entity. Arizona Supreme Court Rule 31(a)2A.

Review the list of QDRO issues likely to arise in divorce cases set forth in section 14.8B. Almost all of them are issues of law concerning the proper drafting and interpretation of legal documents and court orders. Only an experienced pension lawyer can offer competent and credible testimony on the meaning and construction of legal documents, including court orders. Any actuary or accountant who purports to testify to the legal effect or interpretation of the language of a "Qualified Domestic Relations *Order*" is not qualified to do so. If opposing counsel tries to use an accountant or actuary as a QDRO expert on these issues, consider making a motion in limine to bar any testimony from that person due to his or her lack of proper qualifications.

In summary, retain your QDRO expert as early as possible to assist you with pretrial discovery and the negotiation or litigation of every family law case involving a pension plan. Make sure your QDRO expert is a qualified pension lawyer unless the only issue in the case is the present value of future pension payments, in which case the services of an accountant or actuary may be useful. Make sure your QDRO expert is prepared to testify about all the issues listed in this section and to assist you in drafting a QDRO at the conclusion of the case, whether it is settled or tried.

14.9 Follow Through, Follow Through, Follow Through!

It's not unusual to have to revise a DRO once or twice to get it qualified. Make sure that you or your office staff anticipates that this will happen, and structure your office procedures to *follow through* on every single DRO until it is accepted by the plan as a QDRO.

This is an easy task to delegate to a paralegal, administrative assistant, or secretary. Prepare a simple form letter reminding the plan that you have submitted a DRO and have not yet had a response from the plan. Designate someone in your office to be responsible for sending these letters to plan officials every 30 days until your DRO is qualified. If more than six months go by without some kind of action by the plan, you need to get personally involved in communications with the plan and perhaps draw the matter to the attention of the trial judge.

Don't give up. This is an area where persistence is essential. Eventually your persistence will pay off, and you will succeed in getting every one of your DROs qualified.

14.10 Review QDROs Every Three to Five Years

Plans are terminated; Participants and Alternate Payees remarry or die or win the lottery; goals and circumstances change.

Whenever you obtain a QDRO for a client, you should make a notation on the file to review it at least once every five years, and more frequently if circumstances warrant. Prepare a form letter to be sent to clients asking if they would like you to review the status of the QDRO to make sure no material changes have occurred and no problems have arisen. It's a good idea to confirm with the plan that it still has the approval of your QDRO on file and that the Participant hasn't made any changes in his Beneficiary designations or elected any retirement options that are contrary to the terms of the QDRO or the divorce decree. This work is separate from the original divorce or support proceeding and should be billed accordingly.

This procedure is critical with defined benefit plans where the benefits will be paid sometime in the future. This simple procedure helps to ensure that any necessary adjustments are made to old clients' QDROs. Your clients will be grateful that you remember their situation and have taken the time and trouble to contact them. This leads to increased client satisfaction, which helps you avoid malpractice and professional complaints and results in the pleasant prospect of repeat business and referrals. Experts in law practice marketing universally agree that it is easier and far less costly to get additional work from existing clients than it is to locate and secure new clients. Contacting your existing clients about old QDROs every few years is a graceful way to stay in touch and cross-market your practice's legal services.

QDROs: From Headache to Enhanced Employee Benefit for Plan Administrators and Their Lawyers

15

15.1 Write User-Friendly QDRO Procedures

The main objective of Qualified Domestic Relations Order (QDRO) Procedures is *to help lawyers and judges draft acceptable DROs with minimum difficulty.* Write your QDRO Procedures in a user-friendly fashion. Think about the audience that will read and use this document. You are not addressing the contents of the QDRO Procedures to a sophisticated audience of actuaries or a panel of Employee Retirement Income Security Act (ERISA) experts. You are addressing your words to divorce lawyers, state trial judges, your own employees, and their spouses. While the vast majority of these people dealing with the QDRO Procedures are well-versed in legalese and complicated procedural matters, many have had little to no contact with ERISA or QDRO issues. Your goal should be to explain to them—in simple, practical, and easily understandable terms—how to draft a DRO and get it approved by your office. Use language like that in your Summary Plan Description, which ERISA requires to be written "in a manner calculated to be understood by the average Participant." 29 U.S.C. § 1022(a).

Think of your QDRO Procedures as an instruction manual for your company's best-selling product. Your company wants customers to be able to read, use, and understand the directions so they will enjoy the product, buy more of it, and recommend it to their friends. You don't want to make your customers angry or frustrated by giving them an incomprehensible or overly technical user's manual. Or, think of your QDRO Procedures as a recipe to be followed by an amateur chef who has never prepared this particular dish before. You want that recipe to be clear and easy to follow so that it is prepared properly.

Write the QDRO Procedures in that spirit.

Your QDRO Procedures have to set certain legal standards, and the recommendations here are not an argument to water down those safeguards or jeopardize the ERISA-qualified status of your plan. But all legal standards for QDROs can be expressed in plain English and user-friendly language.

In drafting and implementing your QDRO Procedures, follow the Department of Labor requirements. These requirements are contained in the *EBSA Booklet*, the basic mandate of which, to Plan Administrators, is that their QDRO Procedures and their interaction with Participants, Alternate Payees, state IV-D agencies, lawyers, and state courts should be "friendly" rather than adversarial.

The provisions of the *EBSA Booklet* require Plan Administrators to design and administer their QDRO Procedures in the following manner:

1. Provide information about plans, plan benefits, and Participants' actual benefit entitlements as early as possible to Alternate Payees and their lawyers (Question 2-1).
2. Design your QDRO Procedures so that they do not "unduly inhibit or hamper" the process of obtaining qualification of a DRO or making payments under QDROs, so that such determinations and payments are made in a "timely, efficient and cost-effective manner" (Questions 2-4, 2-5, and 2-10).
3. Provide information in your QDRO Procedures concerning the plan and the benefits available under it; describe any time limits for making QDRO determinations; explain

what steps you will take to protect and preserve pension assets or benefits upon receipt of a DRO; and explain any internal appeal or review procedures for QDRO determinations (Question 2-5).

4. Don't charge a Participant or Alternate Payee a fee for determining whether a DRO is a QDRO (Question 2-6). *See* DOL Advisory Opinion 94-32A. This position was reversed, at least for defined contribution plans, by DOL Field Assistance Bulletin 2003-3 (May 19, 2003), which seems to allow the imposition of expenses that can be justified by their actual cost on the parties to a QDRO, but only for defined contribution plans. The right to impose such costs on the Participant and Alternate Payee must be disclosed in the text of the plan and the Summary Plan Description (DOL Regulation § 2520.102–3(l)). This change in position has resulted in the adoption of such fees by several Plan Administrators for defined contribution plans.
5. Provide model QDRO forms to the parties. However, you cannot refuse to qualify a DRO that otherwise meets the requirements of ERISA merely because it does not follow your preferred model DRO form (Question 2-7). Some plans, however, will charge additional "review" or "processing" fees when the submitted DRO does not specifically match the model form. This is a means of encouraging use of the model DRO form.
6. Do not inquire into matters of state law (such as personal and subject matter jurisdiction, service of process, and correct interpretation or application of state domestic relations law, whether the Alternate Payee is in fact the former spouse or child of the Participant) if a DRO is regular on its face (Question 2-8). *See also Blue v. UAL Corp.*, 160 F.3d 383 (7th Cir. 1998); *Fortmann v. Avon Products,* 1999 U.S. Dist. LEXIS 3451 (N.D. Ill. 1999). It isn't uncommon to have both the Participant and Alternate Payee initial each page and sign the final page, much like a Settlement Agreement, to avoid these issues coming up later.
7. Don't reject a DRO solely for failure to specify certain factual information that is readily available to you, such as the Participant's name and address (Question 2-9).

8. State in your QDRO Procedures that the 18-month escrow period described in subsection 2.3F(2) will remain in effect during any short periods during the qualification process after a DRO has been rejected but before an amended DRO has been resubmitted. Don't allow Participants to make immediate withdrawals of plan benefits during that amendment period (Question 2-12).

15.2 Take an Educational Approach, Not an Adversarial Approach

If a DRO isn't properly drafted the first time, the plan's main task is to help the parties get a properly drafted and conforming draft correct. Remember, one of the parties whose life is going to be affected by this document is often a valued employee of your company.

If you must reject a DRO, explain as clearly as you can exactly what is wrong with it. Suggest amendments to existing language, or new clauses, to fix whatever is wrong. Send helpful letters to counsel for both parties. Suggest that they follow up with a face-to-face meeting with you, if they are nearby, or a conference telephone call involving the lawyers for both parties and you (and, if necessary, the trial judge) to discuss the problems with the DRO and your suggested fixes. It is incredibly helpful for attorneys to have a direct link, whether an email address or direct dial, to the plan representative handling the DRO at issue. The attorneys involved are much more likely to be eager to fix anything that needs attention when they can quickly get a response, especially a helpful one, rather than having to call an 800 number, speak with multiple different people, and never actually get their simple question answered. If you make yourself more available, the attorneys are probably going to make your job easier as well. Think of yourself as a teacher who is going to help some students learn to do a task correctly, perhaps for the first time. Take satisfaction in your ability to instruct them and take pride in their progress.

You are familiar with your Employee Benefit Plans and their unique features and options because you deal with them every day. Many lawyers and judges you deal with have never seen your plans before and are totally unfamiliar with their benefits, features, and options. In many circumstances, this may be the one and only time they are involved with the plan. You want them to have a pleasant experience, whether it is the first of many interactions or the only one. Oftentimes, even if it is the only interaction with this particular attorney, the attorney likely knows someone else who will be involved with the plan at some point.

The *EBSA Booklet on QDROs* referred to previously strongly encourages Plan Administrators to follow this educational approach, particularly in Question 2-14, which requires plans, when rejecting DROs, to act as follows.

If you cannot accept a DRO as a QDRO, give prompt written notice of your rejection to all parties. The notice should not simply state that the DRO is not acceptable as a QDRO but should also

1. Specify the reasons why the order is not a QDRO.
2. Refer to specific provisions of the plan on which your decision was based.
3. Explain any time limits that apply to the rights of the parties (such as the duration of any protective action you will take to prevent withdrawal of the Alternate Payee's share by the Participant).
4. Describe any additional material, information, or modifications of the DRO to make it a QDRO, and explain why they are necessary (*EBSA Booklet*, Question 2-14). *See also* 29 C.F.R. §§ 2560.503-1(f)(1)–(4) (similar requirement for Plan Administrators giving notice of denial of claimed benefit). Follow the spirit of this approach in all your dealings with Participants, Alternate Payees, their lawyers, and state court judges.

15.3 Follow Your Own QDRO Procedures and Document Your Actions

A sure recipe for disaster and litigation is failure to follow your own QDRO Procedures. This will often result in litigation against the plan and its administrators as well as the Plan Sponsor and individuals involved in the decision-making process. In *Schoonmaker v. Employee Savings Plan of Amoco Corp.*, 987 F.2d 410 (7th Cir. 1993), for example, the plan's QDRO Procedures stated that employees would not be able to direct purchases or sales of company stock in their accounts after a DRO had been submitted for qualification. The plan also followed an informal and unwritten practice of placing a "hold" on such transactions at a much earlier time—once it learned that a divorce action was pending and that a DRO would be submitted "soon."

In the *Schoonmaker* case, the lawyer for Mrs. Schoonmaker, the Alternate Payee, informally advised a legal assistant at the plan that a DRO was "forthcoming" on August 27, 1987, and an informal "hold" was placed on the Participant's entire account on that day. During September and October the Participant twice sought to sell his company stock, but his transaction requests were blocked because of the hold. (Unfortunately for the Participant and the plan, a major stock market crash occurred during this period.) The DRO was finally submitted to the plan on November 12, 1987, and qualified on November 17. Mr. Schoonmaker, the Participant, then sued the plan (and Amoco's Director of Corporate Benefit Plans and its Vice President for Human Resources as plan fiduciaries), seeking compensation for the losses he incurred as a result of the informal hold that prevented him from selling his Amoco stock before the market crashed.

The Seventh Circuit held that the plan had acted improperly in placing the informal hold on the Participant's account in violation of its own written QDRO Procedures and that the Participant could recover from the plan his losses stemming from the unconsummated stock sales. The court held that the actions of the individual defendants, while wrong, did not rise to the level of a breach of fiduciary duty and granted summary judgment in their favor.

In *Fortmann v. Avon Products, Inc.*, 1999 U.S. Dist. LEXIS 3451 (N.D. Ill. 1999), the plan was not sure which one of two conflicting DROs it had accepted as a QDRO! Its ten-year-old records on the issue were incomplete. A plan employee who reviewed DROs stated that "during his tenure at Avon from 1994 to 1997 he did not work off of written plans and procedures," and another employee stated that she did not know whether the plan's written QDRO Procedures had been followed in qualifying this particular DRO. (A plan's written QDRO Procedures should be drafted to make sure this type of confusion is avoided by attaching a copy of the DRO to your certification that it is qualified.) And in *Day v. Wall*, 2000 U.S. Dist. LEXIS 13388 (E.D. Wis. 2000), a plan that paid benefits to an Alternate Payee under a proposed unsigned draft QDRO (!) was held liable for its erroneous payment and had to honor a (signed) QDRO presented by the Alternate Payee four years later.

These sorts of things should never happen. Train your staff to follow your own QDRO Procedures and document your work.

15.4 Establish a Personal Relationship with Every Participant

Divorces and child support proceedings are mysterious and stressful experiences for many of your company's employees. While you are familiar with QDROs and how they work because you deal with them every day, your coworkers are not. For them the process of dividing up their pension and benefit plans is unfamiliar, threatening, and even alarming—as frightening as the prospect of major surgery. Employees don't know what to expect in their divorce proceedings and feel helpless because events often seem out of their control. Most are quite worried that the division of their pension will have a dramatically negative effect on their financial security. Anger and resentment stemming from other aspects of the divorce itself often spill over into their QDRO dealings with your office.

Too many corporate legal departments ignore the Participant and deal only with the lawyers—or just send the Participant a copy of the plan's QDRO Procedures if he knows enough to ask for one. This is a sure recipe for employee dissatisfaction and often leads to litigation against the plan and its officials.

A far better approach is to ask yourself how you would like to have your QDRO handled if you were going through a divorce, and then make sure you treat your fellow employees the same way. As soon as you learn an employee is going through a divorce or child support proceeding that may involve a QDRO, invite him to visit your office in person. Introduce the Participant to the lawyers, paralegals, and support staff in your department who will be handling his QDRO. Give him a copy of your QDRO Procedures, and spend a few moments explaining the basics of pension divisions. Offer to answer any questions he may have about them. Make sure he has your phone numbers, and encourage him to call at any time during the state court proceedings with any questions or problems he encounters. (If the Participant is in a distant corporate office and it is impossible for him to visit you personally, try to accomplish the same things by telephone or email.) Finally, make sure you send the Participant copies of all correspondence concerning his case that flows into or out of your office. You can be friendly and accessible to your employees without violating the important principle of neutrality discussed in section 15.5.

If you follow these practices, the result will be an employee who appreciates your efforts and hard work and is far less likely to complain about his QDRO or file a potentially expensive ERISA lawsuit against the plan and its officials.

15.5 Don't Take Sides

Especially in a small company, the Participant may be someone you have known well for years—even a close friend—and the Alternate Payee may be someone you have never met. When the divorce or support case is over, you're going to have to work side by side in the same office with the Participant and will probably never see the Alternate Payee again.

Consequently, you may be tempted to lean, just a bit, in the Participant's favor in providing (or not providing) information to his spouse's lawyer, in giving him hints about favorable QDRO provisions, in approving or disapproving the DRO, and in similar matters. Even if you're not tempted to do this, the Participant may try to put pressure on you to take his side during his divorce or support hearings on QDRO issues.

Explain to the Participant that ERISA requires you to be neutral between Participants and Beneficiaries, and that as much as you would like to help him, you just can't do it. Also explain that this can open you, and his employer, up to liability that could impact everyone's future. That's why he has a lawyer to represent his interests; the plan can't take sides, and neither can you personally.

It's often helpful to remind the Participant that the plan does not make any recommendations or decisions about how much, if any, the Alternate Payee is going to receive from the plan. Remind the Participant that this is entirely up to his lawyer and the state court, and that the plan has to honor any QDRO awarding the Alternate Payee anything between 0 percent and 100 percent of his plan benefits.

Your duty is to keep the plan qualified under ERISA, to help both parties draft QDROs that meet the requirements of ERISA, and to avoid paying out duplicate benefits. Perform those obligations, and don't go beyond them.

15.6 Always Show Respect for the Trial Judge

Here's a scene from an actual Texas divorce case, *Jones v. American Airlines*, that should never have happened and should never be repeated:

> On May 20, 1996, Tarrant County, Texas, Trial Judge James K. Walker entered a Domestic Relations Order awarding Mrs. Sharon E. Jones part of her former husband's pension benefits. On January 15, 1997—8 months later—the Plan Administrator wrote to Judge Walker that his May 20, 1996, DRO did not qualify as a QDRO under the Retirement Equity Act.
>
> Judge Walker then entered an amended DRO on February 28, 1997, which provided, in part, "IT IS FURTHER ORDERED that the plan shall comply with this order on or before 10:00 a.m. on March 26, 1997, and the Plan Administrator shall certify to the Court in writing compliance with this order by said date and time. Absent compliance by said date and time the court on its own motion or the motion of any party will join the plan, the Plan Administrator [a named "legal administrator" for the plan], and possibly others . . . as parties to this case."
>
> On the same day he entered the amended DRO, Judge Walker sent a copy of it to the plan with a cover letter to the "legal administrator," specifically directing her attention to the compliance deadline of March 26, 1997.
>
> On March 27, 1997—one day after Judge Walker's deadline—the "legal administrator" responded by acknowledging receipt of the amended DRO from the court. Her letter advised the judge that such orders were reviewed on a "first come, first serve basis" and she instructed Judge Walker and the Joneses not to contact the Plan Administrator about the matter again because it would not expedite the qualification process.
>
> On April 21 Judge Walker held another hearing, during which he issued an order determining that his amended DRO was a QDRO and ordering the Plan Administrator to comply with it immediately.
>
> On April 29, when the plan had still not complied with his order, Judge Walker held a final hearing. The transcript of that hearing reveals his exasperation with the Plan Administrator's failure to comply with his orders. Judge Walker also described the efforts by plan personnel to evade his subpoenas.
>
> Judge Walker then sent certain plan personnel (whom he had subpoenaed into appearing before him and who were present in his courtroom) in the custody of his bailiff to a telephone in the courthouse. After they telephoned back to their office and explained their plight, the Plan Administrator promptly agreed to comply with Judge Walker's order. *Jones v. American Airlines, Inc.*, 1999 U.S. Dist. LEXIS 11507 (D. Wyo. 1999), at 6–10.

Fortunately, this sort of thing happens only rarely. It should never happen.

Take a moment to think about some of the characteristics and concerns of the state court judges with whom you have to deal. Judges are persons who have a substantial amount of power at their disposal. They have bailiffs whom they can send out to arrest people and drag them into their courtrooms, and awesome powers of contempt and imprisonment over parties, lawyers, and witnesses. Every day they don impressive robes, and when they enter their courtrooms everyone must rise and stand in respectful silence until they are seated behind their elevated benches.

Judges are busy. In almost every state, they are overworked and have enormous caseloads. Many of them are weary, or even burnt out, from hearing highly emotional divorce, custody, and support cases.

They have the final say on who will get custody of the parties' children; how much alimony and child support will be paid; and how marital property, including pensions, will be divided. This power is subject to review only by the state appellate courts, and trial judges in domestic relations courts have great discretionary authority, so their decisions are rarely reversed on appeal.

Judges also regularly interact with "experts." An expert is someone who appears in their courtroom like any other witness, can be cross-examined by lawyers, and must obey the judge's orders about which questions to answer and how to conduct himself or herself on the witness stand. Trial judges are the final authorities in their courtrooms.

Just like any other person interacting with the plan, whether attorney, Participant, or Alternate Payee, make all efforts to assist in any way you can, educate, and fully explain what is required or allowed under the plan. If you must disagree with a judge, or even his or her staff, do so as respectfully as possible. Generally, if a state court judge is incorrect about a QDRO issue or how a plan should dictate the division of an account, federal law under ERISA generally will dictate finality on the issue in another forum. *AT&T Management Pension Plan v. Tucker,* 902 F. Supp. 1168 (C.D. Cal. 1995); *Dickerson v. Dickerson,* 803 F. Supp. 127 (E.D. Tenn. 1992); *Stott v. Bunge Corp.,* 800 F. Supp. 567 (E.D. Tenn. 1992); *Custer v. Custer,* 776 S.W.2d 92 (Tenn. Ct. App. 1988), *cert. denied,* 493 U.S. 933 (1989).

15.7 Don't Give Legal or Tax Advice to the Participant or the Alternate Payee

You will frequently be asked for legal or tax advice by one of the litigants, and it is inappropriate to do so. These are questions that should be directed toward his or her attorney and/or tax professional. It is appropriate to refer litigants to provisions of the Summary Plan Description or other plan documents covering the issues they have inquired about, or to make statements regarding the plan. You can answer questions regarding the plan, but do not stray into the area of giving advice. Oftentimes this can be gray area as to what is answering questions and what is giving advice. While you certainly do not want it to appear as if the plan is refusing to provide information, explain that the question asked essentially asks for legal or tax advice and this needs to be directed to the person(s) representing him or her on that end.

15.8 Don't Undercut the Participant's Lawyer

There is a constant temptation to demonstrate your own knowledge and expertise about your company's plan and how that is superior to that of the attorney(s) involved. After all, you work with it every day and have seen and examined dozens or perhaps hundreds of DROs and QDROs for it. You know its features, requirements, and subtleties better than a divorce lawyer who has never seen or dealt with it before. Still, it's not your job to represent the interests of either party—your job is to help the lawyers and the trial judge draft a QDRO acceptable to the plan and not to take sides. Once in a while you are going to run into a lawyer for one of your valued employees who is giving his client awful advice or handling the case unprofessionally. The first thing I would try to do as a Plan Administrator or lawyer representing a Plan Administrator in such a situation is to speak privately with that lawyer and try to work out any problems with him or her in confidence. If that doesn't work, as a last resort you can send a letter to that lawyer, with copies to the Participant and to opposing counsel if necessary, saying, "You have asked the plan to do *X*. We will reluctantly do *X*, because we believe it has the following adverse consequences for Participant: . . ." (You can't do this when the Alternate Payee is being poorly advised; it's difficult to justify taking any action that might harm the interests of the Participant, one of your fellow employees, in the course of representing the interests of your mutual employee benefit plan. The most an Alternate Payee can expect from you is neutrality.) Always start with the telephone call approach first. This generally will cure any issues, and the attorney will appreciate not being undercut in front of a client. If this is ineffective, put it in writing.

If neither one of these approaches works and you see your valued employee is headed for disaster, the most you can do is take your colleague aside and say, "You know, if someone gave me that advice in my own divorce case, I would definitely get a second opinion." Giving this kind of warning should be a rare exception to your general conduct, and you must never go beyond it. Use good judgment in deciding when you might take this extraordinary step. Any interference beyond this with the attorney-client relationship has the potential to cause enormous trouble for you personally and for your plan.

15.9 Don't Review the State Law Aspects of the DRO

As Judge Richard Posner said in *Blue v. UAL Corp.*, 160 F.3d 383 (7th Cir. 1998):

> ERISA does not require, or even permit, a pension fund to look beneath the surface of the [DRO]. . . . ERISA's allocation of functions—in which State Courts apply State laws to the facts, and pension plans determine whether the resulting orders adequately identify the payee and fall within the limits of benefits available under the plan—is eminently sensible.

The *Blue* case required a pension plan to honor a child support DRO that was regular on its face, even though it was undisputed that part of the sum payable under the DRO entered by the state court was for the custodial parent's lawyers' fees, and lawyers' fees cannot be the subject of a QDRO. (See *EBSA Booklet* Question 2-8, which states that plans should not review such state law matters.)

The federal Office of Personnel Management (OPM) has adopted a sound approach in dealing with federal civil service pensions. OPM regulations expressly state that if the employee, former employee, or retiree contests the validity of a state court order, he must submit to OPM a state court order that declares the earlier order invalid or sets it aside. OPM is required to honor court orders that are regular on their face and that are certified to be currently in force by the former spouse unless the employee, former employee, or retiree can submit a superseding court order. (See Chapter 12 and the regulations cited therein.) I recommend you include a similar statement in your QDRO Procedures and follow this sensible approach.

15.10 Pay Compliments When They Are Deserved

Once in a while you will run into a divorce lawyer, or a lawyer representing a state IV-D agency collecting child support from your plan, who understands ERISA and QDROs, is a polite but firm and effective advocate for his or her client's interests, and helps resolve a difficult QDRO issue in a creative way.

Send that lawyer a letter acknowledging these things. Compliment his or her professional skills and demeanor. Make sure you send a copy to his or her client or IV-D agency employer and to the trial judge. Even if you never deal with that particular lawyer again, you have just created a lifelong fan who is going to spread compliments about you and your plan throughout the legal community. It takes only a few minutes to do this, and it will make your life easier in the future.

Managing IV-D Agencies to Collect Child Support with QDROs

16

16.1 Advantages of QDROs for Child Support Enforcement

Proper use of Qualified Domestic Relations Orders (QDROs) by IV-D agencies can lead to an increase in both the percentage of cases in which support is collected and the amount collected per case. *See, e.g.*, *Blue v. UAL Corp.*, 160 F.3d 383 (7th Cir. 1998), in which QDROs were used to collect more than $200,000 in child support and lawyers' fees from an airline pension plan. Collection of child support by QDROs and direct payment to IV-D agencies, guardians, or custodial parents is authorized under the Employee Retirement Income Security Act (ERISA). *EBSA Booklet* Question 1-10; Staff of the Joint Committee on Taxation, *Explanation of Technical Corrections to the Tax Reform Act of 1984 and Other Recent Tax Legislation*, 100th Cong., 1st Sess. (Comm. Print 1987), at 222; *Baird v. Baird*, 843 S.W.2d 388 (Mo. App. 1992); *Iannotti v. Iannotti*, 1997 Conn. LEXIS 146 (Conn. Super. 1997).

There are six major advantages to an IV-D agency's using QDROs to collect child support:

1. *QDROs are permanent remedies.* Payments under a QDRO continue uninterrupted even if the obligor changes jobs, becomes unemployed or disabled, or passes away. Bear in mind, though, that often these have to be readdressed once the child support obligation is terminated or modified.
2. *QDROs are immediate remedies.* They may be used at any time; even long before the support obligor actually retires. In many cases an obligor's pension may be tapped for child support immediately, or when the obligor turns 50. Use of a QDRO as an immediate remedy more often than not is determined by the plan's guidelines and procedures. If this is your desired route, then make sure you review the QDRO Procedures as well as the employment status and age of the payor to determine whether this is a viable option.
3. *QDROs are direct remedies.* Because QDROs tap funds at their source, they are unlike license revocations, incarceration, and so on, remedies that only encourage obligors to pay.
4. *QDROs are secure remedies.* Once a QDRO has been accepted by a plan, the obligor loses all control over the funds.
5. *QDROs can be entered against pension plans anywhere in the United States.* Local jurisdiction over the plan is not required. Just as any state court's order will be recognized for property division, so should a QDRO for child support purposes.
6. *Once approved, QDROs are easy to modify.* The amount of monthly support payments can be increased every few years as a Participant's accrued plan benefits mount. Similarly, as mentioned previously, whether a child support modification or termination of the obligation, it is generally easy to get these modifications or terminations properly handled with the plan.

16.2 Misconceptions about Child Support QDROs

A common misconception about QDROs is that they may be used to collect child support only after a support obligor has already retired and is actually receiving payments from a pension plan. The earliest date on which an Alternate Payee can withdraw funds from a plan varies from plan to plan. Many plans provide options allowing child support to be withdrawn directly from a plan by a QDRO, even if the Participant is many years away from retirement because of the inherently different nature of the purpose of the QDRO. As mentioned previously, this requires review of the plan's guidelines. For example, many plans provide that a Participant may begin receiving payments as soon as he or she ceases to be employed by the plan's sponsoring company. Since Participants might quit or be fired at any time, a child support QDRO under such a plan may call for immediate payments. Even plans that do not provide for payments that early often allow Participants to take early retirement at age 50. In such plans, the Alternate Payee may begin receiving plan benefits as soon as the Participant reaches age 50—whether the Participant actually retires at that age or keeps on working. And, of course, if a Participant has already retired and is receiving plan benefits, payments to the Alternate Payee may begin immediately (see Chapters 6 and 8).

A second common misconception is that QDROs are unduly complex and difficult to draft and qualify. It is not necessary for IV-D agency enforcement staff and lawyers who draft DROs for child support purposes to study "actuarial value" or to make sophisticated mathematical calculations. In practice, this requirement can be dealt with in either of two simple ways. The first method is to ask the plan what is the maximum amount it can pay the IV-D agency without violating this prohibition and then to use that figure. The second is to phrase the DRO to require payment of child support "in the amount of the lesser of (a) $258 per month [or whatever the appropriate monthly support level would be], or (b) the maximum amount of plan benefit that the plan may legally pay to the Alternate Payee without having to provide increased benefits (determined on the basis of Actuarial Value)." Both methods force the plan to do the actuarial calculations for you. Using either method, you will be able to extract the maximum amount legally available from the plan without having to hire actuaries or develop the mathematical expertise necessary to calculate actuarial equivalence.

16.3 Strengths and Weaknesses of QDROs

Like all child support enforcement techniques, QDROs have their limitations as well as their advantages. One limitation is that ERISA does not require uniform plan design. Private pension plans are permitted to structure as they see fit their benefits, forms of payment, normal and early retirement ages, payment options, and so on, as long as they meet certain minimum standards of ERISA. Consequently, no two plans are alike. From the perspective of child support enforcement, this means that unlike wage attachments, which can use a standard format under the Uniform Interstate Family Support Act (UIFSA), each QDRO must be custom-tailored to meet the particular requirements of the plan in question.

A second perceived drawback of QDROs is that plan language, the multitude of options (target benefit plans, money purchase plans, 401(k) plans, vesting, QPSAs, QJSAs), and the specialized jargon of ERISA can seem complex and confusing at first. However, as in dealing with any new subject, familiarity usually leads to expertise, and the process of drafting QDROs becomes easier as an IV-D agency's staff gains experience in dealing with QDROs.

If a child support obligor has only a Defined Contribution Plan, based upon payment options of the plan, payment is generally limited. Most plans will not allow regular and/or scheduled payments from a Defined Contribution Plan. This will likely require you to get a little more creative and stay on top of these types of matters on a more regular basis, for example, once per year. In very limited circumstances, you may be able to obtain the entirety of the child support obligation through a QDRO.

A final limitation is that QDROs cover only private employers' pension plans. They cannot be used to collect child support from federal, state, or local government plans, or from military pensions. However, for all military and federal civil service pension plans, and for many state and local plans, there are comparable statutory procedures enabling IV-D agencies to collect child support from them. For example, if you are seeking to implement payments from a service member's military retired pay, the Military Pension Division Order would need to specify it is for the purpose of child support, and you must submit a properly filled-out DD Form 2293 that specifies in section 3 that the payment is for child support rather than property division (or alimony). Also, bear in mind that most federal government–based pensions will have a maximum allowable cap to be allocated to the child support obligee.

16.4 When Should IV-D Agencies Use QDROs?

QDROs are most suitable for use in the following types of cases:

- The Participant is already retired and receiving payments from the plan (the pension is In Pay Status as described in subsection 2.3D).
- The Participant is currently unemployed but has pension or other vested retirement rights from previous employment.
- The Participant has evaded previous enforcement efforts. QDROs are particularly effective remedies against obligors who habitually quit their jobs whenever a wage attachment catches up with them, or who have left the country.
- Most or all of the Participant's assets are located in another state.

QDROs are probably not the first remedy an IV-D agency should choose in most support cases. A QDRO is only one of several weapons in the arsenal of enforcement techniques available to IV-D agencies. A large part of properly managing an IV-D agency's collection program involves (1) screening cases to determine which enforcement tools are most appropriate for that case, and (2) deciding which alternative should be tried first and in what sequence other remedies should be tried if earlier ones do not work. To do so requires thorough and professional knowledge of the advantages and drawbacks of each available child support enforcement method.

How do QDROs compare to other child support enforcement techniques? QDROs are usually harder to obtain than wage attachments. However, once they are in place they are permanent and cannot be defeated by any act of the obligor. Unlike license revocations, incarceration, and other deterrent-based outcomes, which can only encourage obligors to pay, QDROs have the advantage of directly tapping child support funds at their source. While QDROs require custom tailoring more than wage attachments or asset forfeitures, they are no more complex, time consuming, or difficult than an average contempt proceeding, or obtaining a Qualified Medical Child Support Order (QMCSO).

16.5 How Can an IV-D Agency Begin to Use QDROs?

Putting QDROs to work for an IV-D agency requires three steps:

1. Redesign intake procedures and client information forms in order to gather retirement/pension information about

support obligors. This can be difficult in many cases where the parties may not have ever been married or in a long-term relationship and, therefore, may not have as much background knowledge as to the retirement options of the Participant/obligor. To the extent that the IV-D agency is able to obtain income information for the obligor, retirement contributions can generally be seen on pay stubs and other documents like this. This will be addressed further later.

2. Designate "QDRO specialists" among your child support enforcement staff and attorneys to perform three key tasks:
   (a) Identify child support cases suitable for QDROs.
   (b) Draft DROs.
   (c) Shepherd DROs through the plans' qualification processes.

   Agency staff members and lawyers who already deal with QMCSOs are usually excellent candidates for training as QDRO specialists due to the similarity of the procedures involved.

3. Train your QDRO specialists and the local Family Court judiciary in using QDROs for child support enforcement. Most Family Court judges are already familiar with QDROs from divorce cases, where they are commonly used in property divisions between divorcing spouses, but these judges still can benefit from training in the special child support aspects of QDROs.

16.6 Costs and Benefits

A single QDRO at a reasonable average level of $200 per month will generate, over 18 years, additional child support collections of $43,200. At that level, 11 or 12 QDROs will produce $500,000 in gross additional collections. This increased revenue must be balanced against the cost of training and redesign of information-gathering and intake procedures, but these are relatively modest when compared to the potential for increased collections. This is particularly true because QDROs can be used to collect support in cases where no other remedy might work—for example, if the obligor has no current income and no assets other than his pension rights.

QDROs are a valuable supplement to traditional child support enforcement techniques. In some cases QDROs may be the only method of collecting any support from an obligor. In other cases QDROs will succeed where other remedies have been tried and have failed. Unfortunately, and more often that not, the use of a QDRO for child support recovery purposes is not even addressed. To improve collection rates and amounts, IV-D agencies should give serious consideration to adding QDROs to their repertoire of enforcement techniques.

16.7 Practical Tips and Techniques

Here are ten practical techniques for putting QDROs to work to collect child support at an IV-D agency.

A. Know the Law

There's no substitute and no shortcut. Fortunately, everything you need to draft a child support QDRO is contained in this handbook.

B. Redesign Your Case Intake and Information-Gathering Procedures

If your current intake and information-gathering procedures do not identify pension and other employee benefits that support obligors may have, you will have to redesign the procedures to ask for this information. Asking the obligor is the most direct way to gather this information, obviously. However, most cases that end up at an IV-D agency are the result of the obligor evading his support obligation, being in another state, or being missing. Fortunately, the custodial parent or guardian of the child can often provide useful leads regarding this information. Lawyers representing your agency should also be trained to ask about pensions and other employee benefits in pretrial discovery or during child support hearings. Most child support offices are able to access Department of Labor (DOL) employment information. This can provide significant insight and information as to current or prior employment of the obligor, which gives you direction to explore. Further, use of discovery procedures to nonparties (plans) can be a useful tool in finding information that may otherwise be lacking or not readily available. Information obtained from DOL searches is generally a great starting point for discovery.

If you find a support obligor through new hire reporting or the Federal Parent Locator Service, in addition to seeking wage or salary information and entering a wage attachment, request that the new employer ask about any employee pension or benefit plans and the obligor's eligibility for benefits. If he is not eligible to participate in the employer's benefit plans, or his benefits are not yet vested, ask the employer about its plans' vesting schedules and then mark the file for review when the obligor will become vested in any plan benefits (which must begin at some time between his second and fifth year of employment by his new employer).

C. Identify and Designate QDRO Specialists

Not every child support enforcement staff member and lawyer needs to know how to draft DROs and get them qualified by plans. A minimum of 5 to 10 percent of your staff and lawyers should be designated as QDRO specialists and trained in this area. Many IV-D agencies designate as QDRO specialists those staff members and lawyers who are already familiar with QMCSOs; since the procedures for obtaining QMCSOs and QDROs are quite similar, cross-training is much easier. QDRO training may also include QMCSO training either as a refresher or as a new topic.

D. Train Your QDRO Specialists and the Judiciary

QDROs are not a simple subject. Proper training is essential for your QDRO specialists to make full use of the ideas in this handbook. A single day of instruction is usually enough to get agency staff off to a good start in QDROs—most of them can return to work the next morning and immediately start drafting DROs.

Starting a QDRO program for an IV-D agency means a major change in several areas, including intake and information gathering, case evaluation, and case evaluation, special drafting, qualification follow-up, and case management. Good training is necessary to ensure those changes are fully and properly implemented.

Family Court judges are already quite familiar with QDROs from their divorce property-division cases. I always recommend including the judges in agency staff and lawyers' training sessions so they will learn some of the special features of using QDROs for child support enforcement. Because of their divorce property-division experience, these judges often have QDRO experience to share with the other participants in the training sessions. Inviting the Family Court judiciary to the training sessions is a good practice to help make sure they are aware that your IV-D agency is making a major commitment to using QDROs for child support enforcement. As previously discussed in this book, often it will be your responsibility as the attorney to educate all persons involved, including the court and court staff, because of the more nuanced approach here. This requires you to be able to properly and accurately cite the authority for the QDRO and the plan-specific available options.

E. Set Policy Guidelines to Decide When You Should Use QDROs

With the help of your QDRO specialists, conduct an analysis of your caseload. Determine which cases are suitable for using QDROs (see section 16.4).

F. Be Persistent

It takes time, effort, and energy to make sure your DROs are accepted by plans and turned into QDROs. Follow the suggestions in section 14.9 about setting up an administrative mechanism for continuing contact with the plan until your DRO has been accepted as a QDRO. Don't hesitate to get the trial judge involved if you encounter a stone wall; ask the judge to schedule a telephone conference call with your staff or your lawyers and the plan.

G. Draft Your DROs to Start the Payments as Soon as Possible

Most cases, and most of the literature on QDROs, are concerned with their role as a provider of retirement security for the old ages of divorced husbands and wives. Unlike the child support clauses in this handbook, the model clauses and discussion in such authorities are skewed in that direction.

IV-D agencies collecting child support have an entirely different set of priorities. They are not concerned with someone's retirement security 20 or 30 years from now. Their goal is to get the maximum amount of child support payments flowing as soon as possible so that children can receive support when it is most needed—when they are growing up. It is far better for an IV-D agency to get an immediate QDRO (which might be able to collect payment only at a level below what your child support guidelines might indicate) than to wait several years and start collecting monthly payments at a possibly higher level.

If there is a current shortfall between the indicated level of child support and the amount available under a QDRO, get the QDRO entered anyway and collect the deficiency from the obligor's salary or assets as a supplement to the QDRO. You can go back every few years to amend the QDRO to seek a higher level of current payments or arrears, and you can enter a new QDRO after the child is emancipated to collect any accumulated arrears. Do your best to get a QDRO in effect now; child support obligations will end on the Participant's death, and if there is no QDRO in place before he dies, the IV-D agency may get nothing at all from the plan.

H. Periodically Review Each QDRO Case

Collect what you can right now by getting a QDRO in place for the maximum amount the plan can give. Then every three to five years, and when the child is 17, review your file to see if any arrears have accumulated or if any increase in the monthly support payment is indicated. If so, get back in touch with the plan to see if the passage of time has created more accrued benefits for the Participant. (If the Participant is still employed by the same Plan Sponsor, his Accrued Benefit will increase every year, so an increased payment to cover increases mandated by your state child support guidelines or the collection of arrears should be possible.) Then you can draft and qualify a new DRO for the increase or the arrears and have it in place before the old QDRO expires.

If the Participant has changed jobs in the meantime, track him down through Federal Parent Locator Service and get in touch with the employee benefits department at his new job to see if he is covered by a pension or benefit plan there. If he is, draft a new DRO to attach those benefits for increases or arrears.

I. Be Creative

Explore the payment options and variations allowed by each plan, and deal with them in the context of child support. As noted earlier, for example, it is slightly awkward to try to collect current child support from defined contribution plans because typically they do not provide for monthly payments, but rather lump sums. This is one reason why these are very suited for collecting child support arrears. It is, however, usually possible to provide for annual withdrawals from a Defined Contribution Plan for child support, either in advance or in arrears. You may have to recast the normal monthly or bimonthly payment schedule to achieve this, but it can be done.

J. Training Is Not an Event—It's a Process

QDROs are a difficult and complex subject. Constant training is required to ensure that new staff members and lawyers are properly trained to mitigate the effect of staff turnover. Periodic refresher courses should be held for both new and experienced staff members—whether taught by your own staff, or the initial QDRO consultants, or some combination of the two—so they can hone their QDRO skills and receive updates on new legal and management developments in using QDROs for child support enforcement.

16.8 Model Child Support QDRO for IV-D Agencies

This child support QDRO is fundamentally similar to the general model QDRO set forth in section 8.5. However, certain alternative clauses applicable only to property divisions between spouses or alimony payments have been omitted, and certain comments on child support issues have been expanded.

[Normal State Court or Agency Caption]

Order

This order is entered this ___ day of ___, 20__ [after a hearing] [by stipulation of the parties]. This order is intended to be a Qualified Domestic Relations Order as that term is used in ERISA, 29 U.S.C. § 1056(d)(3).

COMMENT: Under ERISA, only an order may be a DRO or a QDRO. ERISA requires a "judgment, decree or order (including approval of a property settlement agreement)." 29 U.S.C. § 1056(d)(3)(B)(ii). A state court or a state agency authorized to issue child support orders may issue a DRO. *EBSA Booklet* Question 1-3.

1. *Parties.* The names and last known mailing addresses of the parties are:

Participant:

Name: John C. Burns

Address: 123 Broad Street, Augusta, GA 30910

Social Security Number: XXX-XX-6789 (Full SSN provided under separate cover)

Year of Birth: 1975 (Full DOB provided under separate cover)

Alternate Payee:

Name: Alyssa S. Burns, c/o Division of Child Support Enforcement

Address: P.O. Box 5340, Augusta, GA 39099

Social Security Number: XXX-XX-4321 (Full SSN provided under separate cover)

Year of Birth: 1975 (Full DOB provided under separate cover)

[OR ALTERNATIVELY, if paid directly to the custodial parent or guardian of the children for whom the obligation is paid, then it could show something like the following:]

Alternate Payee No. 1:

Name: Amanda S. Burns

Address: P.O. Box 5340, Augusta, GA 39099

Social Security Number: Full SSN provided under separate cover

Year of Birth: Full DOB provided under separate cover

Alternate Payee No. 2:

Name: John C. Burns, Jr.

Address: P.O. Box 5340, Augusta, GA 39099

Social Security Number: Full SSN provided under separate cover

Year of Birth: Full DOB provided under separate cover

Custodial Parent/Guardian of the Alternate Payee(s):

Name: Alyssa S. Burns, c/o Division of Child Support Enforcement

Address: P.O. Box 5340, Augusta, GA 39099

Social Security Number: XXX-XX-4321 (Full SSN provided under separate cover)

Year of Birth: 1975 (Full DOB provided under separate cover)

COMMENT: The names and last known mailing addresses of the Participant and the Alternate Payee are expressly required by ERISA, 29 U.S.C. § 1056(d)(3)(C)(i). If the information is known or readily ascertainable by the Plan Administrator, there should be no problem with omitting it, although the better practice is to include it. *Hawkins v. Comm'r*, 86 F.3d 982 (10th Cir. 1996); *In re Williams*, 1999 U.S. Dist. LEXIS 8650 (C.D. Cal. 1999); *EBSA Booklet* Question 2-9. While ERISA does not require the Social Security numbers or dates of birth for the Participant or the Alternate Payee, including them helps the Plan Administrator make sure it is dealing with the correct party and is a reasonable request. Always include them. Also make sure that you do not include sensitive identifying information such as these in the order that becomes part of the public record. Plans will always accept QDROs with identifying figures drafted as above and submitting the full information under separate cover. This can be in a letter included when submitting the QDRO or an addendum to the QDRO not filed with the public record but also submitted to the plan. If including *any* information, ensure that you are complying with the applicable state law regarding what is included.

2. *Domestic Relations Law.* This order is entered pursuant to the domestic relations laws of the State of _____, in particular [State] Code Section _____ concerning *child support,* to recognize and assign to the Alternate Payee the right to receive that portion of plan benefits otherwise payable to the Participant that is specified below.

COMMENT: Under ERISA, DROs may be entered only pursuant to a "state domestic relations law (including a community property law)," 29 U.S.C. § 1056(d)(3)(B)(ii)(II), and it is useful to recite the specific domestic relations law under which the order is made.

ERISA also requires that a DRO "relates to the provision of *child support,* alimony payments or marital property rights." 29 U.S.C. § 1056(d)(3)(B)(ii)(I) (emphasis added). It is desirable to state the nature of the payments as child support in the DRO for three reasons:

1. To satisfy the plan that the DRO meets this requirement of ERISA;
2. To make sure that the proper and intended tax consequences are achieved by the DRO; and

3. To establish the background for identifying the events (death, eighteenth birthday, emancipation, and such) that may terminate the payments under the DRO (see clauses 6 and 7) where paid from a Defined Benefit Plan.

3. *Relationship of Alternate Payee to Participant.* The Alternate Payee(s) is (are) the child(ren) of the Participant.

COMMENT: ERISA requires that an Alternate Payee be a *child,* spouse, former spouse, or other dependent of the Participant. 29 U.S.C. §§ 1056(d)(3)(B)(ii)(I); 1056(d)(3)(K) (emphasis added).

OPTIONAL ADDITIONAL CLAUSE

3A. The Alternate Payee was born in 2010.

COMMENT: While not required by ERISA, this clause contains useful information that may be needed by the Plan Administrator. Clause 3A is essential in a QDRO for child support if the payments will automatically terminate upon the Alternate Payee's reaching a certain age. If this information is not in the DRO itself, the plan will have to be notified of it in some reliable and acceptable fashion; it is easier simply to insert it in the DRO. Many jurisdictions prohibit including a minor child's complete date of birth in a pleading or order. Avoid doing this. As mentioned previously, all identifying information like this can otherwise be submitted to the plan.

4. *Identity of Plan.* This order applies to the Global MegaCorp Employee Retirement Plan (hereinafter referred to as the "Plan"). This order applies to the Plan and any amended, successor, substitute, or replacement plan that subsequently takes the place of that plan or into which the benefits payable to the Participant by that plan are transferred. The address of the plan is 222 West Corporate Drive, Santa Barbara, California 99099.

COMMENT 1: ERISA requires that QDROs "clearly specify . . . each plan to which the order applies." 29 U.S.C. § 1056(d)(3)(C)(iv). It is imperative that the specific name is listed in the QDRO, otherwise it will get rejected.

COMMENT 2: It is important to provide that the QDRO also applies to successor, substitute, or replacement plans. It is not unusual for Plan Sponsors to redesign their employee benefits packages every few years, and the redesign often involves terminating one plan and substituting a new one in its place. A QDRO should automatically apply to such new plans, as it will if this language is used.

COMMENT 3: The address of the plan is not required by ERISA, but it is useful to include it in the QDRO for ease of future reference.

5. *Division of Payments.*

COMMENT: The wording of this clause will vary greatly depending on whether the plan is a Defined Contribution or Defined Benefit Plan, and, in the case of a Defined Benefit Plan, whether a "Shared Interest" or "Separate Interest" approach is used. (Review Chapter 6 and the model DRO in section 8.5 before drafting this part of the DRO.)

Part A: Division of Defined Benefit Plan: Plan Already In Pay Status or Shared Interest Approach

INTRODUCTORY COMMENT: Note that under this Shared Interest Approach the Alternate Payee or IV-D agency cannot begin receiving benefits until the date the Participant chooses to actually retire, and that all payments (other than death benefits provided in a separate clause) to the Alternate Payee must end—at the latest, if not earlier terminated by another specified event on the Participant's death. For this reason, most IV-D agencies prefer the recommended Separate Interest Approach as set out in Part B. Nonetheless, which approach is utilized must be determined on a case-by-case basis to ensure that the obligee is taken care of in the best way possible.

However, if the Participant has already retired and is already receiving monthly payments from the plan, the end result of these two approaches is the same. Participants should be indifferent as to which approach is taken because the monthly amount payable to the Participant and its starting and ending dates are generally the same under either the Shared Interest or Separate Interest Approach.

The Shared Interest Approach used here is well suited to the provision of child support to an Alternate Payee if such payments have been made from a Participant's salary and the Participant retires and replaces his wage or salary income with monthly pension payments. Unless a Qualified Joint and Survivor Annuity (QJSA) has been elected and the Alternate Payee is a former spouse of the Participant (which is not applicable to child support QDROs), all payments end automatically on the Participant's death under most state laws, so nothing is lost by using this approach in child support orders. (If a Participant dies and leaves a surviving spouse or Alternate Payee under another QDRO to whom payments are made after his death, it should be possible to collect arrears—but not current support—from those payments made by the Participant's pension plan to his survivor, just as arrears can be collected from the estates of deceased obligors.)

5A. Alternate Payee shall be entitled to receive from each monthly payment of benefits made to Participant by the plan:

1. . . . FOUR HUNDRED TWENTY-THREE DOLLARS AND FIFTY-EIGHT CENTS ($423.58).

COMMENT: If a fixed dollar amount is used, the Participant's benefit must be equal to at least that much. An alternative is to phrase the figure as ". . . the lesser of (a) $423.58, or (b) the maximum total monthly amount payable to the Participant by the plan." It is not uncommon for plans to reject a QDRO or require clarification on language that they interpret to mean the plan is required to pay a greater figure than the total benefits due to the Participant, which is not allowable . This will eliminate that ambiguity and be more agreeable to the plan.

2. . . . FORTY AND THIRTY-THREE HUNDREDTHS PERCENT (40.33%) of each such monthly payment.

COMMENT 1: A percentage or a fraction may be used here.

COMMENT 2: If the information given by the plan about available monthly payments is based on the premise that the Participant is currently unmarried, if the Participant later remarries and elects to receive a QJSA with his new spouse, *the monthly payments to the Alternate Payee will be lower, and perhaps significantly lower,* than if the Participant had remained single and elected, on retirement, a Single Life Annuity for his life alone. To protect the Alternate Payee from such a potentially significant reduction in the amount payable to the Alternate Payee, the following clause should be added.

5B. In the event Participant elects any form of payment of benefits other than a Single Life Annuity for his life alone, the phrase "each such monthly payment" as used above shall be interpreted to mean the monthly payment the Participant would have received had he (a) retired on the same date he actually retired, and (b) elected on that date to receive plan benefits in the form of a Single Life Annuity for his life alone, and Alternate Payee's monthly payment shall be computed by multiplying the [fraction] [percentage] set forth above by that level of monthly payments, and not by the actual monthly amount paid to Participant. If the Alternate Payee's monthly payment calculated under this method is more than 100 percent of the actual amount paid to the Participant, she shall receive 100 percent of the amount actually paid to the Participant.

COMMENT: One hundred percent is possible. Pension and other employee benefit payments are not "wages" as that term is used in garnishment statutes, and it is often possible to seize 100 percent of a Participant's payments. *See* 29 U.S.C. § 1056(d)(3)(M). This clause maximizes the current payment level that the Alternate Payee can receive—always desirable in child support collections.

Part B: Division of Defined Benefit Plan: Separate Interest Approach

INTRODUCTORY COMMENT 1: Under the Separate Interest Approach, unlike the Shared Interest Approach of clause 5A, the Alternate Payee may begin receiving benefits on a date of the IV-D agency's own choosing (within the limits established by ERISA and the plan terms), and payments to the Alternate Payee will not be affected by the Participant's death but will end only on the Alternate Payee's death or emancipation. For this reason, most IV-D agencies prefer the Separate Interest Approach as set out in the clauses in this section. Participants should be indifferent as to which approach is taken because the monthly amount payable to the Participant and its starting and ending dates are generally the same under either approach.

INTRODUCTORY COMMENT 2: To use the Separate Interest Approach, you must determine the Participant's "accrued benefit" as of the date of the order. This is an actuarial calculation that the plan (or a consulting actuary) should be able to make for you very readily. The Participant's current Accrued Benefit is not necessarily the amount shown on the Participant's Annual Benefits Statement, because those statements often contain assumptions about future salary increases, interest rates, and retirement ages. The Participant's real current Accrued Benefit is often a much lesser figure.

5C. Alternate Payee shall be entitled to receive from the plan an amount actuarially equivalent to the value of:

1. . . . the Participant's entire accrued benefit . . .

2. . . . the lesser of (a) the Participant's entire accrued benefit, or (b) that portion of the Participant's accrued benefit sufficient to fund monthly payments of $287 from now until the Alternate Payee's eighteenth birthday . . .

3. . . . 40 percent of Participant's accrued benefit. . . .

COMMENT: Payments from pension plans are not always subject to the ceiling and restrictions imposed on garnishment of wages or salary for child support. Consequently, consider using clause 5C(2) instead of limiting the order to a percentage of the Participant's accrued benefit.

4. . . . and the value of the Participant's accrued benefit shall be determined as of the date of this order.

COMMENT: If you need to specify the date as of which the Participant's Accrued Benefit will be valued, use the date of the order and not any earlier date. The more recent the date, the greater the value of the Accrued Benefit.

Part C: Division of Defined Contribution Plan

INTRODUCTORY COMMENT: It is slightly awkward to try to collect current child support payments from defined contribution plans because typically they do not allow for monthly withdrawals or payments but rather for lump sums. (They are, however, very suited to collecting arrears for that reason.) It is, however, possible to provide for annual withdrawals from a Defined Contribution Plan for current child support. If this is possible and desired, the following clause may be used.

5D. . . . from the plan on January 1, 20__, and January 1 of each calendar year thereafter, the lesser of (a) $24,000, or (b) Participant's entire vested plan benefit as of that date, until . . .

COMMENT 1: So long as the Participant continues to work for the Plan Sponsor, more contributions will be made to his account every year, so additional sums may be collected.

COMMENT 2: Do not rely on the Plan to allow for scheduled payments from a Defined Contribution Plan. Most plans do not want to be burdened with issuing payments in this fashion if this is outside of the regular course of business.

Appropriate termination events (see clause 6) should be added here.

If the DRO is used only to collect arrears, you can use the following clause.

5E. Alternate Payee's share of Participant's plan benefits from the plan described in clause 4 above is $23,408.96. . . .

COMMENT 1: If a fixed dollar amount is stated, consider stating here whether the Alternate Payee should receive interest at a stated rate on her share from the date of the order to the date of payment by the plan as: ". . . plus interest on the unpaid balance due the Alternate Payee at 6 percent per year from the date of this order until the date the Alternate Payee has been paid in full."

COMMENT 2: In limited circumstances, whether this is significant recovery issues in the past or a relatively limited remaining child support obligation, courts may be inclined to "prepay" the remainder of the child support obligation where allowed by state law. This obviously can have the potential to create further issues down the road with modifications, so be very cautious with this approach.

6. *Duration of Payments.* The Alternate Payee shall receive the payments provided by this order:

(i) *Commencement date for payments*:

6A. . . . immediately. . . .

COMMENT: This is desirable if the terms of the plan permit it. It is particularly appropriate in dividing defined contribution plans or defined benefit plans already In Pay Status.

6B. . . . as soon as the plan allows payments or distributions to be made to an Alternate Payee. . . .

COMMENT: This is also a very desirable clause.

6C. . . . as soon as the Participant attains, or would have attained, the Earliest Retirement Age permitted under the plan, or the plan allows payments or distributions to be made to an Alternate Payee, whichever occurs first. . . .

COMMENT: Often this will be the same date as in clause 6B. Sometimes the Earliest Retirement Age is the first date on which a plan will allow payments to be made to an Alternate Payee, but some plans allow Alternate Payees to receive payments earlier than a Participant could.

6D. . . . as soon as the Participant actually begins receiving payments of plan benefits. . . .

COMMENT: This clause is not desirable and should rarely, if ever, be used. It leaves the timing of the payment of benefits to the Alternate Payee entirely to the whim of the Participant. Clauses 6A, 6B, or 6C provide better arrangements.

(ii) *Termination date for payments*:

6E. . . . until a total of $127,500 is paid to the Alternate Payee.

COMMENT: This clause is most suited to dividing a Defined Contribution Plan with a specific account balance or if the QDRO is going to be used to collect child support arrears. Also, keep in mind that many jurisdictions do allow for the use of a lump-sum child support award by determining the monthly amount and duration of the child support obligation. This can be extremely useful in situations where you may be hesitant about the continuing payments of the obligor and there is a sufficient amount of funds at hand. For example, in a certain case recently, there was a professional athlete who previously was very inconsistent with his child support payments. There was a sum sufficient to cover the entire child support obligation in his retirement account allowing for a lump-sum obligation satisfaction. It was worth it to the spouse to get that sum upfront and ensure that the children were taken care of. To her, even if she had to go back to modify later, there was already enough in place that amending the QDRO was a rather simple process. It is not generally suited to defined benefit plans. If the distribution is likely to take more than a year under this clause, it is desirable to state the amount payable as "$127,500 plus 6 percent per year simple interest on the unpaid balance due the Alternate Payee from time to time."

6F. . . . until the first to occur of (a) the death of the Participant, or (b) the following events in the life of the Alternate Payee: (i) reaching her eighteenth birthday (or if, on her eighteenth birthday, she is still enrolled in high school and likely to graduate, then on the earlier of (A) her nineteenth birthday, or (B) her graduation from high school), (ii) dying, (iii) marrying, (iv) enlisting in the armed forces, (v) being otherwise emancipated, or (vi) being placed in the permanent custody of the Participant, *provided, however,* that payments shall continue under this order beyond the occurrence of any such event until any arrears of unpaid child support and interest thereon have been paid in full.

COMMENT 1: This clause is generally suitable for use in child support QDROs and recites the standard events under the laws of most states that terminate child support. However, in some states, child support may be ordered to continue after the obligor's death. *See* J. Thomas Oldham, *What Does the U.S. System Regarding Inheritance Rights of Children Reveal about American Families?* 33 FAM. L.Q. 265, 271 (1999). In such jurisdictions, subclause (a) should be deleted. The change of custody clause, (vi), is often omitted because children often change custody more than once before attaining their majority. The plan may also require a more specific statement of the amount of arrears, and any interest payable on arrears, in this clause.

If this clause is used, clause 6G should also be used.

COMMENT 2: Some plans may insist that they cannot make the actuarial calculations required by ERISA unless the order has a definite stop date, such as the child's eighteenth birthday. If so, the best practice is to delete all of the other emancipating events from clause 6F. The order can always be amended later should one of the other emancipating events occur, or extended if state law permits child support through the nineteenth birthday if still in high school, or even into college years.

6G. . . . but the plan shall not be considered to have received notice of any of the occurrence of any of these events, and shall continue to make payments under this order, until the state court that entered the original DRO or another court of competent jurisdiction or the IV-D agency identified in clause 9 below sends a further order or written statement to the plan stating that such a terminating event has occurred and that the plan should cease making payments under the DRO or receipt of a certified official death or marriage certificate.

COMMENT: If clause 6F is used, the question arises as to how the plan is to be officially notified of the occurrence of one of the terminating events. Plans are reluctant to accept informal notice—or even sworn statements—from Participants, who have an obvious financial interest in terminating payments made under a QDRO. Requiring informal notice or a sworn statement from an Alternate Payee may be equally troublesome because the Alternate Payee may have other difficulties with the Participant that might lead her to refuse to provide verification of the occurrence of a terminating event even though she should. From the plan's perspective, the most satisfactory method of notice is a supplemental court order from the court that originally entered the DRO or another court of competent jurisdiction, or, in the case of marriage or death, a certified copy of the official certificate. Another possibility is receipt of official written notice from the IV-D agency. In the case of child support QDROs, this clause might state that the plan may cease payments on the child's eighteenth (or later) birthday without further notice if the child's date of birth is stated in the original DRO.

7. *Recomputation of Participant's Benefits.* In the event the Alternate Payee predeceases the Participant or for any other reason permanently ceases to be eligible to receive payments from the plan before the full amount assigned to her by this order has been paid to her by the plan, the Participant may apply to the plan to increase the remaining benefits to be paid to him or his beneficiaries if, and to the extent that, the terms of the plan permit him to apply for and receive such an adjustment.

COMMENT: This clause costs the Alternate Payee nothing and may allow the Participant to receive more from the plan. Not all plans allow for this kind of recalculation. It is, however, an important clause for which counsel for the Participant may bargain during negotiations with the IV-D agency or argue for in court. *In re Marriage of Rich*, 73 Cal. App. 4th 419 (Cal. Ct. App. 1999) (Alternate Payee's share of pension reverted to Participant after Alternate Payee's death).

8. *Effect of Order.* This order shall not be construed or interpreted to

A. Require the plan to provide any type or form of benefit, or any option, not otherwise provided under the plan;

B. Require the plan to provide increased benefits (determined on the basis of actuarial value); or

C. Require the payment of benefits to the Alternate Payee that are required to be paid to another Alternate Payee under an order previously determined to be a Qualified Domestic Relations Order.

COMMENT: This clause simply repeats the "3 Don'ts" contained in ERISA, 29 U.S.C. § 1056(d)(3)(D). Including this clause places the burden of determining whether there is any conflict in these areas on the plan, which is where it belongs. Counsel for the Participant or the IV-D agency do not need to say more than this in their draft DRO to protect their respective clients' interests.

OPTIONAL ADDITIONAL CLAUSE

D. In the event of any conflict between this clause and any other clause of this order, the provisions of this clause shall prevail.

COMMENT: Plans often request this clause to ensure that they do not have to pay out more than they should or violate the existing payment options provided by the plan.

9. *Role of IV-D Agency.* The payments to be made for the benefit of the Alternate Payee hereunder shall be made to the "Division of Child Support Enforcement" and mailed to P.O. Box 5340, Augusta, GA 39099 as the entity designated by law to receive and disburse child support payments for the Alternate Payee pursuant to _____.

COMMENT: *See EBSA Booklet* Question 1-9; *Metropolitan Life Ins. Co. v. Woodham*, 1995 U.S. Dist. 7620 (E.D. Mich. 1995) (payments to guardian); *Baird v. Baird*, 843 S.W.2d 388 (Mo. Ct. App. 1992).

The Division of Child Support Enforcement is also designated as the Representative of the Alternate Payee pursuant to section 1056(d)(3)(G)(ii)(III) of ERISA to receive copies of all notices sent to the Alternate Payee during the qualification of this order as a QDRO.

10. *Participant Not to Interfere with Alternate Payee's Rights.* The Participant is hereby ordered not to do, or fail to do, any act, or to make any choice or election, or by inaction fail to make any choice or election under the plan, that would interfere in any way with the payment to the Alternate Payee of the share of his plan benefits assigned to the Alternate Payee by this order. In the event any payment assigned to the Alternate Payee by this order is paid to or received by the Participant, the Participant shall be deemed to have received such payments as trustee for the benefit of the Alternate Payee and shall immediately pay the same to the Alternate Payee.

COMMENT: This clause is really directed at the Participant, not the plan, so arguably it does not belong in a QDRO but in the original divorce decree. It is good to have it in the QDRO, however, if only to put the Plan Administrator on notice of it.

11. *Pension Benefit Guaranty Corporation Takeover.* In the event the Pension Benefit Guaranty Corporation (PBGC) becomes the trustee of the plan and the total amount available for payment to the Participant and the Alternate Payee is reduced by the PBGC,

any necessary reduction will be applied by decreasing [each party's payments by the same percentage as the percentage by which the PBGC directs total payments with respect to both parties to be reduced] [by decreasing the Participant's payments first] [by decreasing the Alternate Payee's payments first].

COMMENT: Insolvent defined benefit plans may be taken over by the PBGC. However, the PBGC will not pay plan benefits above certain limits, so it is possible that the payments to one or both of the parties would have to be reduced. The PBGC maximum in 2009 for a Single Life Annuity at age 65 was $4,500 per month; this figure is adjusted annually to reflect changes in the Social Security taxable wage base.

This clause is not necessary in a DRO dividing a Defined Contribution Plan.

12. *Tax Effect.* Since the Alternate Payee is not the spouse or former spouse of the Participant, under section 402(e)(1)(A) of the Internal Revenue Code it is the intention of the court [and the parties] that federal and state income taxes on all payments received by the Alternate Payee under this order shall be borne by the Participant and not by the Alternate Payee, and the Participant is ordered to indemnify and hold the Alternate Payee harmless with respect to any federal or state income tax imposed on the Alternate Payee as a result of the Alternate Payee's receipt of her payments—*provided, however,* that the plan's obligations to any party shall not be affected in any way by this clause.

COMMENT: In most child support QDROs, this clause is omitted. While not binding on the Internal Revenue Service or state tax authorities, however, this clause should always be included. First, it expressly states the intent of the trial court (and the parties, if the order is entered by stipulation) as to the tax effect of the payments to the Alternate Payee. Second, it requires the appropriate party to indemnify the other in case the intended tax consequences do not occur.

The general rule for federal income taxes is that Participants are taxable on all distributions from their plans. The only limited exception is for Alternate Payees who received payments under a QDRO—and even then the Alternate Payee must be a spouse or former spouse of the Participant. *See* 26 U.S.C. § 402(a)(9); *Hawkins v. Comm'r,* 86 F.3d 982 (10th Cir. 1996); *Brotman v. Comm'r,* 105 T.C. 141 (1995). Payments to, or for the benefit of, an Alternate Payee who is a child of the Participant are always taxable income to the Participant and never to the Alternate Payee.

13. *Reservation of Jurisdiction.*

A. This court reserves jurisdiction to amend or modify the provisions of this order in light of comments received from (1) the plan, (2) a court of competent jurisdiction, or (3) any other organization or party during the process of deciding whether this order is a Qualified Domestic Relations Order.

B. This court also reserves jurisdiction to amend or modify the provisions of this order, even after it has been determined to be a Qualified Domestic Relations Order by the plan, to terminate or suspend the payment of benefits to the Alternate Payee as a result of attainment of a certain age, emancipation, change of custody, or other events justifying a change in payments, or to modify this order (subject to clause 8) to deal with any unforeseen tax consequences or other effects of this order.

COMMENT: This is a vitally important clause. It is often necessary to revise a DRO several times during the qualification process, and it is vitally important that the state trial court retain jurisdiction under clause 13A to do so. In many states, the trial court loses jurisdiction over a divorce or support case once the final order in the case has been entered if an express reservation of jurisdiction like this is not made. *Edwards v. Edwards*, 838 S.W.2d 494 (Mo. Ct. App. 1992); *Rohrbeck v. Rohrbeck*, 566 A.2d 767 (Md. 1989). The result can be a nightmare of protracted litigation and malpractice claims. Clause 13B is much broader. It is always desirable in alimony QDROs, and it is very desirable in case of future difficulties with the Internal Revenue Service about the intended and actual tax consequences of the DRO, bankruptcy, or other problems. *See Hawkins v. Comm'r*, 86 F.3d 982 (10th Cir. 1996) (failure of trial court to reserve jurisdiction meant DRO could not be revised).

Use the broadest reservation of jurisdiction clause permitted by state law to deal with all potential modifications, revisions, or other unforeseen contingencies. *Wilson v. Wilson*, 492 S.E.2d 495 (Va. Ct. App. 1997).

If appropriate, add a clause indicating each party has waived his or her right to appeal.

SO ORDERED:

____

Judge

COMMENT: Under ERISA, only an order may be a DRO or a QDRO. A state agency authorized to issue child support orders may also issue a DRO. *EBSA Booklet* Question 1-3.

[Signature of counsel for Participant and IV-D agency

[Signature of Participant]

COMMENT: While not required by ERISA, signature of counsel for both parties and the Participant helps to counter later claims that they had not approved, or at least read, the provisions of the order. For further protection on this end, include initial lines for the parties on every page, similar to a settlement agreement.

16.9 Final Quality Control Check

Once you have drafted a DRO following the guidelines and model clauses in this chapter, check your work.

Does your draft DRO contain all of the required information and clauses set forth in the preceding example and per the plan guidelines and procedures? Use the checklist in the next section. Then offer it to the trial court or send it to the plan for a preliminary and informal review.

16.10 Child Support DRO Checklist

___ 1. Order contains the necessary information of the Participant and Alternate Payee(s), including names, addresses, dates of birth, and Social Security numbers. As previously mentioned in other chapters, do not include the dates of birth and Social Security numbers in an order that will be part of the public record of the court. This information can be included in a cover letter to the plan.

___ 2. Order identifies state domestic relations law section involved and specifies that the QDRO is for child support.

___ 3. Order identifies Alternate Payee(s) as child(ren) of Participant.

___ 4. Order states age(s) for the child(ren) (may have to be included in cover letter/addendum to comply with state law).

___ 5. Order clearly specifies *exact* name of each plan to which it applies.

___ 6. Order clearly specifies what plan benefits, or what fraction of plan benefits, it is dividing.

___ 7. *For defined contribution plans*: Order covers vesting, forfeitures, interest, and Alternate Payee's control over investments while funds remain in plan.

___ 8. *For defined benefit plans*: Order clearly follows Shared Interest Approach or Separate Interest Approach.

___ 9. If Shared Interest Approach is used, it is understood that payments cannot begin until Participant retires, unless otherwise allowable under the plan, and payments must end on Participant's death. This is why a Separate Interest Approach is far more advisable for purposes of child support.

___ 10. Order clearly specifies starting and ending dates (or amounts or events) for receipt of payments by IV-D agency on behalf of Alternate Payee(s).

___ 11. Order clearly specifies amount of each payment, or formula for calculating that amount.

___ 12. Order allows for recomputation of Participant's benefit if Alternate Payee(s) does not collect entire share (optional).

___ 13. Order states that IV-D agency is to receive payments for Alternate Payee(s).

___ 14. Order appoints IV-D agency as Representative.

___ 15. Order directs Participant not to interfere with Alternate Payee(s)'s rights.

___ 16. Order contains appropriate PBGC takeover clause (Defined Benefit Plan only).

___ 17. Order specifies its intended tax effect (optional). Given that child support generally does not have any sort of tax implication, this should be minimal. To the extent that a tax effect is present, specify that it should be the responsibility of the Participant.

___ 18. Order contains appropriate reservation of jurisdiction clause allowing trial court to modify as needed during qualification and afterward.

___ 19. Order clearly specifies what happens if Alternate Payee(s) dies before receiving any benefits from plan.

___ 20. Order clearly specifies what happens if Participant dies before receiving any benefits from plan.

___ 21. Order contains any special features unique to this case (specify):

Family Court Judges and QDROs

17

17.1 Introduction

This chapter is addressed to the Family Court judges who issue Domestic Relations Orders (DROs) and deal with Qualified Domestic Relations Orders (QDROs) in divorce and child support proceedings. If you are a state court judge with jurisdiction over domestic relations matters, I recommend that you read, or at least skim, the rest of this handbook before starting this chapter.

17.2 Require Early Discovery and Prompt Disclosure

Under the best of circumstances, it takes a substantial amount of time to discover, analyze, and cope with the complexities of employee pension and benefit plans. The earlier this process is started, the better for the parties, their lawyers, and the trial court.

If a Participant or his plan is stonewalling the Alternate Payee and her lawyer, take prompt and strong action to move the case along. It is not necessarily common that a plan will create issues, as the plans generally do not want to be caught in the middle of litigation or otherwise fail to comply in some way. It is, however, extremely common that the Defense Finance and Accounting Service (DFAS) will make it difficult to obtain information if you do not represent the service member.

It is beyond dispute that pension and other employee benefit rights are marital or community property in every state. Every divorce or support litigant has an obligation to disclose information about his or her pension rights and employee benefits to the other party to make sure justice is done. One of the most useful tools in a judge's arsenal is ordering the Participant to produce plan documents and to sign release of information forms so that pension rights can be properly explored, valued, and divided. Furthermore, the implementation of financial and other sanctions for failure to cooperate in pretrial discovery is a significant deterrent at a judge's disposal. A daily fine until information is disclosed often produces quick results. Another possible sanction is announcing that you will refuse to consider a recalcitrant party's form of DRO and will accept the opposing party's form if prompt and full disclosure is not made.

Finally, an order from the court requiring the plan to produce relevant information for the Participant's enrollment in each applicable plan and other relevant information, like a Summary Plan Description, helps to provide direction for QDRO preparation.

If the trial court is too lax about enforcing timely disclosure of information and responses to legitimate discovery requests, the result will be unnecessary delay and expense, repeated hearings on discovery motions, and poor case management. Develop a reputation as a judge who takes immediate and firm steps to compel disclosure of QDRO information, and this sort of conduct in your courtroom will come to a rapid halt.

17.3 Enlist the Plan's Cooperation

Unless your state permits or requires joinder of an employee benefit as a party and this is actually done, the plan occupies a unique status in your domestic relations cases. The plan is something less than a full-fledged party to the litigation, but something more than an ordinary witness, because it will be bound to pay out significant sums of money under a QDRO.

Plan officials are a valuable source of information, advice, and guidance on what benefits and options are available from a plan and how QDROs may be worded and structured. Don't hesitate to ask plan officials for advice and guidance on QDRO issues. This advice may take several forms. If the plan is a local one, plan officials may appear either voluntarily or in response to a subpoena as a witness at property-division or support hearings. Plan officials often welcome the opportunity to work with the court and counsel by correspondence or by telephone conference call to provide information about plan benefits and QDRO requirements.

I recommend that you read Chapter 15 to gain a better understanding of the goals and concerns of plan officials. As noted previously, very few plans want to stonewall; most want to help the court and the parties draft a proper DRO and get it qualified with a minimum of friction. It is not going to make their job any easier or more efficient to refuse to assist. Try to work with plan officials in that spirit and with those mutual goals in mind. Oftentimes, this can be as easy as picking up the phone, explaining your role in the litigation, and requesting information. That being said, there are many times where the attorneys involved may get no traction in seeking information directly from the plan because plans are worried about issues of disclosure. This is generally cured with an order from the court or a subpoena.

17.4 Make the Parties and Their Lawyers Come to Court Prepared

In many cases, the trial court first establishes the percentage of employee benefits to be awarded to each party and then, and only then, asks the parties or their lawyers to prepare a DRO. This might initially seem to be a sensible approach, but in my view, it is putting the cart before the horse and is a constant source of friction, neglect, and further litigation (see section 10.4). QDROs are much easier to deal with and much better in quality if you require the parties and their lawyers to come to property-division and support hearings with draft QDROs, preapproved by the plan and ready to present to the court, in hand.

If you require the parties and the lawyers to do their homework before the hearing (or even 30 days in advance, as some trial judges prefer), your hearings will run much more smoothly, and the quality of the DROs you are asked to sign will significantly improve. Litigants and their counsel will be better prepared when they appear before you. Encourage or order the lawyers to try to come up with a single, mutually agreed-upon form of order with the amount left blank if necessary. If the lawyers cannot agree on a single form of order, require each to come to court with a separate one. In either case, push the lawyers to take as many initial steps as possible before anything is presented, including having the plan review and approve the DRO prior to presentation with the court. Let the local lawyers know that if only one of them appears at the hearing with a draft DRO approved by the plan, you will sign that one and ignore any late submissions from the other side. Before long, every lawyer who appears before you will come to court better prepared out of concern that if he or she does not present you with a draft DRO favoring his or her client, you will simply sign the other party's version. There will be far fewer cases in which the parties must return to the court for a second or third hearing to argue over collateral QDRO issues (death benefits, annuity starting dates, tax effect, and so on) if you require all these things to be worked out and presented to you at (or before) the initial property-division or support hearing. It is also important that everyone involved have an understanding as to the aforementioned collateral QDRO issues, because these may vary from plan to plan, and arguing about the issues may not even be applicable due to what the plan will allow.

The work of drafting a DRO must be done sometime. The earlier you require it to be done, the better the final result will be. This, of course, is going to be on a case-by-case basis, but it is something very helpful to include in various steps from the court, including consolidated pretrial orders.

In most circumstances, the most important question that can be asked of the lawyer(s) presenting a proposed DRO is whether it was *preapproved*. If the answer is yes, then the court knows that there should be no further issues with submission of the DRO to the plan. If the answer is no, then I recommend that this be made a requirement before a DRO is signed by the court.

17.5 Be Creative

QDROs can present unique opportunities for finding creative solutions to domestic relations cases. For example, if the plan is a small local one (such as a medical or dental practice) and the Plan Administrator, who may be a partner of the Participant or even the Participant him- or herself, is acting irrationally or improperly, consider appointing the Alternate Payee or her lawyer as the temporary Plan Administrator for the purpose of qualifying the DRO. *In re Williams,* 1999 U.S. Dist. LEXIS 8650 (C.D. Cal. 1999); *Lynn v. Lynn,* 25 F.3d 280 (5th Cir. 1994). As previously discussed, financial sanctions, contempt, and/or the threat of incarceration are generally very strong deterrents from engaging in this sort of unproductive and difficult behavior.

17.6 A Quick Test for Evaluating DROs

Some state court judges like to play an active role in family law cases, probing and questioning to make sure the parties and their counsel have fully explored and understand every aspect of a settlement. Other judges adopt a more laissez-faire approach, approving any arrangement knowingly and voluntarily agreed to by the parties. Whatever your own personal judicial methodology, how can you quickly tell if a DRO has been properly drafted or needs further thought and revision before you will sign it?

There are a few key areas in QDROs where probing questions will rapidly reveal if the parties and their lawyers fully understand what they are doing.

Ask the lawyers in open court, while their clients are present:

- Who will pay the income taxes on distributions to the Alternate Payee?
- What happens if the Participant dies before he retires? Will the Alternate Payee get anything?
- What happens to the Alternate Payee's share of benefits if she dies before collecting all of them? Will they revert to the Participant, will someone else get them, or will the plan just stop paying them?
- Will the Alternate Payee share in any postretirement cost-of-living increases that the Participant gets?

If the answers to any of these key questions are vague or unresponsive, or if either of the parties seem surprised at any of the answers that their lawyers are giving you, these are red (or at least yellow) flags indicating the DRO has not been properly prepared with the clients' best interests in mind. You may wish to encourage or require further discussion and negotiation before you sign a DRO that evokes this kind of response.

I also encourage you to question the Alternate Payee directly any time you see a DRO using a Shared Interest Approach (see Chapter 6 and the discussion of the alternative versions of clause 5 in the model DRO in section 8.5) prior to the Participant being In Pay Status to make sure that is really what the Alternate Payee wants. Is the Alternate Payee aware that a Separate Interest Approach is generally possible (with the exception of military retired pay and the Federal Employee Retirement System), so that payments may begin when she chooses and last for the rest of her life—and not begin only when the Participant chooses to retire and terminate on his death, as the Shared Interest Approach requires? It is very, very common that when our office is hired for QDRO purposes on a pension, the Alternate Payee has zero knowledge as to any options available. A few questions to the Alternate Payee on this topic will rapidly reveal whether her lawyer has chosen the Shared Interest Approach because it is what that client really wants or merely because it is the easiest alternative for lawyers to draft, or because the lawyers did not fully understand.

17.7 Recognize That ERISA Is a Power-Sharing Arrangement

QDROs are a unique area of family law. In every other aspect of divorce or support cases, state courts have complete power to make all decisions and enter all orders necessary to finally resolve the case. However, when QDROs are used, that power is shared with both the Plan Administrator and the federal courts.

As Judge Richard Posner said in *Blue v. UAL Corp.*, 160 F.3d 383 (7th Cir. 1998, page 385):

> ERISA does not require, or even permit, a pension fund to look beneath the surface of the order. . . . ERISA's allocation of functions—in which State Courts apply State laws to the facts, and pension plans determine whether the resulting orders adequately identify the payee and fall within the limits of benefits available under the plan—is eminently sensible. (*See also EBSA Booklet* Question 2-8.)

State courts have most of the power in QDRO cases. You, and you alone, will decide whether an Alternate Payee gets 0 percent, 50 percent, or 100 percent of a Participant's plan benefits (note there will sometimes be limits as to what may be allocated, so read your plan procedures and guidelines). But that power must be exercised within the boundaries prescribed by ERISA, and those boundaries must be understood and respected by all state courts (see Chapter 10 on QDRO and ERISA litigation).

17.8 Help the Lawyers Who Appear Before You Improve Their Professional Skills

If a lawyer appearing before you in a divorce or support matter does a poor job of dealing with the QDRO issues in the case, don't hesitate to take corrective action. Take the lawyer aside and recommend further Continuing Legal Education training. QDROs are a difficult subject for new and experienced lawyers alike, and regular training is required to stay abreast of developing trends in this area.

Most state bar associations offer periodic seminars on QDROs and other aspects of family law. An alternative is private training and law office management consulting services from firms such as QDRO Solutions. You may not wish to recommend any particular consulting firm or program, but it is entirely appropriate to point out to a lawyer who is not dealing adequately with QDRO issues that he or she is heading for trouble, and to recommend that he or she take prompt action to learn the law in this area better and adopt some sound case management techniques.

Depending on how the case before you has transpired (i.e., whether an agreement was reached, a trial was required, or a combination), requiring the parties to sign to reflect their consent, whether by the party or each party's respective counsel, can be extremely helpful so neither party can later argue that the court issued the QDRO without that party's consent.

17.9 Retain Jurisdiction over the DRO

When you approve and sign a DRO, be sure to include a clause that you will retain jurisdiction over the DRO so that if the Plan Administrator fails to properly implement the QDRO, you have the jurisdiction and authority to modify the QDRO to effect your intent or the parties' intent for division. Savvy lawyers will have this clause in their proposed DROs, but if you ensure that it is there, it will allow you the ability to ensure that the plan properly executes your order.

Current Trends and Future Developments in QDROs

18

18.1 Introduction

This chapter discusses recent trends and projected future developments affecting Qualified Domestic Relations Order (QDRO) drafting and processing.

18.2 Employers Outsource Their QDRO Processing

In recent years, many employers who sponsor pension plans have concluded that it would be more efficient and economical for them to hire third-party specialists to review and approve QDROs rather than performing this task themselves. The family law attorney drafting QDROs now is more likely to deal with a large, impersonal financial institution that handles the review, approval, and processing of thousands of QDROs rather than the legal department or human resources department of the employer sponsoring the plan. However, on a positive end, there are many companies that when sending out the correspondence regarding review of the DRO will include contact information for the representative who previously reviewed your DRO. This provides a personal touch and a much quicker means of communication regarding the DRO.

While this development has saved employers some money, the result has been a mixed blessing from the perspectives of Participants, Alternate Payees, and the family law bar. On the one hand, many external QDRO processing firms give prompt, consistent responses to QDRO submissions and request reasonable changes when appropriate. However, their QDRO processing is often done by clerical personnel, not lawyers, who perform their tasks by comparing QDROs with standardized checklists and have no discretion to negotiate reasonable changes to their oversimplified standard format and clauses. This often results in the rejection of QDROs that should be approved if the language of the QDRO departs significantly from the standard form QDRO used by the plan (see section 15.2). It may take two or three written complaints to get such issues out of the hands of the clerical personnel and into the hands of a qualified Employee Retirement Income Security Act (ERISA) plan lawyer who can understand and approve nonstandard QDRO clauses.

QDROs are complex and sophisticated legal documents requiring the expertise of a qualified lawyer to draft and evaluate. Efforts by some QDRO processing firms to standardize QDRO drafting and evaluation are misguided to a large degree because not every case, agreement, or order can be "standardized." In the short run this perspective may save employers a few dollars. But in the long run this small savings is greatly outweighed by the additional expense and delay generated in persuading a QDRO processing firm to accept a nonstandard QDRO, as well as the frustration that divorcing employees and their spouses experience as a result.

The upside to the growth of QDRO processing companies is that these companies become experts in the processing and handling of QDROs. This can make the process less costly and less time consuming for the client. This also makes it easier when dealing with small employers that do not have the resources or the internal knowledge on how to process or handle a QDRO.

18.3 Fewer Defined Benefit Plans, More Defined Contribution Plans

For a variety of economic motives (primarily constantly increasing funding and administrative expenses, including Pension Benefit Guaranty Corporation insurance premiums, and the desire of corporate plan sponsors to shift investment risk from themselves to their employees), the number of employees covered by Defined

Benefit Plans has dropped precipitously in the last 20 years (defined benefit plans: pensions). While 80 percent of the full-time employees of large- and medium-sized companies in America were covered by defined benefit plans in 1985, by 2004 that figure had decreased to just 34 percent and the number of defined benefit plans had dwindled from 128,000 to just 26,000—a large, dramatic, and irreversible decline. During that same time, the percentage of employees of large- and medium-sized companies covered by defined contribution plans (defined contribution plans: 401(k) and similar plans) increased from 41 to 53 percent, with the number of plans more than doubling from 300,000 to 683,000.

No employers are starting new defined benefit plans. Many are freezing or closing their existing defined benefit plans and replacing them with defined contribution plans. You are also seeing some companies and entities introducing "hybrid" or "blended" retirement plans for a certain period of time or class of employee. Overall, many companies are putting more emphasis on the Participant contributions to retirement. One notable example of this is the new military retired pay system that was recently implemented and is addressed in Chapter 11. Many state, county, and municipal plans have followed a similar trend in recent years. The Federal Pension Protection Act of 2006 is likely to accelerate the trend by making Defined Benefit Plan sponsorship more expensive and Defined Contribution Plan sponsorship more attractive to employers.

QDROs dividing defined benefit plans are necessarily more complex and difficult to draft than QDROs dividing defined contribution plans. A Defined Benefit Plan QDRO must address an increased number of variables and issues, including survivor benefits or annuities, early retirement subsidies, cost-of-living increases, the different forms of annuity payments, and similar difficult issues. In contrast, Defined Contribution QDROs need only divide the vested account balance in a plan, generally just simply by a dollar figure or percentage, and then resolve the issues usually presented, such as whether the Alternate Payee's awarded interest will be adjusted for dividends, interest, gains and losses from the date of division to the date of distribution, and the correct treatment of plan loans. Dividing a defined contribution plan is not as complex as the issues presented by dividing defined benefit plans. That does not mean that the amount of care and attention should be any less. It is vitally important for Participants and Alternate Payees and their lawyers to realize that Defined Contribution QDROs remain complex legal instruments and that a mistake in their language can result in a difference of several hundred thousand dollars.

18.4 Erroneous Use of "Interpretation Letters"

Many QDRO processors have begun the practice of sending "interpretation letters" when they approve QDROs, which set forth the Plan Administrator's interpretation of the meaning and effect of the QDRO. As precise legal documents, QDROs speak for themselves and are not susceptible to completely accurate summarization or rewording. "Interpretation letters" are not mentioned in or authorized by ERISA.

Interpretation letters are not all bad, however. For example, oftentimes you will have extremely complicated awards or agreements factoring multiple variables, and it is foreseeable that regardless of the care and specific drafting, the QDRO could be interpreted in an alternate fashion. The interpretation letters can act as a verification and safeguard that everyone is on the same page and that the QDRO is going to be processed as intended.

QDRO drafters receiving such letters have a few choices. If everything is in order, you can simply ignore the letter and put it into the file. If there is an issue down the road with processing, then you have the letter reflecting the plan's interpretation and how everything should have been processed. Alternatively, you can send a simple form response stating that the language of the QDRO speaks for itself and that the parties are not legally required by ERISA to either agree or disagree with the contents of the interpretation letter. Most of the time, if an interpretation letter is received and the draft DRO was approved, the interpretation will be consistent with the intent. While unusual, in the event that an award is complicated, was approved, but was misinterpreted, then this can easily be corrected with the plan to make sure that all involved parties, including the plan, are on the same page.

18.5 Imposition of QDRO Processing Fees

In 2003, the U.S. Department of Labor (DOL) reversed one of its long-standing policies and for the first time allowed defined contribution plans (but not defined benefit plans) to impose fees for the review and approval of QDROs on individual Participants and Alternate Payees. *See* Field Assistance Bulletin 2003-3 (May 19, 2003) (hereinafter FAB 2003-3).

No one disputes that QDRO processors should be paid for their work. Before 2003, their fees were paid, like other plan administrative expenses, either by the plan sponsor or by deduction from the entire pool of the plan's assets, thus spreading the cost over all plan Participants, costing each individual a very small percentage of his or her account. After the issuance of FAB 2003-3, plans have imposed fees ranging from $300 to $1,200. Fortunately, many plans have continued the pre-2003 practice of paying QDRO approval expenses by the corporate sponsor of the plan or from the plan's large pool of assets.

Compounding the problems created by FAB 2003-3, many plans have failed to comply with its two key provisions. First, it requires that plan expenses charged to Participants and Alternate Payees be reasonable. For some plans, the fees have been excessive. Others have engaged in the practice of charging more to review custom-tailored QDROs than they charge to review QDROs based on their own recommended model forms. This effectively ties the drafting attorney's hands in being able to include more specified language and having to address costing one or both of the parties up to or more than $1,000 for the QDRO to be reviewed and processed. This is a result of many processors just being paid for the involvement of review and processing the QDROs. When fees are not paid from the entire pool of the plan's assets, then the costs are "justified" because the originally drafted QDROs require more attention and care in review.

The second requirement of FAB 2003-3 is that any fees charged to individual Participants and Alternate Payees for QDRO approval be expressly disclosed in the plan's Summary Plan Description (see section 15.1). A significant number of plans have simply ignored this regulatory requirement. If requested in writing to provide a copy of the Summary Plan Description disclosing the proposed fee in compliance with FAB 2003-3, many plans simply withdraw their fee request. An additional factor that should always be weighed in attempting to argue with a plan is how much time that effort is going to take and what the likely outcome is.

18.6 Regulatory Failure: Department of Labor Indifference to QDRO Processing Problems

ERISA gives the Department of Labor jurisdiction (concurrent with the Internal Revenue Service) over making and implementing regulations under ERISA and making sure that employee benefit plans are operated "solely in the interests of participants and their beneficiaries." ERISA section 404(a)(1). The DOL may have achieved some measure of success in other areas, but it has failed to do so in the QDRO area. While it has issued a very helpful booklet (discussed in subsection 3.2C and section 15.1) to guide Plan Administrators in how to process and administer QDROs, it has never adopted the rules and principles set forth in its booklet as regulations, which has resulted in a failure to enforce anything against Plan Administrators who defy the regulatory guidance set forth in the booklet.

18.7 The Rise and Spread of Unqualified Internet QDRO-Drafting Firms

The dramatic surge in Internet use has encouraged the growth of Internet advertising by QDRO preparation firms. While some of them are operated by qualified lawyers, a host of unqualified and unregulated QDRO preparation firms have taken advantage of this advertising medium to offer their services to the public. This leads to the risk of unqualified persons drafting and handling a very important and complex legal document with significant financial ramifications.

Bar associations seem to be at a loss regarding how to regulate such firms, namely because they operate in multiple jurisdictions and seem to exist out in hyperspace with no physical presence in the concerned state. The Internet is full of claims about charging the lowest fees and offering the quickest turnaround time. Several Internet QDRO mills now offer a fill-in-the-blank QDRO form on the theory that one size fits all in QDRO drafting—indisputably not the case.

The correct emphasis in QDRO drafting is on accurately reflecting the underlying separation agreement or court order, dealing with the complex requirements of ERISA, and obtaining the best possible result for the client—not in offering cheap services or hasty preparation. Naturally, most Alternate Payees have a desire to get things handled as quickly as possible for a number of reasons; whether they're trying to purchase a home, qualify for a property refinancing, or pay off certain debts, it is important to stress to this client the quality and assurance that things are done correctly the first time. The quality of a QDRO directly affects how well the Participant and Alternate Payee will be able to live in retirement, and the allocation of payments over several decades is not a task to be undertaken hastily or superficially. Unfortunately, there are a significant number of people who willingly settle for these mass-produced and untailored orders because of the cost. These people oftentimes end up calling you again later when things were botched the first time. Unfortunately, as long as these services are available online, it is likely this trend will continue, to the detriment of many Participants and Alternate Payees.

Conclusion

QDROs (and similar division documents) are a complex and difficult area of the law. It is important to review all applicable regulations and address all issues that could arise. It is vitally important to make sure that the parties involved are informed of the process and what is required each step along the way. Ideally, this book can be used to help you in all of these steps and answer questions that may arise.

Any comments you have on the handbook and any suggestions you have for improvements in the next edition are always welcome. As I'm sure every practicing attorney has experienced, a case will come along with a fact pattern you've never seen before. These are excellent to include as examples of what to do or what not to do. Please write to Shewmaker & Lewis, LLC, 50 Technology Parkway South, Peachtree Corners, GA 30092, or in care of the American Bar Association Family Law Section Book Publications, 321 North Clark Street, 20th Floor, Chicago, IL 60654; or email Patricia Shewmaker at PShewmaker@ShewmakerandLewis.com and James Lewis at JLewis@ShewmakerandLewis.com.

APPENDIX A

Text of Sections 1055 and 1056(d) of ERISA

Section 1055. *Requirement of joint and survivor annuity and preretirement survivor annuity*

(a) *Required contents for applicable plans.* Each pension plan to which this section applies shall provide that—

(1) in the case of a vested participant who does not die before the annuity starting date, the accrued benefit payable to such participant shall be provided in the form of a qualified joint and survivor annuity, and

(2) in the case of a vested participant who dies before the annuity starting date and who has a surviving spouse, a qualified preretirement survivor annuity shall be provided to the surviving spouse of such participant.

(b) *Applicable plans.*

(1) This section shall apply to—

(A) any defined benefit plan,

(B) any individual account plan which is subject to the funding standards of section 302 [29 U.S.C. § 1082], and

(C) any participant under any other individual account plan unless—

(i) such plan provides that the participant's nonforfeitable accrued benefit (reduced by any security interest held by the plan by reason of a loan outstanding to such participant) is payable in full, on the death of the participant, to the participant's surviving spouse (or, if there is no surviving spouse or the surviving spouse consents in the manner required under subsection (c)(2), to a designated beneficiary),

(ii) such participant does not elect the payment of benefits in the form of a life annuity, and

(iii) with respect to such participant, such plan is not a direct or indirect transferee (in a transfer after December 31, 1984) of a plan which is described in subparagraph (A) or (B) or to which this clause applied with respect to the participant.

Clause (iii) of subparagraph (C) shall apply only with respect to the transferred assets (and income therefrom) if the plan separately accounts for such assets and any income therefrom.

(2) (A) In the case of—

(i) a tax credit employee stock ownership plan (as defined in section 409(a) of the Internal Revenue Code of 1986 [26 U.S.C. § 409(a)]), or

(ii) an employee stock ownership plan (as defined in section 4975(e)(7) of such Code [26 U.S.C. § 4975(e)(7)]),

subsection (a) shall not apply to that portion of the employee's accrued benefit to which the requirements of section 409(h) of such Code [26 U.S.C. § 409(h)] apply.

(B) Subparagraph (A) shall not apply with respect to any participant unless the requirements of clause [clauses] (i), (ii), and (iii) of paragraph (1)(C) are met with respect to such participant.

[(3)](4) This section shall not apply to a plan which the Secretary of the Treasury or his delegate has determined is a plan described in section 404(c) of the Internal Revenue Code of 1986 (or a continuation thereof) in which participation is substantially limited to individuals who, before January 1, 1976, ceased employment covered by the plan.

(4) A plan shall not be treated as failing to meet the requirements of paragraph (1)(C) or (2) merely because the plan provides that benefits will not be payable to the surviving spouse of the participant unless the participant and such spouse had been married throughout the 1-year period ending on the earlier of the

participant's annuity starting date or the date of the participant's death.

(c) *Plans meeting requirements of section.*

(1) A plan meets the requirements of this section only if

(A) under the plan, each participant—

(i) may elect at any time during the applicable election period to waive the qualified joint and survivor annuity form of benefit or the qualified preretirement survivor annuity form of benefit (or both), and

(ii) if the participant elects a waiver under clause (i), may elect the qualified optional survivor annuity at any time during the applicable period, and

(iii) may revoke any such election at any time during the applicable election period, and

(B) the plan meets the requirements of paragraphs (2), (3), and (4).

(2) Each plan shall provide that an election under paragraph (1)(A)(i) shall not take effect unless—

(A) (i) the spouse of the participant consents in writing to such election, (ii) such election designates a beneficiary (or a form of benefits) which may not be changed without spousal consent (or the consent of the spouse expressly permits designations by the participant without any requirement of further consent by the spouse), and (iii) the spouse's consent acknowledges the effect of such election and is witnessed by a plan representative or a notary public, or

(B) it is established to the satisfaction of a plan representative that the consent required under subparagraph (A) may not be obtained because there is no spouse, because the spouse cannot be located, or because of such other circumstances as the Secretary of the Treasury may by regulations prescribe.

Any consent by a spouse (or establishment that the consent of a spouse may not be obtained) under the preceding sentence shall be effective only with respect to such spouse.

(3) (A) Each plan shall provide to each participant within a reasonable period of time before the annuity starting date (and consistent with such regulations as the Secretary of the Treasury may prescribe) a written explanation of—

(i) the terms and conditions of the qualified joint and survivor annuity,

(ii) the participant's right to make, and the effect of, an election under paragraph (1) to waive the joint and survivor annuity form of benefit,

(iii) the rights of the participant's spouse under paragraph (2), and

(iv) the right to make, and the effect of, a revocation of an election under paragraph (1).

(B) (i) Each plan shall provide to each participant, within the applicable period with respect to such participant (and consistent with such regulations as the Secretary may prescribe), a written explanation with respect to the qualified preretirement survivor annuity comparable to that required under subparagraph (A).

(ii) For purposes of clause (i), the term "applicable period" means, with respect to a participant, whichever of the following periods ends last:

(I) The period beginning with the first day of the plan year in which the participant attains age 32 and ending with the close of the plan year preceding the plan year in which the participant attains age 35.

(II) A reasonable period after the individual becomes a participant.

(III) A reasonable period ending after paragraph (5) ceases to apply to the participant.

(IV) A reasonable period ending after section 205 [this section] applies to the participant.

In the case of a participant who separates from service before attaining age 35, the applicable period shall be a reasonable period after separation.

(4) Each plan shall provide that, if this section applies to a participant when part or all of the participant's accrued benefit is to be used as security for a loan, no portion of the participant's accrued benefit may be used as security for such loan unless—

(A) the spouse of the participant (if any) consents in writing to such use during the 90-day period ending on the date on which the loan is to be so secured, and

(B) requirements comparable to the requirements of paragraph (2) are met with respect to such consent.

(5) (A) The requirements of this subsection shall not apply with respect to the qualified joint and survivor annuity form of benefit or the qualified preretirement survivor annuity form of benefit, as the case may be, if such benefit may not be waived (or another beneficiary selected) and if the plan fully subsidizes the costs of such benefit.

(B) For purposes of subparagraph (A), a plan fully subsidizes the costs of a benefit if under the plan the failure to waive such benefit by a participant would not result in a decrease in any plan benefits with respect to such participant and would not result in increased contributions from such participant.

(6) If a plan fiduciary acts in accordance with part 4 of this subtitle [29 U.S.C. §§ 1101 *et seq.*] in—

(A) relying on a consent or revocation referred to in paragraph (1)(A), or

(B) making a determination under paragraph (2),

then such consent, revocation, or determination shall be treated as valid for purposes of discharging the plan from liability to the extent of payments made pursuant to such Act.

(7) For purposes of this subsection, the term "applicable election period" means—

(A) in the case of an election to waive the qualified joint and survivor annuity form of benefit, the 0-day period ending on the annuity starting date, or

(B) in the case of an election to waive the qualified preretirement survivor annuity, the period which begins on the first day of the plan year in which the participant attains age 35 and ends on the date of the participant's death.

In the case of a participant who is separated from service, the applicable election period under subparagraph (B) with respect to benefits accrued before the date of such separation from service shall not begin later than such date.

(8) Notwithstanding any other provision of this subsection—

(A) (i) A plan may provide the written explanation described in paragraph (3)(A) after the annuity starting date. In any case to which this subparagraph applies, the applicable election period under paragraph (7) shall not end before the 30th day after the date on which such explanation is provided.

(ii) The Secretary of the Treasury may by regulations limit the application of clause (i), except that such regulations may not limit the period of time by which the annuity starting date precedes the provision of the written explanation other than by providing that the annuity starting date may not be earlier than termination of employment.

(B) A plan may permit a participant to elect (with any applicable spousal consent) to waive any requirement that the written explanation be provided at least 30 days before the annuity starting date (or to waive the 30-day requirement under subparagraph (A)) if the distribution commences more than 7 days after such explanation is provided.

(d) *"Qualified joint and survivor annuity" defined.*

(1) For purposes of this section, the term "qualified joint and survivor annuity" means an annuity—

(A) for the life of the participant with a survivor annuity for the life of the spouse which is not less than 50 percent of (and is not greater than 100 percent of) the amount of the annuity which is payable during the joint lives of the participant and the spouse, and

(B) which is the actuarial equivalent of a single annuity for the life of the participant.

Such term also includes any annuity in a form having the effect of an annuity described in the preceding sentence.

(2) (A) For purposes of this section, the term "qualified optional survivor annuity" means an annuity—

(i) for the life of the participant with a survivor annuity for the life of the spouse which is equal to the applicable percentage of the amount of the annuity which is payable during the joint lives of the participant and the spouse, and

(ii) which is the actuarial equivalent of a single annuity for the life of the participant. Such term also includes any annuity in a form having the effect of an annuity described in the preceding sentence.

(B) (i) For purposes of subparagraph (A), if the survivor annuity percentage—

(I) is less than 75 percent, the applicable percentage is 75 percent, and

(II) is greater than or equal to 75 percent, the applicable percentage is 50 percent.

(ii) For purposes of clause (i), the term "survivor annuity percentage" means the percentage which the survivor annuity under the plan's qualified joint and survivor annuity bears to the annuity payable during the joint lives of the participant and the spouse.

(e) *"Qualified preretirement survivor annuity" defined.* For purposes of this section—

(1) Except as provided in paragraph (2), the term "qualified preretirement survivor annuity" means a survivor annuity for the life of the surviving spouse of the participant if—

(A) the payments to the surviving spouse under such annuity are not less than the amounts which would be payable as a survivor annuity under the qualified joint and survivor annuity under the plan (or the actuarial equivalent thereof) if—

(i) in the case of a participant who dies after the date on which the participant attained the earliest retirement age, such participant had retired with an immediate qualified joint and survivor annuity on the day before the participant's date of death, or

(ii) in the case of a participant who dies on or before the date on which the participant would have attained the earliest retirement age, such participant had—

(I) separated from service on the date of death,

(II) survived to the earliest retirement age,

(III) retired with an immediate qualified joint and survivor annuity at the earliest retirement age, and

(IV) died on the day after the day on which such participant would have attained the earliest retirement age, and

(B) under the plan, the earliest period for which the surviving spouse may receive a payment under such annuity is not later than the month in which the participant would have attained the earliest retirement age under the plan.

In the case of an individual who separated from service before the date of such individual's death, subparagraph (A)(ii)(I) shall not apply.

(2) In the case of any individual account plan or participant described in subparagraph (B) or (C) of subsection (b)(1), the term "qualified preretirement survivor annuity" means an annuity for the life of the surviving spouse the actuarial equivalent of which is not less than 50 percent of the portion of the account balance of the participant (as of the date of death) to which the participant had a nonforfeitable right (within the meaning of section 203 [29 U.S.C. § 1053]).

(3) For purposes of paragraphs (1) and (2), any security interest held by the plan by reason of a loan outstanding to the participant shall be taken into account in determining the amount of the qualified preretirement survivor annuity.

(f) *Marriage requirements for plan.*

(1) Except as provided in paragraph (2), a plan may provide that a qualified joint and survivor annuity (or a qualified preretirement survivor annuity) will not be provided unless the participant and spouse had been married throughout the 1-year period ending on the earlier of

(A) the participant's annuity starting date, or

(B) the date of the participant's death.

(2) For purposes of paragraph (1), if—

(A) A participant marries within 1 year before the annuity starting date, and

(B) the participant and the participant's spouse in such marriage have been married for at least a 1-year period ending on or before the date of the participant's death,

such participant and such spouse shall be treated as having been married throughout the 1-year period ending on the participant's annuity starting date.

(g) *Distribution of present value of annuity; written consent; determination of present value.*

(1) A plan may provide that the present value of a qualified joint and survivor annuity or a qualified preretirement survivor annuity will be immediately distributed if such value does not exceed the dollar limit under section 203(e) [29 U.S.C. § 1053(e)]. No distribution may be made under the preceding sentence after the annuity starting date unless the participant and the spouse of the participant (or where the participant has died, the surviving spouse) consent in writing to such distribution.

(2) If—

(A) the present value of the qualified joint and survivor annuity or the qualified preretirement survivor annuity exceeds the amount that can be distributed without the participant's consent under section 203(e) [29 U.S.C. § 1053(e)], and

(B) the participant and the spouse of the participant (or where the participant has died, the surviving spouse) consent in writing to the distribution,

the plan may immediately distribute the present value of such annuity.

(3) (A) For purposes of paragraphs (1) and (2), the present value shall not be less than the present value calculated by using the applicable mortality table and the applicable interest rate.

(B) For purposes of subparagraph (A)—

(i) The term "applicable mortality table" means a mortality table, modified as appropriate by the Secretary of the Treasury, based on the mortality table specified for the plan year under subparagraph (A) of section 303(h)(3) [29 U.S.C.S. § 1083(h)(3)] (without regard to subparagraph (C) or (D) of such section).

(ii) The term "applicable interest rate" means the adjusted first, second, and third segment rates applied under rules similar to the rules of section 303(h)(2)(C) [29 U.S.C.S. § 1083(h)(2)(C)] (determined by not taking into account any adjustment under clause (iv) thereof) for the month before the date of the distribution or such other time as the Secretary of Treasury may by regulations prescribe.

(iii) For purposes of clause (ii), the adjusted first, second, and third segment rates are the first, second, and third segment rates which would be determined under section 303(h)(2)(C) [29 U.S.C.S. § 1083(h)(2)(C)] (determined by not taking into account any adjustment under (iv) thereof) if section 303(h)(2)(D) [29 U.S.C.S. § 1083(h)(2)(D)] were applied by substituting the average yields for the month described in clause (ii) for the average yields for the 24-month period described in such section.

(h) *Definitions.* For purposes of this section—

(1) The term "vested participant" means any participant who has a nonforfeitable right (within the meaning of section 3(19) [29 U.S.C. § 1002(19)]) to any portion of such participant's accrued benefit.

(2) (A) The term "annuity starting date" means—

(i) the first day of the first period for which an amount is payable as an annuity, or

(ii) in the case of a benefit not payable in the form of an annuity, the first day on which all events have occurred which entitle the participant to such benefit.

(B) For purposes of subparagraph (A), the first day of the first period for which a benefit is to be received by reason of disability shall be treated as the annuity starting date only if such benefit is not an auxiliary benefit.

(3) The term "earliest retirement age" means the earliest date on which, under the plan, the participant could elect to receive retirement benefits.

(i) *Increased costs from providing annuity.* A plan may take into account in any equitable manner (as determined by the Secretary of the Treasury) any increased costs resulting from providing a qualified joint or survivor annuity or a qualified preretirement survivor annuity.

(j) *Use of participant's accrued benefit as security for loan as not preventing distribution.* If the use of any participant's accrued benefit (or any portion thereof) as security for a loan meets the requirements of subsection (c)(4), nothing in this section shall prevent any distribution required by reason of a failure to comply with the terms of such loan.

(k) *Spousal consent.* No consent of a spouse shall be effective for purposes of subsection (g)(1) or (g)(2) (as the case may be) unless requirements comparable to the requirements for spousal consent to an election under subsection (c)(1)(A) are met.

(l) *Regulations; consultation of Secretary of the Treasury with Secretary of Labor.* In prescribing regulations under this section, the Secretary of the Treasury shall consult with the Secretary of Labor.

Section 1056(d). *Form and payment of benefits*

(d) *Assignment or alienation of plan benefits.*

(1) Each pension plan shall provide that benefits provided under the plan may not be assigned or alienated.

(2) For the purposes of paragraph (1) of this subsection, there shall not be taken into account any voluntary and revocable assignment of not to exceed 10 percent of any benefit payment, or of any irrevocable assignment or alienation of benefits executed before the

date of enactment of this Act [enacted Sept. 2, 1974]. The preceding sentence shall not apply to any assignment or alienation made for the purposes of defraying plan administration costs. For purposes of this paragraph a loan made to a participant or beneficiary shall not be treated as an assignment or alienation if such loan is secured by the participant's accrued nonforfeitable benefit and is exempt from the tax imposed by section 4975 of the Internal Revenue Code of 1986 [26 U.S.C. § 4975] (relating to tax on prohibited transactions) by reason of section 4975(d)(1) of such Code [26 U.S.C. § 4975(d)(1)].

(3) (A) Paragraph (1) shall apply to the creation, assignment, or recognition of a right to any benefit payable with respect to a participant pursuant to a domestic relations order, except that paragraph (1) shall not apply if the order is determined to be a qualified domestic relations order. Each pension plan shall provide for the payment of benefits in accordance with the applicable requirements of any qualified domestic relations order.

(B) For purposes of this paragraph—

(i) the term "qualified domestic relations order" means a domestic relations order—

(I) which creates or recognizes the existence of an alternate payee's right to, or assigns to an alternate payee the right to, receive all or a portion of the benefits payable with respect to a participant under a plan, and

(II) with respect to which the requirements of subparagraphs (C) and (D) are met, and

(ii) the term "domestic relations order" means any judgment, decree, or order (including approval of a property settlement agreement) which—

(I) relates to the provision of child support, alimony payments, or marital property rights to a spouse, former spouse, child, or other dependent of a participant, and

(II) is made pursuant to a State or Tribal domestic relations law (including a community property law).

For purposes of clause (ii)(II), the term "Tribal" with respect to a domestic relations law means such a law which is issued by or under the laws of an Indian tribal government (as defined in section 7701(a)(40) of the Internal Revenue Code of 1986 [26 U.S.C.S. § 7701(a)(40)]), a subdivision of such an Indian tribal government, or an agency or instrumentality of either.

(C) A domestic relations order meets the requirements of this subparagraph only if such order clearly specifies—

(i) the name and the last known mailing address (if any) of the participant and the name and mailing address of each alternate payee covered by the order,

(ii) the amount or percentage of the participant's benefits to be paid by the plan to each such alternate payee, or the manner in which such amount or percentage is to be determined,

(iii) the number of payments or period to which such order applies, and

(iv) each plan to which such order applies.

(D) A domestic relations order meets the requirements of this subparagraph only if such order—

(i) does not require a plan to provide any type or form of benefit, or any option, not otherwise provided under the plan,

(ii) does not require the plan to provide increased benefits (determined on the basis of actuarial value), and

(iii) does not require the payment of benefits to an alternate payee which are required to be paid to another alternate payee under another order previously determined to be a qualified domestic relations order.

(E) (i) A domestic relations order shall not be treated as failing to meet the requirements of clause (i) of subparagraph (D) solely because such order requires that payment of benefits be made to an alternate payee—

(I) on or in the case of any payment before a participant has separated from service, after the date on which the participant attains (or would have attained) the earliest retirement age,

(II) as if the participant had retired on the date on which such payment is to begin under such order (but taking into account only the present value of benefits actually accrued and not taking into account the present value of any employer subsidy for early retirement), and

(III) in any form in which such benefits may be paid under the plan to the participant (other than in the form of a joint and survivor annuity with respect to the alternate payee and his or her subsequent spouse).

For purposes of subclause (II), the interest rate assumption used in determining the present value shall be the interest rate specified in the plan or, if no rate is specified, 5 percent.

(ii) For purposes of this subparagraph, the term "earliest retirement age" means the earlier of—

(I) the date on which the participant is entitled to a distribution under the plan, or

(II) the later of the date of [on which] the participant attains age 50 or the earliest date on which the participant could begin receiving benefits under the plan if the participant separated from service.

(F) To the extent provided in any qualified domestic relations order—

(i) the former spouse of a participant shall be treated as a surviving spouse of such participant for purposes of section 205 [29 U.S.C. § 1055] (and any spouse of the participant shall not be treated as a spouse of the participant for such purposes), and

(ii) if married for at least 1 year, the surviving former spouse shall be treated as meeting the requirements of section 205(f) [29 U.S.C. § 1055(f)].

(G) (i) In the case of any domestic relations order received by a plan—

(I) the plan administrator shall promptly notify the participant and each alternate payee of the receipt of such order and the plan's procedures for determining the qualified status of domestic relations orders, and

(II) within a reasonable period after receipt of such order, the plan administrator shall determine whether such order is a qualified domestic relations order and notify the participant and each alternate payee of such determination.

(ii) Each plan shall establish reasonable procedures to determine the qualified status of domestic relations orders and to administer distributions under such qualified orders. Such procedures—

(I) shall be in writing,

(II) shall provide for the notification of each person specified in a domestic relations order as entitled to payment of benefits under the plan (at the address included in the domestic relations order) of such procedures promptly upon receipt by the plan of the domestic relations order, and

(III) shall permit an alternate payee to designate a representative for receipt of copies of notices that are sent to the alternate payee with respect to a domestic relations order.

(H) (i) During any period in which the issue of whether a domestic relations order is a qualified domestic relations order is being determined (by the plan administrator, by a court of competent jurisdiction, or otherwise), the plan administrator shall separately account for the amounts (hereinafter in this subparagraph referred to as the "segregated amounts") which would have been payable to the alternate payee during such period if the order had been determined to be a qualified domestic relations order.

(ii) If within the 18-month period described in clause (v) the order (or modification thereof) is determined to be a qualified domestic relations order, the plan administrator shall pay the segregated amounts (including any interest thereon) to the person or persons entitled thereto.

(iii) If within the 18-month period described in clause (v)—

(I) it is determined that the order is not a qualified domestic relations order, or

(II) the issue as to whether such order is a qualified domestic relations order is not resolved, then the plan administrator shall pay the segregated amounts (including any interest thereon) to the person or persons who would have been entitled to such amounts if there had been no order.

(iv) Any determination that an order is a qualified domestic relations order which is made after the close of the 18-month period described in clause (v) shall be applied prospectively only.

(v) For purposes of this subparagraph, the 18-month period described in this clause is the 18-month period beginning with the date on which the first payment would be required to be made under the domestic relations order.

(I) If a plan fiduciary acts in accordance with part 4 of this subtitle [29 U.S.C. §§ 1101 *et seq.*] in—

(i) treating a domestic relations order as being (or not being) a qualified domestic relations order, or

(ii) taking action under subparagraph (H),

then the plan's obligation to the participant and each alternate payee shall be discharged to the extent of any payment made pursuant to such Act.

(J) A person who is an alternate payee under a qualified domestic relations order shall be considered for purposes of any provision of this Act a beneficiary under the plan. Nothing in the preceding sentence shall permit a requirement under section 4001 [29 U.S.C. § 1301] of the payment of more than 1 premium with respect to a participant for any period.

(K) The term "alternate payee" means any spouse, former spouse, child, or other dependent of a participant who is recognized by a domestic relations order as having a right to receive all, or a portion of, the benefits payable under a plan with respect to such participant.

(L) This paragraph shall not apply to any plan to which paragraph (1) does not apply.

(M) Payment of benefits by a pension plan, in accordance with the applicable requirements of a qualified domestic relations order shall not be treated as garnishment for purposes of section 303(a) of the Consumer Credit Protection Act [15 U.S.C. § 1673(a)].

(N) In prescribing regulations under this paragraph, the Secretary shall consult with the Secretary of the Treasury.

(4) Paragraph (1) shall not apply to any offset of a participant's benefits provided under an employee pension benefit plan against an amount that the participant is ordered or required to pay to the plan if—

(A) the order or requirement to pay arises—

(i) under a judgment of conviction for a crime involving such plan,

(ii) under a civil judgment (including a consent order or decree) entered by a court in an action brought in connection with a violation (or alleged violation) of part 4 of this subtitle [29 U.S.C. §§ 1101 *et seq.*], or

(iii) pursuant to a settlement agreement between the Secretary and the participant, or a settlement agreement between the Pension Benefit Guaranty Corporation and the participant, in connection with a violation (or alleged violation) of part 4 of this subtitle [29 U.S.C. §§ 1101 *et seq.*] by a fiduciary or any other person.

(B) the judgment, order, decree, or settlement agreement expressly provides for the offset of all or part of the amount ordered or required to be paid to the plan against the participant's benefits provided under the plan, and

(C) in a case in which the survivor annuity requirements of section 205 [29 U.S.C. § 1055] apply with respect to distributions from the plan to the participant, if the participant has a spouse at the time at which the offset is to be made—

(i) either—

(I) such spouse has consented in writing to such offset and such consent is witnessed by a notary public or representative of the plan (or it is established to the satisfaction of a plan representative that such consent may not be obtained by reason of circumstances described in section 205(c)(2)(B) [29 U.S.C. § 1055(c)(2)(B)]), or

(II) an election to waive the right of the spouse to a qualified joint and survivor annuity or a qualified preretirement survivor annuity is in effect in accordance with the requirements of section 205(c) [29 U.S.C. § 1055(c)],

(ii) such spouse is ordered or required in such judgment, order, decree, or settlement to pay an amount to the plan in connection with a violation of part 4 of this subtitle [29 U.S.C. §§ 1101 *et seq.*], or

(iii) in such judgment, order, decree, or settlement, such spouse retains the right to receive the survivor annuity under a qualified joint and survivor annuity provided pursuant to section 205(a)(1) [29 U.S.C. § 1055(a)(1)] and under a qualified preretirement survivor annuity provided pursuant to section 205(a)(2) [29 U.S.C. § 1055(a)(2)], determined in accordance with paragraph (5).

A plan shall not be treated as failing to meet the requirements of section 205 [29 U.S.C. § 1055] solely by reason of an offset under this paragraph.

(5) (A) The survivor annuity described in paragraph (4)(C)(iii) shall be determined as if—

(i) the participant terminated employment on the date of the offset,

(ii) there was no offset,

(iii) the plan permitted commencement of benefits only on or after normal retirement age,

(iv) the plan provided only the minimum-required qualified joint and survivor annuity, and

(v) the amount of the qualified preretirement survivor annuity under the plan is equal to the amount of the survivor annuity payable under the minimum-required qualified joint and survivor annuity.

(B) For purposes of this paragraph, the term "minimum-required qualified joint and survivor annuity" means the qualified joint and survivor annuity which is the actuarial equivalent of the participant's accrued benefit (within the meaning of section 3(23) [29 U.S.C. § 1002(23)]) and under which the survivor annuity is 50 percent of the amount of the annuity which is payable during the joint lives of the participant and the spouse.

APPENDIX B

Model Letter to Plan Requesting Disclosure of Benefits Information

Maikkula & Teague, P.C.
Attorneys at Law
123 Main Street
Augusta, Georgia 30909
Telephone: (706) 123-4567

June __, 20__

Ms. Olivia Official, Benefits Specialist
Global MegaCorp Employee Retirement Plan
222 West Corporate Drive
Santa Barbara, California 99099

RE: *Pension and Employee Benefits Information (David L. Zoelle)*

Dear Ms. Official:

This letter follows our telephone discussion earlier today. At that time I advised you that we represent Mrs. Arlene Zoelle in divorce action No. 123-45 in Clayton County Superior Court. The defendant in that case is her husband, Mr. David L. Zoelle, who is employed by your company and is a participant in various pension and employee benefit plans sponsored by Global MegaCorp.

Under Georgia law, all employee pension rights and benefits accumulated during the marriage of the parties are considered divisible marital property and the two spouses are considered co-owners thereof. Such assets may also be used to satisfy alimony and child support obligations of plan participants. We are asking the Court to award custody of the parties' children to Mrs. Zoelle and may seek payment of alimony or child support or both from Global MegaCorp's pension and employee benefit plans in addition to a division of them as marital property.

I am enclosing with this letter a copy of the divorce complaint we have filed on behalf of Mrs. Zoelle, the prospective Alternate Payee. This should constitute reasonable assurance to your plans that the information we are requesting is made in connection with a domestic relations proceeding.

With these considerations in mind, I am writing to renew my request that you send to our office as soon as possible the following documents relating to Mr. Zoelle for *each plan* sponsored by Global MegaCorp in which he is or ever was a Participant:

1. Full text of the plan
2. Most recent Summary Plan Description
3. Written QDRO Procedures
4. Mr. Zoelle's three (3) most recent annual benefits statements

If your Written QDRO Procedures do not include a model or sample QDRO form, I would appreciate it if you would send us a QDRO that your plans recently approved (with the names and other identifying information blacked out, of course) and the names and addresses of some attorneys from any jurisdictions who have recently gotten QDROs approved by your plans.

If there are any booklets or pamphlets that you distribute to employees informally explaining your benefit plans and various types and forms of benefits available and any election options, we would appreciate it if you would send us copies of that material as well.

Our goal is to work with you to draft and qualify a QDRO in this case. We want to achieve that goal as efficiently and promptly as possible and to minimize any burdens on the plans during the qualification process. However, we cannot do this without your assistance in providing copies of these materials that we believe you are obligated by law to provide to us.

Should you decline to produce any or all of these documents to us immediately, we would appreciate your providing us with a written statement of your specific grounds for refusing to do so. In such a case, we reserve the right to notify the Department of Labor and the Internal Revenue Service of your actions, to seek appropriate monetary sanctions against the pension and employee benefit plans involved, and to seek personal monetary sanctions against the appropriate plan officials and fiduciaries.

Sincerely yours,

Eileen G. Maikkula
Maikkula & Teague

cc: Mrs. Arlene Zoelle

APPENDIX C

Model Letter to Plan Transmitting DRO for Qualification and Asking for Confirmation of Payment Features

Maikkula & Teague, P.C.
Attorneys at Law
123 Main Street
Augusta, Georgia 30909
Telephone: (706) 123-4567

September __, 20__

Ms. Olivia Official, Benefits Specialist
Global MegaCorp Employee Retirement Plan
222 West Corporate Drive
Santa Barbara, California 99099

RE: *QDRO (Zoelle v. Zoelle, No. 123-04)*

Dear Ms. Official:

Thanks to your cooperation and assistance, we have been able to settle this case. As part of the settlement we will be asking the trial court to enter a DRO covering your employee benefit plans. A draft of that DRO is enclosed for your informal review and comments.

If you do see any problems with accepting this DRO as a QDRO, we would appreciate it if in your correspondence with us you could:

1. Specify the reasons why the order is not a QDRO;
2. Refer to specific provisions of the plan on which your decision was based;
3. Explain any time limits that apply to the rights of the parties (such as the duration of any protective action you will take to prevent withdrawal of the Alternate Payee's share by the Participant); and
4. Describe any additional material, information, or modifications of the DRO to make it a QDRO, and explain why they are necessary as suggested in the Department of Labor's *EBSA Booklet* (1997) in Question 2-14.

In addition to reviewing the enclosed DRO for compliance with ERISA, please also confirm our understanding of the following matters that are based on our analysis of Mr. Zoelle's current and projected plan benefits and our conversations with you and other plan officials in the last few months:

1. There is currently enough in the Global MegaCorp Savings Plan account for Mr. Zoelle to allow an immediate distribution of $28,900 to Mrs. Zoelle.
2. That distribution of $28,900 from the Savings Plan may be made as soon as you accept the DRO as a QDRO.
3. As far as the Global MegaCorp Employee Pension Plan is concerned, it could begin paying Mrs. Zoelle's share of plan benefits in the form of a Single Life Annuity to her with monthly payments beginning at any time of her choosing after the Participant attains age 55, which will be four years and three months from now.
4. Payments of that annuity to her as worded in the enclosed draft DRO would not be affected by the death of Mr. Zoelle at any time, either before or after she began collecting monthly payments, once the DRO is accepted as a QDRO by your plan.
5. Based on Mr. Zoelle's current accrued plan benefit, the amount of the Single Life Annuity payable to Mrs. Zoelle

would be approximately $557 per month if she elects to begin payments on his 55th birthday, and a higher amount if she elects to begin receiving payments later.

6. The terms of your plan permit her to elect to receive an actuarially equivalent lump-sum payment in lieu of an annuity at any time after the Participant's 55th birthday.

Please let me know at once if any of these statements is incorrect. We hope to receive your response to this letter before October 23, when we have a hearing scheduled before Judge Equiter to present the terms of the agreed settlement of this matter.

Sincerely yours,

Eileen G. Maikkula
Maikkula & Teague

cc: Mrs. Arlene Zoelle
Daniel Reese, Esq., Attorney for Participant

APPENDIX D

Model Document Discovery Request/Subpoena Duces Tecum

INTRODUCTORY COMMENT: This request may be used either at the deposition of the Participant or as a subpoena duces tecum at the deposition of a plan official.

For each pension, profit-sharing, savings, stock option, or other employee benefit plan, employee welfare plan, or employee pension plan of any type sponsored by your current employer and every previous employer of yours, whether during your marriage or at any other time, whether full-time or part-time, and whether ERISA plans, military pensions, federal, state, or local pension or retirement plans, or any other type of employee benefit or retirement plan whatsoever, produce for each such plan:

1. All Annual Benefits Statements received by you during the past three (3) years.
2. The plan's QDRO Procedures.
3. The full text of the plan itself.
4. The Summary Plan Description.
5. Any written materials comparable to items 1 through 4 above for any non-ERISA plans,

such as military retirement benefits or federal, state, and local government pension and benefit plans.

6. Any booklets, pamphlets, information sheets, or other written materials distributed by the plan or the Plan Sponsor to employees or participants generally concerning rights to receive plan benefits, types and forms of benefits payable, options, and elections available under any plan.
7. Any other documents concerning rights to receive plan benefits, types and forms of benefits payable, options, and elections available under any plan.
8. Any correspondence you or your attorneys have had with any plan concerning any elections of types of benefits, investment options and alternatives, this court proceeding, or any other topic or matter in the last months.

APPENDIX E

Model Interrogatories

For each of your employers, whether full-time or part-time, commencing with the time you reached age eighteen and continuing to the present day, state:

1. The name, address, and telephone number of that employer;
2. When you began work there and when you left;
3. Your starting title or job description and salary;
4. Your ending title or job description and salary;
5. The reason you left such employment;
6. Whether as a result of such employment you have any pension rights or other employee benefits, whether currently payable to you or payable to you commencing at some future date.
7. If your answer to Interrogatory 6 was affirmative, describe completely:

   (a) The name of each employee benefit plan under which you are entitled to receive pension or other benefits;

(b) The amount of benefit payable to you under each such plan;

(c) The name, address, and telephone number of a person at the employer who sponsors such an employee benefit plan who is knowledgeable about that employee benefit plan and your entitlement to benefits thereunder; and

(d) The name, address, and telephone number of a person at the Plan Administrator for each plan who is knowledgeable about that employee benefit plan and your entitlement to benefits thereunder.

APPENDIX F

Model Deposition Questions for Participant

INTRODUCTORY COMMENT: Many Participants do not understand how their employee benefit plans work, what benefits they are entitled to, what options are available, and so on. Some Participants have serious misconceptions about their benefits and will adamantly insist on their version even when confronted with written plan documents to the contrary. These deposition questions focus on identifying as many possible sources of pension or employee benefits as possible. You should then follow through and get the appropriate documents and information directly from the plans and not rely on the Participant's vague or incorrect notions of what he might be entitled to.

Part 1: Current employment.

By whom are you presently employed?

How long have you been employed there?

What is the address and telephone number of that employer?

Are you entitled to any pension, profit sharing, stock option, or any other form of employee benefit plan or any kind of retirement benefits as a result of your employment there?

Describe to the best of your knowledge what employee and retirement benefits you are currently entitled to as a result of your employment there.

What person or department at that employer is in charge of administering employee benefits? What is their address and telephone number?

Who is currently designated as the Beneficiary in each plan to receive benefits in the event of your death? When was that designation last changed? Who was it before?

Have you had any correspondence with, or spoken orally with, any person in that department in the last five (5) years? Describe that conversation to me in full.

Part 2: Previous employment.

By whom were you employed before your current employer?

[Ask the same questions as in Part 1 for each employer going back to the first employment by the deponent after leaving school.]

Part 3: Part-time employment.

Do you have any part-time employment, such as National Guard, military Reserves, firefighter, police, or such?

Do you have any pension rights or other benefits as a result of such part-time employment?

[Ask the same questions as in Part 1 for each part-time employer going back to the first part-time employment by the deponent after leaving school.]

Part 4: Pensions currently In Pay Status.

Are you currently receiving or entitled to receive any pension payments or other employee benefits from any source?

From whom?

What is their address and telephone number?

How much do you receive or are you entitled to receive?

Part 5: Immediate plans.

Are you currently in the process of making arrangements to retire, or to begin receiving any retirement benefits, or to make any withdrawals from any savings plan, or to make any changes in the current investments or investment policies in any of your employee benefit plans?

Which employee benefit plans are affected?

Identify each person at each plan with whom you have spoken about your retirement or election of benefits forms or change of investments.

What retirement date have you advised them you will take or are you considering taking?

What choice or election-of-benefit forms have you already made or considered making?

How much are you planning on withdrawing from any savings or investment plan?

What changes in investments have you requested or considered requesting?

Why have you made those decisions or choices?

Are those decisions revocable or irrevocable as far as the employee benefit plan is concerned?

Are you considering changing the Beneficiary designation for any of these plans? Who is the current Beneficiary? To whom are you considering changing that designation?

Are you willing to state on the record today that you will not make any election to retire, or any election to change benefit forms, or change any investment policies or the designation of any Beneficiary as long as this action is pending without first giving 30 days' advance written notice to the court and to me as opposing counsel of your desire or intent to do so?

If not, why not?

Part 6: Wrap-up question.

I have asked you several questions about your pension rights and other employee benefits, past and present. I want you to take a moment and think whether there are any other pension rights or other employee benefits to which you are presently entitled, or to which you may become entitled in the future. If there are any such rights that you have not already told me about in response to my earlier questions, I want you to disclose them to me now. Remember that you are under oath and sworn to tell the whole truth about all of these matters.

APPENDIX G

Model Deposition Questions for Plan Official

INTRODUCTORY COMMENT: These are general questions to be asked of an official of the Plan Administrator or an employee of the Plan Sponsor who is familiar with employee benefits. If you can get the text of the plan, the Summary Plan Description, the Participant's Annual Benefits Statements, the plan's written QDRO Procedures, and other written materials from the plan before this deposition is taken, read them over and ask any specific questions you have about them in addition to the questions set forth below. Analogous questions may be asked of the officials of military and civil service plans.

Part 1: Qualifications of Deponent.

What is your name?

What is your educational background?

What is your employment history?

Are you employed by the Plan Administrator or the Plan Sponsor?

How long have you been so employed?

What is your current job title?

What are your current job responsibilities concerning QDROs?

Who else in your department works on QDROs? What are their duties?

State the mailing addresses, telephone, fax, and email contact details for each person.

Are there any other departments at the Plan Administrator or the Plan Sponsor that deal with QDROs and QDRO issues? What are they? Where are they located? Who works there?

State the mailing addresses, telephone, fax, and email contact details for each such department.

[If the deponent does not know the answer to any question, ask who in his or her department or elsewhere would know the answer.]

Part 2: Plans.

Describe each employee benefit plan, whether ERISA-qualified or not, by which Mr. Participant is currently covered.

Is that a Defined Benefit Plan or a Defined Contribution Plan?

How many years must an employee work to be eligible to retire under that plan?

What is the Earliest Retirement Age under that plan?

What is the Normal Retirement Age under that plan?

What is the vesting schedule for that plan?

In what form may benefits be paid from that plan?

What options or benefit choices may a Participant or a Beneficiary or an Alternate Payee make in that plan?

Who is Mr. Participant's current Beneficiary designated to receive benefits if he dies?

When was that Beneficiary designation most recently changed? Who was it before?

A. Questions for Defined Benefit Plans:

What interest rate assumption does that plan use in actuarial calculations?

What mortality tables does that plan use in actuarial calculations?

What other assumptions does that plan use in actuarial calculations?

How are benefits calculated if a Participant takes early retirement?

Is there an employer subsidy for early retirement in this plan? If so, how is it calculated? How much would it be at the Earliest Retirement Age in the specific case of Mr. Participant?

How are benefits calculated if a Participant takes normal retirement?

What is the current actuarial value of Mr. Participant's accrued benefit in that plan?

If Mr. Participant were to continue to be employed by the Plan Sponsor but receive only $1 per year in salary between now and the plan's Early Retirement Age, how much per month would he receive in a Single Life Annuity on his life alone?

If Mr. Participant were to continue to be employed by the Plan Sponsor but receive only $1 per year in salary between now and the plan's Early Retirement Age, how much per month would he receive in a Qualified Joint and Survivor Annuity with his spouse?

If Mr. Participant were to continue to be employed by the Plan Sponsor but receive only $1 per year in salary between now and the plan's Normal Retirement Age, how much per month would he receive in a Single Life Annuity on his life alone?

If Mr. Participant were to continue to be employed by the Plan Sponsor but receive only $1 per year in salary between now and the plan's Normal Retirement Age, how much per month would he receive in a Qualified Joint and Survivor Annuity with his spouse?

If Mr. Participant were to remarry before retiring and elect a Qualified Joint and Survivor Annuity with his new spouse, would your plan honor a QDRO that called for the Alternate Payee to receive payments for the entire duration of that Qualified Joint and Survivor Annuity with his new spouse, or would you require payments to the Alternate Payee to stop when the Participant died if he died before his new spouse?

What justification do you have for that position?

Do you allow a designate of a Contingent Alternate Payee in a QDRO to receive the Alternate Payee's share of plan benefits if she dies before receiving all of them?

If not, what justification do you have for that position?

If so, are there any restrictions on the groups or categories of persons who may be named as a Contingent Alternate Payee? For example, may the estate of the Alternate Payee be designated as a Contingent Alternate Payee? May a child or other relative of the

Alternate Payee be designated as a Contingent Alternate Payee even if that person is not a blood relation of the Participant? If not, why not?

B. Questions for Defined Contribution Plans:

What is the current value of Mr. Participant's plan account?

In what form of investments are his funds held?

May a Participant borrow money from that plan? May an Alternate Payee do so?

May a Participant make investment choices about the investments made in that plan? What are the investment alternatives offered by the plan? What are the restrictions on those alternatives or how frequently changes in investments may be made?

If an Alternate Payee is awarded an interest in this plan, may she leave her share on deposit with the plan? For how long? May she make her own investment decisions about her share of plan benefits that you will be holding for her?

What is the earliest possible date on which an Alternate Payee could withdraw any benefits from that plan?

Part 3: Pensions currently In Pay Status.

Is Mr. Participant currently receiving any payments or benefits from any of these plans?

How much is he receiving or entitled to receive?

When were the elections to start receiving these benefits made? Are those elections irrevocable?

If so, why?

If not, how can they be revoked?

Part 4: Participant's recent discussions with plan.

Have you or anyone else involved with QDROs at the Plan Administrator or Plan Sponsor had any correspondence with, or spoken orally with, Mr. Participant or his lawyer about his plan benefits, or the subject of QDROs, or this case in the last months? Describe that conversation to me in full.

Has Mr. Participant or his lawyer indicated to you or anyone else at the Plan Administrator or the Plan Sponsor that he is about to make any retirement decisions or elections, or to change any of his investment alternatives in any plan? Describe that conversation to me in full.

Is Mr. Participant currently in the process of making arrangements to retire, or to begin receiving any retirement benefits, or to make any changes in the current investments or investment policies, or to change any Beneficiaries in any of your plans?

Which plans are affected?

Identify each person at each plan with whom Mr. Participant has spoken about retirement or election of benefits forms or change of investments or Beneficiaries.

What retirement dates has Mr. Participant advised the plans he will take or is considering taking?

What choice or election of benefit forms has Mr. Participant already made or considered making?

What changes in investments has Mr. Participant requested or discussed?

Why has he made those decisions or choices?

Are those decisions revocable or irrevocable as far as the plan is concerned?

APPENDIX H

Model Release of Information Form

Authorization to Release Information

I, ____ ____________________________, Social Security number __ __ __-__ __-__ __ __ __, am now or have in the past been employed by ______________________________ ____________ ("Employer") and am a participant in, or am covered by, one or more of its pension, retirement, or other employee pension benefit, employee welfare, or employee benefit plans. I hereby authorize the Employee Benefits Department, or any other department, agent, officer, or employee of Employer or the Plan Administrators of all such plans to provide copies of any and all documents relating or pertaining in any way to my employee and retirement benefits (including, without limitation, any and all pension, retirement, profit sharing, employee savings, 401(k), benefit, or similar plans of every type and description) to Eileen G. Maikkula, Esquire, Maikkula & Teague, Attorneys at Law, 123 Main Street, Augusta, Georgia 30909.

This Release shall also be deemed to apply to any military pension rights or other benefits arising out of military service, and any federal (including CSRS and FERS), state, or local government civil service pension or other employee benefit plans.

A photocopy of this form shall have the same force and effect as the signed original.

____

(Signature of employee)

State of _________________

County of _______________

SWORN TO AND SUBSCRIBED before me this ___ day of __________, 20__. _______________________________, Notary Public.

APPENDIX I

Model Client Letter and Questionnaire

Maikkula & Teague, P.C.
Attorneys at Law
123 Main Street
Augusta, Georgia 30909
Telephone: (706) 123-4567

RE: *Pension and Employee Benefits Information*

Dear Client:

The purpose of this letter and the attached questionnaire is to help you understand the importance of pension plans in the context of the divorce action you have asked our firm to handle for you. It is *very important* for your future financial security that you read this letter very carefully and complete the attached questionnaire to the best of your ability. Please try to complete these forms yourself; the more information you provide us, the more you can save in legal fees. However, if you need help in completing the enclosed questionnaire, please call our office and we will arrange for a paralegal or an attorney to assist you.

Pensions and employee benefit plans are unusually valuable assets. Often they are the second most valuable asset a couple has after the equity in their family home—and sometimes they are the most valuable asset a couple has. *Even though the pension may be in your spouse's name alone through his or her employment, under state and federal law you may be entitled to a share in it.* That is why we need this information to help you.

To the extent this questionnaire calls for information about yourself and your pensions or employee benefits, be honest, accurate, and complete in your answers. You have a duty to disclose all significant information about your assets, including these types of plans, to us and to the Court. We cannot represent you effectively if you are not candid about these matters.

To the extent this questionnaire calls for information about your spouse's pension rights and employee benefits, it is to your financial advantage to help us learn as much as possible about these benefits as you are probably entitled to a share of them. While there are many ways for us to find out about such benefits, the most efficient and inexpensive way for us to get the information we need is for you to help us obtain it. If you can do so without creating problems at home, please obtain copies of the documents requested below and provide them to us, leaving the original documents in place.

Part B of this questionnaire asks you to write down your preferences about when and how you would like to receive a share of your spouse's pension or employee benefits. Please give this careful thought, and make a note to discuss the alternatives with us if you would like to do so.

We need the completed questionnaires back from you on or before __________ in order to serve you properly. Please meet this deadline.

Once again, please do your best to complete this questionnaire accurately and completely by yourself, but if you have any questions or need help in completing it, give us a call and we will assign someone to assist you.

Sincerely yours,

Eileen G. Maikkula
Maikkula & Teague

Part A: Employee benefit plan questionnaire.

Your full name: ____

Have you ever been known by any other name? If so, state here: ___

____

Your Social Security number: __ __ __-__ __-__ __ __ __

Your spouse's full name: ____________________________________

Has your spouse ever been known by any other name? If so, state here: ____

Your spouse's Social Security number: __ __ __-__ __-__ __ __ __

(*Note:* If you are not sure of your spouse's Social Security number, look on your old federal or state income tax returns. Pay stubs and driver's licenses usually also show Social Security numbers. They are in the form of a 9-digit number such as 123-45-6789.)

Date of marriage: _______________

Date of separation: _______________ (leave blank if not separated yet)

Date of divorce: _______________ (leave blank if not divorced yet)

Part A-1: Your employment.

The form on this page relates to YOUR EMPLOYMENT during your marriage. If you worked for more than one employer, please make extra copies of this page and fill out a separate page for EACH JOB you held during the marriage. INCLUDE PART-TIME JOBS and SECOND JOBS (National Guard/Reserves, etc.). Do the best you can to complete every item.

1. Employed from _______________ to _________________
2. Employer's name: ________________________
3. Employer's address: ___________________________________

   ____

   ____
4. Employer's telephone and fax numbers:

   ____

   ____
5. Name of person to contact there about employee benefits: ____________________ and their address and telephone number:

____

____

____

____

6. To your knowledge are you entitled to any pension or retirement benefits as a result of this employment? If so, please describe in as much detail as you can.
7. To your knowledge, did you participate in a 401(k) plan with this employment? If so, who was the 401(k) with?
8. Are you entitled to the proceeds of any employer-sponsored savings plan, stock option plan, stock bonus plan, or any other form of employee benefit? If so, please describe in as much detail as you can on a separate sheet.
9. If you have received any information from this employer about pension or retirement benefits, please provide us with a copy or the original of that information when you return this questionnaire to us.
10. If you are currently employed, please attach a copy of a recent paycheck stub from your job, showing gross pay, take-home pay, deductions, etc.

Part A-2: Your spouse's employment.

The form on this page relates to YOUR SPOUSE'S EMPLOYMENT during your marriage. If he or she worked for more than one employer, please make extra copies of this page and fill out a separate page for EACH JOB your spouse held during the marriage. INCLUDE PART-TIME JOBS and SECOND JOBS (National Guard/Reserves, etc.). Do the best you can to complete every item.

1. Employed from ______________ to ________________
2. Employer's name: ______________________
3. Employer's address: ________________________________

   ____

   ____

4. Employer's telephone and fax numbers:

   ____

   ____

5. Person to contact there about employee benefits: __________ ___________ and their address and telephone number: ________

   ____

   ____

6. To your knowledge is your spouse entitled to any pension or retirement benefits as a result of this employment? If so, please describe in as much detail as you can on a separate sheet.

7. To your knowledge, did your spouse have a 401(k) or other similar plan with this employment? If so, do you know who the account was with?
8. To your knowledge is your spouse entitled to the proceeds of any employer-sponsored savings plan, stock option plan, stock bonus plan, or any other form of employee benefit? If so, please describe in as much detail as you can.
9. If your spouse has received any information from this employer about pension or retirement benefits, or any form of employee benefit plan, *and if you can obtain a copy of it without creating problems at home,* please provide us with a copy of that information when you return this questionnaire to us.
10. *If you can obtain a copy of it without creating problems at home,* please attach a copy of a recent paycheck stub from your spouse's current job, showing gross pay, take-home pay, deductions, etc.

Part B: When and in what form you would like to receive your share of your spouse's pension?

In this part of the questionnaire, we would like you to set down your personal goals and your thoughts and comments about when and in what form you would like to receive your share of your spouse's pension rights and other employee benefits. Many employee pension and benefit plans only offer a few alternative methods of distribution, so an alternative you want (such as a lump-sum payment) may not be available from the plan. We cannot guarantee that we will be able to arrange for payment in any particular form, but we will do our best to obtain what you want for you.

Please rank the following alternatives from 1 to 6, with *1 being the best* alternative (the one you would prefer the most) and *6 being the worst* alternative (the one you would least like to have):

___ Lump-sum payment from the plan right away, or as soon as possible, even though I understand I will have to pay taxes on it

___ Rollover of part of my spouse's benefits into an IRA I can establish (no tax payable until I make withdrawals from the IRA)

___ Award of a larger share of other assets (such as more equity in the family home, vehicles, cash, stocks, or bonds) to be given to me immediately in exchange for my waiving any interest in my spouse's pension rights

___ A pension to provide for my own retirement security, starting when my spouse retires and ending on his or her death

___ A pension to provide for my own retirement security, starting when my spouse retires and ending on my death even if my spouse dies first

___ A pension to provide for my own retirement security starting when I choose and continuing until my death even if my spouse dies first

Please write any questions or comments you have about pension divisions in your case so that we can discuss these matters with you later:

____

____

____

____

____

____

____

____

____

APPENDIX J

QDRO Management Procedures Checklist for IV-D Agencies and Private Law Practices

This checklist is suitable for use by state IV-D agencies and private law practices to monitor QDRO cases. Following this checklist ensures that you will have all important information in one place and can tell, at a single glance, whether your QDRO work is done. You should maintain *one (1) checklist for each plan involved in the case.* If more than one plan is involved, use a checklist for each plan. Keep all checklists in the front of each client's file.

1. Name of Participant: ____________________
2. Address of Participant: ____________________

   ____
3. Social Security number of Participant: ______

   ____
4. Name of Alternate Payee: ________________
5. Address of Alternate Payee: ______________

   ____
6. Social Security number of Alternate Payee:

   ____

   (Indicate our client by asterisk next to item 1 or item 4 above)

7. Alternate Payee's relationship to Participant (check one):
   ____ Spouse
   ____ Former spouse
   ____ Child
   ____ Other dependent
8. Date of marriage: ____________________
9. Date of separation: ____________________
10. Date of divorce: ____________________
11. Date of birth (if Alternate Payee is child): ______________
12. Date Participant started work: ______________________
13A. Date Participant retired: ___________________________ OR
13B. Normal Retirement Age: ____________________________
13C. Early Retirement Age: _____________________________
14. Full and accurate name of benefit plan:
    ____
15. Contact person at plan: ____________________________
16. Address of plan contact person: _____________________
17. Telephone, fax, and email contact details: ______________
    ____
18. Plan is (check one):
    ____ ERISA Defined Benefit
    ____ ERISA Defined Contribution
    ____ Military
    ____ Federal Civil Service
    ____ Other (specify) __________________
19. Type of benefits available from plan (check all that apply):
    ____ Lump sum
    ____ Company stock (ESOP Plan)
    ____ QJSA
    ____ QPSA Single Life Annuity
    ____ Fixed Term Annuity
    ____ Death benefit
    ____ Health insurance
    ____ Other (specify)

20. Amount, form, and type of benefits sought by client: ______
    ______
    ______

21. Opposing counsel name and contact details: ______
    ______

22. DRO entered in ______ Court.
23. DRO sent to plan on ______.
24. Details of follow-up correspondence with plan *(every 30 days until file is closed!)* ______
    ______
    ______

25. DRO approved by plan as a QDRO on ______.
26. Copy of qualification letter or document from plan sent to client on ______.
27. File closed on ______.
28. File review date: ______ (three to five years after date in item 27).

APPENDIX K

Plan Administrator's or Counsel's QDRO Management Procedures Checklist

This checklist is suitable for use by Plan Administrators and their lawyers to monitor QDRO cases. Following this checklist ensures that you will have all important information in one place and can tell, at a single glance, whether your QDRO work is done. You should maintain *one (1) checklist for each DRO for each plan involved in the case.* If more than one plan is involved, use a separate sheet of paper for each plan. Keep all checklists in the front of each employee's file.

1. Name of Participant: ____________________
2. Address of Participant: ____________________
3. Social Security number of Participant: ______
   ____
4. Name, address, contact numbers, and email address for Participant's lawyer: ____________
   ____
   ____
   ____
5. Name of Alternate Payee: ______________
6. Address of Alternate Payee: ______________
   ____

7. Social Security number of Alternate Payee: ____________
8. Name, address, contact numbers, and email address for Alternate Payee's lawyer: ______________________________

   ____

   ____

9. Alternate Payee's relationship to Participant (check one):
   ____ Spouse
   ____ Former spouse
   ____ Child
   ____ IV-D agency
   ____ Other dependent
10. Date of marriage: __________________
11. Date of separation: ________________
12. Date of divorce: ___________________
13. Date of birth (if Alternate Payee is child): ______________
14. Date Participant started work: ______________________
15A. Date Participant retired: ________________________ OR
15B. Early Retirement Age: ____________________________
15C. Normal Retirement Age: ___________________________
16. Plan involved: ____________________________________

   ____

17. Amount, form, and type of benefits sought by Alternate Payee: ____

   ____

   ____

18. DRO entered in ____________ Court.
19. Case caption: ______________________
20. Case number: ____________________
21. DRO dated: ________________
22. DRO received by plan on ____________________.
23. Name, address, contact numbers, and email address for Alternate Payee's Representative named in DRO (if different from lawyer in item 8): __________________________

   ____

   ____

24. Notice of receipt of DRO sent to ______________________
    Participant ______________________________
    Alternate Payee ___________________________
    Counsel for Participant ____________________
    Counsel for Alternate Payee ________________
    Representative for Alternate Payee __________
    Trial Court ______________________________
25. Preliminary Review completion deadline: ______________
26. Preliminary Review Notice(s) of Deficiency sent:

	Response due
____________________	____________
____________________	____________
____________________	____________
____________________	____________
____________________	____________
____________________	____________

27. Notice of Abandonment sent: __________________
28. Preliminary Review passed: ____________________
29. Final Review completion deadline: _____________
30. Final Review Notice(s) of Deficiency sent:

	Response due
____________________	____________
____________________	____________
____________________	____________
____________________	____________
____________________	____________
____________________	____________

31. Notice of Abandonment sent: ________________________
32. Final Review passed: _______________________________
33. Certificate of Qualification dated: __________________
34. Sent to all addresses: ______________________________
35. File review date: ____________________

APPENDIX L

How to Read an Annual Benefits Statement

Global MegaCorp Savings Plan
Global MegaCorp Retirement Plan

Statement for:	Mr. David L. Zoelle, 111-22-3344
Date of birth:	May 19, 1964
Date of Statement:	March 31, 20__.
Years of credited service:	4.67

1. *Your account with the Global MegaCorp Savings Plan:*

	Vested	*Unvested*
Stock Fund	$2,112.38	$557.94
Bond Fund	$0	$0
Company Stock	53 shares	114 shares

During the year the Company contributed $797.68 to your Stock Fund account and 98 shares of Company Stock to your Company Stock account. You were also credited with $102.50 and 24 shares of Company Stock in forfeitures from Plan Participants who left the plan.

COMMENT: Participants are always 100 percent vested in their own contributions but may be only partially vested in employer contributions (see Chapter 5).

There's a lot that this part of the statement does not adequately reveal. How are forfeitures allocated?

How long does it take for them to be allocated? When will this Participant be fully vested? How frequently are contributions made to the plan by the employer and the employee? Is the Participant contributing at the maximum level? See generally the discussion in Chapter 5. These points need to be cleared up with a plan official.

2. *Your benefits with the Global MegaCorp Retirement Plan:*

Your current salary is $57,600. Assuming that you continue to work at Global MegaCorp until retirement and that your salary increases at 6 percent per year, at Normal Retirement Age (65) you would be able to retire with a monthly pension of $1,837. You could also retire earlier, at Early Retirement Age (age 55 with ten years of service or more) and receive a pension of $949 per month.

You are currently 40 percent vested in your Retirement Plan benefits.

COMMENT: This part of the statement also raises a lot of questions. First, note the *assumptions* at the beginning (continuing employment, 6 percent salary increases every year). These inflate the value of the Participant's Accrued Benefit as described in this statement. You will need to ascertain from plan officials what the monthly payment at age 65 would be if the Participant continued working until age 65 but received only a nominal salary, say $1, per year.

Second, there is no indication of whether the early retirement monthly figure includes an employer subsidy for early retirement.

Third, there is no indication of whether the monthly annuity figures are for a Single Life Annuity or for a Qualified Joint and Survivor Annuity for the Participant and his current spouse or for the Participant and the Alternate Payee. Further information from the plan is required to do proper actuarial calculations on these points.

APPENDIX M

Text of the Uniformed Services Former Spouses Protection Act, 10 U.S.C. § 1408

§ 1408. Payment of retired or retainer pay in compliance with court orders

(a) Definitions. In this section:

(1) The term "court" means—

(A) any court of competent jurisdiction of any State, the District of Columbia, the Commonwealth of Puerto Rico, Guam, American Samoa, the Virgin Islands, the Northern Mariana Islands, and the Trust Territory of the Pacific Islands;

(B) any court of the United States (as defined in section 451 of title 28) having competent jurisdiction;

(C) any court of competent jurisdiction of a foreign country with which the United States has an agreement requiring the United States to honor any court order of such country; and

(D) any administrative or judicial tribunal of a State competent to enter orders for support or maintenance (including a State agency administering a program under a State plan approved under part D of title IV of the Social Security Act [42 U.S.C.S. §§ 651 *et seq.*]), and, for purposes of this subparagraph, the term "State" includes the District of Columbia, the Commonwealth of Puerto Rico, the Virgin Islands, Guam, and American Samoa.

(2) The term "court order" means a final decree of divorce, dissolution, annulment, or legal separation issued by a court, or a court ordered, ratified, or approved property settlement incident to such a decree (including a final decree modifying the terms of a previously issued decree of divorce, dissolution, annulment, or legal separation, or a court ordered, ratified, or approved property settlement incident to such previously issued decree), or a support order, as defined in section 453(p) of the Social Security Act (42 U.S.C. 653(p)), which—

(A) is issued in accordance with the laws of the jurisdiction of that court;

(B) provides for—

(i) payment of child support (as defined in section 459(i)(2) of the Social Security Act (42 U.S.C. 659(i)(2)));

(ii) payment of alimony (as defined in section 459(i)(3) of the Social Security Act (42 U.S.C. 659(i)(3))); or

(iii) division of property (including a division of community property); and

(C) in the case of a division of property, specifically provides for the payment of an amount, expressed in dollars or as a percentage of disposable retired pay, from the disposable retired pay of a member to the spouse or former spouse of that member.

(3) The term "final decree" means a decree from which no appeal may be taken or from which no appeal has been taken within the time allowed for taking such appeals under the laws applicable to such appeals, or a decree from which timely appeal has been taken and such appeal has been finally decided under the laws applicable to such appeals.

(4) (A) The term "disposable retired pay" means the total monthly retired pay to which a member is entitled less amounts which—

(i) are owed by that member to the United States for previous overpayments of retired pay and for recoupments required by law resulting from entitlement to retired pay;

(ii) are deducted from the retired pay of such member as a result of forfeitures of retired pay ordered by a court-martial or as a result of a waiver of retired pay required by law in order to receive compensation under title 5 or title 38;

(iii) in the case of a member entitled to retired pay under chapter 61 of this title [10 U.S.C.S. §§ 1201 *et seq.*], are equal to the amount of retired pay of the member under that chapter computed using the percentage of the member's disability on the date when the member was retired (or the date on which the member's name was placed on the temporary disability retired list); or

(iv) are deducted because of an election under chapter 73 of this title [10 U.S.C.S. §§ 1431 *et seq.*] to provide an annuity to a spouse or former spouse to whom payment of a portion of such member's retired pay is being made pursuant to a court order under this section.

(B) For purposes of subparagraph (A), in the case of a division of property as part of a final decree of divorce, dissolution, annulment, or legal separation that becomes final prior to the date of a member's retirement, the total monthly retired pay to which the member is entitled shall be—

(i) in the case of a member not described in clause (ii), the amount of retired pay to which the member would have been entitled using the member's retired pay base and years of service on the date of the decree of divorce, dissolution, annulment, or legal separation, as computed under section 1406 or 1407 of this title [10 U.S.C.S. § 1406 or 1407], whichever is applicable, increased by the sum of the cost-of-living adjustments that—

(I) would have occurred under section 1401a(b) of this title [10 U.S.C.S. § 1401a] between the date of the decree of divorce, dissolution, annulment, or legal separation and the time of the member's retirement using the adjustment provisions under section 1401a of this title [10 U.S.C.S. § 1401a] applicable to the member upon retirement; and

(II) occur under 1401a of this title [10 U.S.C.S. § 1401a] after the member's retirement; or

(ii) in the case of a member who becomes entitled to retired pay pursuant to chapter 1223 of this title [10 U.S.C.S. §§ 12731 *et seq.*], the amount of retired pay to which the member would have been entitled using the member's retired pay base and creditable service points on the date of the decree of divorce, dissolution, annulment, or legal separation, as computed [sic] under chapter 1223 of this title [10 U.S.C.S. §§ 12731 *et seq.*], increased by the sum of the cost-of-living adjustments as described in clause (i) that apply with respect to the member.

(5) The term "member" includes a former member entitled to retired pay under section 12731 of this title [10 U.S.C.S. § 12731].

(6) The term "spouse or former spouse" means the husband or wife, or former husband or wife, respectively, of a member who, on or before the date of a court order, was married to that member.

(7) The term "retired pay" includes retainer pay.

(b) Effective service of process. For the purposes of this section—

(1) service of a court order is effective if—

(A) an appropriate agent of the Secretary concerned designated for receipt of service court orders under regulations prescribed pursuant to subsection (i) or, if no agent has been so designated, the Secretary concerned, is personally served or is served by facsimile or electronic transmission or by mail;

(B) the court order is regular on its face;

(C) the court order or other documents served with the court order identify the member concerned and include, if possible, the social security number of such member; and

(D) the court order or other documents served with the court order certify that the rights of the member under the Servicemembers Civil Relief Act (50 U.S.C. 3901 *et seq.*) were observed; and

(2) a court order is regular on its face if the order—

(A) is issued by a court of competent jurisdiction;

(B) is legal in form; and

(C) includes nothing on its face that provides reasonable notice that it is issued without authority of law.

(c) Authority for court to treat retired pay as property of the member and spouse.

(1) Subject to the limitations of this section, a court may treat disposable retired pay payable to a member for pay periods beginning after June 25, 1981, either as property solely of the member or as property of the member and his spouse in accordance with the law of the jurisdiction of such court. A court may not treat retired pay as property in any proceeding to divide or partition any amount of retired pay of a member as the property of the member

and the member's spouse or former spouse if a final decree of divorce, dissolution, annulment, or legal separation (including a court ordered, ratified, or approved property settlement incident to such decree) affecting the member and the member's spouse or former spouse (A) was issued before June 25, 1981, and (B) did not treat (or reserve jurisdiction to treat) any amount of retired pay of the member as property of the member and the member's spouse or former spouse.

(2) Notwithstanding any other provision of law, this section does not create any right, title, or interest which can be sold, assigned, transferred, or otherwise disposed of (including by inheritance) by a spouse or former spouse. Payments by the Secretary concerned under subsection (d) to a spouse or former spouse with respect to a division of retired pay as the property of a member and the member's spouse under this subsection may not be treated as amounts received as retired pay for service in the uniformed services.

(3) This section does not authorize any court to order a member to apply for retirement or retire at a particular time in order to effectuate any payment under this section.

(4) A court may not treat the disposable retired pay of a member in the manner described in paragraph (1) unless the court has jurisdiction over the member by reason of (A) his residence, other than because of military assignment, in the territorial jurisdiction of the court, (B) his domicile in the territorial jurisdiction of the court, or (C) his consent to the jurisdiction of the court.

(d) Payments by Secretary concerned to (or for benefit of) spouse or former spouse.

(1) After effective service on the Secretary concerned of a court order providing for the payment of child support or alimony or, with respect to a division of property, specifically providing for the payment of an amount of the disposable retired pay from a member to the spouse or a former spouse of the member, the Secretary shall make payments (subject to the limitations of this section) from the disposable retired pay of the member to the spouse or former spouse (or for the benefit of such spouse or former spouse to a State disbursement unit established pursuant to section 454B of the Social Security Act [42 U.S.C.S. § 654b] or other public payee designated by a State, in accordance with part D of title IV of the Social Security Act [42 U.S.C.S. §§ 651 *et seq.*], as directed by court order, or as

otherwise directed in accordance with such part D) in an amount sufficient to satisfy the amount of child support and alimony set forth in the court order and, with respect to a division of property, in the amount of disposable retired pay specifically provided for in the court order. In the case of a spouse or former spouse who, pursuant to section 408(a)(3) of the Social Security Act (42 U.S.C. 608(a)[(3)](4)), assigns to a State the rights of the spouse or former spouse to receive support, the Secretary concerned may make the child support payments referred to in the preceding sentence to that State in amounts consistent with that assignment of rights. In the case of a member entitled to receive retired pay on the date of the effective service of the court order, such payments shall begin not later than 90 days after the date of effective service. In the case of a member not entitled to receive retired pay on the date of the effective service of the court order, such payments shall begin not later than 90 days after the date on which the member first becomes entitled to retired pay.

(2) If the spouse or former spouse to whom payments are to be made under this section was not married to the member for a period of 10 years or more during which the member performed at least 10 years of service creditable in determining the member's eligibility for retired pay, payments may not be made under this section to the extent that they include an amount resulting from the treatment by the court under subsection (c) of disposable retired pay of the member as property of the member or property of the member and his spouse.

(3) Payments under this section shall not be made more frequently than once each month, and the Secretary concerned shall not be required to vary normal pay and disbursement cycles for retired pay in order to comply with a court order.

(4) Payments from the disposable retired pay of a member pursuant to this section shall terminate in accordance with the terms of the applicable court order, but not later than the date of the death of the member or the date of the death of the spouse or former spouse to whom payments are being made, whichever occurs first.

(5) If a court order described in paragraph (1) provides for a division of property (including a division of community property) in addition to an amount of child support or alimony or the payment of an amount of disposable retired pay as the result of the court's treatment of such pay under subsection (c) as property of the

member and his spouse, the Secretary concerned shall pay (subject to the limitations of this section) from the disposable retired pay of the member to the spouse or former spouse of the member, any part of the amount payable to the spouse or former spouse under the division of property upon effective service of a final court order of garnishment of such amount from such retired pay.

(6) In the case of a court order for which effective service is made on the Secretary concerned on or after August 22, 1996, and which provides for payments from the disposable retired pay of a member to satisfy the amount of child support set forth in the order, the authority provided in paragraph (1) to make payments from the disposable retired pay of a member to satisfy the amount of child support set forth in a court order shall apply to payment of any amount of child support arrearages set forth in that order as well as to amounts of child support that currently become due.

(7) (A) The Secretary concerned may not accept service of a court order that is an out-of-State modification, or comply with the provisions of such a court order, unless the court issuing that order has jurisdiction in the manner specified in subsection (c)(4) over both the member and the spouse or former spouse involved.

(B) A court order shall be considered to be an out-of-State modification for purposes of this paragraph if the order—

(i) modifies a previous court order under this section upon which payments under this subsection are based; and

(ii) is issued by a court of a State other than the State of the court that issued the previous court order.

(8) A division of property award computed as a percentage of a member's disposable retired pay shall be increased by the same percentage as any cost-of-living adjustment made under section 1401a after the member's retirement.

(e) Limitations.

(1) The total amount of the disposable retired pay of a member payable under all court orders pursuant to subsection (c) may not exceed 50 percent of such disposable retired pay.

(2) In the event of effective service of more than one court order which provide for payment to a spouse and one or more former spouses or to more than one former spouse, the disposable retired pay of the member shall be used to satisfy (subject to the limitations of paragraph (1)) such court orders on a first-come,

first-served basis. Such court orders shall be satisfied (subject to the limitations of paragraph (1)) out of that amount of disposable retired pay which remains after the satisfaction of all court orders which have been previously served.

(3) (A) In the event of effective service of conflicting court orders under this section which assert to direct that different amounts be paid during a month to the same spouse or former spouse of the same member, the Secretary concerned shall—

(i) pay to that spouse from the member's disposable retired pay the least amount directed to be paid during that month by any such conflicting court order, but not more than the amount of disposable retired pay which remains available for payment of such court orders based on when such court orders were effectively served and the limitations of paragraph (1) and subparagraph (B) of paragraph (4);

(ii) retain an amount of disposable retired pay that is equal to the lesser of—

(I) the difference between the largest amount required by any conflicting court order to be paid to the spouse or former spouse and the amount payable to the spouse or former spouse under clause (i); and

(II) the amount of disposable retired pay which remains available for payment of any conflicting court order based on when such court order was effectively served and the limitations of paragraph (1) and subparagraph (B) of paragraph (4); and

(iii) pay to that member the amount which is equal to the amount of that member's disposable retired pay (less any amount paid during such month pursuant to legal process served under section 459 of the Social Security Act (42 U.S.C. 659) and any amount paid during such month pursuant to court orders effectively served under this section, other than such conflicting court orders) minus—

(I) the amount of disposable retired pay paid under clause (i); and

(II) the amount of disposable retired pay retained under clause (ii).

(B) The Secretary concerned shall hold the amount retained under clause (ii) of subparagraph (A) until such time as that Secretary is provided with a court order which has been certified by the member and the spouse or former spouse to be valid and applicable to the retained amount. Upon being provided with such an order, the Secretary shall pay the retained amount in accordance with the order.

(4) (A) In the event of effective service of a court order under this section and the service of legal process pursuant to section 459 of the Social Security Act (42 U.S.C. 659), both of which provide for payments during a month from the same member, satisfaction of such court orders and legal process from the retired pay of the member shall be on a first-come, first-served basis. Such court orders and legal process shall be satisfied out of monies which are subject to such orders and legal process and which remain available in accordance with the limitations of paragraph (1) and subparagraph (B) of this paragraph during such month after the satisfaction of all court orders or legal process which have been previously served.

(B) Notwithstanding any other provision of law, the total amount of the disposable retired pay of a member payable by the Secretary concerned under all court orders pursuant to this section and all legal processes pursuant to section 459 of the Social Security Act (42 U.S.C. 659) with respect to a member may not exceed 65 percent of the amount of the retired pay payable to such member that is considered under section 462 of the Social Security Act (42 U.S.C. 662) to be remuneration for employment that is payable by the United States.

(5) A court order which itself or because of previously served court orders provides for the payment of an amount which exceeds the amount of disposable retired pay available for payment because of the limit set forth in paragraph (1), or which, because of previously served court orders or legal process previously served under section 459 of the Social Security Act (42 U.S.C. 659), provides for payment of an amount that exceeds the maximum amount permitted under paragraph (1) or subparagraph (B) of paragraph (4), shall not be considered to be irregular on its face solely for that reason. However, such order shall be considered to be fully satisfied for purposes of this section by the payment to the spouse or former spouse of the maximum amount of disposable retired pay permitted under paragraph (1) and subparagraph (B) of paragraph (4).

(6) Nothing in this section shall be construed to relieve a member of liability for the payment of alimony, child support, or other payments required by a court order on the grounds that payments made out of disposable retired pay under this section have been made in the maximum amount permitted under paragraph (1) or subparagraph (B) of paragraph (4). Any such unsatisfied obligation of a member may be enforced by any means available under law other than the means provided under this section in any case in which the maximum amount permitted under paragraph (1) has been paid and under section 459 of the Social Security Act (42 U.S.C. 659) in any case in which the maximum amount permitted under subparagraph (B) of paragraph (4) has been paid.

(f) Immunity of officers and employees of United States.

(1) The United States and any officer or employee of the United States shall not be liable with respect to any payment made from retired pay to any member, spouse, or former spouse pursuant to a court order that is regular on its face if such payment is made in accordance with this section and the regulations prescribed pursuant to subsection (i).

(2) An officer or employee of the United States who, under regulations prescribed pursuant to subsection (i), has the duty to respond to interrogatories shall not be subject under any law to any disciplinary action or civil or criminal liability or penalty for, or because of, any disclosure of information made by him in carrying out any of his duties which directly or indirectly pertain to answering such interrogatories.

(g) Notice to member of service of court order on Secretary concerned. A person receiving effective service of a court order under this section shall, as soon as possible, but not later than 30 days after the date on which effective service is made, send a written notice of such court order (together with a copy of such order) to the member affected by the court order at his last known address.

(h) Benefits for dependents who are victims of abuse by members losing right to retired pay.

(1) (A) If, in the case of a member or former member of the armed forces referred to in paragraph (2)(A), a court order provides (in the manner applicable to a division of property) for the payment of an amount from the disposable retired pay of that member or former member (as certified under paragraph (4)) to an eligible spouse or former spouse of that member or former

member, the Secretary concerned, beginning upon effective service of such court order, shall pay that amount in accordance with this subsection to such spouse or former spouse.

(B) If, in the case of a member or former member of the armed forces referred to in paragraph (2)(A), a court order provides for the payment as child support of an amount from the disposable retired pay of that member or former member (as certified under paragraph (4)) to an eligible dependent child of the member or former member, the Secretary concerned, beginning upon effective service of such court order, shall pay that amount in accordance with this subsection to such dependent child.

(2) A spouse or former spouse, or a dependent child, of a member or former member of the armed forces is eligible to receive payment under this subsection if—

(A) the member or former member, while a member of the armed forces and after becoming eligible to be retired from the armed forces on the basis of years of service, has eligibility to receive retired pay terminated as a result of misconduct while a member involving abuse of a spouse or dependent child (as defined in regulations prescribed by the Secretary of Defense or, for the Coast Guard when it is not operating as a service in the Navy, by the Secretary of Homeland Security);

(B) in the case of eligibility of a spouse or former spouse under paragraph (1)(A), the spouse or former spouse—

(i) was the victim of the abuse and was married to the member or former member at the time of that abuse; or

(ii) is a natural or adopted parent of a dependent child of the member or former member who was the victim of the abuse; and

(C) in the case of eligibility of a dependent child under paragraph (1)(B), the other parent of the child died as a result of the misconduct that resulted in the termination of retired pay.

(3) The amount certified by the Secretary concerned under paragraph (4) with respect to a member or former member of the armed forces referred to in paragraph (2)(A) shall be deemed to be the disposable retired pay of that member or former member for the purposes of this subsection.

(4) Upon the request of a court or an eligible spouse or former spouse, or an eligible dependent child, of a member or former

member of the armed forces referred to in paragraph (2)(A) in connection with a civil action for the issuance of a court order in the case of that member or former member, the Secretary concerned shall determine and certify the amount of the monthly retired pay that the member or former member would have been entitled to receive as of the date of the certification—

(A) if the member or former member's eligibility for retired pay had not been terminated as described in paragraph (2)(A); and

(B) if, in the case of a member or former member not in receipt of retired pay immediately before that termination of eligibility for retired pay, the member or former member had retired on the effective date of that termination of eligibility.

(5) A court order under this subsection may provide that whenever retired pay is increased under section 1401a of this title [10 U.S.C.S. § 1401a] (or any other provision of law), the amount payable under the court order to the spouse or former spouse, or the dependent child, of a member or former member described in paragraph (2)(A) shall be increased at the same time by the percent by which the retired pay of the member or former member would have been increased if the member or former member were receiving retired pay.

(6) Notwithstanding any other provision of law, a member or former member of the armed forces referred to in paragraph (2)(A) shall have no ownership interest in, or claim against, any amount payable under this section to a spouse or former spouse, or to a dependent child, of the member or former member.

(7) (A) If a former spouse receiving payments under this subsection with respect to a member or former member referred to in paragraph (2)(A) marries again after such payments begin, the eligibility of the former spouse to receive further payments under this subsection shall terminate on the date of such marriage.

(B) A person's eligibility to receive payments under this subsection that is terminated under subparagraph (A) by reason of remarriage shall be resumed in the event of the termination of that marriage by the death of that person's spouse or by annulment or divorce. The resumption of payments shall begin as of the first day of the month in which that marriage is so terminated. The monthly amount of the payments shall be the amount that would have been paid if the continuity of the payments had not been interrupted by the marriage.

(8) Payments in accordance with this subsection shall be made out of funds in the Department of Defense Military Retirement Fund established by section 1461 of this title [10 U.S.C.S. § 1461] or, in the case of the Coast Guard, out of funds appropriated to the Department of Homeland Security for payment of retired pay for the Coast Guard.

(9) (A) A spouse or former spouse of a member or former member of the armed forces referred to in paragraph (2)(A), while receiving payments in accordance with this subsection, shall be entitled to receive medical and dental care, to use commissary and exchange stores, and to receive any other benefit that a spouse or a former spouse of a retired member of the armed forces is entitled to receive on the basis of being a spouse or former spouse, as the case may be, of a retired member of the armed forces in the same manner as if the member or former member referred to in paragraph (2)(A) was entitled to retired pay.

(B) A dependent child of a member or former member referred to in paragraph (2)(A) who was a member of the household of the member or former member at the time of the misconduct described in paragraph (2)(A) shall be entitled to receive medical and dental care, to use commissary and exchange stores, and to have other benefits provided to dependents of retired members of the armed forces in the same manner as if the member or former member referred to in paragraph (2)(A) was entitled to retired pay.

(C) If a spouse or former spouse or a dependent child eligible or entitled to receive a particular benefit under this paragraph is eligible or entitled to receive that benefit under another provision of law, the eligibility or entitlement of that spouse or former spouse or dependent child to such benefit shall be determined under such other provision of law instead of this paragraph.

(10) (A) For purposes of this subsection, in the case of a member of the armed forces who has been sentenced by a court-martial to receive a punishment that will terminate the eligibility of that member to receive retired pay if executed, the eligibility of that member to receive retired pay may, as determined by the Secretary concerned, be considered terminated effective upon entry of judgment under section 860c of this title (article 60c of the Uniform Code of Military Justice) [10 U.S.C.S. § 860c].

(B) If each form of the punishment that would result in the termination of eligibility to receive retired pay is later remitted, set aside, or mitigated to a punishment that does not result in the termination of that eligibility, a payment of benefits to the eligible recipient under this subsection that is based on the punishment so vacated, set aside, or mitigated shall cease. The cessation of payments shall be effective as of the first day of the first month following the month in which the Secretary concerned notifies the recipient of such benefits in writing that payment of the benefits will cease. The recipient may not be required to repay the benefits received before that effective date (except to the extent necessary to recoup any amount that was erroneous when paid).

(11) In this subsection, the term "dependent child", with respect to a member or former member of the armed forces referred to in paragraph (2)(A), means an unmarried legitimate child, including an adopted child or a stepchild of the member or former member, who—

(A) is under 18 years of age;

(B) is incapable of self-support because of a mental or physical incapacity that existed before becoming 18 years of age and is dependent on the member or former member for over one-half of the child's support; or

(C) if enrolled in a full-time course of study in an institution of higher education recognized by the Secretary of Defense for the purposes of this subparagraph, is under 23 years of age and is dependent on the member or former member for over one-half of the child's support.

(i) Certification date. It is not necessary that the date of a certification of the authenticity or completeness of a copy of a court order for child support received by the Secretary concerned for the purposes of this section be recent in relation to the date of receipt by the Secretary.

(j) Regulations. The Secretaries concerned shall prescribe uniform regulations for the administration of this section.

(k) Relationship to other laws. In any case involving an order providing for payment of child support (as defined in section 459(i)(2) of the Social Security Act [42 U.S.C.S. § 659(i)(2)]) by a member who has never been married to the other parent of the child, the provisions of this section shall not apply, and the case shall be subject to the provisions of section 459 of such Act [42 U.S.C.S. § 659].

(l) Garnishment to satisfy a judgment rendered for physically, sexually, or emotionally abusing a child.

(1) Subject to paragraph (2), any payment of retired pay that would otherwise be made to a member shall be paid (in whole or in part) by the Secretary concerned to another person if and to the extent expressly provided for in the terms of a child abuse garnishment order.

(2) A court order providing for the payment of child support or alimony or, with respect to a division of property, specifically providing for the payment of an amount of the disposable retired pay from a member to the spouse or a former spouse of the member, shall be given priority over a child abuse garnishment order. The total amount of the disposable retired pay of a member payable under a child abuse garnishment order shall not exceed 25 percent of the member's disposable retired pay.

(3) In this subsection, the term "court order" includes a child abuse garnishment order.

(4) In this subsection, the term "child abuse garnishment order" means a final decree issued by a court that—

(A) is issued in accordance with the laws of the jurisdiction of that court; and

(B) provides in the nature of garnishment for the enforcement of a judgment rendered against the member for physically, sexually, or emotionally abusing a child.

(5) For purposes of this subsection, a judgment rendered for physically, sexually, or emotionally abusing a child is any legal claim perfected through a final enforceable judgment, which claim is based in whole or in part upon the physical, sexual, or emotional abuse of an individual under 18 years of age, whether or not that abuse is accompanied by other actionable wrongdoing, such as sexual exploitation or gross negligence.

(6) If the Secretary concerned is served with more than one court order with respect to the retired pay of a member, the disposable retired pay of the member shall be available to satisfy such court orders on a first-come, first-served basis, subject to the order of precedence specified in paragraph (2), with any such process being satisfied out of such monies as remain after the satisfaction of all such processes which have been previously served.

(7) The Secretary concerned shall not be required to vary normal pay and disbursement cycles for retired pay in order to comply with a child abuse garnishment order.

APPENDIX N

DoD Financial Management Regulation, Volume 7B, Chapter 29

FORMER SPOUSE PAYMENTS FROM RETIRED PAY

1.0 GENERAL

1.1 Purpose. This chapter explains how a former spouse can apply for direct payments from a military member's military retired pay and how the former spouse's payments will be administered.

1.2 Authoritative Guidance. The pay policies and requirements established by DoD in this chapter are derived primarily from, and prepared in accordance with the United States Code (U.S.C.), including Titles 10, 15, 28, 31, 38, 42 and 50. Due to the subject matter in this chapter, the list of authoritative sources is extensive. The specific statutes, regulations, and other applicable guidance that govern each individual section are listed in a reference section at the end of the chapter.

2.0 DEFINITIONS

2.1 Alimony. Alimony is a legal obligation where a member is ordered to pay an amount for the support and maintenance of a spouse or former spouse. This definition includes attorney's fees, interest, and court costs. Alimony does not include child support, property settlement, equitable distribution of property, or any other division of property.

2.2 Child Support. Child support is a legal obligation where a member is ordered to pay an amount for the support and maintenance of a child. This definition includes costs for health care, arrearages, attorney's fees, interest, penalties, and other related relief.

2.3 Court. Court means any court of competent jurisdiction of any state (in the United States), the District of Columbia, the Commonwealth of Puerto Rico, Guam, American Samoa, the Virgin Islands, the Northern Mariana Islands, and the Trust Territory of the Pacific Islands and any court of the United States, as defined in 28 U.S.C. § 451. Court also includes a court of a foreign country with which the United States has an agreement requiring the United States to honor any court order of such country.

2.4 Court Order. Court order means a final decree of divorce, dissolution, annulment, or legal separation issued by a court, or a property settlement incorporated into such an order. Court order also includes orders issued incident to a divorce, such as an order dividing military retired pay or a domestic relations order (DRO) that divides military retired pay. NOTE: A DRO is not required, but will be accepted. A court order also includes a support order as defined in section 453 of the Social Security Act (42 U.S.C. § 653(p)).

2.5 Creditable Service. Creditable service means years and full months of military service creditable for the purpose of computing a member's retired pay entitlement if the member is on active duty or the Reserve retirement points creditable if the member is a Reserve component member. See 10 U.S.C. §§ 1405 and 12733, and Volume 7B, Chapter 1 and Chapter 3.

2.6 Designated Agent. Designated agent is the agent authorized to review applications for direct payments made. See paragraph 4.0 for specific designations.

2.7 Disposable Retired Pay. Disposable retired pay is defined in paragraphs 7.1 and 8.2.

2.8 Entitlement. Entitlement is the legal right of a military member to receive military retired pay. The term refers to members who actually receive retired pay rather than those who qualify by completing the required years of service.

2.9 Final Decree. A final decree is an order from which no appeal may be taken or from which no appeal has been taken within the time allowed for taking such appeals under the laws applicable to such appeals, or a decree from which timely appeal has been taken and such appeal has been finally decided under the laws applicable to such appeals.

2.10 Former Spouse. Former spouse is the former husband or wife, or if the parties are legally separated, the current husband or wife, of a military member.

2.11 Formula Award. A formula award computes a former spouse's property interest in a military member's retired pay based on the relationship of a period of time (i.e., the length of the parties' marriage through the date of separation or total marriage through the date of divorce) during the member's creditable service (numerator) to the member's total service that is creditable toward retirement (denominator). A formula award is stated as a marital fraction in which the numerator and denominator are multiplied by a given percentage.

2.11.1. For members qualifying for an active duty (i.e., regular service) retirement, the numerator is the number of months the parties were married while the member was performing creditable military service and the denominator is the number of months of the member's total creditable military service. The elements must be expressed in terms of whole months. The former spouse's award is usually calculated by multiplying the marital fraction by one-half or 50 percent, or any other given percentage amount. See paragraph 6.7 for acceptable active duty formula award language.

2.11.2. For members qualifying for a Reserve (i.e., non-regular service) retirement, the numerator is the number of Reserve retirement points earned during the parties' marriage, and the denominator is the member's total number of Reserve retirement points. The elements must be expressed in terms of Reserve retirement points. The former spouse's award is usually calculated by multiplying the marital fraction by one-half or 50 percent, or any other given percentage amount. See subparagraph 6.7.3 for acceptable Reserve formula award language.

2.12 Garnishment Order. A garnishment order is an order directing the designated agent to issue payments from a member's pay to satisfy a legal obligation for child support, alimony, or division of property other than a division of military retired pay, or a monetary judgment rendered against a member for the physical, sexual, or emotional abuse of a child. See Public Law (PL) 115-91, section 534.

2.13 Hypothetical Retired Pay Award. Hypothetical retired pay award is an award based on a percentage of retired pay that is calculated using variables provided in a court order that are different from the member's actual retirement variables (i.e., hypothetically what would the member's retired pay be if the member retired on this date). The retired pay calculated using the court ordered variables is called the member's hypothetical retired pay. A hypothetical award typically attempts to define the property interest in the retired pay as if the member had retired at the time the court divided the member's military retired pay based upon the member's rank, or high-3 amount, and years of service accrued to that point in time. Thus, the former spouse does not benefit from the member's pay increases due to promotions or increased service time after the divorce.

2.14 Member. A member is an individual who is on active duty, one who is a reservist, or one who is retired from military service.

2.15 Renounced Pay. Renounced pay is military retired pay to which a member is entitled, but which the member has waived receipt.

2.16 Retired Pay. Retired pay is the statutory entitlement due a member based on conditions of the retirement law, pay grade or high-3 pay amount, years of service, and the date of retirement. Retired pay includes "retainer pay." NOTE: A Reserve member is generally not eligible to start receiving retired pay until they reach age 60. However, the National Defense Authorization Act (NDAA) for Fiscal Year 2008 enacted the Reduced Retirement Age for Reserve Component (RC) soldiers based on Active Duty (AD) performance. The NDAA for 2008 reduces the retirement age for RC soldiers from 60 to a lesser age, but not below age 50, for those who have served on AD in an eligible status (qualifying service) after January 8, 2008.

2.17 Retired Pay Award. Retired pay award is a portion of a member's disposable military retired pay awarded to a former spouse or current spouse by a court of competent jurisdiction as a property division.

2.18 Standard Retired Pay Multiplier. The standard retired pay multiplier used to compute retired pay for members with a Date of

Initial Entry into Military Service (DIEMS) prior to January 1, 2018 who have not elected to participate in the Blended Retirement System (BRS) is 2.5 percent times the member's years of creditable service. See Chapter 3. The retired pay or retainer pay multiplier for a member with a DIEMS on or after January 1, 2018, or a member with a DIEMS before January 1, 2018, who elected to enroll in the BRS, is 2 percent times the years of creditable service. See Chapter 3.

2.19 Uniformed Services Former Spouses' Protection Act (USFSPA). PL 97-252, enacted on September 8, 1982, states that the section of Title 10 addressing former spouse protection may be cited as the "USFSPA." Therefore, USFSPA is used throughout and refers to the provisions of 10 U.S.C. § 1408.

3.0 AWARDS THAT CAN BE COLLECTED UNDER THE USFSPA

3.1 Child Support. A former spouse can collect child support if there is a court order that awards child support, and the former spouse and military member have ever been married to each other.

3.2 Child Support Arrearages. To collect child support arrearages, a former spouse must submit a recent court order that lists the total arrearages. The order cannot be older than two years from the date the designated agent receives it.

3.3 Alimony. A former spouse can collect current alimony under the USFSPA, but not alimony arrearages.

3.4 Retired Pay Award. A former spouse can collect current retired pay award payments, but not retired pay award arrearages through DFAS.

3.5 Property Other than a Division of Retired Pay. A former spouse can collect a property division, other than a retired pay award, by garnishment if an order awards it to the former spouse and if the former spouse was also awarded alimony, child support, or a division of retired pay. A former spouse must be receiving at least one type of payment (i.e., division of property, alimony, or child support) from the designated agent and must provide the designated agent a garnishment writ to commence payments under this provision. See subparagraph 4.1.2 for more information.

3.6 Child Abuse Garnishments. Garnishment of a military retiree's retired pay in satisfaction of a judgment for physical, sexual or emotional abuse of a child under 18 years of age.

3.6.1. Subject to a court order, any payment of retired pay that would otherwise be made to a member shall be paid (in whole or in part) by the designated agent to another person as provided for in the terms of a child abuse garnishment order. The total amount payable under a child abuse garnishment order cannot exceed 25 percent of the member's disposable retired pay.

3.6.2. A court order providing for the payment of child support, alimony, or division of property, to the spouse or a former spouse of the member, is given priority over a child abuse garnishment order.

3.7 Blended Retirement System (BRS) Lump Sum Awards.

3.7.1. A member who retires under the BRS has the option of electing to receive a lump sum of a portion of their retired pay (either 25 or 50 percent) as a "discounted present value of his or her retired pay." The lump sum amount is classified as retired pay and therefore is subject to division between a member and a spouse or former spouse pursuant to the provisions of a court order. A member has several options of how to receive the lump sum, including a number of annual payments. A spouse or former spouse who is entitled to receive a portion of those payments will be paid at the time the member receives each payment.

3.7.2. In order for a spouse or former spouse to receive a portion of lump sum payments made to a member pursuant to the member's election under the BRS, the designated agent must have received and approved the application for former spouse payments prior to the member's receipt of the lump sum amount. Lump sum payments will not be divided retroactively if the application for former spouse payments was not received prior to the members' receipt of the lump sum payment. For example, if the retiree elects to receive the lump sum amount in four annual payments, (June 2026, 2027, 2028 and 2029) but the former spouse does not submit an application for former spouse payments until January 2028, the designated agent upon approval of the application, will only divide the June 2028 and June 2029 annual lump sum payments. See 10 U.S.C. § 1415 and Chapter 3 for complete information on the BRS.

4.0 APPLICATION BY FORMER SPOUSE

4.1 Application Process.

4.1.1. The former spouse must submit a completed DoD (DD) Form 2293, Application for Former Spouse Payments From Retired Pay, and a certified copy of the court order awarding alimony, child support, or military retired pay. A court order for child support arrearages cannot be older than 2 years from the date the designated agent receives it. The court order must be certified by the clerk of the court that issued the order.

4.1.2. If the former spouse is applying for a property division other than a retired pay award, the former spouse must submit a garnishment order (writ of garnishment) in addition to the DD Form 2293 and the court order. To be eligible for payments under this section, a former spouse must be receiving at least one type of payment (i.e., division of property, alimony, or child support) from the designated agent.

4.1.3. The former spouse may mail the application to the appropriate designated agent given in paragraph 4.3, or may fax it to the number provided in paragraph 4.3. Please read the instructions and certification on the DD Form 2293 carefully.

4.2 Additional Documentation.

4.2.1. A former spouse may need to provide additional documentation if the designated agent cannot determine whether the former spouse is eligible for USFSPA payments based solely on the DD Form 2293 and the court order.

4.2.2. A person designated by the former spouse in a Power of Attorney (POA) form may assist the former spouse in completing the DD Form 2293 and in notifying the designated agent of address changes. However, a person designated in the POA form cannot change the payment account number. Only the former spouse can request such changes. Additionally, payments can only be made to the account in the name of the former spouse. A copy of a POA form that properly references entitlement of payments under USFSPA must be provided.

4.2.3. A person appointed by the court to hold fiduciary responsibilities over the estate and/or property of the former spouse may make address and account changes on behalf of the former spouse. A certified copy of the order (i.e., conservatorship and guardianship) must be provided within one year of the appointment or before the specified termination date.

4.3 Where to Send an Application for USFSPA Payments. The former spouse should send the application and all supporting documents to the following designated agent for the appropriate Uniformed Service.

4.3.1. For Army, Navy, Air Force, Space Force, and Marine Corps mail to:

DFAS Office of General Counsel
Attn: Garnishment Law Directorate
P.O. Box 998002
Cleveland, OH 44199-8002
Fax: 877-622-5930

4.3.2. For U.S. Coast Guard, Public Health Services, and National Oceanic and Atmospheric Administration mail to:

Commanding Officer (LGL)
Pay and Personnel Center
444 S.E. Quincy Street
Topeka, KS 66683-3591
Fax: 785-339-3788

4.4 When to Apply for USFSPA Payments. A former spouse may apply for payments any time after the court has issued a court order enforceable under the USFSPA. Although payments will not start under the USFSPA until after the member starts to receive retired pay, the designated agent can conditionally approve a former spouse's application prior to that, and retain the application pending the member's retirement.

4.5 Conditional Preapproval.

4.5.1. If the former spouse applies prior to the member receiving retired pay, the designated agent will perform a legal review of the application, and may conditionally approve it based on information available at the time of the review concerning the member's duty status (active or Reserve).

4.5.2. At the time the member begins to receive retired pay, the designated agent will perform a second review prior to establishing the former spouse's direct payments. If the former spouse's award was based on a formula or hypothetical retired pay amount, and the member's status has changed since the initial legal review, it may be necessary to reject the application and require the former spouse to submit a clarifying order providing the necessary information. For example, if the formula or hypothetical award lists the Reserve retirement points, but the member retires from active duty, the designated agent will need a new court order that lists a valid active duty formula. See paragraph 6.7 concerning formula awards and paragraph 6.8 concerning hypothetical retired pay awards.

5.0 NOTIFICATION

5.1 Notification to Former Spouse of Approval or Disapproval. Within 30 days of the date of receipt of a former spouse's application, the designated agent will notify the former spouse if his or her application has been approved or disapproved. If approved, the designated agent will state the month the former spouse's payments will tentatively begin. If the designated agent cannot approve the application, the notice will include an explanation regarding the reason(s) why.

5.2 Notification to the Member of Approval of an Application. If a former spouse's application is approved, the designated agent will notify the member affected within 30 days of the date of receipt of the application. The member will not be notified if the application is not approved.

5.3 Second Notice. If the designated agent notified the member as part of a conditional preapproval more than 90 days prior to the member's becoming entitled to receive retired pay, the designated agent will provide a second notice to the member when the designated agent establishes the former spouse's payments at the time the member begins to receive retired pay.

5.4 Contents of Notice to Member.

5.4.1. The notice will explain that payments issued under the USFSPA cannot exceed 50 percent of the member's disposable retired pay (or 65 percent of the member's disposable pay when also withholding for an income withholding order issued pursuant to 42 U.S.C. § 659), and will contain the month that the payments will tentatively begin.

5.4.2. The notice will inform the member that he or she must notify the designated agent if the court order has been amended, superseded, or set aside.

5.4.3. The notice will inform the member that if he or she submits information in response to this notice, he or she consents to the disclosure of that information.

5.4.4. The notice will include a copy of the court order.

5.4.5. The notice will advise that the member's failure to respond within 30 days of the date that the notification is mailed may result in the payment of a portion of the member's retired pay to a spouse or former spouse as set out in the notice to the member.

5.5 How to Prevent USFSPA Payments from Starting. The member must provide documentary evidence that a former spouse's court order is legally defective or has been appealed, amended, or set aside. If the designated agent determines that the documentary evidence is sufficient to bar payments to a former spouse, the designated agent will not start the payments. The designated agent will then inform the former spouse that payments will not start, and provide copies of the documentary evidence to the former spouse.

6.0 COURT ORDERS

6.1 Contents of Court Order.

6.1.1. The court order must be regular on its face. This means that a court of competent jurisdiction issued the order and nothing on its face provides reasonable notice that it was issued without authority of law.

6.1.2. If the court order awarding child support or alimony appears on its face to conform to the laws of the jurisdiction from which it was issued, the designated agent will not be required to ascertain whether the court had obtained personal jurisdiction over the member.

6.1.3. The court order must award former spouse alimony, child support, or a retired pay award. There is no requirement in Federal law that specifies how military retired pay is to be divided.

6.1.4. If the order contains a retired pay award, that award must be expressed as a fixed dollar amount or as a percentage of disposable retired pay. A retired pay award expressed as a percentage will automatically receive a proportionate share of the member's cost-of-living adjustments (COLA), while one expressed as a fixed amount will not. There is no authority for a retired pay award to state a fixed dollar amount and also order COLAs. Retired pay awards phrased in that manner will be construed as a fixed dollar amount and will not receive COLAs.

6.1.5. The designated agent will construe percentage awards such as a percentage of gross retired pay, as a percentage of disposable retired pay regardless of the language in the order.

6.1.6. If the former spouse and the member were divorced before the member became entitled to receive military retired pay, the retired pay award may be expressed as a formula or hypothetical retired pay award in accordance with paragraphs 6.7 and 6.8. Since the computation of formula and hypothetical retired pay awards result in a percentage, they are considered a type of percentage award, and would automatically receive a proportionate share of the member's retired pay COLAs.

6.2 Divorces Finalized While the Member is Still on Active Duty.

6.2.1. For court orders issued prior to December 19, 2003, the court order must show that the member's rights under the Soldiers' and Sailors' Civil Relief Act of 1940 (50 U.S.C. Appendix 501 *et. seq.*) were complied with.

6.2.2. For court orders issued on or after December 19, 2003, the court order must show that the member's rights under the Servicemembers Civil Relief Act 50 U.S.C. § 3901 et. seq. (formerly cited as 50 U.S.C. Appendix 501 *et. seq.*) were complied with.

6.3 Domestic Relations Order (DRO). There is no requirement in USFSPA that a former spouse submit a DRO, but the designated agent will accept one if it is submitted and if it meets the requirements of the USFSPA. If the divorce decree or dissolution order states a DRO was entered, it must be submitted to the designated agent unless a subsequent court order has been entered and provided.

6.4 Requirements Specific to a Retired Pay Award.

6.4.1. In the case of a retired pay award, the designated agent must be able to determine from the court order that the court dividing military retired pay had jurisdiction over the member in one of the following ways:

6.4.1.1. The member resided in the territorial jurisdiction of the court at the time of the legal proceeding due to other than military assignment;

6.4.1.2. The court finds that member's domicile was in the territorial jurisdiction of the court at the time of the legal proceeding; or

6.4.1.3. The member consented to the jurisdiction of the court. If the court order does not "explicitly" state that the member consented to the court's jurisdiction, the designated agent will regard the member's participation in the legal proceeding, other than to contest the court's jurisdiction, as evidence of the member's consent to the court's jurisdiction in the proceeding dividing the member's military retired pay.

6.4.2. Also, in the case of a retired pay award, the designated agent must be able to determine from the application that the former spouse and the member were married for at least 10 years during which the member performed 10 years or more of service creditable toward retirement eligibility (the "10/10" requirement). The 10 years of creditable service is determined upon the effective date of the divorce, dissolution, legal separation, or annulment. There is no "10/10" requirement for payment of alimony, child support awards, or child abuse garnishments under USFSPA.

6.5 State Law Jurisdiction. The satisfaction of state law jurisdictional requirements is not sufficient alone to satisfy the additional jurisdictional requirement stated in paragraph 6.4. If the court states that it has USFSPA jurisdiction, it must state the basis for the finding, i.e., member's residence, member's domicile or member's consent.

6.6 Member's Consent to a Separation Agreement. If the member signed a separation agreement, the designated agent will presume that the member consented to the jurisdiction of any court that at any time incorporates the agreement into a court order.

6.7 Acceptable Formula Awards.

6.7.1. If the former spouse's award is expressed in terms of a formula, all the variables needed to calculate the formula must be included in the court order, with the exception of a member's total number of months of creditable service or total number of Reserve retirement points, which the designated agent will provide in accordance with subparagraphs 6.7.2 and 6.7.3. If the order provides all the variables needed to do the calculation, including total months of military service or total Reserve retirement points, the designated agent will calculate the formula using the variables provided, even if the figure is different from the member's actual total. If the member disagrees with the number listed in the court order (i.e., the denominator), the member will have to petition the court to get the order corrected to show the member's actual total months or points of military service. If any needed variable besides the total number of months of creditable service or total number of Reserve retirement points is not provided in the order, the applicant will have to provide the designated agent with a clarifying court order, which provides the necessary variable. The designated agent will carry out any percentages derived from formulas to four decimal places.

6.7.2. If the court order requires the designated agent to supply the denominator of a marital or coverture fraction, and the member qualifies for an active duty (i.e., regular service) retirement, the formula award must be expressed in terms of whole months. The numerator of the formula fraction is the number of months of marriage during military service. This number must specifically be provided in the court order. The denominator of the formula is the member's total number of months of creditable military service. If needed, the designated agent will provide the denominator if the order states it represents the member's total number of months of creditable military service. If the denominator represents anything other than the member's total number of months of creditable service at the time of retirement (for example, number of months of creditable service as of the date of the separation or divorce), the designated agent is unable to provide it. Any days or partial months of service will not be considered. If the award is expressed in terms of years instead of months, the designated agent will convert years into whole months by rounding down to the nearest month.

6.7.3. If the court order requires the designated agent to supply the denominator of a marital or coverture fraction, and the member qualifies for a Reserve (i.e., non-regular service) retirement, the formula award must be expressed in terms of Reserve retirement points. In the case of a Reserve retirement, the numerator of the formula is the number of Reserve retirement points earned during the marriage. The Reserve retirement points that are to be used for the numerator must be provided in the court order. The denominator of the formula is the member's total number of Reserve retirement points at the time of retirement. If needed, the designated agent will provide the denominator if the order states it represents the member's total number of Reserve retirement points at the time of retirement. If the denominator represents anything other than the member's total Reserve retirement points at the time of the retirement (for example, Reserve retirement points as of the date of divorce), the designated agent is unable to provide it. The designated agent cannot honor a formula award for a member that qualifies for Reserve retirement that is expressed in terms of whole months, even if both the numerator and denominator are provided.

6.7.4. The sample Military Retired Pay Division Orders (see Figures 29-1 and 29-2 [in Chapter 29 of the DODFMR, Vol. 7b]) provide examples of acceptable formula award language. All the blanks in the sample awards represent variables that must be provided in the court order. The sample language is not required, but any award expressed using the applicable sample language will be acceptable.

> Example of active duty formula: The court order awarded the former spouse a percentage of the member's disposable retired pay calculated by multiplying 50 percent times a fraction, where the numerator is 144 months of marriage during military service, and the denominator is the member's total months of active duty service. The member later retired after 20 years (or 240 months) of creditable service. The former spouse's award would be computed as follows: 50% x 144 months/240 months = 30%. The designated agent would pay 30 percent of the member's disposable retired pay.

6.8 Hypothetical Retired Pay Awards.

6.8.1. Military retired pay is computed at the time the member retires and it is based on two possible methods depending on when the member initially enters service. It will either be computed by using the member's rank and total years of service at the time of retirement, or the member's retired pay base, also known as high-3 (highest 36 months of earnings), and total years of service at the time of retirement. For members who entered military service before September 8, 1980, the member's rank is used. For members who entered military service on or after September 8, 1980, the member's retired pay base (high-3) is used.

6.8.2. A hypothetical retired pay award determines the amount awarded to a former spouse by using retirement information different from what will exist at the time a member actually retires. Typically, the court will use variables to determine the retired pay award as though the member had retired at the time of the court order dividing military retired pay or some other date prior to the member's actual retirement. In this manner, the former spouse is awarded a portion of the member's retirement without accounting for promotions or service completed after the date of the order.

6.8.3. The hypothetical retired pay amount is calculated by multiplying the hypothetical retired pay multiplier (see subparagraph 6.8.4) times the hypothetical retired pay base (i.e., the member's active duty pay based on their rank and years of service or the average of their monthly pay for their highest 36 months of pay;

their "high-3"). If the initial retired pay computation is not a multiple of $1, it is rounded down to the next lower multiple of $1. See Chapter 3 for retired pay calculations.

6.8.4. Retired Pay Multiplier.

6.8.4.1. The standard retired pay multiplier is 2.5 percent multiplied by the member's years of creditable service. For example, the retired pay multiplier for an active duty member who serves 20 years will be 50 percent (2.5% x 20 years = 50%). In the case of a hypothetical retired pay award, the hypothetical retired pay multiplier is determined by multiplying 2.5 percent times the hypothetical years of creditable service provided in the court order. The hypothetical years of creditable service must only include years and full months. If the figure provided in the court order includes days of service, the designated agent will round down to the nearest month. For example, if the hypothetical years of service provided is 14.57, since this figure includes more than 14 years, 6 months of service but not enough for 14 years 7 months of service, 14 years, 6 months (or 14.5) will be used for the calculation. See paragraph 2.5. The resulting percentage is rounded to two decimal places. See Chapter 3 for retired pay calculations.

6.8.4.2. For members who retire under the BRS, the retired pay multiplier is 2 percent multiplied by the member's years of creditable service.

6.8.4.3. A hypothetical retired pay award for a reservist must be expressed in terms of Reserve retirement points rather than years of creditable service. The Reserve retirement points are converted into years of creditable service by dividing the Reserve retirement points on which the award is based by 360. The resultant figure is carried to three decimal places; then rounded to two. (See Chapter 3.) This resultant figure is used to compute the hypothetical retired pay multiplier. For example: 5,258 Reserve retirement points would convert to 14.61 years of service for multiplier purposes (5,258 points/360 = 14.61 years).

6.8.5. Retired Pay Base.

6.8.5.1. For members entering military service before September 8, 1980, the retired pay base is the member's basic pay at retirement based on the member's rank and years of service for basic pay purposes. See Chapter 3. When computing a hypothetical award for one of these members, their hypothetical retired pay base would usually be their basic pay as of the hypothetical retirement date.

6.8.5.2. For members entering military service on or after September 8, 1980, the retired pay base is the average of the member's highest 36 months of basic pay at retirement (high-3 amount). See Chapter 3. For these members, their hypothetical retired pay base would usually be their average basic pay for the most recent 36 months prior to the hypothetical retirement date. If the court order provides the annual amount of retired pay base (high-3), the designated agent will convert it to a monthly amount by dividing the yearly amount by 12 to arrive at the monthly average.

6.8.6. In order to enable the designated agent to calculate the hypothetical retired pay amount, the court order must provide:

6.8.6.1. The percentage the former spouse was awarded;

6.8.6.2. The hypothetical years of creditable service, or, in the case of a reservist, the Reserve retirement points on which the hypothetical retired pay is to be based;

6.8.6.3. The hypothetical retired pay base (high-3). In the case of members entering military service before September 8, 1980, the court order may provide either the member's hypothetical retired pay base or the member's hypothetical rank and years of service for basic pay purposes; and

6.8.6.4. The hypothetical retirement date.

6.8.7. For members whose divorce, dissolution, legal separation, or annulment was effective on or before December 23, 2016 (the effective date of the NDAA 2017), if the court intends that the hypothetical retired pay be calculated based on the pay tables in effect at the time the member becomes entitled to receive military retired pay, the designated agent will use as the retired pay base either the basic pay for the hypothetical rank and years of service as of the date the member becomes eligible to receive retired pay, or the member's actual retired pay base, whichever is lower. The court order must provide:

6.8.7.1. The percentage the former spouse is awarded;

6.8.7.2. The hypothetical years of creditable service, or, in the case of a reservist, the Reserve retirement points on which the hypothetical retired pay is to be based and the member's years of service for basic pay purposes;

6.8.7.3. The member's hypothetical rank; and

6.8.7.4. An unequivocal statement that the calculation is to be made as of the member's actual retirement date.

6.8.7.5. If the court order awards a Reserve hypothetical calculated as of the time the member attains age 60, but the reserve member begins to receive retirement pay earlier based upon the Reduced Retirement Age provision of NDAA 2008, the designated agent cannot pay the former spouse until the member turns age 60. Additionally, the designated agent cannot compute the award if the member has not turned 60 years of age because the pay tables for a future date are not published until that date. The applicant will need to either wait until the member turns age 60 to start receiving the division of property award or obtain a clarifying court order.

6.8.8. If the award language is missing any necessary variables, the court will have to clarify the award. See the sample Military Retired Pay Division Order (Figures 29-1 and 29-2 [in Chapter 29 of the DODFMR, Vol. 7b]) for examples of acceptable hypothetical retired pay award language.

6.8.9. All percentage hypothetical retired pay awards will be converted into a percentage of a member's actual retired pay according to the following example:

> The court order awarded the former spouse 50 percent of the disposable retired pay the member would have received had the member retired with 17 years of creditable service, a retired pay base of $2,200.00 per month, and a hypothetical retirement date of June 1, 1999. The member actually retired on June 1, 2002, with 20 years of creditable service, a retired pay base of $2,400.00 per month, and an initial gross retired pay of $1,200.00 per month (2.5% x 20 years = 50%; 50% x $2,400.00 = $1,200.00).
>
> First, the designated agent will calculate the member's hypothetical retired pay multiplier, which in this example is 42.5 percent (2.5% x 17 years = 42.5%).
>
> Next, the designated agent will calculate the hypothetical retired pay amount, which in this example is $935.00 per month (42.5% x $2,200.00 = $935.00).
>
> Then, the designated agent will apply retired pay COLAs to the hypothetical retired pay amount from the hypothetical retirement date to the date the member became eligible to receive retired pay, unless the court order directs otherwise. This cal-

culation will determine the present value of the hypothetical retired pay as of the member's actual retirement date. In this case, if the member had become eligible to receive retired pay on June 1, 1999, the hypothetical retirement date, the hypothetical retired pay, after adding the COLAs, would have been $1,008 per month on June 1, 2002, the actual retirement date.

In these examples, the addition of the partial annual COLAs would be as follows:

Year	COLA	Formula
12/1/1999	1.7 percent	$935.00 x 1.017 = $950.00 (rounded down)
12/1/2000	3.5 percent	$950.00 x 1.035 = $983.00 (rounded down)
12/1/2001	2.6 percent	$983.00 x 1.026 = $1,008.00 (rounded down)

Finally, the designated agent will convert the former spouse's percentage of hypothetical retired pay to a percentage of the member's actual retired pay as follows: 50% x 1,008,00/$1,200.00 = 42%. (All percentages derived from hypothetical computations will be carried out to four decimal places if applicable without rounding.) In this example, 42 percent is the amount that the designated agent would enter into the retired pay system as the spouse/former spouse's retired pay award.

6.8.10. The military retired pay of a post-July 1986 member who has accepted a Career Status Bonus (CSB) is calculated using a reduced multiplier. (See Chapter 3.) However, when computing a retired pay award based on a hypothetical, the CSB member's hypothetical retired pay will be calculated using the standard multiplier. The retired pay of a member who has accepted a CSB will be recomputed using a standard multiplier effective the first day of the month after the member attains age 62. The former spouse's percentage will also be adjusted at the same time in accordance with subparagraph 6.8.8, using the member's recomputed retired pay in the denominator of the conversion fraction. This adjustment will result in a lower percentage being applied to a higher disposable pay figure, and will ensure that the former spouse continues to receive the amount intended in the court order.

6.8.11. When computing hypothetical awards for members under the BRS the former spouse's hypothetical award (percentage) will be calculated in accordance with subparagraph 6.8.8. However, since the actual military retired pay for members who retire under the BRS is calculated using the 2 percent multiplier, the BRS member's hypothetical retired pay will also be calculated using the 2 percent multiplier. Additionally, the designated agent will use the unreduced gross retired pay in the denominator of the conversion fraction, even if the member elects to receive a lump sum payment. Using the unreduced gross retired pay for the denominator ensures that the numerator and denominator are computed in an equalized manner (i.e., the same variables are used and one is not reduced).

6.9 Orders Issued before June 26, 1981 That Did Not Divide Retired Pay. Any court order that contains a retired pay award that was issued before June 26, 1981 will be honored if it otherwise satisfies the requirements and conditions shown in this chapter. If a pre-June 26, 1981 decree or property settlement incident to the decree did not divide the member's military retired pay, and did not reserve jurisdiction to divide it, the designated agent cannot honor an application for payment based on a subsequent order issued on or after June 26, 1981, dividing retired pay as property.

6.10 Survivor Benefit Plan (SBP) Premium.

6.10.1. Pursuant to 10 U.S.C. § 1452, the SBP premium must be deducted from the member's retired pay. The SBP premium cannot be deducted from the former spouse's portion of the member's retired pay. Any provision in a court order stating that the premium should be deducted from the former spouse's portion is unenforceable by the designated agent. Any adjustments between the parties for the SBP premium payment will need to be made outside of the stated procedures. However, those adjustments will not be considered by the designated agent when computing the retired pay award.

6.10.2. SBP premiums for members who elect a lump sum payment or payments will not be collected from the lump sum payment. Premiums will be deducted from the portion of retired pay that the member receives as regular retired pay after the lump sum payment. For more information on SBP premiums and BRS see Chapters 3, 42, and 45.

NOTE: A court order associated with a divorce that requires a retired member to establish former spouse SBP coverage is not self-executing. If a former spouse seeks to be deemed as the former spouse SBP beneficiary (to commence or continue SBP coverage after a divorce) (s)he must complete a DD Form 2656-10 ("Survivor Benefit Plan (SBP) Former Spouse Request for Deemed Election") and submit it along with a copy of the relevant court order, within one year of the order requiring the member to elect former spouse coverage. See Volume 7B, Chapter 43, paragraphs 4.4.3 and 5.2.

6.11 Conflicting Retired Pay Awards.

6.11.1. If the designated agent is served with court orders issued by different jurisdictions which contain conflicting awards enforceable under the USFSPA, the designated agent will deduct an amount equal to the largest amount required to be paid to the former spouse by either order, but will pay to the former spouse the least amount directed to be paid. The designated agent will retain the difference between the upper and lower ordered amounts until served with an order certified by the member and former spouse to be valid, and then pay the retained funds in accordance with the order.

6.11.2. If the designated agent is served with a court order containing conflicting retired pay award language within the same court order, or two orders issued on the same date that do not contain a time stamp, the designated agent will pay the former spouse the lower award amount; if the orders contain a time stamp, the order issued last controls. If one of the parties disagrees with the amount being paid, that party must provide the designated agent with a new court order stating the correct amount.

6.12 Court Orders Modifying Retired Pay Awards.

6.12.1. If the designated agent is served with a court order containing valid award language in accordance with this chapter and the USFSPA, that modifies or clarifies a retired pay award, the designated agent will implement the order issued most recently. The order with valid award language issued most recently supersedes all prior orders.

6.12.2. If the designated agent is served with a court order containing valid award language that modifies or clarifies a retired pay award that was issued by a court of a state other than the state that issued the prior court order, the designated agent may implement the new order containing valid award language only if the court issuing this order had jurisdiction over both the member and former spouse in the manner specified in subparagraph 6.4.1.

6.12.3. If the designated agent is served with a court order containing invalid award language that modifies or clarifies a retired pay award and the order does not vacate or set aside a prior order with valid award language, the designated agent will continue to honor the prior valid court order. If the designated agent is served with a subsequent court order containing invalid award language that vacates or sets aside a prior order with valid award language, the designated agent will terminate former spouse payments until served with a subsequent order containing valid award language.

6.13 Conditional Awards. The designated agent cannot honor a court order that makes the former spouse's payments conditional on the occurrence of some other event. There is no authority for the designated agent to ascertain whether a condition in a court order has been satisfied. The former spouse will need to obtain a modified court order without the condition.

6.14 Awards Based on Retired Pay Accrued During Marriage. The designated agent cannot honor awards based on the value of the member's retired pay that has "accrued" during the marriage because military retired pay does not accrue over time. Military retired pay is not a pension. Rather, it is a statutory entitlement computed at the time the member retires and it is based on the member's rank and total years of service at the time of retirement, or member's high-3 and total years of service.

6.15 Awards of a Percentage of the Marital Portion. The designated agent cannot honor an award of a percentage of the "marital portion" or "marital share" of a member's retired pay unless the court order also provides all variables necessary for the calculation of the marital portion/share. See paragraphs 6.7 and 6.8 for examples.

6.16 Factual Errors in Court Orders. If a party submits documentary evidence that shows a factual error in a court order, this will not be sufficient to modify or stop payments being made pursuant to the court order. Subject to compliance with existing law, if a court order provides elements needed to calculate a former spouse award, including but not limited to, formulas, hypotheticals, and/or NDAA awards, the designated agent will use the elements provided even if the elements vary from the member's actual figures. The party asserting the error must petition the court to correct the order. The designated agent does not have the authority to correct errors in court orders.

7.0 DISPOSABLE RETIRED PAY

7.1 Disposable Retired Pay for Regular and Non-Regular Retirements.

7.1.1. Disposable retired pay is defined by the USFSPA as a member's total monthly retired pay (gross pay) entitlement minus authorized deductions. See 10 U.S.C. § 1408(a)(4).

7.1.2. If the former spouse and member were divorced on or before February 2, 1991, then USFSPA authorizes the following deductions:

7.1.2.1. Amounts owed to the United States;

7.1.2.2. Amounts withheld as Federal and state income tax withholding, consistent with the member's current actual tax liability;

7.1.2.3. Fines and forfeitures ordered by a court-martial;

7.1.2.4. Amounts waived in order to receive compensation under Titles 5 or 38 of the U.S.C.;

7.1.2.5. SBP premiums paid, but only if the former spouse applying for a retired pay award payment under USFSPA is the beneficiary of the SBP; and

7.1.2.6. The amount of retired pay for a member retired under Title 10, Chapter 61 computed based on percentage of disability.

7.1.3. If the former spouse and member were divorced on or after February 3, 1991, then the USFSPA authorizes the following deductions:

7.1.3.1. Amounts owed to the United States due to the overpayment of retired pay, or amounts required to be recouped due to the member's entitlement to retired pay;

7.1.3.2. Fines and forfeitures ordered by a court-martial;

7.1.3.3. Amounts waived in order to receive compensation under Titles 5 or 38 of the U.S.C.;

7.1.3.4. SBP premiums paid but only if the former spouse applying for a retired pay award payment under USFSPA is the beneficiary of the SBP; and

7.1.3.5. The amount of retired pay for a member retired under Title 10, Chapter 61 computed based on percentage of disability.

7.2 Computing Disposable Retired Pay for Disability Retirements.

7.2.1. Effective January 1, 2004, pursuant to Pub. L. 108-136, div. A, title VI, § 641(e) (Nov. 24, 2003), codified at 10 U.S.C. § 1414 certain retired members may receive both disability compensation from the Department of Veterans Affairs (VA) and military retired pay concurrently. When a retired member qualifies for concurrent payments, the military retired pay provided to the member must be included in the member's gross retired pay. The disposable retired pay may then be computed in accordance with paragraphs 7.1 and 8.0. The disposable pay is subject to division under the USFSPA. See Chapter 64 for additional information on concurrent receipt of both retired pay and VA disability compensation.

7.2.2. Members who were retired for disability under Title 10, Chapter 61 for being found unfit to perform the duties of their office because of physical disability are entitled to disability retired pay. The amount to which a member is entitled is determined by applying a percentage multiplier to the member's basic pay (or high-36 month average) at the time of retirement. There are two possible multipliers and the choice of which multiplier to use is made by the member. The percentage multiplier may be either:

7.2.2.1. The number of years of the member's creditable service, or

7.2.2.2. The disability percentage assigned by the Service.

7.2.3. In general, the disposable retired pay equals a member's total gross monthly retired pay entitlement minus certain authorized deductions. One of the authorized deductions is "[t]he amount of retired pay for a member retired under Title 10, Chapter 61 computed based on percentage of disability." Accordingly, to compute disposable retired pay for members retired for disability under Title 10, Chapter 61, it is necessary to segregate the portion of gross monthly retired pay attributable to the percentage of disability from that attributable to years of creditable service:

7.2.3.1. Example 1 – disposable retired pay using years of creditable service. A disability retiree who selected disability retired pay computed using creditable service in the monthly amount of $900 and declined disability retired pay computed using the percentage of disability in the monthly amount of $700. In this case, no other deductions apply.

Assumptions	**Member's Option**	**Entitlement Amount for Each Option**	**Member's Choice**	**Gross Retired Pay as Chosen by Member (Monthly)**	**Amount That May be Deducted***	**Disposable Retired Pay**
Disability retiree* with an option between a retired pay multiplier based on years of service and a retired pay multiplier based on percentage of disability.	Option 1: Retired pay based on years of service	$900	Elect	$900	$700	$200 ($900 – $700)**
	Option 2: Retired pay based on percentage of disability	$700	Decline			

7.2.3.2. Example 2 – disposable retired pay using percentage of disability. A disability retiree who selected disability retired pay using the percentage of disability in the monthly amount of $1000 and declined disability retired pay using years of creditable service in the monthly amount of $500. In this case, no other deductions apply.

Assumptions	Member's Option	Entitlement Amount for Each Option	Member's Choice	Gross Retired Pay as Chosen by Member (Monthly)	Amount That May be Deducted*	Disposable Retired Pay
Disability retiree* with an option between a retired pay multiplier based on years of service and a retired pay multiplier based on percentage of disability.	Option 1: Retired pay based on years of service	$500	Decline	$1000	$1000	$0 ($1000 – $1000)**
	Option 2: Retired pay based on percentage of disability	$1000	Elect			

* Examples 1 and 2 include disability retirees who are entitled to receive both disability compensation from the VA and military retired pay concurrently. Under subparagraph 7.2.1, when a retired member qualifies for concurrent payments, the military retired pay provided to the member must be included in the member's gross retired pay.

** Examples 1 and 2 are computed assuming no other authorized deductions apply.

7.2.4. Only disposable retired pay is subject to division under the USFSPA. If a disability retiree is entitled to receive both military disability retired pay from the DoD and disability compensation from the VA concurrently and the deduction under 10 U.S.C. § 1408(a)(4)(A)(iii) for "The amount of retired pay . . . computed based on percentage of disability" results in disposable retired pay of $0, then no direct payments from a military member's military retired pay will be made.

7.2.5. Under 10 U.S.C. § 1414, certain retired members may receive both disability compensation from the VA and military retired pay concurrently. When a member who was retired for disability under Title 10, Chapter 61, is in receipt of both disability compensation from the VA and military disability retired pay, the retired pay is still disability retired pay and it is no different than disability retired pay paid to a retired member who is not eligible for concurrent receipt under 10 U.S.C. § 1414. The nature of the disability retired pay is not changed simply because the retiree is found by the DVA to have a service-connected disability that entitles the member to receive both benefits concurrently under 10 U.S.C. § 1414 even though the amount of disability retired pay that can be received concurrently with DVA disability compensation may be limited. For more information about concurrent receipt of disability compensation from the VA and military disability retired pay, see Chapter 64.

7.3 Other Deductions Included in Court Order. If a court order directs the use of deductions other than those authorized in paragraph 7.1 to compute the former spouse's award, that provision of the court order is unenforceable. The designated agent will use only the deductions authorized in paragraph 7.1 for the computation of disposable retired pay.

8.0 DISPOSABLE RETIRED PAY UNDER THE NDAA

8.1 Application of the NDAA. The provision of the NDAA FY 2017, section 641, applies to divorces, dissolutions, annulments, and legal separations effective after December 23, 2016, that award the former spouse a retired pay award and:

8.1.1. That occur prior to an active duty member becoming entitled to military retirement pay, or

8.1.2. That occur prior to a reserve member becoming entitled to retired pay (generally 60).

8.2 NDAA FY 2017 Disposable Pay Limits. In addition to the definition of disposable retired pay in paragraph 7.1, and the authorized deductions in subparagraph 7.1.2, the NDAA also limits disposable retired pay as follows:

8.2.1. The amount of retired pay is limited to that which the member would have been entitled using the member's retired pay base (rank or high-3) and years of service on the date of the final decree of divorce, dissolution, annulment, or legal separation; and

8.2.2. Increased by any COLA awards added from the effective date of divorce, dissolution, annulment, or legal separation to the member's date of retirement. A provision in a court order purporting to restrict COLAs from being applied to a former spouse's award of retired pay is not enforceable and will not be honored.

8.3 Variables Required to Calculate the NDAA FY 2017 Disposable Retired Pay. In order to enable the designated agent to calculate the NDAA FY 2017 disposable retired pay amount, the court order must provide the variables listed in subparagraphs 8.3.1 or

8.3.2. See Figures 29-1 and 29-2 [in Chapter 29 of the DODFMR, Vol. 7b] for examples of acceptable NDAA required language.

8.3.1. If the member entered the service before September 8, 1980:

8.3.1.1. The fixed amount, the percentage, the formula, or the hypothetical award that the former spouse is granted;

8.3.1.2. The member's pay grade (rank) at the time of divorce, dissolution, legal separation, or annulment; and

8.3.1.3. The member's years of creditable service, on the date of divorce, dissolution, annulment, or legal separation. In the case of a reservist, the Reserve retirement points, on the date of divorce, dissolution, annulment, or legal separation and years of creditable service for basic pay purposes.

8.3.2. If the member entered the service on or after September 8, 1980:

8.3.2.1. The fixed amount, the percentage, the formula, or the hypothetical award that the former spouse is granted;

8.3.2.2. The member's retired pay base (high-3) amount at the time of divorce, dissolution, legal separation, or annulment (the actual dollar figure); and

8.3.2.3. The member's years of creditable service, on the date of divorce, dissolution, annulment, or legal separation. In the case of a reservist, the Reserve retirement points, on the date of divorce, dissolution, annulment, or legal separation.

8.4 Clarification Order. If the award language in the court order is missing any of the listed variables in paragraph 8.3, then the applicant will need to obtain a clarifying court order that provides the variables as described in paragraph 8.3.

9.0 STARTING PAYMENTS

9.1 Starting Payments. If the former spouse's application is approved, payments will start no later than 90 days after the date the designated agent received the former spouse's complete application, or no later than 90 days after the date the member becomes entitled to receive military retired pay, whichever is later.

9.2 Timing of Payments. Payments will be issued in conformity with normal pay and disbursement cycles, which mean that payments will be issued monthly. Payments will be deducted from the month's pay and paid on the first business day of the following month. For example, a payment issued for the month of March would be sent at the beginning of April.

10.0 PAYMENT AMOUNT

10.1 Limitations.

10.1.1. If the spouse or former spouse applies for payments under the USFSPA only, the maximum amount a former spouse can receive is 50 percent of the member's disposable retired pay.

10.1.2. If the spouse or former spouse applies for payments under the USFSPA and there is also a garnishment order for support, the maximum amount that can be paid toward both obligations is 65 percent of the member's disposable earnings calculated in accordance with 42 U.S.C. § 659 (child and spousal support statute) and its implementing regulation.

10.1.3. For garnishments for property other than a retired pay award, the maximum amount payable is 25 percent of disposable earnings in accordance with 15 U.S.C. § 1673.

10.1.4. In the event a member receives a retroactive award for disability compensation (under Title 38 of the U.S. Code) or a retroactive award for Combat-Related Special Compensation (under 10 U.S.C. § 1413a), the payments of retired pay previously made to a former spouse pursuant to a valid court order that were proper when paid do not become erroneous overpayments.

10.2 COLA. If a retired pay award is expressed as a percentage of disposable retired pay, the former spouse will automatically receive a proportionate share of the member's COLAs regardless of any language in a court order to the contrary. Formula and hypothetical retired pay awards are considered a type of percentage award, and thus will automatically include a proportionate share of the member's COLAs. If the retired pay award is a fixed amount, COLAs cannot be added, even if awarded in the court order, and the former spouse's payments will remain fixed. In an NDAA applicable case, COLAs will be added to the disposable income calculation on all awards regardless of what the court order states. Also, the former spouse will automatically receive a proportionate share of the member's COLAs on all NDAA applicable cases in which the award is a percentage, formula, or hypothetical regardless of what the court order states.

10.3 Offset of Former Spouse's Payment for Garnishment or Other Obligation. A former spouse's payment cannot be offset or garnished by the designated agent for any legal obligation, including child support owed to the member.

11.0 PRIORITY OF PAYMENTS

11.1 Multiple Awards. If a court order includes multiple types of awards to a former spouse, the former spouse may designate the priority of payments on the DD Form 2293. If the former spouse does not specify otherwise, the designated agent will pay the retired pay award first, child support second and spousal support third.

11.2 Multiple Former Spouses. If the designated agent is served with applications from more than one former spouse, the designated agent will honor the applications on a first-come, first-served basis. Subsequently served USFSPA applications shall be satisfied out of the disposable retired pay that remains after the satisfaction of all previously served court orders, subject to the limitations of paragraph 10.1.

11.3 Garnishment Orders for Support and Applications under USFSPA. If the designated agent is served with both a garnishment for support and an application under USFSPA, the designated agent will pay whichever is served first. If the garnishment is served first and is payable directly to the former spouse, the former spouse may reverse the priority of payments by instructing the designated agent to terminate deductions pursuant to the garnishment, and then later requesting that garnishment deductions be reestablished. The designated agent will not change the priority of payments between a retired pay award and a support garnishment if the garnishment was served by an IV-D agency unless the agency agrees to withdraw (terminate) the support order in order to allow the retired pay award to have priority over the support order.

12.0 STOPPING PAYMENTS

12.1 Erroneous Payment Information from Former Spouse. The former spouse has a continuing duty to provide the designated agent with correct payment instructions and current contact information. If a former spouse's payments are returned due to erroneous payment instructions (i.e., invalid address or incorrect account number for direct deposit payments), the designated agent will send notice to the last known correspondence address that, unless new payment instructions are received within 30 days of the date of the notice, payments will stop. If the former spouse submits new payment instructions after the payments have terminated, the designated agent will restart the payments on a current basis, and will not make up any missed payments.

12.2 Termination and Suspension of Retired Pay Award Payments.

12.2.1. Unless the court order specifies otherwise, payments will stop upon the designated agent's receipt of notice of the death of either party. Payments will be prorated for the month of the death of either party.

12.2.2. Unless the court order specifies otherwise, retired pay award payments will not stop upon the designated agent's receipt of notice of the former spouse's remarriage.

12.2.3. If the designated agent is served with an order staying payments, the designated agent will stop the payments until served with an order indicating that the former spouse's payments are to resume.

12.2.4. If the designated agent has already started payments and is served with documentation showing that an appeal of the order has been filed within the forum state's appeal timeframe, payments will stop. The designated agent will not recoup any payments already issued.

12.2.5. A former spouse may stop payments under USFSPA by sending the designated agent a letter with his or her signature notarized withdrawing their application for payments under the USFSPA. A former spouse can later reapply for payments by submitting a new DD Form 2293 and a certified copy of the court order that awards him/her the division of military retired pay.

12.2.6. If the designated agent has already started payments and the member goes into a non-pay status (thus is no longer receiving pay from DFAS), payments will stop. If the member goes back into a pay status, payments will resume.

12.3 Termination of Child Support Payments under USFSPA. Child support payments will stop in accordance with the provisions of the court order. If the court order is silent as to when the payments should stop, payments will stop in accordance with the law of the state that issued the court order. The member has the burden of providing sufficient documentation to justify stopping payments on or before a child's age of majority. The former spouse has the burden of providing sufficient documentation to justify continuing payments after a child's age of majority.

12.4 Termination of Alimony Payments under USFSPA. Alimony payments will stop in accordance with the provisions of the court order. If the court order is silent as to when the payments should stop, payments will stop in accordance with the law of the state that issued the court order, or upon receiving a court order terminating the alimony payments. (NOTE: The law of some states does not provide that an alimony obligation automatically terminates upon a former spouse's remarriage. For such states, a court order terminating the alimony will need to be provided.) If the designated agent does not already have sufficient documentation to stop payments, additional evidence such as a marriage certificate will be required.

12.5 Payments and Bankruptcy. Absent a court order, there is no authority to stop a former spouse's retired pay award, current and arrearage child support payments, and current spousal support payments, if a member files bankruptcy.

12.6 Certification of Eligibility. The designated agent may request that a former spouse submit a signed certification of continued eligibility to receive payments under USFSPA. The certificate of eligibility should include notice of a change in status or circumstance that affects eligibility, if any such change exists. If the former spouse fails or refuses to comply with the certification requirement, the designated agent may stop the payments after notice to the former spouse.

13.0 RETIRED PAY ARREARS OWED A DECEASED FORMER SPOUSE

13.1 Applicability. This section applies to the settlement of arrears of a retired pay award that may be due a deceased former spouse pursuant to a previous application for direct payment completed under section 4.0. Arrears of a retired pay award may result from prorating a member's disposable retired pay for the month of the former spouse's death, from checks not negotiated before the former spouse's death, or the designated agent's failure to establish and/or make payments to the former spouse in the correct amount prior to the former spouse's death for a period that the former spouse was entitled to a property division.

13.2 Documentation. To settle the arrears of retired pay owed a deceased former spouse, the following documentation must be on file:

13.2.1. Copy of Death Certificate. A notification of death from any source (next of kin, post office, or neighbor) is sufficient to suspend future payment of the retired pay award. However, an official copy of a certificate of death for the former spouse is required before the arrears of a retired pay award are paid under this section.

13.2.2. Written Claim. A written claim must contain the claimant's signature and address, or that of the claimant's authorized agent or attorney. A Standard Form 1174, Claim for Unpaid Compensation of Deceased Member of the Uniformed Service, is not required, but may be used for this purpose, as long as the claim specifies the claimant's relationship to the deceased former spouse and documents other living relatives of the deceased former spouse.

13.2.3. Additional Documentation as Required. A claimant may be required to submit any additional documentation the designated agent deems necessary to establish the claimant's status and entitlement to the retired pay award arrears including, but not limited to, marriage certificates, birth certificates, divorce decrees, or other documentation that validates the living beneficiaries of a former spouse in any class of persons entitled to the arrears pursuant to paragraph 13.4.

13.3 Recoupment of Outstanding Payments. All outstanding checks or direct deposits (not negotiated before the former spouse's death or made after the former spouse's death) or the proceeds thereof must be returned to the designated agent before a settlement of arrears may be made.

13.4 Payment of the Arrears. Former spouse payments from retired pay are prorated for the month of the former spouse's death. When all documentation has been received and all outstanding payments have been recouped, payment of the arrears is made to the person living on the date of the former spouse's death who is highest on the order of precedence set forth in Chapter 30. For the purpose of payment of arrears under this paragraph, the provisions of Chapter 30, subparagraphs 2.4.3, 2.4.4, and 2.4.5 apply, and all references to a "retiree" in subparagraphs 2.4.1.2 through 2.4.1.6, 2.4.3, 2.4.4, and 2.4.5 should be considered as referring to a deceased former spouse rather than a retiree.

13.5 Indebtedness Resulting from Overpayment to a Former Spouse. Any indebtedness resulting from overpayment to a deceased former spouse must be liquidated before retired pay award arrears can be settled.

13.6 Claim for Arrears. A claim for arrears must be filed within the 6-year statute-of-limitation restriction. See 31 U.S.C. § 3702(b)(1). Any claim received 6 years after the date of the former spouse's death is barred.

13.7 Taxability. In the case of deceased former spouses, one or more Treasury Department (TD) Forms 1099-R, Distributions From Pensions, Annuities, Retirement or Profit-Sharing Plans, IRAs, Insurance Contracts, etc., may be used. If no former spouse arrears are paid, one TD 1099-R will be issued in the former spouse's name to cover any entitlement through date of death. If arrears are paid, an additional TD 1099-R is issued to each claimant to whom the arrears were paid.

14.0 ADMINISTRATIVE APPEAL PROCESS

14.1 Either Party Disagrees. If either party disagrees with the designated agent's determination concerning a former spouse's entitlement to payments under the USFSPA, that party may request reconsideration by writing to the designated agent. If the party requesting reconsideration asserts that the designated agent has erroneously overpaid the other party, the request for reconsideration will be considered a claim against the designated agent. An attorney will review the request and issue a decision in writing.

14.2 Party Requesting Reconsideration Disagrees. If the party requesting reconsideration disagrees with the attorney's determination, that party may submit an appeal to the designated agent, which must be received within 30 days of the date of the initial determination. The designated agent will forward the appeal to the Defense Office of Hearings and Appeals for their decision.

14.3 Additional Information. Parties are referred to Department of Defense Instruction (DoDI) 1340.21 for additional information concerning the submission of claims and appeals.

15.0 LIABILITY

15.1 Payments Made in Accordance with the USFSPA. Neither the United States nor any employee of the United States shall be liable regarding any payment made from retired pay to a retiree or former spouse pursuant to a court order that is regular on its face, if such payment is made in accordance with the USFSPA.

15.2 Designated Agent Liability. If the designated agent processes a former spouse's USFSPA application and administers the former spouse's payments in accordance with the USFSPA and in accordance with all documentation in its files, the designated agent is not liable for any former spouse payments issued after a former spouse's eligibility to receive payments has ended. Nor is the designated agent liable for any payments that the former spouse may have been entitled to prior to the designated agent's beginning direct payments pursuant to the former spouse's USFSPA application.

APPENDIX O

QDRO Provisions of the Pension Protection Act of 2006

Section 1001. Regulations on Time and Order of Issuance of Domestic Relations Orders.

Not later than 1 year after the date of the enactment of this Act, the Secretary of Labor shall issue regulations under Section 206(d)(3) of the Employee Retirement [Income] Security Act of 1974 and Section 414(p) of the Internal Revenue Code of 1986, which clarify that—

(1) a domestic relations order otherwise meeting the requirements to be a qualified domestic relations order, including the requirements of Section 206(d)(3)(D) of such Act and Section 414(p)(3) of such Code, shall not fail to be treated as a qualified domestic relations order solely because—

(A) the order is issued after, or revises, another domestic relations order or qualified domestic relations order; or

(B) of the time at which it is issued; and

(2) any order described in paragraph (1) shall be subject to the same requirements and protections which apply to qualified domestic relations orders, including the provisions of Section 206(d)(3)(H) of such Act and Section 414(p)(7) of such Code.

APPENDIX P

Interim Final Rule Relating to Time and Order of Issuance of Domestic Relations Orders

DEPARTMENT OF LABOR
Employee Benefits Security Administration
29 C.F.R. Part 2530
RIN 1210–AB15

AGENCY: Employee Benefits Security Administration, Department of Labor.

ACTION: Interim final rule with request for comments.

SUMMARY: This document contains an interim final rule issued under section 1001 of the Pension Protection Act of 2006, Public Law 109–280 (PPA), which requires the Secretary of Labor to issue, not later than 1 year after the date of the enactment of the PPA, regulations clarifying certain issues relating to the timing and order of domestic relations orders under section 206(d)(3) of the Employee Retirement Income Security Act of 1974, as amended (ERISA). The rule contained in this document provides guidance to plan administrators, service providers, participants, and alternate payees on the qualified domestic relations order (QDRO) requirements under ERISA. The rule is being adopted in response to the specific statutory directive contained in the PPA. Interested persons are invited to submit comments on the interim final rule for consideration by the Department of Labor in developing a final rule.

DATES: *Effective date*: The interim final rule is effective on April 6, 2007.
Comment date: Written comments on the interim final rule must be received by May 7, 2007.

ADDRESSES: To facilitate the receipt and processing of comments, EBSA encourages interested persons to submit their comments electronically to *e-ORI@dol.gov*, or by using the Federal eRulemaking portal *http://www.regulations.gov* (follow instructions for submission of comments). Persons submitting comments electronically are encouraged not to submit paper copies. Persons interested in submitting comments on paper should send or deliver their comments (preferably three copies) to: Office of Regulations and Interpretations, Employee Benefits Security Administration, Room N–5669, U.S. Department of Labor, 200 Constitution Avenue NW, Washington, DC 20210, Attention: QDRO Regulation. All comments will be available to the public, without charge, online at *http://www.regulations.gov* and *http://www.dol.gov/ebsa*, and at the Public Disclosure Room, Employee Benefits Security Administration, U.S. Department of Labor, Room N–1513, 200 Constitution Avenue NW, Washington, DC 20210.

FOR FURTHER INFORMATION CONTACT: Yolanda R. Wartenberg, Office of Regulations and Interpretations, Employee Benefits Security Administration, U.S. Department of Labor, Washington, DC 20210, (202) 693-8510. This is not a toll-free number.

SUPPLEMENTARY INFORMATION:

A. Qualified Domestic Relations Order Provisions

Section 206(d)(3) of title I of ERISA, and the related provisions of section 414(p) of the Internal Revenue Code of 1986 (Code), establish a limited exception to the prohibitions against assignment and alienation contained in ERISA section 206(d)(1) and Code section 401(a)(13).[1] Under this limited exception, a participant's benefits under a pension plan may be assigned to an alternate payee, defined as the participant's spouse, former spouse, child, or other dependent, pursuant to an order that constitutes a qualified domestic relations order (QDRO) within the meaning of those provisions. Such QDROs, in addition, survive the federal preemption of State law imposed by ERISA section 514(a) by virtue of ERISA section 514(b)(7).

Pursuant to the QDRO provisions, a plan administrator must determine, in accordance with specified procedures, whether an order purporting to divide a participant's benefits under a plan meets the applicable requirements set forth in section 206(d)(3) of ERISA. If the plan administrator determines that the order meets these requirements and is, accordingly, a QDRO within the meaning of section 206(d)(3), the plan administrator must distribute the assigned portion of the participant's benefits to the alternate payee or payees named in the order in accordance with the terms of the order.

Subparagraphs (G) and (H) of ERISA section 206(d)(3) set forth provisions relating to the procedures that a plan must establish, and a plan administrator must observe, in determining whether an order is a QDRO and in administering the plan and the participant's benefits during the period in which the plan administrator is making such a determination. The plan's procedures must be reasonable, must be in writing, must require prompt notification and disclosure of the procedures to participants and alternate payees upon receipt of an order, and must permit alternate payees to designate representatives for notice purposes. In addition, the plan administrator must complete the determination process

1. The QDRO provisions were added to ERISA and the Code by the Retirement Equity Act of 1984 (REA), Public Law 96–397, 96 Stat. 1438 (1984). Except where no corresponding provision exists, all references to paragraphs of ERISA section 206(d)(3) should be read to refer to corresponding provisions of Code section 414(p). The Secretary of Labor has authority to interpret the QDRO provisions, section 206(d)(3), and its parallel provision at section 414(p) of the Code, and to issue QDRO regulations in consultation with the Secretary of the Treasury. 29 U.S.C. 1056(d)(3)(N). The Secretary of the Treasury has authority to issue rules and regulations necessary to coordinate the requirements of section 414(p) (and the regulations issued by the Secretary of Labor thereunder) with the other provisions of Chapter I of Subtitle A of the Code. 26 U.S.C. 401(n). The Secretary of the Treasury has been consulted on this interim final rule.

and notify participants and alternate payees of its determination within a reasonable period after receipt of the order.

Subparagraph (H) of section 206(d)(3) provides specific procedural protection of a potential alternate payee's interest in a participant's benefits during the plan's determination process and for a period of up to 18 months (the 18-month period) during which the issue of the qualified status of a domestic relations order is being determined—whether by the plan administrator, by a court of competent jurisdiction, or otherwise. During the 18-month period, a plan administrator must separately account for any amounts that would have been payable to the alternate payee if the order had been immediately treated as a QDRO and must pay these amounts (including any interest thereon) to the alternate payee if the order is deemed qualified within such period. If the issue as to whether the order is a QDRO is not resolved within the 18-month period, the plan administrator is to pay such amounts to the person or persons who would have been entitled to the amounts if there had been no order. Any determination that an order is a QDRO that is made after the close of the 18-month period is to be applied prospectively only.

If a plan fiduciary, acting in accordance with the fiduciary responsibility provisions of part 4 of title I of ERISA, treats an order as a QDRO (or determines that such an order is not a QDRO) and distributes benefits in accordance with that determination, paragraph (I) of section 206(d)(3) provides that the obligations of the plan and its fiduciaries to the affected participants and alternate payees with respect to the distribution shall be treated as discharged.

The QDRO provisions detail specific requirements that an order must satisfy in order to constitute a QDRO. The order must be a "domestic relations order" issued pursuant to a State domestic relations law (including a community property law) that relates to the provision of child support, alimony payments, or marital property rights to a spouse, former spouse, child, or other dependent of a participant. Section 206(d)(3)(B)(ii). It must create or recognize the existence of an alternate payee's right to receive all or a portion of the benefits payable to a participant under a plan. Section 206(d)(3)(B)(i). Further, it must clearly specify the name and last known mailing address (if any) of the participant and the name and mailing address of each alternate payee covered by the order; the amount or percentage of the participant's benefits to be paid by the plan(s) to each such alternate payee, or the manner in which such amount or percentage is to be determined; the number of payments or period to which the order applies; and each plan to which the order applies. Section 206(d)(3)(C). An order will fail to be a QDRO, however, if it requires the plan to provide any type or form of benefit, or any option, not otherwise provided under the plan; to provide increased benefits determined on the basis of actuarial value; or to pay benefits to an alternate payee that are required to be paid to another alternate payee under another order previously determined to be a QDRO. Section 206(d)(3)(D).

B. Pension Protection Act of 2006

Under section 1001 of the Pension Protection Act of 2006 (PPA), Public Law 109–280, section 1001, 120 Stat. 780 (2006), Congress instructed the Secretary of Labor to issue regulations, not later than 1 year after the date of the enactment, under section 206(d)(3) of ERISA and section 414(p) of the Code, to clarify that—(1) a domestic relations order otherwise meeting the requirements to be a QDRO, including the requirements of section 206(d)(3)(D) of ERISA and section 414(p)(3) of the Code, shall not fail to be treated as a QDRO solely because—(A) the order is issued after, or revises, another domestic relations order or QDRO; or (B) of the time at which it is issued. Section 1001 of the PPA also requires that the regulations clarify that such orders are subject to all of the same requirements and protections that apply to QDROs, including the provisions of section 206(d)(3)(H) of ERISA and section 414(p)(7) of the Code.

C. Overview of Interim Final Rule

Scope of the Regulation
Paragraph (a) of the regulation provides that the scope of the regulation is to implement the directive contained in section 1001 of the PPA to clarify certain timing issues with respect to domestic relations orders and qualified domestic relations orders under ERISA.

Subsequent Domestic Relations Orders
Paragraph (b)(1) of the regulation provides that a domestic relations order otherwise meeting ERISA's requirements to be a QDRO shall not fail to be treated as a QDRO solely because the order is

issued after, or revises, another domestic relations order or QDRO. Paragraph (b)(2) provides examples of this rule.[2] Example 1 illustrates this rule as applied to a subsequent order revising an earlier QDRO involving the same parties. Example 2 illustrates this rule in the context of a subsequent order involving the same participant and a different alternate payee.

Timing of Domestic Relations Order

Paragraph (c)(1) of the regulation provides that a domestic relations order otherwise meeting ERISA's requirements to be a QDRO shall not fail to be treated as a QDRO solely because of the time at which it is issued. Paragraph (c)(2) provides examples of this rule. Example 1 illustrates the principle that a domestic relations order will not fail to be a QDRO solely because it is issued after the death of the participant. Example 2 illustrates that a domestic relations order will not fail to be a QDRO solely because it is issued after the parties divorce. Example 3 illustrates that an order would not fail to be a QDRO solely because it is issued after the participant's annuity starting date.

Requirements and Protections

Paragraph (d)(1) of the regulation provides that any domestic relations order described in paragraph (b) or (c) of the regulation shall be subject to the same requirements and protections that apply to all QDROs under section 206(d)(3) of ERISA. Paragraph (d)(2) provides examples of this rule. Example 1 illustrates that, although an order will not fail to be a QDRO solely because it is issued after the death of the participant, the order would fail to be a QDRO if it requires the plan to provide a type or form of benefit, or any option, not otherwise provided under the plan. Example 2 illustrates application of the protective rules regarding segregation of payable benefits to a second order involving the same participant and alternate payee. Example 3 illustrates that, although an order will not fail to be a QDRO solely because it is issued after another QDRO, the order would fail to be a QDRO if it assigns benefits already assigned to another alternate payee under another QDRO.

2. The examples in paragraphs (b)(2), (c)(2), and (d)(2) of the regulation show how the rules in paragraphs (b)(1), (c)(1), and (d)(1), respectively, apply to specific facts. They do not represent the only circumstances for which these rules would provide clarification.

D. Effective Date

The interim final regulation will be effective 30 days after the date of publication in the **Federal Register**. The guidance provided by the interim final regulation is in response to the direction from Congress in section 1001 of the PPA to the Secretary of Labor to issue regulations to clarify current law under section 206(d)(3) of ERISA. The Department, therefore, has determined it is necessary and appropriate to proceed with an interim final rule to provide the clarification mandated by Congress, while also requesting public comments on the matter for the purpose of drafting a final rule.

E. Justification for Interim Final Rulemaking

This regulation incorporates, with minor changes, language in section 1001 of the Pension Protection Act. The changes do not modify the meaning of the statutory language. In the Department's view, Congress directed the Secretary to adopt the substance of this language as a clarification of current law. In issuing these regulations, the Secretary has not deviated from the narrow Congressional directive. The examples included in the regulation merely provide interpretive guidance by explaining how the statutory language would apply to particular facts. Therefore, in accordance with section 553(b) of the Administrative Procedure Act, 5 U.S.C. 553(b), the Department finds for good cause that notice and public procedure on this regulation is unnecessary. To the extent that the examples go beyond the statutory language, they are purely interpretive and are not subject to the notice and public procedure requirements of section 553(b).

F. Request for Comments

The Department invites comments from interested persons on all aspects of the interim final rule, including whether, and to what extent, there are additional factual scenarios that should be added to the examples already in the interim final rule. To facilitate the receipt and processing of comments, EBSA encourages interested persons to submit their comments electronically by e-mail to *e-ORI@dol.gov*, or by using the Federal eRulemaking portal at *http://www.regulations.gov* (follow instructions for submission of comments). Persons submitting comments electronically are encouraged not to submit paper copies. Persons interested in submitting comments on paper should send or deliver their comments (preferably three copies) to: Office of Regulations and Interpretations, Employee Benefits Security Administration, Room N–5669, U.S. Department of Labor, 200 Constitution Avenue NW, Washington, DC 20210, Attention: QDRO Regulation. All comments will be available to the public, without charge, online at *http://www.regulations.gov* and *http://www.dol.gov/ebsa*, and at the Public Disclosure Room, Employee Benefits Security Administration, U.S. Department of Labor, Room N–1513, 200 Constitution Avenue NW, Washington, DC, 20210.

G. Regulatory Impact Analysis

Executive Order 12866 Statement

Under Executive Order 12866 (58 FR 51735), the Department must determine whether a regulatory action is "significant" and therefore subject to review by the Office of Management and Budget (OMB). Section 3(f) of the Executive Order defines a "significant regulatory action" as an action that is likely to result in a rule (1) having an annual effect on the economy of $100 million or more, or adversely and materially affecting a sector of the economy, productivity, competition, jobs, the environment, public health or safety, or State, local, or tribal governments or communities (also referred to as "economically significant"); (2) creating serious inconsistency or otherwise interfering with an action taken or planned by another agency; (3) materially altering the budgetary impacts of entitlement grants, user fees, or loan programs or the rights and obligations of recipients thereof; or (4) raising novel legal or policy issues arising out of legal mandates, the President's priorities, or the principles set forth in the Executive Order. The Department has determined that this regulatory action is not economically significant within the meaning of section 3(f)(1) of the Executive Order. However, the Office of Management and Budget (OMB) has determined that the action is significant within the meaning of section 3(f)(4) [of] the Executive Order, and the Department accordingly provides the following assessment of its potential costs and benefits.

This interim final rule is intended to clarify the statutory requirements for QDROs under section 206(d)(3) of ERISA and section 414(p) of the Code. The provisions of section 206(d)(3) generally assist State authorities in deciding permissible ways in which pension benefits may be divided in domestic relations matters. The rules and processes under section 206(d)(3) make it possible for plan administrators to determine whether a State order seeking to assign pension benefits to an alternate payee should be given effect under the plan; clear rules concerning what constitutes a QDRO have the effect of assisting plan administrators in reviewing orders received by the plan, as well as participants and alternate payees in planning how to take pension assets into account when significant events require making a division of marital assets.

In directing the Department, in section 1001 of the Pension Protection Act, to clarify the application of the QDRO provisions, Congress expressed the view that existing uncertainty about the application of those provisions has caused difficulties meriting resolution through regulatory action. Uncertainty concerning the application of the QDRO provisions can impose litigation and other costs on plans, participants, and alternate payees, as well as on State domestic relations authorities, that will be reduced through the promulgation of this rule. Consistent with the view of Congress, the rule clarifies, first, that the sequence in which multiple orders may be issued does not in itself affect whether the orders are QDROs, and, second, that the time at which an order is issued does not, in itself, determine whether an order is or is not a QDRO. The rule further reiterates that an order must meet the specific requirements of sections 206(d)(3) of ERISA and section 414(p) of the Code.

By reducing uncertainty over the application of the statutory requirements in specific circumstances, the rule is expected to reduce costs that might otherwise arise from the necessity of resolving uncertainty in such circumstances. By providing clearer rules for plan administrators, the rule is also expected to increase the efficiency of plan administration. In addition, the Department is issuing this rule in direct response to a Congressional directive. As described above, section 1001 of the Pension Protection Act requires the Department to issue regulations clarifying that an order otherwise meeting the requirements of section 206(d)(3) of ERISA for a QDRO should not fail to be treated as a QDRO solely because it was issued after or revised another order, or because of the time at which it was issued. In issuing this interim final rule, therefore, the Department is fulfilling objectives expressly endorsed by Congress. Because the rule applies only in certain specific circumstances and affects only a small subset of domestic relations orders, the Department believes that its economic impact will be small, overall, but positive.

The rule is not anticipated to impose increased compliance costs, since it merely establishes the legal effect of certain sequences of events. Although it may cause some orders to be treated as QDROs that otherwise might be disputed (or fail to be treated as a QDRO), the rule provides certainty with respect to the circumstances it covers, which will aid State authorities seeking to divide pension benefits and assist plan administrators seeking to discharge their obligations under section 206(d)(3) of ERISA, without limiting the power of State authorities to determine the proper division of marital assets. The rule is expected generally to provide benefits to pension plans, plan participants and alternate payees, and State domestic relations authorities by increasing the clarity of the rules that apply to QDROs.

Based on the foregoing assessment, the Department concludes that promulgation of this interim final rule will provide substantial benefits without imposing major costs.

Paperwork Reduction Act

The interim final regulation being issued here is not subject to the requirements of the Paperwork Reduction Act of 1980 (44 U.S.C. 3501 *et seq.*) because it does not contain an "information collection" as defined in 44 U.S.C. 3502 (11).

Regulatory Flexibility Act

The Regulatory Flexibility Act (5 U.S.C. 601 *et seq.*) (RFA) imposes certain requirements with respect to federal rules that are subject to the notice and comment requirements of section 553(b) of the Administrative Procedure Act (5 U.S.C. 551 *et seq.*) and that are likely to have a significant economic impact on a substantial number of small entities. Unless an agency certifies that a proposed rule will not have a significant economic impact on a substantial number of small entities, section 603 of the RFA requires that the agency present an initial regulatory flexibility analysis at the time of the publication of the notice of proposed rule-making describing the impact of the rule on small entities and seeking public comment on such impact. Because this rule is being issued as an interim final rule, the RFA does not apply and the Department is not required to either certify that the rule will not have a significant impact on a substantial number of small businesses or conduct an initial regulatory flexibility analysis. Nevertheless, the Department has considered the likely impact of the interim rule on small entities in connection with its assessment under Executive Order 12866, described above, and believes this rule will not have a significant impact on a substantial number of small entities. For purposes of this discussion, the Department deemed a small entity to be an employee benefit plan with fewer than 100 participants. The basis of this definition is found in section 104(a)(2) of ERISA, which permits the Secretary of Labor to prescribe simplified annual reports for pension plans [that] cover fewer than 100 participants. The Department invites comments on the effect of the interim final rule on small entities.

Congressional Review Act

The interim final rule being issued here is subject to the Congressional Review Act provisions of the Small Business Regulatory Enforcement Fairness Act of 1996 (5 U.S.C. 801 *et seq.*) and will be transmitted to Congress and the Comptroller General for review. The interim final rule is not a "major rule" as that term is defined in 5 U.S.C. 804, because it does not result in (1) an annual effect on the economy of $100 million or more; (2) a major increase in costs or prices for consumers, individual industries, or federal, State, or local government agencies, or geographic regions; or (3) significant adverse effects on competition, employment, investment, productivity, innovation, or on the ability of United States–based enterprises to compete with foreign-based enterprises in domestic and export markets.

Unfunded Mandates Reform Act

For purposes of the Unfunded Mandates Reform Act of 1995 (Pub. L. 104–4), the interim final rule does not include any federal mandate that may result in expenditures by State, local, or tribal governments, or impose an annual burden exceeding $100 million on the private sector.

Federalism Statement

Executive Order 13132 (August 4, 1999) outlines fundamental principles of federalism and requires federal agencies to adhere to specific criteria in the process of their formulation and implementation of policies that have substantial direct effects on the States, the relationship between the national government and the States, or on the distribution of power and responsibilities among the various levels of government. This interim final rule does not have federalism implications because it has no substantial direct effect on the States, on the relationship between the national government and the States, or on the distribution of power and responsibilities among the various levels of government. Section 514 of ERISA provides, with certain exceptions specifically enumerated, that the provisions of titles I and IV of ERISA supersede any and all laws of the States as they relate to any employee benefit plan covered under ERISA. One exception described in section 514(b)(7) is for qualified domestic relations orders, as defined in section 206(d)(3) of ERISA. The interim rule does not alter the provisions of the statute, but merely clarifies the status of certain types of domestic relations orders under ERISA.

List of Subjects in 29 C.F.R. Part 2530

Alternate payee, Divorce, Domestic relations orders, Employee benefit plans, Marital property, Pensions, Plan administrator, Qualified domestic relations orders, Spouse.

- For the reasons set forth in the preamble, the Department amends Subchapter D, Part 2530 of Title 29 of the Code of Federal Regulations as follows:

Subchapter D—Minimum Standards for Employee Pension Benefit Plans Under the Employee Retirement Income Security Act of 1974

Part 2530—Rules and Regulations for Minimum Standards for Employee Pension Benefit Plans

1. The authority citation for part 2530 is revised to read as follows:

Authority: Secs. 201, 202, 203, 204, 210, 505, 1011, 1012, 1014, and 1015, Pub. L. 93–406, 88 Stat. 852–862, 866–867, 894, 898–913, 924–929 (29 U.S.C. 1051–4, 1060, 1135, 26 U.S.C. 410, 411, 413, 414); Secretary of Labor's Order No. 13–76. Section 2530.206 also issued under sec. 1001, Pub. L. 109–280, 120 Stat. 780.

2. Add § 2530.206 to read as follows:

§ 2530.206 Time and order of issuance of domestic relations orders.

(a) *Scope.* This section implements section 1001 of the Pension Protection Act of 2006 by clarifying certain timing issues with respect to domestic relations orders and qualified domestic relations orders under the Employee Retirement Income Security Act of 1974, as amended (ERISA), 29 U.S.C. 1001 *et seq.*

(b) *Subsequent domestic relations orders.* (1) Subject to paragraph (d)(1) of this section, a domestic relations order shall not fail to be treated as a qualified domestic relations order solely because the order is issued after, or revises, another domestic relations order or qualified domestic relations order.

(2) The rule described in paragraph (b)(1) of this section is illustrated by the following examples:

Example (1). Subsequent domestic relations order between the same parties. Participant and Spouse divorce, and the administrator of Participant's 401(k) plan receives a domestic relations order. The administrator determines that the order is a QDRO. The QDRO allocates a portion of Participant's benefits to Spouse as the alternate payee. Subsequently, before benefit payments have commenced, Participant and Spouse seek and receive a second domestic relations order. The second order reduces the portion of Participant's benefits that Spouse was to receive under the QDRO. The second order does not fail to be treated as a QDRO solely because the second order is issued after, and reduces the prior assignment contained in, the first order.

Example (2). Subsequent domestic relations order between different parties. Participant and Spouse divorce, and the administrator of Participant's 401(k) plan receives a domestic relations order. The administrator determines that the order is a QDRO. The QDRO allocates a portion of Participant's benefits to Spouse as the alternate payee. Participant marries Spouse 2, and then they divorce. Participant's 401(k) plan administrator subsequently receives a domestic relations order pertaining to Spouse 2. The order assigns to Spouse 2 a portion of Participant's 401(k) benefits not already allocated to Spouse 1. The second order does not fail to be a QDRO solely because the second order is issued after the plan administrator has determined that an earlier order pertaining to Spouse 1 is a QDRO.

(c) *Timing.* (1) Subject to paragraph (d)(1) of this section, a domestic relations order shall not fail to be treated as a qualified domestic relations order solely because of the time at which it is issued.

(2) The rule described in paragraph (c)(1) of this section is illustrated by the following examples:

Example (1). Orders issued after death. Participant and Spouse divorce, and the administrator of Participant's plan receives a domestic relations order, but the administrator finds the order deficient and determines that it is not a QDRO. Shortly thereafter, Participant dies while actively employed. A second domestic relations order correcting the defects in the first order is subsequently submitted to the plan. The second order does not fail to be treated as a QDRO solely because it is issued after the death of the Participant.

Example (2). Orders issued after divorce. Participant and Spouse divorce. As a result, Spouse no longer meets the definition of "surviving spouse" under the terms of the plan. Subsequently, the plan administrator receives a domestic relations order requiring that Spouse be treated as the Participant's surviving spouse for purposes of receiving a death benefit payable under the terms of the plan only to a participant's surviving spouse. The order does not fail to be treated as a QDRO solely because, at the time it is issued, Spouse no longer meets the definition of a "surviving spouse" under the terms of the plan.

Example (3). Orders issued after annuity starting date. Participant retires and commences benefit payments in the form of a straight life annuity, with respect to which Spouse waives the surviving spousal rights provided under the plan and section 205 of ERISA. Participant and Spouse divorce after Participant's annuity starting date and present the plan with a domestic relations order providing for Spouse, as alternate payee, to receive half of the benefit payments that are made to Participant after a specified future date. Pursuant to paragraph (c)(1) of this section, the order does not fail to be a QDRO solely because it is issued after the annuity starting date.

(d) *Requirements and protections.* (1) Any domestic relations order described in this section shall be subject to the same requirements and protections that apply to qualified domestic relations orders under section 206(d)(3) of ERISA.

(2) The rule described in paragraph (d)(1) of this section is illustrated by the following examples:

Example (1). Type or form of benefit. Participant and Spouse divorce, and their divorce decree provides that the parties will prepare a domestic relations order assigning 50 percent of Participant's benefits under a 401(k) plan to Spouse to be paid in monthly installments over a ten-year period. Shortly thereafter, Participant dies while actively employed. A domestic relations order consistent with the decree is subsequently submitted to the 401(k) plan; however, the plan does not provide for ten-year installment payments of the type described in the order. Pursuant to paragraph (c)(1) of this section, the order does not fail to be treated as a QDRO solely because it is issued after the death of Participant, but the order would fail to be a QDRO under section 206(d)(3)(D)(i) and paragraph (d)(1) of this section because the order requires the plan to provide a type or form of benefit, or any option, not otherwise provided under the plan.

Example (2). Segregation of payable benefits. Participant and Spouse divorce, and the administrator of Participant's plan receives a domestic relations order under which Spouse would begin to receive benefits immediately if the order is determined to be a QDRO. The plan administrator separately accounts for the amounts covered by the domestic relations order as is required under section 206(d)(3)(H)(v) of ERISA. The plan administrator finds the order deficient and determines that it is not a QDRO. Subsequently, after the expiration of the segregation period pertaining to that order, the plan administrator receives a second domestic relations order relating to the same parties under which Spouse would begin to receive benefits immediately if the second order is determined to be a QDRO. Notwithstanding the expiration of the first segregation period, the amounts covered by the second order must be separately accounted for by the plan administrator for an 18-month period, in accordance with section 206(d)(3)(H) of ERISA and paragraph (d)(1) of this section.

Example (3). Previously assigned benefits. Participant and Spouse divorce, and the administrator of Participant's 401(k) plan receives a domestic relations order. The administrator determines that the order is a QDRO. The QDRO assigns a portion of Participant's benefits to Spouse as the alternate payee. Participant marries Spouse 2, and then they divorce. Participant's 401(k) plan administrator subsequently receives a domestic relations order pertaining to Spouse 2. The order assigns to Spouse 2 a portion of Participant's 401(k) benefits already assigned to Spouse 1. The second order does not fail to be treated as a QDRO solely because the second order is issued after the plan administrator has determined that an earlier order pertaining to Spouse 1 is a QDRO. The second order, however, would fail to be a QDRO under section 206(d)(3)(D)(iii) and paragraph (d)(1) of this section because it assigns all or a portion of Participant's benefits that are already assigned to Spouse 1 by the prior QDRO.

Signed at Washington, DC, this 28th day of February, 2007.

Bradford P. Campbell,

Acting Assistant Secretary, Employee Benefits Security Administration, Department of Labor.

[FR Doc. E7–3820 Filed 3–6–07; 8:45 am]

BILLING CODE 4510–29–P

Table of Cases

M

N

O

P

Q

R

Index

E

F

G

H

I

J

K

L

M

T